P9-CDY-426

Examining Global Social Welfare Issues

Using MicroCase®

Andrew L. Cherry, Jr.
Barry University

THOMSON

BROOKS/COLE

Australia • Canada • Mexico • Singapore • Spain • United Kingdom • United States

THOMSON

BROOKS/COLE

Executive Editor: Lisa Gebo
Editorial Assistant: Sheila Walsh
Technology Project Manager: Julie Aguilar
Marketing Manager: Caroline Concilla
Marketing Assistant: Mary Ho
Project Manager, Editorial Production: Stephanie
  Zunich

Print/Media Buyer: Vena Dyer
Permissions Editor: Sue Ewing
Copy Editor: Kristen Cassereau
Cover Designer: Carole Lawson
Printer: Phoenix Color Corporation

COPYRIGHT © 2003 Brooks/Cole, a division of Thomson Learning, Inc. Thomson Learning™ is a trademark used herein under license.

ALL RIGHTS RESERVED. No part of this work covered by the copyright hereon may be reproduced or used in any form or by any means—graphic, electronic, or mechanical, including but not limited to photocopying, recording, taping, Web distribution, information networks, or information storage and retrieval systems—without the written permission of the publisher.

Printed in the United States of America
1 2 3 4 5 6 7 06 05 04 03 02

For more information about our products, contact us at:
Thomson Learning Academic Resource Center
1-800-423-0563
For permission to use material from this text, contact us by:
Phone: 1-800-730-2214
Fax: 1-800-730-2215
Web: http://www.thomsonrights.com

Library of Congress Control Number: 2002111293

Student Edition with InfoTrac College Edition:
  ISBN 0-534-61038-2

Student Edition without InfoTrac College Edition:
  ISBN 0-534-61040-4

Brooks/Cole—Thomson Learning
511 Forest Lodge Road
Pacific Grove, CA 93950
USA

Asia
Thomson Learning
5 Shenton Way #01-01
UIC Building
Singapore 068808

Australia
Nelson Thomson Learning
102 Dodds Street
South Melbourne, Victoria 3205
Australia

Canada
Nelson Thomson Learning
1120 Birchmount Road
Toronto, Ontario M1K 5G4
Canada

Europe/Middle East/Africa
Thomson Learning
High Holborn House
50/51 Bedford Row
London WC1R 4LR
United Kingdom

Latin America
Thomson Learning
Seneca, 53
Colonia Polanco
11560 Mexico D.F.
Mexico

Spain
Paraninfo Thomson Learning
Calle/Magallanes, 25
28015 Madrid, Spain

CONTENTS

About the Author

Andrew Cherry has been working in the helping professions since he received his BS from Troy State University, Troy, Alabama, in 1969. He received his Masters of Social Work from the University of Alabama and worked as a psychiatric social worker at Bryce Hospital, in Tuscaloosa, Alabama, for 5 years. He received his Doctorate from the Columbia University School of Social Work, in New York City. When not teaching research at the master level, the doctoral level, and chairing dissertations at the Barry University School of Social Work, Professor Cherry works and conducts research and evaluations in the areas of homeless, addiction, social services to children and families, and the influence of social bond on human behavior. In addition to numerous professional journal articles and conference presentations, he has authored books titled *The Socialization Instinct: Individual, Family and Social Bonds,* (1994), Praeger Press; *A Research Primer for the Helping Professions: Methods Statistics and Writing,* (2000), Brooks/Cole Pub.; *A Global View of Teenage Pregnancy* (2001), *A Global View of Substance Abuse* (2002), and one book in press, *A Global View of Suicide* (in press), published by Greenwood Press. He also co-authored *Social Bonds and Teen Pregnancy* (1992), Praeger Press. He is currently the series advisor for a set of 18 books being published by Greenwood Press called *A World View of Social Issues.* He is also chair of the Conference on Social Work Education, *Disaster & Traumatic Stress Symposium.*

PREFACE

Although most of us never think too much about it, social welfare programs and policies shape our behavior as surely as physical structures such as interstate highways and roads shape the routes we take to work and to play. Social welfare systems provide family housing, education, employment, and other basic needs that impact our lives on a daily basis. Social welfare covers the broad spectrum of human conditions and circumstances. It is a broad concept, and there are a number of definitions for *social welfare.*

The definition of *social welfare* used in this workbook is inclusive. It begins with the definition of social welfare proposed by Elizabeth Wickenden (1965). For Wickenden, social welfare meant "those laws, programs, benefits, and services which assure or strengthen provisions for meeting social needs recognized as basic to the well being of the population and the better functioning of the social order." This definition includes providing services to help people meet their basic economic, mental, and physical needs. This definition and others like Reid's concept-ualization (1995) are grounded on the assumption that "because society can organize itself to provide its members with services basic to the well being of the population, society is obligated to provide these services." We can answer questions about the impact of social welfare on our lives many differeny ways. One approach is to use quantitative research methods (even with their limitations). Using these approaches, we can organize and analyze numerical data to provide a picture of the differences in, for example, poverty as it exists around the world, in the United States, in your state, and even in your county.

Workbook Design

This workbook and the accompanying databases by MicroCase, provided on the CD-ROM that accompanies the workbook, are designed as an interactive tool that provides you with a platform for exploring current social welfare issues. With this workbook, you will use the latest databases, *the same data that are used by social scientists all over the world to do their research.* With these data files, you will be able to compare states, countries, and public attitudes about some of the most important social welfare issues of our day. As you explore the social welfare issues presented in this workbook, your critical thinking skills will improve as your knowledge of the logical order of data analysis increases. *Critical and independent thinking skills can be developed with practice, and they are far more important than the skills of using computer-based statistical packages.*

Elements of Critical Thinking:

What is the precise question (problem) I am trying to answer?
What is the purpose of my thinking about the problem (e.g., general, specific)?
What point of view (e.g., perspective/paradigm) am I using to think about the question?
What are the central concepts and/or ideas I am using to think about the question?
What assumptions am I making to answer the question?
What information am I using (e.g., data, facts, observations)?
How am I interpreting the information that I have gathered?
What are the most logical and ethical conclusions?
If I accept the conclusion(s), what are the implications?
What would the consequences be if I based future action on my conclusions?
What am I taking for granted?

These questions can result in well-reasoned answers (Gibbs and Gambrill, 1999).

Using the MicroCase databases, you will be better able to understand the conditions that affect social welfare issues in the present and trends that will affect them in the future. As you test your ideas about relationships and build your critical thinking skills, you will become more skilled at learning from asking well-thought-out questions and stating the hypothesis. The data will show how the social welfare of people varies from state to state within the United States, and how it varies among different countries around the world. Using the MicroCase databases, you can compare trends in social welfare. You can determine how people's attitudes have influenced social programs and how they will influence social welfare programs and policy in the future. You will also learn more about how social welfare programs and policy have shaped individual and group attitudes, and behavior. Moreover, you will be able to ask and answer your questions with real-time data.

Exploring Social Welfare Issues

The social welfare issues you will explore using this workbook are real, and in many cases they are *pressing* issues. These data are current. They were complied from real surveys and data files from around the world. The statistical tool to analyze these data (MicroCase) is provided on the CD with the data files that you will need to explore 10 major social welfare issues. For example, Chapter 7 focuses on *gender equality*. This chapter looks at conditions associated with being female: gender discrimination and the progress women have made globally, by state, attitudes in the United States, and from a historical perspective. The *principle of comparable worth* and the impact of poverty on women with families is but one of the focal points.

The use of this computer-based tool for teaching applied social research will increase your learning, understanding, and interest in research, social policy, and human behavior. Based on the experience of using a MicroCase workbook written for sociology, Forte (1998, 1995) reported that MicroCase is relatively easy to use and "lessens the pain and increases the gain associated with teaching and learning" research. This workbook is unlike the earlier books that were written for and by sociologists, political scientists, criminologists, and anthropologists. This is the first MicroCase book written for social workers by a social work researcher. The content of this workbook addresses social issues that are important to practitioners, researchers, and our clients. The methods are typical of those used in social work research and in the human services. The MicroCase software used to analyze the data is intuitive and puts out both graphs and maps that will help maintain your interest and promote learning in an almost painless way. The program is easier to use than most Windows-based programs. This text will walk you through several easy steps until you can do a complete *analysis of a social issue* on your own. At the same time, as you work through the chapters the analytical procedures become more sophisticated, building on previous chapters. Even so, there are straightforward statistical analyses that you can easily do in each chapter to build your knowledge of the social welfare issue and your research skills. This workbook can be used to explore issues in textbooks on social work, social welfare, social policy, and/or books on social research (see the Course Grid in the Appendix).

Acknowledgements

No one works in a vacuum when writing and putting together a project like this one. Numerous people gave freely of their time and ideas. Both colleagues and students contributed to the final product. The process was like working clay into an object of art or useable vessel; one works clay into a form that one has in mind—then reworks it until it has a life of its own. It is not pressed from a mold, but is influenced by the many teachers that one encounters along the way. I would like to thank my students for their indulgence when I was trying out earlier versions of this workbook; my wife and colleague Mary; a friend, student, and now a colleague Douglas Rugh. I would like to thank the following social work educators who reviewed the different versions of the manuscript: Mary Davidson, Columbia-Greene Community College; Glenda Dewberry Rooney, Augsburg College; Chris Faiver, John Carroll University; Doman Lum, California State University-Sacramento; Stephen Marson, University of North Carolina-Pembroke; Allen Rubin, University of Texas-Austin; and Jeff Schrenzel, Western New England College.Their feedback was invaluable. Many thanks also go to Julie Aguilar and her assistance with MicroCase and the databases. As always, Lisa Gebo was understanding and helpful, as were her many associates at Wadsworth Publishing.

References

Forte, J. A., Healey, J., and Campbell, M. H. (1994). Does MicroCase statistical software package increase the statistical competence and comfort of undergraduate social work and social science majors? *Journal of Teaching in Social Work, 10*(1/2), 99–115.

Forte, J. A. (1998). Less pain, more gain: Computer applications for teaching applied social statistics. *Computers in Human Services, 15*(2/3), 71–87.

Reid, P. N. (1995). Social Welfare History. In L. R. Edwards (ed.), *Encyclopedia of Social Work*, Washington, DC: NASW Press, (19th ed.), 2206–2225.

Gibbs, L. and Grambrill, E. (1999). *Critical Thinking for Social Workers,* Thousand Oaks. CA: Pine Forge Press.

Wickenden, E. (1965). Social welfare in a changing world. Washington, DC: Dept. of Health, Education and Welfare. p. vii [For this Reference, see pp. 30 and 51 in Popple and Leighninger (1996), *Social Work and Social Welfare, and American Society.*]

GETTING STARTED

SYSTEM REQUIREMENTS

The software that accompanies this workbook is designed for the Windows 95 operating system or higher. To run the software, it must first be installed on a personal computer.

The minimum computer requirements are
- Windows 95 (or higher)
- 16 MB RAM
- CD-ROM drive
- 20 MB of hard drive space

To run the software on a Macintosh, you will need emulation software or hardware installed. For more information about emulation software or hardware, check with your local Macintosh retailer or try the Web site: machardware.about.com/cs/pcemulation/.

NETWORK VERSIONS OF MICROCASE

A network version of MicroCase is not available with this title.

INSTALLING MICROCASE

To install MicroCase to a hard drive, you will need the CD-ROM that is packaged inside the back cover of this book. Then follow these steps in order:

1. Start your computer and wait until the Windows desktop is displayed on your screen.

2. Insert the CD-ROM disc into the CD-ROM drive of your computer.

3. On most computers the CD-ROM will automatically start and a welcome menu will appear. If the CD-ROM doesn't automatically start, do the following:

   Click [Start] from the Windows desktop, click [Run], type **D:\SETUP**, and click [OK]. (If your CD-ROM drive is not the D drive, replace the letter D with the proper drive letter.)

4. During the installation, you will be presented with several screens, as described below. In most cases you will be required to make a selection or entry and then click [Next] to continue.

   The first screen that appears is the **License Name** screen. Here you are asked to type your name. It is important to type your name correctly, since it cannot be changed after this point. Your name will appear on all printouts, so make sure you spell it completely and correctly. Then click [Next] to continue.

   A **Welcome** screen now appears. This provides some introductory information and suggests that you shut down any other programs that may be running. Click [Next] to continue.

   You are next presented with a **Software License Agreement**. Read this screen and click [Yes] if you accept the terms of the software license.

The next screen has you **Choose the Destination** for the program files. You are strongly advised to use the destination directory that is shown on the screen. Click [Next] to continue.

5. The MicroCase program will now be installed. At the end of the installation, you will be asked if you would like a shortcut icon placed on the Windows desktop. It is recommended that you select [Yes]. You are now informed that the installation of MicroCase is finished. Click the [Finish] button and you will be returned to the opening Welcome screen. To exit completely, click the option "Exit Welcome Screen."

STARTING MICROCASE

To start MicroCase, locate the MicroCase "shortcut" icon on the Windows desktop, which looks something like this:

Student MicroCase

To start MicroCase, position your mouse pointer over the shortcut icon and double-click (that is, click it twice in rapid succession). If you did not permit the shortcut icon to be placed on the desktop during the install process (or if the icon was accidentally deleted), you can alternatively follow these directions to start the software:

> Click [Start] from the Windows desktop.
> Click [Programs].
> Click MicroCase.
> Click Student MicroCase -- SW.

After a few seconds, MicroCase will appear on your screen.

MICROCASE MENUS

MicroCase is very easy to use. All you do is point and click your way through the program. That is, use your mouse arrow to point at the selection you want, and then click the left button on the mouse.

Four menus provide the beginning points for everything you will do in MicroCase. When you start MicroCase, the FILE MANAGEMENT MENU appears first. From this menu you can open a new file, view the file settings, or save any modifications to the file. The DATA MANAGEMENT menu contains the List Data and Codebook tasks. The basic statistical analysis tasks are located on the BASIC STATISTICS menu. The following statistical tasks can be found on this menu: Univariate, Cross-tabulation, t-Test, ANOVA, Mapping, Scatterplot, Correlation, Regression, and Historical Trends. The ADVANCED STATISTICS task provides access to the Logistic Regression, Curve Fitting, Factor Analysis, MANOVA, and Trend Series tasks. You can toggle back and forth among these four menus by clicking the menu names shown on the left side of the screen.

Not all options on a menu are always available. You cannot, for example, do a statistical analysis until you have a data file open. You will be shown a message if you attempt to use a task that is not currently available.

There are some shortcuts for moving through the software as well. From any screen, you can click on File in the Menu bar and click on Open to select a new data file. You are then presented with the list of available files, and once a file is selected you are returned to the current menu. If you find you are switching between the same files during a session, you can access these files directly from the File option on the Menu bar. The last four data files that have been opened during the current session are listed and can be opened directly by selecting them from the list.

A variable list can be obtained by pressing [F3] any time a data file is open.

SOFTWARE GUIDES

Throughout this workbook, "Software Guides" provide the basic information needed to carry out each task. Here is an example:

> ➤ *Data File*: **GLOBAL**
> ➤ *Task*: **Mapping**
> ➤ *Variable 1*: **9) BIRTH RATE**
> ➤ *View:* **Map**

Each line of the software guide is actually an instruction. Let's follow the simple steps to carry out this task.

Step 1: Select a Data File

Before you can do anything in MicroCase, you need to open a data file so that you will have data to analyze. To open a data file, click the Open File task on the FILE MANAGEMENT menu. A list of data files will appear in a window (e.g., GSS, GLOBAL, STATES, etc.). If you click on a file name once, a description of the highlighted file is shown in the window next to this list. In the Software Guide shown above, the arrowhead symbol to the left of the Data File step indicates that you should open the GLOBAL data file. To open the file GLOBAL, click GLOBAL and then click the [Open] button (or just double-click GLOBAL). The next window that appears (labeled File Settings) provides additional information about the data file, including a file description, the number of cases in the file, and the number of variables, among other things. To continue, click the [OK] button. You are now returned to the FILE MANAGEMENT menu of MicroCase. (You won't need to repeat this step until you want to open a different data file.) Notice that by looking at the file name shown on the top line of the screen, you can always see which data file is currently open.

Step 2: Select a Task

Once you open a data file, the next step is to select a program task. Not all tasks will work for each data file, because some tasks are appropriate only for certain kinds of data. Mapping, for example, is a task that applies only to ecological data and thus cannot be used with survey data files.

In the software guide we're following, the arrowhead symbol on the second line indicates that the Mapping task should be selected, so switch to the BASIC STATISTICS menu and click the Mapping option with your left mouse button.

Step 3: Select a Variable

After a task is selected, you will be shown a list of the variables in the open data file. Notice that the first variable is highlighted and a description of that variable is shown in the Variable Description window at the lower right. You can move this highlight through the list of variables by using the up and down cursor keys (as well as the <Page Up> and <Page Down> keys). You can also click once on a variable name to move the highlight and update the variable description. Go ahead—move the highlight to a few other variables and read their descriptions.

If the variable you want to select is not displayed in the variable window, click on the scroll bars located on the right side of the variable list window to move through the list. By the way, Appendix A at the back of this workbook contains a list of the variable names for the data files provided with this book.

Each task requires the selection of one or more variables, and the software guides indicate which variables should be selected. The software guide example here indicates that you should select 9) BIRTH RATE as Variable 1. On the screen, there is a box labeled Variable 1. Inside this box, there is a vertical cursor that indicates that this box is currently an active option.

When you select a variable, it will be placed in this box. Before selecting a variable, be sure that the cursor is in the appropriate box. If it is not, place the cursor inside the appropriate box by clicking the box with your mouse. This is important because in some tasks the software guide will require more than one variable to be selected, and you want to be sure that you put each selected variable in the right place.

To select a variable, use any one of the methods shown below. (If the name of a previously selected variable is in the box, use the <Delete> or <Backspace> key to remove it—or click the [Clear All] button.)

• Type the **number** of the variable and press <Enter>.
• Type the **name** of the variable and press <Enter>. Or you can type just enough of the name to distinguish it from other variables in the data—BIR would be sufficient for this example.
• Double-click the desired variable in the variable list window. This selection will then appear in the variable selection box. (If the name of a previously selected variable is in the box, the newly selected variable will replace it.)
• Highlight the desired variable in the variable list, and then click the arrow that appears to the left of the variable selection box. The variable you selected will now appear in the box. (If the name of a previously selected variable is in the box, the newly selected variable will replace it.)

Once you have selected your variable (or variables), click the [OK] button to continue to the final results screen.

Variable Search Feature

You will often want to find a variable dealing with a particular research issue. In this situation, you may find it useful to search the variable list for certain words, phrases, or partial words that might appear in the variable name or description of the variable. Maybe, for example, you want to find a variable about crime. No problem. Just click the [Search] button below the variable list. Then type the word **crime**, and then either click the [OK] button or press <Enter>. The variable list window now contains only those variables that have *crime* in either the variable name or the variable description. You can select a variable directly from this search list in any of the ways described above. To return to the full list of variables, click the [Full List] button that appears below the variable list window.

Step 4: Select a View

The next screen that appears shows the final results of your analysis. In most cases, the screen that first appears matches the "view" indicated in the software guide. In this example, you are instructed to look at the Map view—that's what is currently showing on the screen. In some instances, however, you may need to make an additional selection to produce the desired screen.

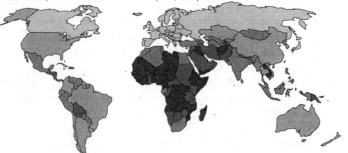

BIRTH RATE -- THE AVERAGE ANNUAL NUMBER OF BIRTHS DURING A YEAR PER 1,000 POPULATION AT MID YEAR; A.K.A. CRUDE BIRTH RATE (TWF, 1997)

(OPTIONAL) Step 5: Select an Additional Display

Some software guides will indicate that an additional "Display" should be selected. In that case, simply click on the option indicated for that additional display. For example, this software guide may have included an additional line that required you to select the Legend display that describes what each map color represents.

Step 6: Continuing to the Next Software Guide

Some instructions in the software guide may be the same for at least two examples in a row. For instance, after you display the map for birth rates in the example above, the following software guide may be given:

> *Data File*: **GLOBAL**
> *Task*: **Mapping**
> ➤ *Variable 1*: **59) FREEDOM**
> ➤ *View*: **Map**

Notice that the first two lines in the software guide do not have the arrowhead symbol located in front of the items. That's because you already have the data file GLOBAL open and you have already selected the Mapping task. With the results of your first analysis showing on the screen, there is no need to return to the main menu to complete this next analysis. Instead, all you need to do is select FREEDOM as your new variable. Click the [⟲] button located in the top left corner of your screen and the variable selection screen for the Mapping task appears again. Replace the variable with 59) FREEDOM and click [OK]. To repeat: you need to do only those items in the software guide that have the arrowhead symbol in front of them. If you start from the top of the software guide, you're simply wasting your time.

If the software guide instructs you to select an entirely new task or data file, you will need to return to the main menu. To return to the main menu, simply click the [Menu] button located at the top left corner of the screen. At this point, select the new data file and/or task that is indicated in the software guide. (Remember, the Open File option is available from File on the menu bar or from the FILE MANAGEMENT menu.) That's all there is to the basic operation of MicroCase. Just follow the instructions given in the software guide and point and click your way through the program.

ONLINE HELP

MicroCase offers extensive online help. You can obtain task-specific help by pressing <F1> at any point in the program. For example, if you are performing a scatterplot analysis, you can press <F1> to see the help for the Scatterplot task.

If you prefer to browse through a list of the available help topics, select Help from the pull-down menu at the top of the screen and select the **Help Topics** option. At this point, you will be provided a list of topic areas. A closed-book icon represents each topic. To see what information is available in a given topic area, double-click on a book to "open" it. When you double-click on a book graphic, a list of help topics is shown. A help topic is represented by a graphic with a piece of paper with a question mark on it. Double-click on a help topic to view it. If you have questions about MicroCase, try the online help described above. If you are not very familiar with software or computers, you may want to ask a classmate or your instructor for assistance.

EXITING FROM MICROCASE

If you are continuing to the next section of this workbook, it is not necessary to exit from MicroCase quite yet. But when you are finished using the program, it is very important that you properly exit the software—do not just walk away from the computer. To exit MicroCase, return to the main menu and select the [Exit Program] button that appears on the screen.

Chapter 1

POPULATION GROWTH AS A FORCE FOR SOCIAL CHANGE

Tasks: Mapping
Data Files: GLOBAL, STATES

Overview of Chapter 1

Chapter 1 and subsequent chapters will add to your knowledge of 10 important social welfare issues at the global, national, and local levels. These topics were selected because of their prevalence, severity, and current importance. The chapters cover subjects that are important to families, children, and older people. You will examine some of the problems faced by these groups: acquiring health care and dealing with substance abuse. The second section covers some important issues related to justice and equality. This section has chapters on gender equality, diversity, poverty, and crime and justice. As you move through each chapter, you will also learn how to use research methods and statistical procedures to discover new information and answer questions that occur to you. Each chapter builds on the last chapter to increase your understanding and ability to systematically think through a research question. The chapters start out with basic concepts and walk you through new procedures as you move from chapter to chapter. These chapters are designed as an interactive tool when used with MicroCase. You will use the latest databases—*the same data are used by social scientists and social researchers around the world.* With these data files, as you explore these important social welfare issues, your critical thinking skills will improve as your knowledge of the logical order of data analysis increases. *You will also notice that each chapter covers a number of topics and subtopics. The treatment of these topics is not exhaustive; there is a great deal more to learn about each topic. The grid in Appendix B will help identify chapters in textbooks that will help your inquiry and give additional information on the topics covered in these chapters. In addition, with the data files that are provided you can answer many of your questions on your own using the skills you will learn in these chapters.*

In Chapter 1, you will explore population issues that affect international and national social welfare. The chapter begins by looking at concerns over the *population explosion*. You will find that the impact of both rapid population growth and a drop in population has widespread consequences. In this chapter, you will learn the importance of asking thoughtful research questions. You will also learn how to identify variables in a database that can be used to answer these questions. As you create maps of global and national population distributions, you will be able to see the utility of different levels of analyses such as univariate and bivariate. So, prepare to have some fun.

I s the population explosion fizzling out? In 1974, the world population hit 4 billion and nearly everyone panicked. Prognosticators were forecasting a world population of 8 billion by the year 2000. A doomsday mentality took over. It was a worldwide crisis. Money and scientific talent focused on improving grains and farming techniques. The world food supply grew. Major efforts were funded to persuade women to have fewer children. Women around the world were offered birth control methods. Some programs seemed to work, others did not. Nevertheless, by the year 2000, the world's human population was slightly over 6 billion—a large number of people, but 50% less of an increase than was predicted in 1974. Let me tell you, being this wrong will drive the prognosticators up a tree.

As we begin the 21st century, rather than the world population growth continuing to increase at an ever-expanding rate, the world growth rate is leveling off. It is still growing, but the rate of growth is slowing. The population explosion is more like a series of blasts from different countries and regions of the world (Furedi, 1999). True, some countries have large populations that are growing rapidly, but others have birth rates that are below population replacement.

One question that may arise after discovering this new information on the population issue is, "What countries have exploding populations and what countries have declining populations?" Don't ponder the question too long. Before you finish with this chapter, you will be able to find out for yourself.

1.1   Definitions

Demographer: A person cross-trained in mathematics and statistics, biology, medicine, sociology, economics, history, geography, and anthropology who compiles and analyzes data that are used to understand various social systems related to populations and for guiding and establishing public policy.

Demography: Demography is a relatively new field of study. It began with the publication *An Essay on the Principle of Population* (1798) by Thomas Robert Malthus. Malthusian theory predicts that there will always be a constant pressure for human population growth to outstrip food production. Malthus proposed both "positive checks" (events such as war, famine, and disease) and "preventive checks" (for example, celibacy and contraception) would act to control population growth.

Today there are two groups of scholars at odds over the question of population growth. One group is often called the Neo-Malthusians. They follow the general ideas of Thomas Malthus (died 1834). They argue that population growth is dangerous and will deplete the world's resources. The opposing group argues that population growth can be controlled without draconian measures. They propose that planned growth, where population numbers and growth are stable, will lead to higher standards of living and economic growth. Let's look at this issue a little closer.

Over Six Billion People

There is no way of knowing when the six billionth human was born. By using population estimates, however, the United Nations set the official date for the birth of the six billionth person as October 12, 1999. The sixth billionth person was probably born in Asia. What type of impact do you think 6 billion people will have on social welfare issues?

1.2   Historical Growth of the World's Population

• 10,000 B.C.	About 5 million people lived on earth.	
• A.D. 100	World population reaches	200 million people.
• A.D. 1250	World population begins to fall.	
• A.D. 1450	World population begins to grow rapidly.	
• A.D. 1700	World population reaches	600 million people.
• A.D. 1850	World population reaches	1 billion people.
• A.D. 1974	World population reaches	4 billion people.
• A.D. 1980	China's population reaches	1 billion people.
• August 1999	India's population reaches	1 billion people.
• October 1999	World population reaches	6 billion people.
• A.D. 2100	World population levels off at	9 billion people.

World Population

So, what do you want to know about the world population? Have you ever wondered which country has the world's densest population? Or which country is succeeding with planned growth? You do not need to guess at the answers. You have the tools and the data to find out for yourself.

To answer some of your questions and perhaps confirm some of the observations made by Thomas Malthus, let's begin by using the database called GLOBAL in your MicroCase data files. Like the other databases that come with this workbook, the GLOBAL database contains data on a number of interesting topics. These topics can be described and analyzed by studying the *variables* in the databases provided with your workbook.

1.3   Definitions

Variable: A variable is the logical grouping of characteristics (i.e., gender is made up the characteristics of female and male). A variable describes characteristics about a person, group, organization, etc.

Units of analysis: A person, group, organization, etc. may also be referred to as *the unit of analysis*. The *units of analysis* in this chapter are nations, states, and communities. Their variables, for example, are *density, population growth, birth rate,* and *death rate.*

Impact of Population Growth on Social Welfare

When studying the impact of a population explosion on individual and social behavior, clearly the variable *density* will have a great impact. The density of the population in the community in which you live affects your economic opportunities, your environment, and your daily life experiences. The demand for land and resources continues to increase. The distribution of the population around the world and the population density in some areas of the world have a major impact on the social welfare of the people living in those areas. The limited habitable land and the problems associated with rapidly growing urban centers threaten the social welfare of us all (Livi-Bacci, 1997).

1.4   Overcrowding

For an interesting experiment on overcrowding among animals, see if you can find Calhoun's (1962) classic study of the impact of high population density. In this experiment, rats were raised under ideal conditions. All the food and water they needed was provided. The pen was always kept clean. The only provision that was not provided was room for expansion as the number of rats grew. The numbers grew rapidly with unlimited water and food supply. However, at a certain point in the increasing population of rats, suddenly the population declined sharply. Some mother rats ate their babies; others exhibited withdrawal and possibly depression. Similar reaction to overcrowding has also been observed in deer, mice, and lemmings that march into the sea when their population becomes too overcrowded.

As the above experiment suggests, overcrowding is a serious social welfare problem for people and governments. Let's use MicroCase to find out what countries have the most serious problem with being overcrowded. Looking at the variable of population density is one approach.

Research Hypothesis/Question   1.1:
What countries have the world's densest population?

Before we do, however, what is your best guess as to the top 10 nations with the densest population?
List your 10 guesses here: _____

_____

To answer this question, we will use the GLOBAL data file and the MicroCase software. The GLOBAL file contains data for 174 nations from around the world. To answer this question we will map the data for the variable 3) DENSITY, the population per square mile.

To answer the above question, look at the map below. Although, this map does not give you the names of each country on the map with the densest populations; you can see that the darker the shade, the denser the population of each country.

> *Data File:* **GLOBAL**
>> *Task:* **Mapping**
> *Variable:* **3) DENSITY**
>> *View:* **Map**

DENSITY -- POPULATION PER SQUARE MILE (SAUS, 1998)

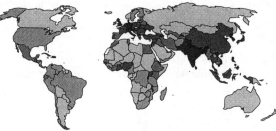

To reproduce this graphic on the computer screen using MicroCase, review the instructions in the *Getting Started* section. For this example, you would open the GLOBAL data file, select the BASIC STATISTICS menu (from the left side of the screen), select the MAPPING task, and select 3) DENSITY for Variable 1. The first view shown is the Map view. (Remember the ➢ symbol indicates which steps you need to perform if you are doing all examples as you follow along in the text. So in the next example, you only need to select a new view—that is, you don't need to repeat the first three steps, because they were already done in this example.)

Note that the darker the color on the map, the denser the population for that country. If you select 'Legend' in the 'Display' block, the values represented by the colors will be displayed. ·

Before you generate a computer list of the countries by the density of their population per square mile, *do you want to change your guess* about the nations you thought had the densest population?

Now let's look at the actual ranking of nations around the world by density.

As indicated by the ➢ symbol, if you are continuing from the previous example, select the [List: Rank] button. The number of rows shown on your screen may be different from that shown here. Use the cursor keys and scroll bar to move through this list if necessary.

How good were your guesses, or in other words, how good were your hypotheses about the top 10 nations with the densest population? Were any of the countries that you thought would be in the top 10 listed among the top 10? For example, did you think China would be in the top 10? How about India? Did you think you would find India in the top 10?

To find the rank of China, India, and the United States, scroll down the list of nations until you find China, India, the United States, and the rank of the countries that you guessed would have the densest population. If you look for India, you will find that India ranks 13th. China ranks 35th and shares that rank with Moldavia.

Data File:	**GLOBAL**		
Task:	**Mapping**		
Variable 1:	**3) Density**		
➢ *View:*	**List: Rank**		

RANK	CASE NAME	VALUE
1	Singapore	14487
2	Malta	3063
3	Bahrain	2579
4	Maldives	2505
5	Bangladesh	2467
6	Taiwan	1759
7	Mauritius	1636
8	Barbados	1560
9	South Korea	1224
10	Netherlands	1200

Can you find the rank of the United States? While you are looking, check out other countries that may interest you. Look at countries that make up regions of the world. We can learn a lot by looking at the regions of the world.

Now look for the nations with the least dense populations. Scroll down the list and find the countries at the bottom of the list that have the least dense population.

1.5	**Population Facts**

- As of 1990, 1.2 billion people lived in the developed nations of the world (approximately 25%).
- Some 4.1 billion people lived in the less-developed countries (approximately 75%).
- If there were 100 people living in a village, and given the proportionate food supply found on earth in the year 2000, we could feed 25 people on a U.S. diet, or all 100 people on a Chinese diet.
- World grain production per capita is about the same as it was in the mid-1970s.

Population Density in the United States

After you have looked at the density of different nations around the world, let's look at the density of the population by state in the United States.

Research Hypothesis/Question   1.2:
How do states in the United States differ in the density of their population?

To answer Research Hypothesis/Question 1.2, create the following map.

➢ *Data File:*	**STATES**
➢ *Task:*	**Mapping**
➢ *Variable 1:*	**11) DENSITY 95**
➢ *View:*	**Map**

DENSITY 95 -- 1995: POPULATION PER SQUARE MILE (SA, 1996)

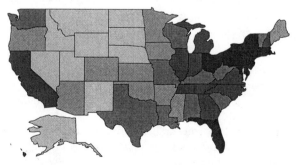

The ➤ symbol on the Data File line indicates that you must return to the FILE MANAGEMENT menu and open a new data file—STATES. Then return to the BASIC STATISTICS menu, select the MAPPING task, and select 11) DENSITY 95 for Variable 1.

Can you identify the most densely populated states? Where are the least densely populated states located? Is this what you expected to find?

For another view of the density of the population in the United States use the *spot fill* function. It gives you a view that can help assess the states with the densest population.

Data File: **STATES**
Task: **Mapping**
Variable 1: **11) DENSITY 95**
View: **Map**
➤ Display: **Spot Fill**

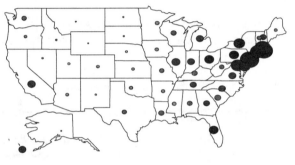

DENSITY 95 -- 1995: POPULATION PER SQUARE MILE (SA, 1996)

The larger the spots, the denser the population. This is a quick reference that helps us easily spot the states with the densest populations and the states with the least dense populations. Again, before you list the states in the United Sates by the density of their population, venture a guess as to what states will be in the top 10 of the most densely populated states. Where does the state in which you live rank in population density?

Data File: **STATES**
Task: **Mapping**
Variable 1: **11) DENSITY 95**
➤ View: **List: Rank**

RANK	CASE NAME	VALUE
1	New Jersey	1070.9
2	Rhode Island	947.2
3	Massachusetts	774.9
4	Connecticut	675.9
5	Maryland	515.9
6	New York	384.0
7	Delaware	366.9
8	Ohio	272.3
9	Pennsylvania	269.3
10	Florida	262.3

Now look for the states with the least dense populations. Scroll down the list and find the states at the bottom of the list that have the least dense population. When you looked at the list above, did you notice that 8 out of the 10 densest states were in the northeast of the United States? **What is the rank of your state?**

Another procedure you can use to find the rank of your state is the MicroCase [**List: Alpha**] procedure. To see the alpha list, point and click the [**List: Alpha**] option while in MicroCase. This will provide you with a list of the states in alphabetical order.

Exploring Global Social Welfare

	Data File:	STATES
	Task:	Mapping
	Variable 1:	11) DENSITY 95
➤	View:	List: ALPHA

RANK	ALPHA NAME	VALUE
25	Alabama	83.8
50	Alaska	1.1
37	Arizona	37.1
34	Arkansas	47.7
12	California	202.5
38	Colorado	36.1
4	Connecticut	675.9
7	Delaware	366.9
10	Florida	262.3
20	Georgia	124.3

The Research Process Depends on Your Asking a Good Question

If you are wondering why your guess about the countries with the densest population was so far off, the reason is that we asked the wrong question of the data. If we wish to study the world population, the first question asked of the data should probably be—**What countries have the largest populations?** This first question makes sense; it is intuitive and gives us basic information to begin exploring the impact of population on social welfare.

As you realize at this point, the question we ask of the data is what determines the findings. True, a dense population can be very problematic. However, it is a different issue. Just because a nation has a dense population does not mean it is has a large population compared to other countries. **In research, it is as important to ask a well-thought-out question as it is to have a good database.**

Now try guessing the 10 nations with the largest populations. If you guess China and India are the most populated countries in the world, you are correct. What is your guess about the 3rd most populated country in the world? Finding the answers about the population of each country will be quick. You already know how to use the mapping procedure. In MicroCase, reopen the **GLOBAL** database.

Research Hypothesis/Question   1.3:
What countries have the largest population?

➤	Data File:	GLOBAL
➤	Task:	Mapping
➤	Variable:	2) POPULATION
➤	View:	Map
➤	Display:	Legend

POPULATION -- POPULATION IN 1000S (IDB, 1998)

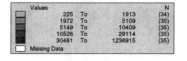

Values				N
	225	To	1913	(34)
	1972	To	5109	(35)
	5149	To	10409	(35)
	10526	To	29114	(35)
	30481	To	1236915	(35)
Missing Data				

Note that this task requires a new data file. *A hint*: **selecting the FILE from the top left of your screen provides you with the option to open a new data file or to open a recently used data file from a list without having to return to the FILE MANAGEMENT menu.**

Select the [Legend] display to view the ranges represented by each color. Now view the ranked list.

<table>
<tr><td>Data File:</td><td>GLOBAL</td></tr>
<tr><td>Task:</td><td>Mapping</td></tr>
<tr><td>Variable 1:</td><td>2) POPULATION</td></tr>
<tr><td>➢ View:</td><td>List: Rank</td></tr>
</table>

RANK	CASE NAME	VALUE
1	China	1236915
2	India	984004
3	United States	270312
4	Indonesia	212942
5	Brazil	169807
6	Russia	146861
7	Pakistan	135135
8	Bangladesh	127567
9	Japan	125932
10	Nigeria	110532

This is how the countries were ranked on the scale called population. The variable *population* is the number of people in thousands. This is a good measure of the population of each country. The list by rank is important because it shows us that China, India, and the United States are the three most populated countries in the world.

I would wager your guesses were better this time. You were aware that China and India were countries with large populations. Nevertheless, you probably did not know that the United States was the 3rd most populated country in the world. In the Americas, Brazil has the 5th largest population in the world. The other surprise for most of us is Nigeria checking in with the 10th largest population of 174 countries, the vast majority of recognized countries. On the other hand, **although Nigeria has the 10th largest population in the world (125 million people), China has 16 times the people (2 billion) and India has 8 times the people (1 billion).** India has approximately 4 times the population of the United States.

Population in the United States

Let's return to the **STATES** file to look at population growth in the United States by state. We have a variable called POP GO 96 that can give us a picture of differences in growth rate from one state to the other. We need there to be some variation from one state to another. If there is no variation, there is nothing in the data to analyze. Not to worry, as you will see, there is plenty of variation in growth from state to state. This raises another question: Why do some states grow in population and other states lose population?

Before we speculate further, let's see for ourselves which states are growing in population and which states are not. The Mapping procedure is still the best procedure to get a good visual picture of the differences.

1.6   The World Bank's Definition of Poverty

Most people in the United States do not know that the World Bank defines poverty as living on less than $1 per day (U.S. currency). For people in the developed world, this is mind-boggling. In most of the highly developed countries, a can of cola or a cup of coffee can cost as much as $1. In India, however, it is estimated that between 300 and 400 million people live on less than $1 a day.

Research Hypothesis/Question   1.4:
Is there a difference in the population growth rates among states in the United States?

> Data File: **STATES**
> Task: **Mapping**
> Variable 1: **3) POP GO 96**
> View: **Map**

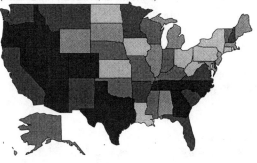

POP GO 96 -- PERCENT CHANGE IN POPULATION FROM JULY, 1995 TO JULY, 1996
(U.S. BUREAU OF THE CENSUS, REPORT ST-96-2)

Data File: **STATES**
Task: **Mapping**
Variable 1: **3) POP GO 96**
> View: **List: Rank**

RANK	CASE NAME	VALUE
1	Nevada	4.50
2	Arizona	2.90
3	Utah	2.20
4	Colorado	2.00
4	Idaho	2.00
4	Georgia	2.00
7	Oregon	1.70
7	Texas	1.70
7	Tennessee	1.70
7	North Carolina	1.70

Nevada had the greatest amount of growth in 1996, with a 4.5% increase in population. Which 10 states had the lowest growth rate in 1996? Where did your state rank?

The Impact of Birth Rate on Population Growth

One of the forces that drives social welfare policy and programming is population growth. Population growth that cannot be supported is a serious problem for any country and the community of nations. Social unrest, disease, and mass starvation have been the result of rapid population growth and scarce national resources or weak political will.

Much the same is true of population growth that is too small to replace those that die and emigrate. Too much growth is a problem, but too little growth is also a problem. Both situations represent a population and both can have grave consequences for the people living in countries experiencing such a crisis. Countries could lose their economic and world power position if the government cannot control and ensure a positive population growth (Cherry, et al., 2001).

At the beginning of the 21st century, Russia continued to lose population because of a significant reduction in birth rate and a significant drop in life expectancy. Both situations are significantly impacted by extremely heavy alcohol consumption (Cherry et al.).

High Birth Rates Equals High Population Growth, or Does It?

Logically, it makes sense that countries with high birth rates will have high population growth. Yet, there is that nagging voice in the back of my head saying, "You better check your assumption, it probably is not true in every case." Even what seems like the most unassailable assumption may have cracks in its armor. So, to do first things first, we need to make sure the variables are related. It is not a given that a country with a high birth rate will also have a high rate of population growth. That also depends on the rate of infant mortality and the general death rate.

To test the hypothesis about population growth in countries with high birth rates, we will again use our **GLOBAL** data file. This is a simple hypothesis that was probably more important in the past. Anyway, let's see how well this relationship held up in the 1990s.

Research Hypothesis/Question   1.5:
Do countries with high birth rates also have high levels of population growth?

To find out if there is a relationship between birth rate and population growth, we will use a bivariate analysis. **Select 9) BIRTH RATE for variable 1 and 7) POP GROWTH for variable 2.**

>   *Data File:*   **GLOBAL**
> >   *Task:*   **Mapping**
>   *Variable 1:*   **7) POP GROWTH**
>   *Variable 2:*   **9) BIRTH RATE**
> >   *Views:*   **Map**

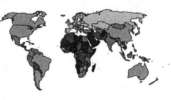

POP GROWTH -- CURRENT ANNUAL POPULATION GROWTH RATE (TWF, 1997)

$r = 0.752**$
BIRTH RATE -- THE AVERAGE ANNUAL NUMBER OF BIRTHS DURING A YEAR PER 1,000 POPULATION AT MID YEAR; A.K.A. CRUDE BIRTH RATE (TWF, 1997)

Is there a relationship between population growth and birth rates among nations around the world? A visual examination of the two world maps produced by MicroCase shows that many of the nations that have high population growth also have high birth rates.

A visual examination provides good information and tells us a great deal, but the question you might ask is, "How do we know that the nations with high birth rates are really the same nations that are experiencing high population growth?"

With this database, we can ask the question, "Are the countries ranked the same or almost the same on both lists?" If they are ranked in the top of the list for countries with high birth rates, will they be ranked on the top of the list in population growth? We can get some idea if they are of a similar ranking on both lists by looking at the *correlation* reported with the **Map**.

In this case, the two conditions are strongly related. Most of the time, when you find a country that has a high birth rate, it will also have a high growth rate. But, there are exceptions. The correlation was not perfect ($r = .75$). See if you can find the correlates in the two *lists*. Correlates can be loosely described as countries found in approximately the same rank on two lists.

> ### 1.7 Definitions
>
> **Univariate analysis:** This is the analysis of one variable at a time. It describes one characteristic of a population or sample at a time. For example, finding out that more men than women get into auto accidents is interesting although it is a univariate analysis. Also, it is interesting to find out that people who drive more than 100 miles a week get into more accidents than people who drive fewer than 100 miles a week. Although this information is based on a univariate analysis, it does help us form some ideas about auto accidents. Combining these two variables, "frequency of accidents by gender" and "frequency of accidents by miles driven," makes it a bivariate analysis. The finding of this bivariate analysis, "more men drive over a 100 miles a week than women," will narrow down and focus our ideas and probably change our earlier explanations for the possible causes for auto accidents (Cherry, 2000).
>
> **Bivariate analysis:** This is the analysis of two variables analyzed at the same time to determine the empirical relationship between the two variables. Remember, the definition of *univariate analysis* is the analysis of one variable at a time. When we analyze two variables at the same time, in this case "frequency of accidents by gender" and "frequency of accidents by miles driven," we are doing a *bivariate analysis*. Statistical procedures such as used in a *cross tabulation* (also called *crosstabs* or a *crossbreak table*), *t-Test,* and the *Pearson's correlation (r^2)* are examples of statistical procedures used to do *bivariate analyses*.
>
> **Correlation:** This is the relationship between two variables where, for instance, when one variable changes the other variable goes through a corresponding and consistent change. Therefore, when two variables are correlated—for example, education and income—we mean that there is an association between education and income. More specifically, we expect to find a positive association or relationship indicating that people with a high school education or less will have lower-paying jobs and that people with college educations will have higher-paying jobs. Typically, we expect to find that the more education a person has, the higher the person's income will be.

Well, there is strong *prima fascia* evidence to suggest that the two characteristics (population growth and birth rates) occur together in the same nations. The evidence is the significant statistical *correlation* between population growth and birth rates ($r = .75$, $p < .01$). This means that most of the countries that report a high birth rate also report high population growth. *The hypothesis that there is a relationship between birth rate and population growth is supported by the analysis.*

You can find the *correlation coefficient* reported from this analysis on the right of the screen directly above the bottom map description. It appears as "$r = .75**$." The *asterisks* (**) indicate the level of significance. In this case, the two asterisks represent a statistically significant relationship of $p < .01$. This means we would expect to find a similar relationship between these two variables (high birth rate and high population growth) in 99 out of 100 similar samples. This is an important finding. A correlation of $r = .75$ could possibly explain as much as 56% of the variation in population growth.

So, although the maps are good visual information, correlations and their level of significance tell us if the two variables are really related. If there is a statistically significant relationship (in this case, $p < .01$), we can find out the strength of the relationship by looking at the *Pearson's r* statistic (in this case, $r = .75$). This indicates that there is a fairly strong relationship between the two variables. It means that these two characteristics occur together in 75% of the countries used in this database. If you find one characteristic in a country, you will probably find the second characteristic. If you find a country with a high birth rate, the country will also have a high rate of population growth.

Now click on [**List: Rank**] for *variable 2* to see what countries had the fastest growth. Again, the list of countries is a little unexpected.

Data File:	**GLOBAL**
Task:	**Mapping**
Variable 1:	**17) BIRTH RATE**
Variable 2:	**7) POP GROWTH**
Views 1:	**Map**
➢ View 2:	**List: Rank**

RANK	CASE NAME	VALUE
1	Rwanda	8.24
2	Liberia	6.92
3	Gaza Strip	6.59
4	Eritrea	6.35
5	Kuwait	5.96
6	Afghanistan	4.48
7	West Bank	4.32
8	Qatar	4.04
9	Libya	3.64
10	Iraq	3.62

Now, look at the tables below to compare the 10 fastest-growing countries to their ranking on birth rate. You can select the [List: Rank] option for the BIRTH RATE variable if you would like to scroll through the list to compare the two lists for yourself. If you do so, you will see that out of the 174 countries for which we have measures of population growth and birth rates, you will see some of the same countries at the top of both lists. They may not be of the same rank on both lists, but the countries that have the highest birth rates will also be countries that tend to have high population growth. The exceptions to this correlation are the countries that have low birth rates and high population growth because of immigration. Some countries are growing because people from poorer countries are migrating to them to improve their and their family's economic conditions.

The reason I predict that countries with growing populations and countries with high birth rates will hold similar ranks on both lists is because the map analysis produced a strong Pearson's r correlation of .75. I am providing the lists below to make it easier for you to see the exact comparison of where the 10 fastest-growing countries stand when it comes to birth rate.

RANK	CASE NAME	VALUE
	10 fastest-growing countries	
1	Rwanda	8.24
2	Liberia	6.92
3	Gaza Strip	6.59
4	Eritrea	6.35
5	Kuwait	5.96
6	Afghanistan	4.48
7	West Bank	4.32
8	Qatar	4.04
9	Libya	3.64
10	Iraq	3.62

RANK	CASE NAME	VALUE
	Rank on birth rate of 10 fastest-growing countries	
45	Rwanda	38.73
30	Liberia	42.30
3	Gaza Strip	49.85
19	Eritrea	43.96
113	Kuwait	19.56
23	Afghanistan	42.72
50	West Bank	37.71
120	Qatar	17.26
20	Libya	43.94
27	Iraq	42.52

As you can see, only one country holds the same rank position in the top 10 on both lists, the Gaza Strip. However, if you look closely you will see that while the countries do not hold the same rank, all but two countries are in the top 25% of countries with high birth rates. These two countries (Kuwait and Qatar) are different from the rest of the countries because they have high population growth and low birth rates. These countries are wealthy and very attractive to people from poor countries looking for work.

This comparison is a good demonstration of what correlation tells us. A strong correlation tells us that the countries that have high population growth *tend* to have high birth rates. As the correlation in this example is not a perfect correlation, the names are not the same on both lists. Even so, if countries rank high on one list they will *tend* to rank high on the other list. In a similar way, if countries rank low on one list they will tend to rank low on the other list.

Environmental Consequences of Continued Population Growth

If consumption patterns and the population continue to grow in developing countries, there will be less water, land, food, and energy for the people in those countries. In many cases, these poor countries actually have adequate resources to care for their people. The problem is that international political interests have led to the diversion of resources from domestic needs to western markets. As a result, there are shortages of food, water, health, education and other important social services (Brown, et al., 1999; Global Issues, 2001).

The Impact of Immigration Rates on Population Growth

The research question that asks, "Is there a relationship between birth rate and population growth?" was answered. Based on the data available, we can say there is a strong relationship between birth rate and population growth. Then again, another condition that can greatly influence a country's population growth is immigration. To this point, I have mentioned that birth rate and immigration are important for a country to maintain its level of population. Nonetheless, this does not make it true. We need to test this hypothesized relation.

Shall we see if there is a relationship between population growth in countries with high immigration rates? This hypothesis is probably more important today than in the past (the exception being immigration to the Americas).

Research Hypothesis/Question   1.6:
Countries with high immigration rates will tend to have high levels of population growth.

Data File:	**GLOBAL**
Task:	**Mapping**
➢ *Variable 1:*	**17) POP GROWTH**
➢ *Variable 2:*	**8) NETMIGRT**
➢ *Views:*	**Map**

POP GROWTH -- CURRENT ANNUAL POPULATION GROWTH RATE (TWF, 1997)

$r = 0.639^{**}$
NETMIGRT -- THE BALANCE BETWEEN THE NUMBER OF PERSONS ENTERING AND LEAVING A COUNTRY DURING THE YEAR PER 1,000 PERSONS (TWF, 1997)

If you thought this was a true hypothesis, you were right. As you can see, there is a statistically significant relationship between *population growth* and *immigration* ($r = .64$, $p < .01$). This relationship does not appear to be as strong as the relationship between birth rate and population growth. This test of the hypothesis, however, suggests that there is a lot of support for immigration being a major contributor to the population growth of many countries. This finding is supported by previous studies on the cost of immigration to the immigrant. It is estimated that because of the high cost of migrating to another country, immigrants never recover the cost of leaving their homeland and making a new life for themselves in another country. For this reason, immigrants place more emphasis on the future of their children. The higher the cost of immigration, the more the emphasis will be placed on the success and future of their children (Cherry et al., 2001).

| 1.8 | The Most Important Resource |

1.8   The Most Important Resource

The most important resource at risk in the 21st century is clean water, not only for drinking, but also for food production and control of hygiene-related disease. Already the supply of clean water is limited in some Third World countries as a result of uncontrolled pollution or overuse in wasteful farming and industrial practices. India is thought to be draining aquifers twice as fast as they are replenished. This means that in the near future India will surely have water shortages (Koretz, 2000).

The Impact of Immigration on the United States

How does the increase of immigration affect the United States? This is an important question for people of the United States in the 21st century, and the responses will drive social welfare policy and programming over the next 50 years or longer. One impact that immigration may have on the United States is suggested by Berman and Rzakhanov (1999). They propose that high-income countries such as the United States, Canada, Israel, Australia, and New Zealand have higher incomes than other nations because they manipulate immigration to produce a moderate population growth.

This may seem a bit counterintuitive, but consider the characteristics of immigrants. Immigrants as a group are more interested in both having children and investing in the future of their children (Koretz, 2000). This encourages fertility and economic development. This process is instrumental in building wealth in the adopted country of the immigrant.

As a hypothesis, the relationship between moderate growth and immigration may sounds interesting, but will this hypothesis hold up when tested with real data? Will this hypothesis be supported when examining data from the United States? One way to begin to test whether immigration has an influence on growth in the United States is to compare the United States with the data we have on the other 173 nations. If we look at birth rate, immigration, and population growth, what might we expect to find?

If this hypothesis is true, we would expect to find the United States ranked low on birth rate as compared to other countries. We would expect the United States to also rank low on population growth rate. We would also expect the United States to rank high on immigration. Use your MicroCase program to find the ranking of the Unites States in relationship to other nations on these three variables.

Where does the United States rank in immigration? Using your **GLOBAL** database, you will find we rank 28 out of 174 nations.

Where does the United States rank in population growth? We rank 126 out of 174.

Where does the United States rank in birth rate? We rank 134 out of 174.

Do the findings about the three variables support the above hypothesis about immigration contributing to the prosperity of the United States? The expected conditions of a prosperous country are present: low population growth, low birth rate, and high immigration. There is no denying that the United States is a prosperous country. There is also no denying that immigrants, their hard work, and their dreams for a better life for their children have helped give all who live and work in the United States a better life.

Controlling Population Growth

One of the population controls observed by Robert Malthus is the death rate. *The numbers of births, deaths, immigrants, and emigrants determine the fluctuation and change in the size of a country's population.* In almost every country on the planet, death rates are much lower than they were 50 to 100 years ago. The new pattern of population fluctuation began to take shape in the 1700s. The traditional population pattern of relatively high birth rates balanced by high death rates began to shift toward lower death rates followed by lower birth rates. At the beginning of the 21st century, most countries' population patterns were ones of lower birth and death rates, even in countries in Sub-Saharan Africa. Although AIDS has had a devastating effect on the Sub-Saharan people, in general, the life expectancy has increased during the last 100 years.

These population changes and fluctuations are still occurring and are expected to continue to change. In the past, they have occurred in different nations at different times and at different rates (Cohen, 1995). This recent population pattern is characterized first by a reduction in death rates while birth rates remained constant or fall slightly. With the passing of time, birth rates continue to fall, which creates an equilibrium of low birth rates and a fairly stable population whose members have a long life expectancy.

1.9   Birth Rates in Asia

Though birth rates are slowing, in some Asian countries overall birth rates are still too high. Half the planet's population growth in the next 50 years will come from countries in Asia—18% will come from India alone (Koretz, 2000).

Factors Contributing to High Birth Rates

One important factor that contributes to the birth rate is a woman's knowledge that her children will live. Stokes (1999) and many others have stated that women around the world who believe that their children will live into adulthood tend to have fewer children than women who expect many of their children to die in childhood. If this condition is true, we expect to find countries with high death rates will tend to have high birth rates. Let's test the above statement or hypothesis with international data.

Research Hypothesis/Question   1.7:
Countries with high death rates tend to have high fertility rates.

Data File: **GLOBAL**
Task: **Mapping**
➤   Variable 1:   **9) BIRTH RATE**
➤   Variable 2:   **16) DEATH RATE**
➤   Views: **Map**

BIRTH RATE -- THE AVERAGE ANNUAL NUMBER OF BIRTHS DURING A YEAR PER 1,000 POPULATION AT MID YEAR; A.K.A. CRUDE BIRTH RATE (TWF, 1997)

r = 0.418**
DEATH RATE -- THE AVERAGE ANNUAL NUMBER OF DEATHS DURING A YEAR PER 1,000 POPULATION AT MIDYEAR; A.K.A. CRUDE DEATH RATE (TWF, 1997)

How strong is the correlation between high fertility rates and high death rates? The correlation between birth rate and death rate is statistically significant, but they are only modestly correlated to each other ($r = .42$, $p < .01$) in the nations around the world. A high correlation is between .70 and .99. A correlation of $r = .42$ does not prove that these nations have high birth rates because of high death rates, but it does lend support to the idea. This finding warrants more research and testing of the hypothesis.

The next step, to continue to test this hypothesis, would be to see if the hypothesis is supported using a *subset* of poor countries. In Chapter 3, you will work with a number of cases where you will analyze data using subsets of a population.

Opportunity and Birth Rate

China was forced to reduce its population growth to move into the modern world. Rapid population growth was outstripping the growth in food and industrial production. China reduced its population growth by using a severe public policy called the "one-child-family" policy. This policy became law in China in the early 1980s; the penalty for disobeying the law was harsh financial penalties imposed on the entire family. It is unlikely this type of policy would be acceptable in a democracy (Cherry et al., 2001).

The "one-child-family" policy in China has had another result that is more ominous. In large numbers, mothers are choosing to abort female fetuses until they are pregnant with a male fetus. The one-child-family policy clashed with traditional Chinese family values that require a male child to care for the parents, carry on the family name, and care for the family's ancestors.

Traditionally, in Chinese culture, and in the cultures of other people around the world, boys were and continue to be favored over girls. In many cases in these cultures, girls were and continue to be killed at birth based on the notion that boys had more value to the family and parents. In February 2000, it was reported that after 20 years of following the one-child per family policy, 67% of all children born in China since the policy was enacted were boys. It was estimated that in China's countryside, where culture and custom are stronger than government policies, the birth rate might be as high as 80% boys (Kwang, 2000).

1.10   Infant Mortality

About 7.7 million children worldwide died before their first birthday in 1998. Infant mortality accounted for about 14% of all deaths. Disparities in conditions, however, distinguishing today's less-developed and more-developed countries are also reflected in the portion of all deaths that occur in infancy. At the extremes, where overall mortality risks are highest, infant deaths will represent 20 to 25% of all deaths occurring in Sub-Saharan Africa, the Near East and North Africa. In contrast, infant deaths will be only 1% of all deaths in the more-developed countries of North America, Europe, Japan, Australia, and New Zealand.
Source: U.S. Bureau of the Census, World Population Profile: 1998, pp. 1–2.

Opportunity Reduces Fertility

There is another proposed proposition about females in relationship to fertility that suggests that females who have more opportunity as girls and young women will choose to postpone childbearing and have fewer children in their lifetime (Gupte, 1999). This proposition suggests that in countries were females have more educational opportunity, more job opportunity, and opportunity in general, teen pregnancy and fertility among adult women will be lower. We will consider this a working hypothesis that, if it holds up under testing, will suggest that perhaps there are less draconian ways of slowing and stabilizing population growth. If this hypothesis is supported, it is also a way that Second and Third world countries can control their population growth.

Let's test this hypothesis with data we have on 174 nations in the **GLOBAL** data file. In addition to the variable that measures fertility in each country, we will also use a variable that measures human development.

Research Hypothesis/Question   1.8:
Countries that have high levels of human development tend to have low fertility rates.

Data File: **GLOBAL**
Task: **Mapping**
➢ Variable 1: **10) FERTILITY**
➢ Variable 2: **23) HUMAN DEV.**
➢ View: **Map**

FERTILITY -- AVERAGE NUMBER OF
CHILDREN BORN TO EACH WOMAN
(SAUS, 1998)

r = -0.864**
HUMAN DEV. -- HUMAN DEVELOPMENT
INDEX. HIGHER SCORE = MORE
DEVELOPED (HDR, 1998)

These two variables, a country's rating on the *Human Development Index* and a country's fertility rate, are strongly and negatively correlated ($r = -.86$, $p < .01$). This supports our hypothesis that the availability of more opportunity and employment options result in women giving birth to fewer children.

Developing Critical Thinking Skills

In this chapter, you used real data (as opposed to mock data) to map out the countries of the world so they could be compared on different characteristics. You also saw how important it is to think critically about your research question and about the best approach for testing the veracity of your beliefs. Knowing that you need to methodically think through a research question or hypothesis is half the battle. Moreover, these thinking skills are transferable. They will be useful to you throughout your career.

1.11 Paradigm

As an undergraduate deep in the throes of psychology, I became concerned in my sophomore year that I was school phobic. Almost every Monday morning when I stayed on campus, I would wake up with a blinding headache. My paradigm for explaining the headaches was a psychological paradigm. I thought that my underlying desire to be free from school doing my own thing (whatever that was) and having a good time (whatever that was) explained my headaches. Years later, I experienced a paradigm shift in my thinking. I found out that many of my headaches were related to a severe allergic reaction to corn and corn by-products. My Monday morning headaches during my undergraduate education took on new meaning. Could it be possible that the traditional dormitory Friday night dinner of fish breaded with corn meal and hush puppies (corn bread) and the beer I drank on Saturday and Sunday (also made from corn mash) contributed to those awful headaches? I still laugh at my carefully thought-out psychological explanation that did not explain my outcome. Would someone who is school phobic attend eight years of college classes and accept a job as a professor? There again, I am trying to explain a long-term behavior using a psychological paradigm. Using the *paradigm* as a way to guide and organize explanations of *observable phenomena* can be learned and used in your professional life. In part, this skill is the ability to stop and pose the question to yourself, "I believe a certain description of reality to be true, but are there other explanations?" For me, the paradigm is a principle that, once understood, gives us another view, the opportunity to step back, and another way to make sure we sought out all competing explanations. It is much like triangulation. You place conditions on your beliefs: "If I think it is true, and in fact it is true, additional true information will verify that truth." Understanding how to use a paradigm to focus our study is important. Understanding that another paradigm might yield a different explanation of reality adds enormous depth to our critical thinking skills.

Highlights from the Census Bureau's *World Population Profile: 1998*

The world population will continue to grow in the 21st century. Despite a decline in fertility rates that began to drop in many countries in the 1970s, world population growth continues to be quite substantial. The Census Bureau (1999) estimated that in the early years of the 21st century, "crude death rates will exceed crude birth rates for the world's more developed countries, and the difference—natural increase—will be negative. At this point, international migration will become the critical variable determining whether the total population of today's more developed countries increases or decreases." These projections lead to the conclusion that "natural increase offset by net international immigration through 2019 but, if present trends continue, the population of the world's more developed countries will slowly begin to decrease from the year 2020 onward."

The increase in global population per year is equivalent to adding the population of Israel, Egypt, Jordan, West Bank, and Gaza to the world total each year. Population growth is being determined by the world's less-developed nations. Approximately 96% of the world's population increase is occurring in the developing regions of Africa, Asia, and Latin America, and the percentage of children born in these countries will continue to increase over the next 25 years.

While fertility and mortality continue to decline in the more-developed countries, substantial gaps exist, and will continue to exist, between the world's more-developed and less-developed countries in terms of the risk of dying at every age faced by children in less-developed countries. A baby born in Sub-Saharan Africa is far more likely to die in infancy than a child born in another developing region and has a lower life expectancy than a child born anywhere else. A child born in Latin America or Asia can expect to live between 7 and 13 fewer years on average than one born in one of the world's countries that are more affluent.

End Note: This chapter has covered a number of subjects and issues that hopefully were informative and interesting. The question is, however, how does Elizabeth Wickenden's definition of social welfare apply to us? She proposes that social welfare are "those laws, programs, benefits, and services which assure or strengthen provisions for meeting social needs recognized as basic to the well being of the population and the better functioning of the social order." In a world where over 90% of the world's population growth is occurring in the less-developed countries, what is the responsibility of the developed countries like the United States and federations like the European Union? Can and should Wickenden's definition and others like Reid's conceptualization (1995) that "because society can organize itself to provide its members with services basic to the well being of the population, society is obligated to provide these services" only apply to those societies within the borders of the developing nations, or are all societies around the world "obligated to provide these services"?

Other Population Issues

There are a number of issues related to population growth and decline that I could not examine in this chapter. However, with the data files provided with this book, you can analyze many of these issues on your own. To learn more about other issues related to world population, you can enter the following search terms in the InfoTrac College Edition.

Urbanization	**Pollution**
Subsistence farming	**Growing elderly population**
Depopulation	**Micro economy**
Deforestation	**Crop failure**
Mass starvation	**Drought**

For a view of how moviemakers in the 1970s saw the results of the population explosion, rent the movie *Soylent Green* (1973), starring Charleston Heston.

Workbook exercises and software are copyrighted. Copying is prohibited by law.

WORKSHEET	EXERCISE

NAME:

COURSE:

DATE:

EXERCISE 1

Review Questions

Based on the work you've done so far on the issue of population, see how well you do on this short True or False quiz.

In 1974, the population on the planet was expected to double by the year 2000. T F

Thomas Malthus is the person recognized as the founder of the field of study
called demography. T F

The United States is the third most populated country on earth. T F

Luckily, explosive population growth in one country cannot affect chances in social
welfare policy in another country. T F

Immigration has a positive influence and often contributes to the wealth of the country
that receives the immigrants. T F

There is a statistically significant relationship between nations with high birth rates and
nations that spend a great deal on public education. T F

MicroCase QUESTIONS

You will need to use the MicroCase software to answer the remainder of the questions in this exercise and the following chapter exercises. Make sure you have already gone through the *Getting Started* section that is located in the beginning of this book. If you have any difficulties using the software to obtain the appropriate information, or if you want to learn additional features of the MAPPING task, use the online help (F1).

Use the following data files, variables, and analytical approaches to answer the MicroCase questions.

1.   Let's look at a few more characteristics of the world population. We will start by looking at urbanization. There are two good measures of urbanization. One is the percentage of a country's population that lives in an urban area. The second is the percentage of yearly urban growth.

Using the **GLOBAL** database, see if there are differences among the countries in terms of the percentage of the population that lives in an urban area. Using MicroCase, map the countries by the percentage of their population living in urban areas.

> *Data File:* **GLOBAL**
> *Task:* **Mapping**
> *Variable 1:* **4) URBAN %**
> *View:* **List: Alpha**

To create this map using MicroCase, open the GLOBAL data file, select the BASIC STATISTICS menu (from the left side of the screen), select the MAPPING task, and select 4) URBAN % for variable 1. After examining the map, note that you need to switch to the [List:Alpha] view to answer the first question.

    a.   What are the ranks of China, India, and the United States in terms of the percentage of people living in urban areas?

        China _____   India _____   United States _____

> *View:* **List: Rank**

    b.   Which three countries had the highest percentage of urban population?

        1. _____   2. _____   3. _____

    c.   Which three countries had the lowest percentage of urban population?

        1. _____   2 . _____   3. _____

Now examine global urban growth using MicroCase to answer the following questions.

      Data File: **GLOBAL**
      Task: **Mapping**
> *Variable 2:* **5) URBAN GRWT**
> *View:* **List: Alpha**

As indicated by the ➤ symbol, if you are continuing from the previous example, select the [List: Rank] button. The number of rows shown on your screen may be different from that shown here. Use the cursor keys and scroll bar to move through this list if necessary.

    d.   Which region is experiencing the greatest amount of urban growth?
          1. North America
          2. Africa
          3. South America
          4. Europe

WORKSHEET

> Data File: **GLOBAL**
> Task: **Mapping**
> Variable 1: **4) URBAN %**
> View: **List: Alpha**

e. What are the ranks of China, India and the United States in terms of the percentage of people living in urban areas?

China _____ India _____ United States _____

> View: **List: Rank**

f. Which three countries had the highest percentage of urban growth?

1. _____ 2. _____ 3. _____

g. Which three countries had the lowest percentage of urban growth?

1. _____ 2. _____ 3. _____

Given the two variables *percent urban* and *urban growth*, do you think the countries with the highest levels of urbanization also have the fastest-growing urban areas? You will need to take note of the Pearson's correlation (*r*) to answer this question. What do you base your answer on?

To answer this question, try the following.

       Data File: **GLOBAL**
       Task: **Mapping**
> Variable 1: **4) URBAN %**
> Variable 2: **5) URBAN GRWT**
> Views: **Map**

h. Which statement best describes the correlation of these two variables?

    1. Strong, significant, and positive.
    2. Moderate, significant, and negative.
    3. Strong, significant, and negative.
    4. Weak, not significant, and positive.

i. What do these maps tell us about urban growth in Third World countries?

2. Now let us turn our attention to population issues that affect social welfare in the United States. High levels of immigration will exert intense pressure on social welfare issues in the United States for many years in the future. One of the assumptions mentioned earlier in this chapter was that the continued wealth of the United States is in part due to controlled immigration. This occurs

because, for the vast majority, immigration is so costly that the immigrant cannot recoup the loss in their lifetime. Intuitively, they invest in the future of their children. If this statement reflects reality for the immigrant, then it should be supported in the data.

First, examine the following map before you begin to answer questions about this very complex phenomenon.

> *Data File:* **STATES**
> > *Task:* **Mapping**
> *Variable 1:* **4) NIM 90-99**
> > *View:* **List: Rank**

    a.   What five states had the highest net immigration rate in the years 1995–1996?

    _____   _____   _____   _____   _____

    b.   What five states had the lowest level of net immigration in 1995–1996?

    _____   _____   _____   _____   _____

Now test the hypothesis that the states with the highest net immigration will be among the states with the largest number of children under 20 years of age. This presupposes that immigrants who invest in their children will also have more children under 20 years of age.

> *Data File:* **STATES**
> *Task:* **Mapping**
> *Variable 1:* **4) NIM 90-99**
> *Variable 2:* **24) POP<18 98**
> > *View:* **Map**

    c.   Well, was our assumption supported by the data?   Yes   No

    d.   What would be two competing hypotheses that would explain the correlation between high immigration in a state with large numbers of children under 20 years of age?

_____

_____

I would like to leave you with a thought. Imagine a scenario where an ultraconservative political party won the presidency and held a majority in both houses of Congress. One of their first actions was to close the borders and stop virtually all legal and illegal immigration. Imagine what life in the United States would be like if for eight years the government stopped immigration and the total population of the United States dropped by 40 to 50 million people. How would this impact our economic and social life? What kind of pressure would such a drop have on social welfare policy and social welfare programming?

Variable List Related to Population Issues

The following is a partial list of the variables for continuing the study of population issues. You can use the MicroCase approaches you learned in this chapter to pose a few questions of your own. To see a list of the variables, the variable descriptions, and the range of values, either select any statistical option in the BASIC STATISTICS menu, or press [F3] at any time to view the variable selection window.

GLOBAL

6) CITY POP
   1995: % OF TOTAL POPULATION IN CITIES OF MORE THAN 750,000 (HDR, 1998)
18) LIFEX MALE
   AVERAGE LIFE EXPECTANCY, MALES (TWF, 1997)
19) LIFEX FEM
   AVERAGE LIFE EXPECTANCY, FEMALES (TWF, 1997)

STATES

10) %>85 96
   1996: PERCENT OF THE POPULATION 85 YEARS OF AGE AND OLDER (U.S. BUREAU OF THE CENSUS, REPORT ST-96-11)
16) %NON-ENG90
   1990: PERCENT OF THOSE OVER 5 SPEAKING LANGUAGE OTHER THAN ENGLISH AT HOME
18) %FOREIGN90
   1990: PERCENT FOREIGN BORN
19) SAME HSE90
   1990: PERCENT OF THOSE OVER 5 WHO LIVED IN THE SAME HOUSE IN 1985

Web Pages Related to Population Issues

If you wish to find a world of resources that are available to you over the Internet, the following list of sites will get you started. Once you visit these Web sites, you will find many interesting links to other useful Web sites.

The Population Council
www.popcouncil.org

United Nation's Home page
www.un.org

U.S. Committee for Refugees
www.Refugees.org

The World Fact Book (by the CIA)
www.odci.gov/cia/publications/factbook/index.html

Bureau of the Census
www.census.gov

Department of Labor
www.dol.gov

References

Berman, E. and Rzakhanov, Z. (1999). *Fertility, Migration and Altruism*. Cambridge, MA: National Bureau of Economic Research.

Brown, L. R., Gardner, G., and Halweil, B. (1999). *Beyond Malthus: Nineteen Dimensions of the Population Challenge*. New York: W.W. Norton & Company.

Calhoun, J. B. (1962). Population density and social pathology. *Scientific America, 206*, 139–148.

Cherry, A. L. (2000). *A research primer for the helping professions: Methods statistics and writing*. Belmont, CA: Brooks/Cole Pub.

Cherry, A., Dillon, M., and Rugh, D. (2001). *Teenage Pregnancy: A World View*. Hartford, CT: Greenwood Publishing, Inc.

Cohen, J. E. (1995). *How Many People Can the Earth Support?* New York: W W Norton & Co.

Furedi, F. (1999). Your number's up. *New Scientist*, Oct. 9, p. 52.

Global Issues. (2001). *Causes of poverty: Poverty around the world*. Retrieved September 18, 2001, from www.globalissues.com.

Gupte, P. (1999). When bigger isn't better. *Newsweek*, August 16, p. 2.

Koretz, G. (2000). A better life for our kids. *Business Week*, April 10, p. 32.

Kwang, M. (2000). 67% of one-child families in China have sons. *The Straits Times* (Singapore). Feb. 1, Section: Asia. p. 19.

Livi-Bacci, M. (1997). *A Concise History of World Population*. Oxford, UK: Blackwell Pub.

McDevitt, T. M. (1999). *World Population Profile: 1998*. Washington, DC: U.S. Bureau of the Census. Retrieved May 15, 2001, from, the World Wide Web: www.census.gov.

Reid, P. N. (1995). Social welfare history. In L. R. Edwards (ed.), *Encyclopedia of Social Work*, Washington, DC: NASW Press (19th ed.), 2206–2225.

Stokes, B. (1999). Here's food for thought. *The National Journal, 31*(37), p. 2570.

Wickenden, E. (1965). *Social Welfare in a Changing World*. Washington DC: Dept. of Health, Education and Welfare. p. vii [For this reference, see pp. 30 and 51 in Popple and Leighninger (1996), *Social Work and Social Welfare, and American Society*.]

Zastrow, C. (2000). *Introduction to Social Work and Social Welfare*, (7th ed.) Belmont, CA: Wadsworth Publishing Co.

Additional Material That May Be of Interest

Chand, S. K. and Jaeger, A. (1996). *Aging Populations and Public Pension Schemes*. Washington, DC: International Monetary Fund.

Ehrlich, P. R. (1990). *The Population Explosion*. New York: Simon and Schuster.

Evans, L. T. (1998). *Feeding the Ten Billion: Plants and Population Growth*. Cambridge, UK: Cambridge University Press.

Harrison, A. (1991). *Black Exodus: The Great Migration from the American South*. Jackson, MS: University Press of Mississippi.

Littman, M. S. (1998). *A Statistical Portrait of the United States: Social Conditions and Trends*. Lanham, MD: Bernan Press.

Markley, O. W. and McCuan, W. R. (eds.). *21st Century Earth: Opposing Viewpoints*. San Diego, CA: Greenhaven Press.

Mattson, M. T. (1992). *Atlas of the 1990 Census*. New York: Macmillan.

Simon, J. L. (1995). *Immigration: The Demographic and Economic Facts*. Washington, DC: Cato Institute: National Immigration Forum.

Chapter 2

THE FAMILY

Tasks: Mapping, Univariate, Scatterplot
Data Files: GLOBAL, STATES

Overview of Chapter 2

In Chapter 1, while learning about population issues that affect social welfare globally and nationally you learned the importance of asking thoughtful and testable research questions. You learned how to select variables from different databases to answer research questions. You used the *mapping* procedure to do both univariate and bivariate analyses.

Chapter 2 starts out with some background information on families that will help you look at families both globally and nationally. You will see if marriage is still an important institution and the impact on families when a female is the head of the household. You will continue to use the *mapping* procedure in this chapter and be introduced to the use of *averages (means)* and dispersion of responses on either the mean *(standard deviation)*. You will also be introduced to the *scatterplot*. The scatterplot will help you develop a visual image of what a bivariate analysis tells us.

T he "Family" in the 21st century is still the basic unit of society. Most sociologists think of the family as a group of people united through bonds of kinship or marriage. They point out that families are found in all societies; however, the structure of the family and the support that the family provides individual members vary from society to society. Even so, families provide essential services to society; they provide protection, companionship, security, and socialization for family members. Families have been doing so without much change to their structure for thousands of years. Nonetheless, in the 21st century, the definition of family is evolving and taking new shapes. "It is a phenomenon of our times that people have discovered so many other ways to come together as 'family'" (Meyer, 1990; Hepworth, Rooney, and Larsen, 1997).

Many people in the helping professions believe that how a society or government defines "family" characterizes the services provided to the family unit and its members. The social definition and the authority of the legal definition for "family" guides the provision of family services, which is related to the legal rights and benefits of family members. Others in the field add that ethics play an important role in determining the kinds and extent of services provided to families, and they believe ethics should play an even greater role in the future (Ashford et al., 2001).

Ethical Foundation of Family Services

To examine the social welfare issues that impact families is impossible without explaining why a *certain level of social services must be provided to all families in a modern world.* One reason is that in this modern world we have no choice but to depend on others. Our lives intertwine. To survive, we depend on each other and the large organizations that have evolved to meet our needs. We begin needing others at conception, and we need the help of others until we die. For others, once we are born or conceived, our lives are a series of accidents in the midst of chaos. There are some things in our lives that we have control of or at least some control over. Then there are circumstances none of us can control. To help reduce the harm to individuals and families caused by *harmful circumstances* or misfortune of all kinds, social welfare policies and programs have been developed.

Family services and the rationale for protecting and providing services to help sustain families have a long tradition in religious teachings and a rich secular philosophical foundation. In the past, most ethical positions and decisions were based on religious teachings. These teachings still affect most ethical thinking. During the era of enlightenment, however, other philosophic positions began to influence government policy and human behavior. Much of this thinking began in the mid-1700s with the effort of Protestant philosophers to discredit the concept of the *divine right of kings*. Over the next 200 years principles based on *natural law* were formulated that defined human behavior, democracy, and its social contract with the individual. Utilitarianism had a great impact on *deontology* (the study of ethics) during this period. Its doctrine, that we should act in ways that provide the greatest good for the greatest number of people, still has great appeal. For many modern deontologists (people who study the history and theory of ethics), the utilitarian position is a threat to the rights of the individual. Philosophers, such as Immanuel Kant and John Rawls, follow in the tradition of Hobbs, Locke, and Rousseau and hold the view that a natural *social contract* exists between individuals and the outside world. They believe that this contract defines the relationship among individuals and their relationship with their governments. In his book, *A Theory of Justice* (1971), Rawls suggests that justice is *fairness*. From this perspective, fairness in social welfare is determined by how evenly and fairly the benefits and burdens of society are distributed (Jansson, 2001).

This sounds good, but the dilemma is how to distribute the benefits fairly and who do we trust to be fair? Rawls (1971) approached the problem of *who determines fairness* by using a simple hypothetical situation familiar to students of philosophy. He asks, if you had to design a world in which to be born, a birth that would be totally random—you could be born anywhere to any woman—what kind of society would you wish to be born into? What kind of society would you design if you had to take that chance? From this perspective, Rawls believes that if we were in the situation above most of us could agree on two positions: (1) every person should have as many rights and privileges as possible without infringing on the rights of others; (2) in the society we design, we would not want anyone to have contrived privileges over others unless the advantage was to help those of us who might be born at a disadvantage.

So, one of the biases that guided my view and reporting on these social welfare issues was a set of simple questions about what social welfare would look like in a good and fair society and what it looks like when we take the world's *vital signs*. In Box 2.1, the question is asked in terms of providing family services.

2.1   Ethics of Family Services

What if by some future invention you could be reborn one more time—you could start over as a newborn child. Would you do it? Would you do it even if you had no control over the family or the place in the world where you would be reborn? If you would *not* take the chance, what would change your mind? If you would take the chance to be reborn again and you were born into a low-strata family in a Third World country, what kind of family services would you want to be available to your family?

What Is a Family?

Although much about the world has changed, there is still a need for families in the 21st century. We still believe, with good reason, that families are the best way to care for and socialize the young, take care of the elderly, and provide a source of affection for the members of the society. To help provide services to families that are different from the traditional family, some in the helping professions have suggested using a broader definition of *family*.

This definition would include "possible alternative structures and sets of functions that constitute *family* for others" (Schriver, 1995).

Family or Household? The United States Bureau of the Census defines family and household differently. The Bureau's definition, like any formal definition, is not always a good fit with the public's view or definition of family. *Family:* a group of two or more persons related by blood, marriage, or adoption and residing together in a household. *Household:* all persons who occupy a "household unit" that is a house, an apartment, or other group of rooms, or a single room that constitutes "separate living quarters." Check out the U.S. Census Bureau's Web site; it has a great deal of information and data that can be downloaded and used for school papers and even journal articles (www.census.gov—see other Web sites at the end of each chapter).

The Census Bureau's definition only considers the family in terms of structure and activities. By this definition, a brother and sister cohabitating are treated like a family, while a man and woman living together in a sexual union are not considered a family but a household. Why? They are not married, nor are they raising children (Longres, 2000).

Traditional Families

Much of the variation in today's families—the differences from the traditional family—has occurred because of the changes in role expectations among family members (Longres, 2000). The traditional family in Western society is the nuclear family. The nuclear family is made up of a married man and woman with their children. Traditional families are organized by gender. Males and females have specific roles and responsibilities. In the traditional family, the responsibilities are divided; the father is the authority figure and the mother is responsible for child care and rearing the children.

Among families in the 21st century, in the postindustrial nations such as the United States, the roles in the family are no longer determined by gender. However, in countries where traditional norms, particularly where religious tradition is strong, there is typically a preference for what we think of as the male-dominated traditional family. Nonetheless, the traditional family as defined in Western society is not the definition of the typical family in many other parts of the world or in other cultures not based on Western traditions (Jansson, 2001; Longres, 2000).

A Global View of Today's Families

Family structure varies somewhat from country to country, and among and within ethnic groups. Customs and religious law originally shaped our view of the traditional family; but today, customs and religious law are themselves affected by secular education, economics, world communications, and individual freedoms. This has opened up the concept, if not the legal definition, of *family*. Moreover, complex physical, familial, and cultural factors that are often poorly understood still determine who will marry and when; who will begin sexual activity before marriage; who will begin childbearing during adolescence; and who will bear children outside marriage. While the needs and experiences of families and family members vary around the world, there are similarities that cross national and regional boundaries (Cherry et al., 2001).

2.2   Japan Spending Billons for Seniors to Live at Home

Japan's elderly population is increasing in numbers faster than any country in the world; and the Japanese government is spending billions to help its elderly citizens live in their own homes. In 2000, 1.2 million elderly Japanese were bedridden, half for three years or more. Nursing homes are in short supply and hospitals are overcrowded with people needing a nursing home because the family was unable to give them proper care. In Japan, the elderly were traditionally cared for by their children. However, today this tradition is impossible for many families to meet and most are conflicted by the double bind they are in. Similar to families in other Western societies, few can afford to stay home to care for an elderly parent (Tolbert, 2000).

To help expand our understanding of how the *family* is viewed in different countries and cultures, we can continue to use MicroCase and the Global database. As you did in Chapter 1, the mapping procedure can again be used to identify differences in the view of *family* from country to country. First, why don't we ask a question about people's view of the family? One question that might inform us about what people think of family is to ask if they still think the family is relevant in today's modern, fast-paced world.

Research Hypothesis/Question   2.1:
Is marriage an outdated institution?

Before you use MicroCase to answer this question, take your best guess as to the percentage of people in the world who agree with the statement that "marriage is an outdated institution." Name 5 countries with the <u>highest</u> score and 5 countries with the <u>lowest</u> score. Write your guess here:

_____

_____

To test your hypothesis by looking at a world map of countries surveyed on this question, in MicroCase you would select the following.

> *Data File:* **GLOBAL**
> *Task:* **Mapping**
> *Variable 1:* **57) WED PASSÉ**
> *View:* **Map**

WED PASSE' -- PERCENT WHO AGREE THAT "MARRIAGE IS AN OUTDATED INSTITUTION." (WVS)

To reproduce this graphic on the computer screen using MicroCase, review the instructions in the *Getting Started* section. For this example, you would open the GLOBAL data file, select the BASIC STATISTICS menu (from the left side of the screen), select the MAPPING task, and select 57) WED PASSÉ for variable 1. The first view shown is the Map view. (Remember the ➢ symbol indicates which steps you need to perform if you are doing all examples as you follow along in the text. So in the next example, you only need to select a new view—that is, you do not need to repeat the first three steps, because they were already done for you in this example.)

If you select 'Legend' in the 'Display' block, the values represented by the colors will be displayed under your map. Again, note that the darker the color on the map, the larger the percentage of people in that country that agree with the statement "marriage is an outdated institution."

As you can see by a visual examination of the world map above, a number of countries in Africa and South America were not surveyed. Nonetheless, given the 40 countries where people did answer this question, it is clear that people living in countries in Western Europe appear to be most likely to agree that marriage as an institution is old-fashioned or outdated. People in Brazil also seem to feel that marriage, at least the way it is practiced in Brazil, is an outdated institution.

This is excellent information, but to be able to see if your guesses were correct we still need to find out how the nations rank on this question.

Data File: **GLOBAL**
Task: **Mapping**
Variable 1: **57) WED PASSÉ**
➤ View: **List: Rank**

RANK	CASE NAME	VALUE
1	France	29%
2	Brazil	27%
3	Belgium	23%
4	Portugal	22%
5	Netherlands	21%
36	Poland	8%
36	United States	8%
38	Japan	7%
39	Iceland	6%
40	India	5%

As indicated by the ➤ symbol, if you are continuing from the previous example, select the [List: Rank] button. The rows shown on your screen will be different from that shown here. Use the cursor keys and scroll bar to move through this list if necessary.

Based on this information, almost 3 out of 10 (29%) French residents view marriage as an outdated institution. Brazil and Portugal also have high percentages of residents who think marriage is passé. Why are the people in these two traditionally religious, Hispanic countries so burned out on marriage? Were the countries with the least number of people who think marriage is passé also a surprise? India, Iceland, Japan, and the United States have the lowest percentages of the 40 nations surveyed.

How Is Family Viewed in the U.S.?

Now that we have some idea about where the United States stands in comparison to other countries around the world on the inviolability of marriage, let's look more closely at how attitudes vary from state to state and from region to region within the United States.

Three major concerns of those promoting traditional family values are (1) the drop in the rate of marriage, (2) the increase in the divorce rate, and (3) the number of girls and women who are having children outside marriage. The major concerns of those promoting flexibility in family styles are (1) the number of single-parent families and (2) the poverty among single female-headed families (Jansson, 2001).

2.3   A Traditional Family Typically Means a Male-Dominated Family

Countries and states whose populations agree with statements about traditional values will typically be made up of families that are male-dominated. This is a long-held assumption by social scientists that you can test using the MicroCase data files provided with this book. In the data files, you will find variables related to family and traditional values such as desire for a large family, abortion, single moms, working moms, etc.

To begin to explore the role of family in the United States, first let us see how much variation there is among the number of marriages per 1,000 people in each state.

Research Hypothesis/Question   2.2:
Which states have the highest rate of marriage per 1,000 population?

Before you run this analysis, however, try to guess one of the top five states for marriage rates and one of the states that will be in the bottom five states in terms of marriage rate.

> *Data File:* **STATES**
> *Task:* **Mapping**
> *Variable 1:* **34) MARRIAG 94**
> *View:* **Map**

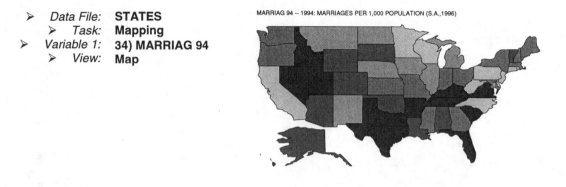

MARRIAG 94 -- 1994: MARRIAGES PER 1,000 POPULATION (S.A.,1996)

There seems to be no clear pattern in the number of marriages based on this map analysis. At best there appears to be several small clusters of states that have similar numbers of married couples. To see how each state compares on the proportion of marriage in its population, switch to the ranked list.

Data File: **STATES**
Task: **Mapping**
Variable 1: **34) MARRIAG 94**
> *View:* **List: Rank**

RANK	CASE NAME	VALUE
1	Nevada	96.3
2	Arkansas	15.6
3	Tennessee	15.5
4	Hawaii	15.2
5	South Carolina	13.9
46*	New Jersey	6.7
46*	Connecticut	6.7
48	California	6.5
49	Pennsylvania	6.3
50	West Virginia	6.0

* Both New Jersey and Connecticut were tied for the rank of 46, so the number 47 is not used in the rankings.

On this list, look closely at Nevada. You will notice that the number of marriages per 1,000 population is 96.3. This is far above the next state. The number two state is Arkansas at 15.6 marriages per 1,000 population. In research, a case like Nevada that is so different is called an *outlier*. This is a case where the data value is so out of line with the other values that it is in a group by itself. Such a case can throw off the *mean,* or *average*, and other statistics such as *standard deviation*. Anyway, I imagine that you pretty much know why there are so many marriages each year in Nevada.

2.4   Definition: Outlier

Usually an *outlier* is at least three deviations from the average mean values of the variable. Extreme *outliers* are typically dropped from the data analysis or analyzed separately because they may be a *measurement error* and may adversely affect the analysis. In this case, the Nevada number per 1,000 who marry is not a measurement error. It is a real number inflated by couples who come from other states to be married in Nevada because of the glamour and covenants of marriage laws in Nevada (Cherry, 2000; Singleton et al., 1993). Since this is a unique and extreme situation, Nevada would most likely be dropped from the analyses by most researchers.

The above rank-order list answers the question about the number of people who marry per 1,000 people in each state. It shows that, with the exception of Nevada, somewhere between 5 and 16 people per 1,000 in the United States marry each year. It also shows that the numbers who marry vary quite a bit from state to state.

What the rank-order list tells us is interesting and adds to our verified knowledge about marriage in the United States. What the list cannot tell us is whether the numbers of marriages have been static over the years or have been increasing or decreasing over the years. From what we hear and read from the popular press, we would believe that the number of marriages per 1,000 people has been dropping over the years. To find out if fewer people married in the United States in 1994 than in 1980, we can find the average for each year and compare them. We can test this assumption with the **STATES** database.

Research Hypothesis/Question   2.3:
What was the average number of marriages in the United States in 1980 and in 1994?

To answer the question, was the marriage rate lower in 1994 than in 1980, we again use the STATES database. This time, however, we will be using two variables and the univariate analysis procedure. First, find the average number per state that married in 1980 and then find the average for 1994. The following will give you the average for both years.

Data File: **STATES**	
➢ *Task:* **Univariate**	
➢ *Primary Variable:* **34) MARRIAG 94**	
➢ *View:* **Summary**	

```
MARRIAG 94 -- 1994: MARRIAGES PER 1,000
POPULATION (S.A.,1996)

Mean: 10.852    Std. Dev.: 12.544   N:    50

Median: 8.500   Variance: 157.3  Missing:  0
```

Now do the following to find the average for number of people who married in 1980.

Data File: **STATES**	
Task: **Univariate**	
➢ *Primary Variable:* **45) MARRIAGE80**	
➢ *View:* **Summary**	

```
MARRIAGE80 -- MARRIAGES PER 1000
POPULATION in 1980.  Omitted case: Nevada 142.8
per 1,000 marriages

Mean: 10.68     Std. Dev.: 2.180   N:    49

Median: 10.500  Variance: 4.75   Missing:  1
```

At first glance there appears to be little change; however, if you look more closely at the table, Nevada was dropped from the 1980 data file because **as an outlier it can distort the average**. In 1980, 142.8 people were married for every 1,000 people living in Nevada. In the rank list above in 1994 Nevada had a rate of marriage almost 7 times that of the state with the next-highest rank at 96.3 marriages per 1,000. To see if Nevada is affecting the average for the number who married in 1994, look at the Variance coefficient from the 1994 data analysis. A variance value or coefficient of 157.3 indicates that there is a great deal of difference in the range of scores between the state with the fewest marriages and the state with the highest number of marriages (Nevada).

Nevada needs to be dropped from the analysis and the analysis run again. When we do the new analysis the average for 1994 will change.

Data File:	STATES		MARRIAG94B-- MARRIAGES PER 1,000 POPULATION
Task:	Univariate		in 1994. Omitted case: Nevada 96.3 per 1,000
➤ Primary Variable:	35) MARRIAG94B		marriages
➤ View:	Summary		

> Data File: **STATES**
> Task: **Univariate**
> ➤ Primary Variable: **35) MARRIAG94B**
> ➤ View: **Summary**

MARRIAG94B-- MARRIAGES PER 1,000 POPULATION in 1994. Omitted case: Nevada 96.3 per 1,000 marriages

Mean: 9.08   Std. Dev.: 2.327   N: 49

Median: 8.400   Variance: 5.13   Missing: 1

Now if we look at the values of the variance reported in the three analyses, clearly the analysis that included Nevada distorted the view of the number of people who marry in the United States. In both years, when Nevada is dropped, the variance is approximately five for each year. This suggests (excluding Nevada) that there is little difference in the range of scores between the state with the fewest marriages and the state with the highest number of marriages. The same is true for standard deviations, which varies little from year to year. That is why Nevada and similar data points are called an outlier.

As you can see, when Nevada is dropped from the analysis, the mean number of marriages dropped to 9.1 from 10.68 in 1994 per 1000 people. The new analysis also shows that the average number of marriages in 1994 (excluding Nevada) was 1.57 less than in 1984 per 1,000 people in the United States.

2.5   Definition: Standard Deviation

The *standard deviation* is a measure of dispersion or distribution of data points around the mean. In the distribution of data that make up a normal distribution, 68% of cases fall within one standard deviation (SD) of the mean. Ninety-five percent (95%) will fall within 2 SD of the mean. If the average age of students in your research class is 30 and the SD is 5 years of age, then 68% of your classmates are between 25 and 35 years old. If you look at the age of students two standard deviations from the mean, 95% of your classmates will be between the ages of 20 and 40 years of age. A large SD typically indicates a flat normal curve where the population is diverse, or heterogeneous. A small SD typically indicates a narrow and peaked normal curve where the population is very similar, or homogeneous.

This is a substantial drop over a short period. Given no other reason for the drop, one could speculate, based on this limited statistical analysis, that marriage was not viewed as being as important in the United States in 1994 as it was in 1980. If the numbers who marry are dropping, that will be a serious concern for those promoting traditional values. If the numbers who marry are dropping, but the number of families headed by a single mom is increasing, that would be a serious concern for the Social Libertarians.

One way to improve the reliability of our findings is to use triangulation to look at the issue in several ways. For example, we know that the number of people marrying per year varies from state to state, and we know that the number of people marrying declined between 1980 and 1994.

2.6   Using Triangulation to Examine Social Welfare Issues

Triangulation is especially useful for dealing with problems related to systematic error. It improves the reliability of the study when several different research methods are used to collect data on the same phenomenon. We tend to have more confidence when data are collected from several sources and they all point to similar descriptions or explanations of the phenomenon. One form of triangulation, when doing qualitative research, is the use of observation data and interview data. Another approach might be using records, observations, and interviews. One of the most ambitious approaches to triangulation is to use qualitative and quantitative methodologies to study a phenomenon. Typically, this is more expensive and time-consuming. Basically, you are doing two different studies (Cherry, 2000).

To determine if the Social Libertarians need to be worrying along with the Traditionalists, let us look at differences among the states in terms of single-parent families. Using this approach, we are looking for other indicators that suggest a decline in the popularity of marriage in the United States.

Research Hypothesis/Question   2.4:
Which states in the U.S. have the highest number of single-parent households?

Data File: **STATES**
➢ Task: **Mapping**
➢ Variable 1:   **43) F HEAD/C90**
➢ View: **Map**

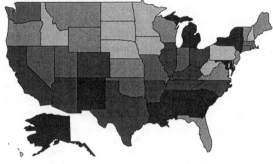

F HEAD/C90 -- 1990: PERCENT OF HOUSEHOLDS THAT ARE FEMALE HEADED WITH OWN CHILDREN, NO SPOUSE PRESENT

Did you think that half of the states with the highest percentage of female-headed households and no spouse present would be in the Deep South? Let's take a look at the rank-order list for the top 5 and bottom 5 states.

2.7	Mr. Mom
•	In 2.2 million households in the United States, fathers are raising their children without a mother in the home. The 2.2 million "father-only" households represent 2% of all households.
•	The number of single-father households increased 62% between 1990 and 2000.
•	"Mother-only" households accounted for 13 million households out of 105 million households and increased 25% between 1990 and 2000 (U.S. Bureau of the Census, 2000).

Data File: **STATES**
Task: **Mapping**
Variable 1:   **43) F HEAD/C90**
➢ View: **List: Rank**

RANK	CASE NAME	VALUE
1	Mississippi*	9.12
1	Louisiana*	9.12
3	Georgia	7.79
4	Michigan	7.68
5	South Carolina	7.49
46	South Dakota	5.13
47	Iowa	4.90
48	Hawaii	4.74
49	New Hampshire	4.72
50	North Dakota	4.68

*Both Mississippi and Louisiana tied for 1st place, so the number 2 was not used in the rankings.

Based on the map and ranking of the states, you will notice that the states with the highest number of single moms tend to be overrepresented by southern states. Although a lot of researchers are reporting high levels of poverty among households headed by females with their own children and no spouse present, this does not mean that poverty is the cause for the large percent of single moms and their children. It does suggest, however, that in the United States families headed by females with no husband present goes hand in hand with living in poverty. You might also suggest, based on the ranks, that poverty among female-headed households tends to be more common in southern states.

Research Hypothesis/Question   2.5:
Is there a correlation between being a single mom and living below the level of poverty?

In this analysis, we will analyze two variables at the same time in what is called a bivariate, Pearson correlation analysis, or scatterplot. In Chapter 1, we compared several maps and used Pearson's r to evaluate the strength of the relationship. The scatterplot task relies on Pearson's r as well, but it also gives us other tools to use to evaluate the relationship.

To take a quick look at how the scatterplot is created, we can draw a horizontal line across the bottom of a piece of paper. This line will represent the variable F Head/C90 or the percent of households that are headed by a woman with her own children present, but without a spouse. So, at the left of this line we will write 4, the lowest value of any state. At the right end of the line we will write 10 for the highest value.

```
 _____
4                              10
```

Now we can draw a vertical line up the left side of the paper. This line will represent the variable POV.LINE, or the percent of the population below the poverty line. At the bottom of this line, we will write 7 to reflect the lowest value, and at the top we will write 26 to represent the highest value.

```
26 |
   |
   |
   |
   |
   |
   |
 7 |_____
   4                              10
```

Now that we have a line with an appropriate scale for each variable, the next thing we need to do is refer to the distributions for each variable in order to learn the value for each state and then locate it on each line according to its score. Let's start with Louisiana. Since it is one of two states with the highest percent of households headed by a woman, we will make a mark at 9.12 on the horizontal line. Since it is also has the highest percentage of people living under the poverty line, we will make a mark at 25.7 on the vertical line. Next we draw a line up from the point on the horizontal line, and a line out from the vertical line, and where these two lines meet we draw a dot. This dot represents the combined map locations of Louisiana.

When reading explanations about statistics and statistical procedures, it is helpful to read slowly.

Let's go ahead and use MicroCase to make a completed scatterplot of these two variables.

➢ Data File:	**STATES**
➢ Task:	**Scatterplot**
➢ Dependent Variable:	**78) POV.LINE**
➢ Independent Variable:	**43) F HEAD/C90**

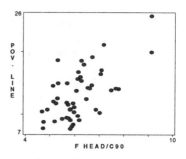

Notice that the Scatterplot task requires two variables.

Special feature: When the scatterplot is showing, you may obtain information on any dot by clicking on it. A little box will appear around the dot, and the values of the two variables will be shown.

The next step is to create a **regression line**.

To show the regression line, select the [Reg. Line] option from the menu.

Data File:	**STATES**
Task:	**Scatterplot**
Dependent Variable:	**78) POV.LINE**
Independent Variable:	**43) F HEAD/C90**
➢ View:	**Reg. Line**

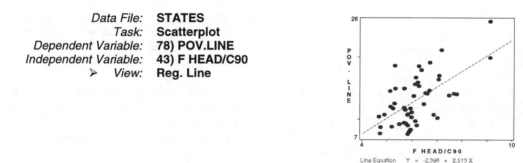

The regression line represents the best effort to draw a straight line that connects all the dots. Since the data from these two variables are similar, but not identical, most of the dots are scattered near, but not on, the regression line. Calculating Pearson's *r* is easy once the regression line is drawn. What it amounts to is measuring the distance from the regression line to every dot.

To show the residuals, select the [Residuals] option from the menu.

Data File:	**STATES**
Task:	**Scatterplot**
Dependent Variable:	**43) F HEAD/C90**
Independent Variable:	**78) POV.LINE**
➢ View:	**Reg. Line/Residuals**

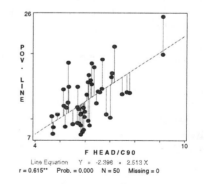

If you add the length of all the lines together, you would have the sum of the deviation of the dots from the regression line. The smaller this sum is, the more alike are the two variables. For example, when the maps are identical and all the dots are on the regression line, the sum of the deviations is 0.

If you look at the lower left of the screen, you will see $r = 0.615**$. This means the same thing it did when you were looking at two maps. This is a moderately strong correlation, and it is significant as Prob. = 0.00. This is also a positive correlation. Positive correlations are shown in scatterplots by the direction of the line; it will always slope upward from left to right. This represents how, if a case has a high value for one variable, it will also have a high value for the other variable. Conversely, for a negative relationship, besides the negative sign before the value for Pearson's r, the line will slope downward from left to right. This represents how, if a case has a high value for one variable, it will have a low value for the other variable

Now let's find Louisiana on this grid. To find Louisiana, you can either click on the dot that has the highest value for both variables, or select the [Case] option on the left of the screen. A list of the cases will appear, and if you select Louisiana off the list, you will see a dot in the top right corner is highlighted.

As we have noticed, this scatterplot shows that the state of Louisiana has the highest rate of single moms and the highest percentage of population below the poverty line of any state in the United States. While this does not prove that being a single mom puts you and your family at risk of being poor, it adds support to the idea. This supports our hypothesis, even though the two conditions (variables) are not perfectly related ($r = .615$, $p < .000$). In other words, at the time the data were collected, about 40% ($r^2 = .38$) of the reason a family would be living in poverty was because it was headed by a female. About four of every five female-headed households were living in poverty in the United States. The 40% is the amount of variance explained by being a single mom. The 40% is found by multiplying the Pearson's correlation ($r = .615$) times itself. Try it.

End Note: In this chapter you were introduced to some important inequities that harm families. The story as the saying goes is *in the numbers*. It is impossible for us and our political leaders to deny these inequities. We can ignore them, but we cannot deny them. With basic univariate and bivariate analyses, a strong case can be made for improving and expanding economic supports for families in general and specifically for families headed by females. The scatterplot was also used to demonstrate how two related variables look and act when used in a bivariate analysis. Correlation, which was introduced briefly, will be used and explained in more detail in the next chapter when we examine the world that children experience.

Other Family Issues

There are a number of issues related to families that I cannot examine in this chapter. However, with the data files provided with this book, once you become familiar with MicroCase you can analyze many of these issues on your own. Remember this is real data about real people like you and me. You may have even responded to the General Social Survey (GSS), which means your opinion is represented in these data files. Anyway, the following is a partial list of additional issues important for understanding the plight of families. These issues have been important in the past and continue to be important today. To learn more about other issues related to families, you can enter the following search terms in the InfoTrac College Edition.

Family advocacy	**Family policy**
Family assessment	**Minority families**
Family medical leave	**Housing**
Family welfare	**Foster parents**
Family violence	**Kinship care**

NAME:

COURSE:

DATE:

Workbook exercises and software are copyrighted. Copying is prohibited by law.

Review Questions

Based on the work you've done so far on the issue of family, see how well you do on this short True or False quiz.

Although families continue to be the basic unit of society, people have discovered many ways to come together as family.	T F
Ethics must play a central role in the provision of family services.	T F
In the analysis using the variable WED PASSÉ there were several countries where more than half of the people thought that marriage was outdated.	T F
The United States falls among the countries that have the fewest people who think marriage is outdated.	T F
An outlier is a data point that can distort the average because its value is so different from the other cases.	T F
In the 50 states, the greatest number of single moms living in poverty in 1994 was in the state of Iowa.	T F

MicroCase QUESTIONS

If you have any difficulties using the software to obtain the appropriate information, or if you want to learn additional features of the MAPPING or SCATTERPLOT tasks, use the online help (F1).

Use the data files, variables, and analytical approaches to answer the following MicroCase questions.

1.   Before we go any further in our examination of the family, we might ask if the family is still important in the lives of people today. The answer may change the way we go about our study. From the following database, map the percent of people surveyed who say the family is very important in their lives.

> ➢   *Data File:*   **GLOBAL**
> ➢   *Task:*   **Mapping**
> ➢   *Variable 1:*   **94) FAMILY IMP**
> ➢   *View:*   **List: Rank**

a.   Which 5 countries surveyed had the highest number of people responding that family was important to them?

_____ _____ _____ _____ _____

b.   Which 5 countries surveyed had the lowest number of people responding that family was important to them?

_____ _____ _____ _____ _____

c.   Is family important to people in the United States?   Yes   No

2.   Divorce is a major problem for families. It affects family members for life and it can have a devastating effect on communities. Many studies have found divorce linked to depression, anxiety, drug use, etc. The 10 leading reasons stated for divorce in the United States are communication problems, basic unhappiness, incompatibility, emotional abuse, financial problems, sexual problems, alcohol abuse by spouse, infidelity, physical abuse, and last but not the least, the in-laws (Ashford et al., 2001).

> ➤ *Data File:*   **STATES**
> ➤ *Task:*   **Mapping**
> ➤ *Variable 1:*   **36) DIVORCE 94**
> ➤ *View:*   **List: Rank**

a.   Which 5 states have the highest rate of divorce?

_____ _____ _____ _____ _____

b.   Which 5 states have the lowest divorce rates?

_____ _____ _____ _____ _____

>   *Data File:*   **STATES**
> ➤ *Task:*   **Scatterplot**
> ➤ *Dependent Variable:*   **36) DIVORCE 94**
> ➤ *Independent Variable:*   **55) CH.MEMB 90**
> ➤ *View:*   **Reg. Line**

Note that the SCATTERPLOT task requires you to choose two variables.

c.   What is the correlation coefficient? $r =$ _____ Is it significant?   Yes   No

d. Which statement best describes these results?

1. There is a weak but statistically significant relationship between states with higher levels of church membership and lower levels of divorce.
2. There is a strong and statistically significant relationship between states with higher levels of church membership and lower levels of divorce.
3. There is no statistically significant relationship between states with higher levels of church membership and lower levels of divorce.

In the chapter we discussed that an *outlier* is a case that is remarkably different from the others to the extent it can affect the results disproportionately. The SCATTERPLOT task provides an easy way to find out if an outlier is affecting the results, and it tells you what your results would be without the outlier. Let's go ahead and check for an outlier here.

> *Find:* **Outlier**

Select the [Outlier] option from the menu.

e. According to the information shown to the left of the scatterplot, what state is the outlier?

_____

f. If this state were removed, what would the new correlation coefficient be?

r = _____ Would it be significant? Yes No

Go ahead and click [Remove] to eliminate this case from the analysis.

g. Now, which statement best describes these results?

1. There is a weak but statistically significant relationship between states with higher levels of church membership and lower levels of divorce.
2. There is a strong and statistically significant relationship between states with higher levels of church membership and lower levels of divorce.
3. There is no statistically significant relationship between states with higher levels of church membership and lower levels of divorce.

One of the reasons often given for getting a divorce is economics. Let's examine the role that poverty plays in the divorce rates.

> Data File: **STATES**
> Task: **Scatterplot**
> Dependent Variable: **36) DIVORCE 94**
> ➤ Independent Variable: **78) POV.LINE**
> ➤ View: **Reg. Line**

h. What is the correlation coefficient? *r* = _____ Is it significant? Yes No

     i.   Which statement best describes these results?

    1. There is a weak but statistically significant relationship between states with higher percentages of the population living in poverty and lower divorce rates.

    2. There is a moderate and statistically significant relationship between states with higher percentages of the population living in poverty and higher divorce rates.

    3. There is no statistically significant relationship between states with higher percentages of the population living in poverty and higher divorce rates.

3.   Let's see if the amount of money countries spend on public education has an impact on the belief that families with more than three children are ideal.

       ➤   *Data File:*   **GLOBAL**
       ➤   *Task:*   **Scatterplot**
    Dependent Variable: **11) LARGE FAML**
  ➤ *Independent Variable:*   **31) PUB EDUCAT**
       ➤   *View:*   **Reg. Line**

    a.   What is the correlation coefficient? *r* = _____ Is it significant?   Yes   No

Let's check for an outlier here.

       ➤   *Find:* **Outlier**

    b.   What case is identified as the outlier? _____

    c.   If this case were removed, what would the new correlation coefficient be?

    r = _____ Would it be significant?   Yes   No

Go ahead and click [Remove] to eliminate this case from the analysis.

    d.   Explain why you think spending on public education does or does not impact attitudes about ideal family size around the world.

    e.   Do these results surprise you?   Yes   No

4.   For some people around the world, among both men and women, there is the belief that the only thing that women want out of life is a home and children.   Yes   No

> Data File: **GLOBAL**
> Task: **Mapping**
> ➤ Variable 1: **56) HOME&KIDS**
> ➤ View: **List: Rank**

a.   Which country ranked highest on this list? _____

b.   What percent agreed with this statement? _____

c.   Which country ranked lowest on the list? _____

d.   What percent agreed with this statement? _____

e.   Where did the United States rank? _____

f.   What percent agreed with this statement? _____

Now do the bivariate analysis to answer the following questions.

> Data File: **GLOBAL**
> ➤ Task: **Mapping**
> ➤ Dependent Variable: **56) HOME&KIDS**
> ➤ Independent Variable: **31) PUB EDUCAT**
> ➤ View: **List: Rank**

g.   What is the correlation coefficient? $r =$ _____ Is it significant?   Yes   No

h.   Which statement best describes these results?

1.   There is a strong and statistically significant relationship between greater spending on education and lower percentages of people who agree that what women really want is a home and children.

2.   There is no statistically significant relationship between greater spending on education and lower percentages of people who agree that what women really want is a home and children.

3.   There is a strong and statistically significant relationship between greater spending on education and higher percentages of people who agree that what women really want is a home and children.

i.   The statement you selected in Question 4.h. is considered a

1.   Positive relationship
2.   Negative relationship
3.   Circular relationship
4.   No relationship

Lesbians and Gay Men as Parents

It is important to remember that in years past, the typical reason most public policy forbid openly gay and lesbian adults from adopting children was the unfounded fear that they would turn their children to the gay lifestyle. Most children, however, in families headed by gays or lesbians are the children's natural parents. Many more gay and lesbian parents never reveal their sexual orientation. Nevertheless, the question was asked by a number of researchers. They consistently found that children raised by homosexual parents were no more likely to become gay than children raised by heterosexual parents. However, they were found to be more accepting of people who were different than themselves (Kirst-Ashman and Hull, 2001).

5.   Using the **GLOBAL** data file, look at how people in different countries reacted to the question of gay sex. Does the level of education affect the attitude of people from different countries?

>   *Data File:* **GLOBAL**
>   ➤ *Task:* **Mapping**
>   ➤   *Variable 1:* **80) ANTI-GAY**
>   ➤ *View:* **List: Rank**

    a.   Which 5 countries tend to have the lowest percent of people who would not want homosexuals as neighbors?

    _____ _____ _____ _____ _____

    b.   Which 5 countries tend to have the highest percent of people who would not want homosexuals as neighbors?

    _____ _____ _____ _____ _____

6.   Next, test the hypothesis that in countries where people agree with the statement that all "women really want is a home and children" will not want homosexuals for neighbors. In other words, we will use this variable as a measure of conservative and/or traditional thinking.

>   *Data File:* **GLOBAL**
>   ➤ *Task:* **Scatterplot**
>   ➤   *Dependent Variable:* **80) ANTI-GAY**
>   ➤   *Independent Variable:* **56) HOME&KIDS**
>   ➤ *View:* **Reg. Line**

    a.   What is the correlation coefficient? *r* = _____ Is it significant?   Yes   No

    b.   Is our hypothesis supported?   Yes   No

c.   Does our variable 56) HOME&KIDS appear to be a good indicator of conservative and/or traditional attitudes?   Yes   No

7.   Now let's hypothesize that the populace will be more tolerant of gays and lesbians in countries where more money is spent on public education.

> Data File: **GLOBAL**
> Task: **Scatterplot**
> Dependent Variable: **80) ANTI-GAY**
> ➢   Independent Variable: **31) PUB EDUCAT**
> ➢   View: **Reg. Line**

a.   What is the correlation coefficient? *r* = _____ Is it significant?   Yes   No

b.   Is our hypothesis supported?   Yes   No

c.   Which statement best explains why PUB EDUCAT is used as an independent variable in this analysis?

1.   The level of spending for public education creates an environment that impacts attitudes toward gays and lesbians.
2.   Attitudes toward gays and lesbians impact the level of spending for public education.
3.   Neither variable influences the other; it was a random choice.

8.   Another hypothesis to consider is that more people will be tolerant of the homosexual lifestyle in countries with a high level of gender equality.

> Data File: **GLOBAL**
> Task: **Scatterplot**
> Dependent Variable: **80) ANTI-GAY**
> ➢   Independent Variable: **52) GENDER EQ**
> ➢   View: **Reg. Line**

a.   What is the correlation coefficient? *r* = _____ Is it significant?   Yes   No

b.   Is our hypothesis supported?   Yes   No

Let's check to see if a single case is disproportionately affecting our results.

> ➢   Find: **Outlier**

c.   Does the outlier change the outcome of our analysis in a way that validates or invalidates the hypothesis?   Yes   No

d. Do you expect that gender equality will be higher in countries that spend more on public education?   Yes   No

Let's find out.

> ➤   *Data File:*   **GLOBAL**
> ➤   *Task:*   **Scatterplot**
> ➤   *Dependent Variable:*   **52) GENDER EQ**
> ➤   *Independent Variable:*   **31) PUB EDUCAT**
> ➤   *View:*   **Reg. Line**

e. What is the correlation coefficient? *r* = _____ Is it significant?   Yes   No

f. Is our hypothesis supported?   Yes   No

Diverse Family Styles

I would like to leave you with this observation. In the United States and Eastern Europe, families have become much more diverse. Working in the human services it is common to work with families who are composed of a parent and stepparent, who are raising some combination of children from one or more marriages. Families where one of the parents is in prison or separated by military service are also common. There are growing numbers of gays and lesbians raising children as single parents and as couples. Grandparent-headed families raising grandchildren are common (Zastrow, 2000).

2.8	Estimates of Children in Lesbian and Gay Homes
•	In the United States, estimates vary widely on the number of adult gay and lesbians with children in their home from 1.5 million to 5 million.
•	Estimates of children being raised in gay and lesbian homes are between 8 and 10 million.

Variable Lists Related to Family

The following is a partial list of the variables in your data files that you might find interesting in your study of families. You can examine them as either individual variables or two variables at a time using the MicroCase approaches you learned in this chapter. To see a list of the variables, the variable descriptions, and the range of values, either select any statistical option in the Basic Statistics menu, or press [F3] at any time to view the variable selection window. Try this with some of the other variables you have already tested.

GLOBAL

12) INF. MORTL
 NUMBER OF INFANT DEATHS PER 1,000 BIRTHS (TWF, 1997)
13) CONTRACEPT
 1990–1995: % OF WOMEN USING CONTRACEPTION (HDR, 1998)
14) ABORTION
 ABORTIONS PER 1,000 LIVE BIRTHS (NBWR, 1991)
15) MOM HEALTH
 PERCENT WHO APPROVE OF AN ABORTION WHEN THE MOTHER'S HEALTH IS AT RISK
55) SINGLE MOM -- PERCENT WHO APPROVE OF A WOMAN CHOOSING TO BE A SINGLE PARENT
 (WVS)

STATES

23) %>17 90
 1990: PERCENT OF POPULATION 18 YEARS OR OLDER
40) %WIDOWS90
 1990: PERCENT OF FEMALES OVER 15 WHO ARE WIDOWED
44) ONE P.HH90
 1990: PERCENT OF HOUSEHOLDS WITH ONE PERSON
96) SEX RAT.96
 1996: NUMBER OF MALES PER 100 FEMALES (U.S. BUREAU OF THE CENSUS)

Web Pages Related to Families

If you wish to find a world of resources that are available to you over the Internet, the following list of Web sites will get you started. Once you visit these Web sites you, will find many interesting links to other useful Web sites.

The American Association of Family and
Consumer Sciences
www.aafcs.org

American Family Association
www.afa.net

Children, Youth and Family Consortium
www.cyfc.umn.edu

Jewish Family.Com
www.jewishfamily.com

Australian Institute of Family Studies
www.aifs.org

Family Health International
www.fhi.org

References

Ashford, J. B., Lecory, C. W. and Lortie, K. L. (2001). *Human Behavior in the Social Environment* (2nd ed.). Belmont, CA: Wadsworth/Thomson Learning.

Cherry, A. L. (2000). *A Research Primer for the Helping Professions: Methods Statistics and Writing.* Belmont, CA: Brooks/Cole Pub.

Cherry, A. L., Dillon, M. E., and Rugh, D. (eds.) (2001). *Teenage Pregnancy: A Global View.* Westport, CT: Greenwood Pub.

Hepworth, D. H., Rooney, R. H. and Larsen, J. A. (1997). *Direct Social Work Practice: Theory and Skills* (4th ed.). Pacific Grove, CA: Brooks/Cole Pub.

Jansson, B. S. (2001). *The Reluctant Welfare State* (4th ed.). Belmont, CA: Wadsworth Publishing Company.

Kirst-Ashman, K. K. and Hull, G. H. (2001). *Generalist Practice with Organizations & Communities* (2nd ed.). Belmont, CA: Wadsworth Publishing Company.

Longres, J. E. (2000). *Human Behavior in the Social Environment* (3rd ed.). Itasca, IL: F. E. Peacock Pub. Inc.

Meyer, C. (1990, April 11). *Can social work keep up with the changing family?* [Monograph] The fifth annual Robert J. O'Leary Memorial Lecture. Columbia, OH: The Ohio State University College of Social Work, 1–24.

Rawls, R. (1971). *A Theory of Justice.* Cambridge, MA: Harvard University Press.

Singleton, R. A., Straits, B. C. and Straits, M. M. (1993). *Approaches to Social Research* (2nd ed.). New York: Oxford Univ. Press.

Schriver, J. M. (1995). *Human Behavior and the Social Environment: Shifting Paradigms in Essential Knowledge for Social Work Practice.* Boston: Allyn & Bacon.

Tolbert, K. (2000). Japan spending billions for seniors to live at home. Miami, FL: *The Miami Herald* (July 9), p. 9a.

U.S. Bureau of the Census. (2001). *No. 60. Households, families, subfamilies, and married couples.* Washington, DC: U.S. Bureau of the Census. Retrieved May 15, 2001, from www.census.gov.

Zastrow, C. (2000). *Introduction to Social Work and Social Welfare.* (7th ed.). Belmont, CA: Wadsworth Publishing Company.

Additional Material That May Be of Interest

Browning D. (2000). *From Culture Wars to Common Ground: Religion and the American Family Debate.* Louisville, KY: Westminster John Knox Press.

Casper, L. and Bianchi, S. (2001). *Continuity and Change in the American Family: Anchoring the Future.* Thousand Oaks, CA: Sage Pub.

Goldenberg, H. and Goldenberg, I. (2002). *Counseling Today's Families* (4th ed.). Belmont, CA: Brooks/Cole Pub.

Hayslip, B. and Goldberg-Glen, R. (eds). (2000). *Grandparents Raising Grandchildren: Theoretical, Empirical, and Clinical Perspectives.* New York: Springer Pub. Co.

Chapter 3

THE CHILDREN

Tasks: Mapping, Univariate, Scatterplot, Correlation
Data Files: GLOBAL, STATES, GSS

Overview of Chapter 3

In Chapter 3 you will continue to build on what you have learned in Chapters 1 and 2. You will first identify the countries and regions of the world where the highest percentage of children live. With this information, you will look at associate conditions such as the degree of economic development in countries with large populations of children. Infant mortality and the role played by public health and education to reduce infant mortality will be examined. Using the *States* database, we will identify the percentage of children living in poverty in the United States. You will also look at children who live in middle-class families by racial and ethnic identity. The General Social Survey (GSS) will be used to examine the public opinion of adults about children in the United States. While studying these issues, you will become familiar with the use of correlations. You will learn how to read a correlation table and learn what correlations tell us.

C hildhood is a period of growth and development. It is a time when our future is bright and hope abounds. Most people of all political and religious persuasions will agree with the cliché, "Our children are the best hope for the future." Having agreed with this statement, however, few people will be able to explain why we provide so little in terms of resources to ensure the best future for our children. The reality is incongruent with the platitudes. One might conclude that as a society we say one thing and do another. If this is true, how does it affect children? Let's see what the facts really are.

Who Are the Children of the World?

The vast majority of children on earth today are growing up in families where both parents must work to support them and their siblings. In the worst situation, parents work to stave off hunger and poverty. In the best situations, parents work to give their children the advantages their children will need to succeed as adults in the 21st century (Zastrow, 2000).

Let's back up; who are we talking about when we say *the children*? Are we talking about the children of the world? If we are, do we have any idea what the *children really look like*? They surely are not the same as children in the United States. We can use the **GLOBAL** data file to get a better picture of the children. We can start by testing the following.

Research Hypothesis/Question   3.1:
What countries have the highest percentage of children who are younger than 15 years of age?

We will use the variable that identified the number of children per country who were under 15 years of age, because at 15 most of the children in the Third World are working to help support their family and are often starting a family of their own (WHO, 2001).

> ➤ *Data File:* **GLOBAL**
> ➤ *Task:* **Mapping**
> ➤ *Variable:* **21) % UNDER 15**
> ➤ *View:* **Map**

% UNDER 15 -- PERCENT OF POPULATION UNDER 15 YEARS OLD (SAUS, 1998)

As you can see from the map, the majority of the world's children under 15 years of age live in Central Africa. The fewest children under 15 live in Italy, Spain, Japan, Germany, Greece, and in countries that made up the former Union of Soviet Socialist Republics (USSR). The transition from a state-controlled economy to a market economy was devastating to more than the Soviet economy. Millions of people died from lack of basic services, while others became distraught, depressed, or (as the majority of the people did) increased their already-heavy consumption of vodka (Cherry et al., 2002).

Based on the map above, one could surmise that countries with larger populations of children under 15 years of age are poor countries. Interesting, but let's test the assumption to see if that is the case. One measure we can use is the countries' level of economic development.

Research Hypothesis/Question   3.2:
Economically underdeveloped countries will have the highest percentage of children younger than 15.

Before we test this hypothesis, write down the outcome you expect.

> *Data File:* **GLOBAL**
> *Task:* **Mapping**
> *Variable 1:* **21) % UNDER 15**
> ➤ *Variable 2:* **24) ECON DEVEL**
> ➤ *View:* **Map**

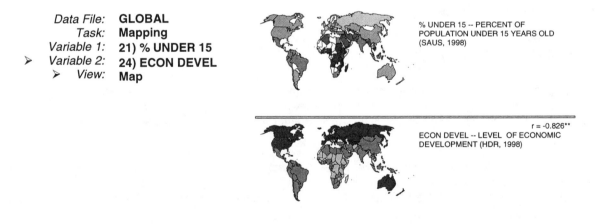

% UNDER 15 -- PERCENT OF POPULATION UNDER 15 YEARS OLD (SAUS, 1998)

$r = -0.826**$
ECON DEVEL -- LEVEL OF ECONOMIC DEVELOPMENT (HDR, 1998)

If you thought there would be a strong correlation between countries with large populations of children under 15 and countries that are underdeveloped economically – you were right. Congratulations! However, did you predict it would be an inverse relationship? It is a strong inverse relationship. In other words, the higher the country's rank in the percentage of children under 15, the lower the country tends to be ranked on level of economic development. As you may already know, correlations can be positive or inverse (negative).

The positive or negative sign tells us the direction of the relationship between the two variables. The correlation coefficient, the Pearson's r, tells us how strongly the two variables are related, or how closely the variables change in concert with one another. If we find a country with a large population of children, we can expect to find that the country will also tend to be economically underdeveloped.

3.1 Definition

A correlation can be positive or inverse. An *inverse correlation* between two variables exists when the values of the first variable increase while the values of the second variable decrease. As an example, when you pay your bills (an independent variable), the money you have in the bank (the dependent variable) goes down. In other words, the more bills you pay, the less money you have (Cherry, 2000).

To this point in our examination, we know that the majority of children under 15 live in countries that are not well developed economically. They may have unique and special cultures, but in terms of survival in the modern world, they are economically underdeveloped.

3.2 Ethics of Services to Children

What if by some truly stroke of bad luck you and your spouse were killed in an auto accident and you left behind three children who are 2, 5, and 8 years of age. Their grandparents have all passed away. You and your wife had no siblings. Distant relatives could not or did not want to take on the responsibility for the three children. The result was that the children had to be placed in foster care. Furthermore, it would be difficult to adopt out without separating the children. If you knew your children would enter the foster care system, what kinds of children's services, health, education, and other social services would you want for your children?

Based on what we know so far, we would expect (or we might hypothesize) that poor countries do not spend much on health care, so infant mortality will be high. High infant mortality puts more pressure on parents to have more children in hopes that a few will live (Cherry et al., 2001). Additionally, leaders in these countries act so irresponsibly in providing adequate public health care for their children, I would expect them to act as irresponsibly in expending resources on public education.

Would you expect the same? Or, would you guess that once a child reached school age in these poor countries, the leaders in these countries want the children to go to school to get an education because these leaders realize that an educated population will help improve their country's economic condition? Given the picture we are developing on fact and speculation, let's try to verify some of our suspicions about how the world's children are treated. We can see if the statements (hypotheses) we make are true by using variables from the **GLOBAL** database to test them.

Given what we know from the data above and our study of children around the world (Cherry et al., 2001; Cherry et al., 2002), *my colleagues believe that the data collected on countries around the world will support our deductions that* (1) countries with the largest percent of children under 15 tend to spend less on public health [**32) PUB HEALTH**] than countries with fewer children under 15 years of age; (2) countries with the largest percent of children under 15 tend to have high rates of infant mortality [**12) INF. MORTL**]; (3) fertility [**10) FERTILITY**] is higher in countries with large percentages of children under 15; and (4) countries with the largest percent of children under 15 spend less on public education [**31) PUB EDUCAT**] than countries with fewer children under 15 years.

To begin to test these stated beliefs or hypotheses using real data, in this case we will use the MicroCase **Scatterplot** procedure to test the hypothesis. We will begin by generating a scatterplot using the two variables called **21) % UNDER 15** and **12) INF. MORTL**.

Research Hypothesis/Question   3.3:
Countries with populations that are younger than 15 years of age (1) will spend less on public health, (2) will spend less on public education, (3) will have some of the highest rates of infant mortality, and (4) will have some of the highest rates of fertility in the world.

Data File:	**GLOBAL**
➤ *Task:*	**Scatterplot**
➤ *Dependent Variable:*	**12) INF MORTL**
➤ *Independent Variable:*	**21) % UNDER 15**
➤ *View:*	**Reg. Line**

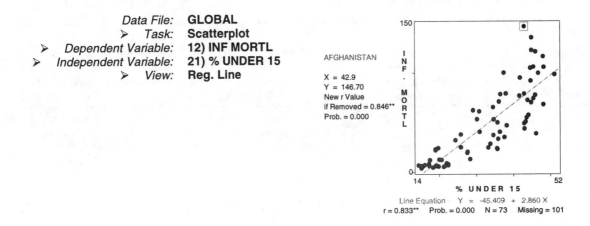

To see what country a dot on the graph represents, click on the dot. The program will give you the name of the country and specifications on that particular country.

The graph above indicates that the countries with large populations of children under 15 are the same countries that have high infant mortality rates ($r = .833$, $p < .01$). As you can see, Uganda has the world's largest percentage of children under 15 years of age and it also has one of the world's highest rates of infant mortality.

Could the high infant mortality rate in these countries be related to spending for public health? We will do another scatterplot to find out.

Data File:	**GLOBAL**
➤ *Task:*	**Scatterplot**
➤ *Independent Variable:*	**21) % UNDER 15**
➤ *Dependent Variable:*	**32) PUB HEALTH**
➤ *View:*	**Reg. Line**

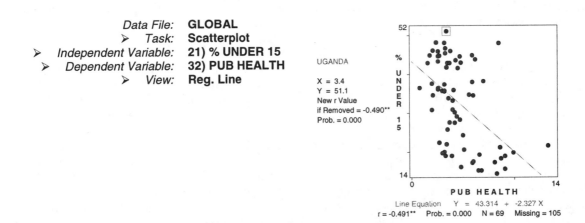

Again, Uganda, with the largest population of children under 15, is one of the nations that spends the least on public health. In spite of this, we do not want to malign Uganda; it is a poor country and like other poor countries, it must make tough decisions about priorities.

The reality is that in the world economy, children under 15 living in poor countries have very little value, influence, and no clout when their interests are competing against those of the industrial countries. How much damage do you think the rapid increase in oil prices in 2001 did to the children of the world? How do you think it affected spending on public health in poor countries like Uganda, Syria, Yemen, and other countries with large populations of children under 15? How many infants would you guess died because of cutbacks in public health expenditures so those poor countries could buy oil to keep their economies from collapsing? Although indirect, I believe the loss of life was great. To quickly answer our questions, we will use the **Correlation** procedure.

Correlation Coefficients Table

Data File: **GLOBAL**		% Under 15	Fertility	Inf. Mort	Pub Educat	Pub Health
Task: **Correlation**	% Under 15	1.000 (*n*=73)	0.932 ** (*n*= 72)	0.833 ** (*n*=73)	-0.092 (*n*=51)	-0.491 ** (*n*=69)
Variables: **21) % UNDER 15** **10) FERTILITY**	Fertility	0.932 ** (*n*=72)	1.000 (*n*=94)	0.847 ** (*n*=94)	-0.195 (*n*=66)	-0.390 ** (*n*=89)
12) INF. MORTL **31) PUB EDUCAT**	Inf. Mortl	0.833 ** (*n*=73)	0.847 ** (*n*=94)	1.000 (*n*=174)	-0.162 * (*n*=123)	-0.381 ** (*n*=145)
32) PUB HEALTH Deletion: **Pairwise**	Pub Educat	-0.092 (*n*=51)	-0.195 (*n*=66)	-0.162 * (*n*=123)	1.000 (*n*=123)	0.275 ** (*n*=108)
Test: **1-tailed**	Pub Health	-0.491 ** (*n*=69)	-0.390 ** (*n*=89)	-0.381 ** (*n*=145)	0.275 ** (*n*=108)	1.000 (*n*=145)

Pairwise deletion (1-tailed test) Significance Levels: ** =.01, * =.05

This correlation procedure will produce a correlation matrix using all five variables. This is still a bivariate analysis. We are simply doing four different bivariate analyses and putting them into a table so we can see if variables are correlated with each other. What kinds of social services for children would we expect if the leaders of those countries thought that *children are our future*? The correlation table provides us with an answer. As you can see, if you can read this correlation table, most of our hypotheses were correct. If you cannot read this correlation table, make sure you read the explanation in Box 3.3.

3.3　Reading a Correlation Table

1.　One thing you need to know about reading a correlation table is that a correlation table is a matrix and is a mirror image of itself along the diagonal running down from the left upper corner to the lower right corner. This diagonal runs through the cells that have the *1.000* in them. The 1.000 reveals that the variable is perfectly correlated with itself. As an example, look at the cell at the bottom right-hand corner of the correlation table. That cell represents the correlation between the *expenditures on public health* at the top of the table with the same variable *expenditures on public health* on the side of the table. All the numbers above the diagonal are the same as the numbers below the diagonal. Take, for example, that spending on public health by countries with large populations of children under 15 is $r = -.491$, $p < .01$, which can be found in a lower left-hand corner cell. This cell has the same numbers in it as the cell in the upper right-hand corner. Like other cells above the diagonal, their values are the same in a mirror-image cells below the diagonal.

2.　There are two numbers in each cell. The number on top is the Pearson's r coefficient; it tells us the direction of the relationship and how strong or weak the relationship is between the two variables represented by the cell. The number below the correlation stands for the number in the sample or population used in the bivariate correlation. In this case, there were 69 countries with information on the number of *children under the age of 15* and each country's *spending on public health*.

3.　When you begin looking at a correlation table, look for one or two asterisks (*) by the numbers. The asterisks tell us that the relationship between the two variables is statistically significant. In the case of *public health spending*, among countries with large populations of children under 15, there is only 1 chance in a 100 that these results are due to random chance.

Based on the correlation table, we were not correct in all our beliefs. I stated that I believed that the leaders in poor countries would spend a smaller percentage of the resources on public education. If you agreed with me, we were both wrong on that one. Some leaders in these economically underdeveloped countries must have realized that saving money by not spending it on public education is "penny wise and pound foolish." Interestingly, they do not have the same attitude about spending on public health. As you can see in the table, there is a moderate but statistically significant inverse relationship between countries with large populations of children under 15 and the amount they spend for public health ($r = -.49$, $p < .01$). As a result, these countries have a high infant mortality rate ($r = .381$, $p < .01$). This means that there is more pressure on women to have more children, resulting in a high correlation between countries with large populations of children under 15 and high fertility rates ($r = .93$, $p < .01$). This is very compelling evidence. It means that in almost 100% of the cases where countries have high rates of infants dying, they will have high rates of children being born.

Please keep in mind when you are working with these variables that these are real data about real people in these countries. When the results of an analysis points to a country as having a high infant mortality rate, this means that the actual number of infants that died were counted. It would be possible to go to any of these countries and count the graves of the dead infants; that is how real the data are in your data files.

It is easy to be critical of these poor countries—the shortcomings are out there for everyone to see—but how does the United States treat its children?

Who Are the Children of the United States?

During the last 25 years of the 1900s, two profound changes occurred to make the process of childhood growth and development more understandable on the one hand, and more complicated on the other hand. During this period of the 20th century, a flood of discoveries and scientific findings increased our understanding of childhood. One of the major changes was the compelling evidence from many sources and scientific fields showing that the life experiences at the earliest stages of development have a crucial impact on the child's ability to learn and the behavioral patterns developed by children. Second, in the United States, the incorporation of this knowledge has been slow to improve the life of children because of a political agenda that relegates children's issues to a lower level of importance. Some researchers refer to the agenda building for children's issues in the United States as a process skewed against this *powerless population* (Jansson, 2001, p. 130).

3.4	U.S. Children Census Facts—2000
	• There were 72 million children and adolescents 17 years old or younger living in the United States.
	• There were 19 million children who were 4 or under living in the United States.
	• Over 43% of the population had completed high school and another 11.4% had finished college.
	• The median household money income in 1997 was $37,000 a year.
	• Approximately 14 million children were living in poverty in the United States in 1997. An income of less than $14,000 a year for a family of three in the year 2000 was considered poverty (U.S. Bureau of the Census, 2001).

First, as we did when beginning to examine the world's children, let's find out a few facts about the children of the United States. We can do this using the **STATES** data file.

The 2000 U.S. census reports that 20% of children live below the poverty level. This should be an embarrassment to us all. It means that every time you see five children, theoretically, one would be living in poverty. Trying to get a better understanding of who these *poor* children are will help our understanding of all the children of the United States (Ambrosino, et al., 2001).

To begin, why don't we map out the percentage of children living in poverty by state? This will give us an idea of whether child poverty is distributed evenly across the United States or whether poverty falls into some type of a pattern.

Research Hypothesis/Question   3.4:
Which states have the highest number of children living in poverty?

> *Data File:* **STATES**
> *Task:* **Mapping**
> *Variable:* **80) CHILD POR89**
> *View:* **Map**

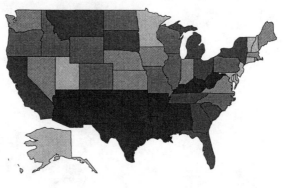

CHLD POR89 -- 1989: PERCENT OF CHILDREN UNDER 18 BELOW POVERTY LEVEL

The pattern we thought might appear could not be clearer. If you are a child, 17 or under, and you live in a southern state, the chances are good that you are living in poverty. Remember, the darker the colors on the map the more children in that state that are living in poverty. This map suggests some real inequities among children living in different regions of the country.

Given the extent of the poverty among these children, we need to look at their situation more closely. A group, such as *children living in poverty,* is considered a subgroup. We can learn a lot about these children as a subgroup. To begin, why don't we speculate as to what other maladies might befall children living in poverty in the United States. We can find some of the information we need about these children and the conditions under which they live in the **STATES** data file.

3.5	Excerpts—The 4th Annual Report to the Nation on Our Most Precious Resource, Our Children
•	In 2000, 25% of the population was 17 years old and under, down from a peak of 36% at the end of the Baby Boom in 1964. The number of children is expected to remain stable. It is projected that children will make up 24% of the population in the United States in 2020.
•	The racial/ethnic diversity of children in the United States has changed and it will continue to change. In 2000, 65% were white non-Hispanic; 15% were black non-Hispanic; 4% were Asian or Pacific Islander; and 1% were American Indian or Alaska Native. The number of Hispanic children increased faster than other racial/ethnic groups, growing from 9% in 1980 to 16% by 2000 (U.S. Bureau of the Census, 2001).

You may remember that in Chapter 2 we found a moderately strong correlation between single moms and families living in poverty ($r = .615$, $p < .01$). This means that if you meet a single mom in the local mall, there is a good chance she and her children are living in poverty. To build on those findings, why don't we see if the kids in households headed by a single mom are the same kids we see as a group living in poverty. They do not have to be the same kids. If poverty were a random occurrence, you would expect to find about the same number of children living in poverty in families with single moms, in families with both a mom and dad, as well as in families with a single dad. Here, however, based on what we think we know, we believe that the kids identified as living in poverty are pretty much the same kids who are living in the household of a single mom. If we are right, we should be able to find a strong correlation between the two variables. Try this analysis.

Research Hypothesis/Question   3.5:
States that have a high percentage of single moms will be states that have a high percentage of children living in poverty.

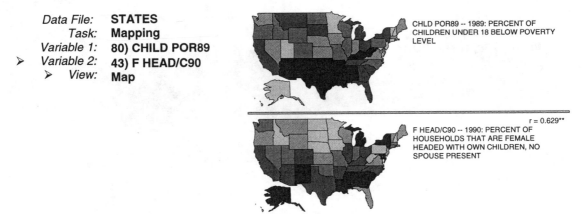

Data File:	**STATES**
Task:	**Mapping**
Variable 1:	**80) CHILD POR89**
➤ *Variable 2:*	**43) F HEAD/C90**
➤ *View:*	**Map**

CHLD POR89 -- 1989: PERCENT OF CHILDREN UNDER 18 BELOW POVERTY LEVEL

r = 0.629**

F HEAD/C90 -- 1990: PERCENT OF HOUSEHOLDS THAT ARE FEMALE HEADED WITH OWN CHILDREN, NO SPOUSE PRESENT

As we saw before, when there was a fairly strong correlation between two variables, such as we have here, we know that while most of the states will not have the same rank number on both lists; they will tend to be close in their ranking on both lists because of the correlation ($r = .63$, $p <.01$). Alabama has a large number of children living in poverty and is ranked 8th on that list. Alabama also has a large population of single moms and ranks 8th on that list.

It is interesting to take notice of the standing of Alaska on these two lists of the states by rank. Alaska ranks 9th in the number of female-headed households with children, right behind Alabama. At the same time it ranked 48th in the number of children living in poverty, just in front of Connecticut (which ranked 30th for single moms) and New Hampshire (which ranked 49th for single moms). Alaska is another very good example of an outlier. Typically, when we find states with large number of single mothers with children, we also expect to find that a good percentage of the children will be living in poverty. Alaska is an exception. Alaska has many single moms with children but very few poor children. We will take one more look at child poverty using the scatterplot procedure and then we will draw some tentative conclusions.

Research Hypothesis/Question   3.6:
The more single moms in a state, the more children in that state who will be living in poverty.

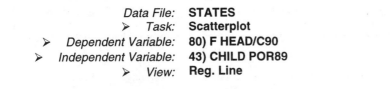

Data File:	**STATES**
➤ *Task:*	**Scatterplot**
➤ *Dependent Variable:*	**80) F HEAD/C90**
➤ *Independent Variable:*	**43) CHILD POR89**
➤ *View:*	**Reg. Line**

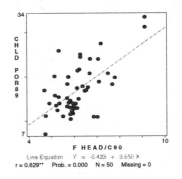

Line Equation   Y = -5.423 + 3.650 X
r = 0.629**   Prob. = 0.000   N = 50   Missing = 0

I am convinced, based on the maps and scatterplot, that our hypothesis is well supported by the facts. Although it is not true in every case, there is a genuine possibility ($r = .63$, $p < .01$) that if you know a child 17 years old or under living in the southern half of the United States, and that child lives in a household headed by a single female, there is a better than even chance that the child is living in poverty.

What these maps and scatterplot also clearly show is the inequity in how the children of the United States are treated from state to state.

The Racial and Ethnic Identity of Children in the United States

To continue to add pieces to the puzzle to reveal the picture that is emerging from the data, next we will examine children in the United States by their racial and ethnic make-up. Approximately 70 million people living in the United States did *not* identify themselves as being *white* in the 2000 census.

In this examination, I will limit the racial and ethnic groups to four. The groups will be made up of people who self-identified as African American, Asian, Hispanics, and white. In the United States, the quality of life of a child depends a lot on the family's income (Popple & Leighnger, 2001). The United States has a large middle class. Its institutions and government are structured to meet the needs of middle-class families and their children. So let's look at the median family income. This time, however, we will look at maps of where these families live by the racial or ethnic group with which they identify.

Research Hypothesis/Question   3.7:
What states have the highest number of middle-class families that self-identified as African American, Asian, Hispanic, or white?

Before we generate the maps that will show us where the racial and ethnic groups of families live, do you think there will be a pattern or cluster of states in similar regions of the country for the different racial and ethnic groups? Or do you think that the distribution will be random or equally divided among the states? Here we will want to consider the role of slavery as creating traditionally African American states, and the traditional role of our nation's borders, and cost lines related to immigration.

Before you read my conclusions about each map, consider what you think causes the different patterns. Do historical immigration patterns explain the differences? Or, do you think the distribution is a random occurrence that has no connection to history?

> ➢   *Data File:*   **STATES**
> ➢   *Task:*   **Mapping**
> ➢   *Variable 1:*   **14) %ASIAN/92**
> ➢   *Subset Variable:*   **75) MED.FAM$96**
> ➢   *Subset Range:*   **25086 - 5277**
> ➢   *View:*   **Map**

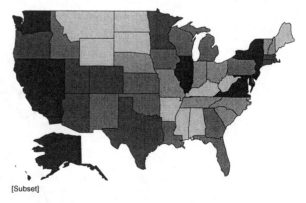

%ASIAN/P92 -- 1992: PERCENT ASIAN OR PACIFIC ISLANDERS (SA,1996)

[Subset]

This map shows us that middle-class Asian families in the United States tend to live around the Pacific Rim, Alaska, Hawaii, and the continental West Coast. These are traditional areas where Asian immigrants have historically settled (Jansson, 2001).

> *Data File:* **STATES**
> *Task:* **Mapping**
> *Variable 1:* **13) %BLACK/92**
> *Subset Variable:* **75) MED.FAM$96**
> *Subset Range:* **25086 - 5277**
> *View:* **Map**

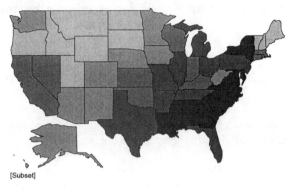

The majority of African American families tend to live in the historically slave states where their families established homesteads after Emancipation. These states have the highest number of middle-class African American families in the country (Jansson, 2001).

> *Data File:* **STATES**
> *Task:* **Mapping**
> *Variable 1:* **28) %HISPANC90**
> *Subset Variable:* **75) MED.FAM$96**
> *Subset Range:* **25086 - 5277**
> *View:* **Map**

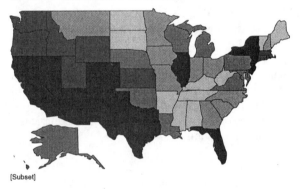

Middle-class Hispanic families also follow a historical and traditional pattern. They continue to live in Florida and the southwestern United States, where their families immigrated to the United States (Jansson).

> *Data File:* **STATES**
> *Task:* **Mapping**
> *Variable 1:* **32) %WHITE92**
> *Subset Variable:* **75) MED.FAM$96**
> *Subset Range:* **25086 - 5277**
> *View:* **Map**

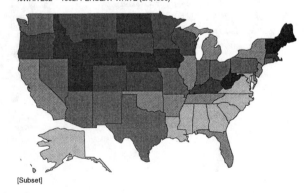

The explanation for the cluster of states where there are large numbers of white middle-class families is not as clear as with the other groups. However, they do cluster in the northwest and the northeastern corner of the United States, and in West Virginia. We do know that many whites left the south and moved west after the Civil War. Moreover, a large number of western Europeans that came to the United States entered the country on the East Coast. What do you think?

Attitudes About Children and Family

The 72 million children living in the United States at the turn of the 21st century faced many threats: (1) their parents had seen changes in the nature and amount of work they had to do to earn a living for their family; (2) even with the increase in overall education of parents, employment opportunities, and a strong economy, there continued to be high rates of children living below the poverty line; (3) there continued to be significant racial and ethnic disparities in health and developmental outcomes among children; (4) there were growing numbers of children who were spending more and more time in child-care settings; and, (5) there was more evidence that the public had come to believe that the negative effects of serious family problems and adverse community conditions had a profound negative impact on our children (Shonkoff & Phillips, 2000). However, as a society, how do we really feel about our children?

To get some understanding of how we really feel about kids, we can use information from the General Social Survey (GSS) found in the **GSS** data file. The GSS data consist of answers to hundreds of questions from thousands of randomly selected people in the United States.

Using this database, we can better understand the public view and opinion about our children. Education plays a major role in the life of a child, both at home and in school. We will start by seeing if people think we are spending enough on education. Then, we will look at our ideas about how children behave, and how we should punish them when they misbehave.

Research Hypothesis/Question 3.8:
Do people think that this country is spending enough on education?

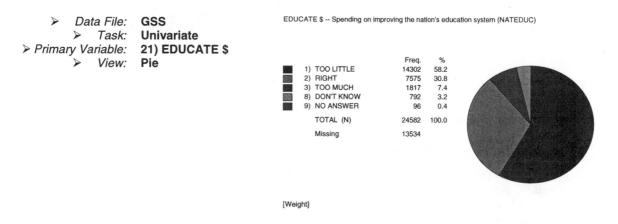

Fortunately, for our children and the country as a whole, 58% of people in this country think we spend too little on education, and another 30% think we are spending the right amount. At least 88% of the people do not want to spend less. Yet, 7.4% of the people surveyed believe that the United States spends too much for education. Who do you think these people are?

Research Hypothesis/Question   3.9:
What do people in the United States think is the ideal number of children?

Data File: **GSS**
Task: **Univariate**
➢ Primary Variable: **60) IDEAL#KIDS**
➢ View: **Pie**

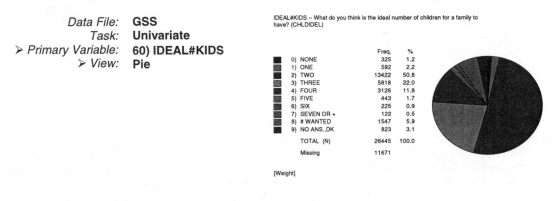

IDEAL#KIDS -- What do you think is the ideal number of children for a family to have? (CHLDIDEL)

		Freq.	%
0)	NONE	325	1.2
1)	ONE	592	2.2
2)	TWO	13422	50.8
3)	THREE	5818	22.0
4)	FOUR	3126	11.8
5)	FIVE	443	1.7
6)	SIX	225	0.9
7)	SEVEN OR +	122	0.5
8)	# WANTED	1547	5.9
9)	NO ANS.,DK	823	3.1
	TOTAL (N)	26445	100.0
	Missing	11671	

[Weight]

This is interesting; most people think the ideal number of children is two (50.8%). In fact, only 2.2% of people think one child is an ideal number of children. More people think that three or even four children per family is more the ideal than one child per family. Based on this survey question, I could safely say China's one-child, one-family policy would probably be as unpopular in the United States as it is in China.

Research Hypothesis/Question   3.10:
How important do we think it is to teach children to help others?

Data File: **GSS**
Task: **Univariate**
➢ Primary Variable: **38) HELP OTH**
➢ View: **Pie**

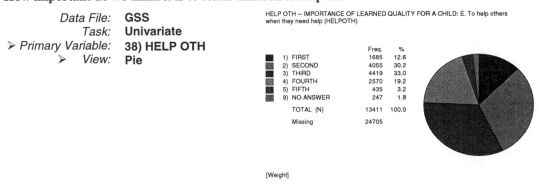

HELP OTH -- IMPORTANCE OF LEARNED QUALITY FOR A CHILD: E. To help others when they need help (HELPOTH)

		Freq.	%
1)	FIRST	1685	12.6
2)	SECOND	4055	30.2
3)	THIRD	4419	33.0
4)	FOURTH	2570	19.2
5)	FIFTH	435	3.2
9)	NO ANSWER	247	1.8
	TOTAL (N)	13411	100.0
	Missing	24705	

[Weight]

Although cynics in this country decry the loss of our moral compass, people still believe that altruism is an admirable trait (Schriver, 1998), so much so that 84% of people think it should be one of the top four qualities that a child should learn when growing up. Only 1.8% of people asked did not have an opinion.

3.6	**Two Theoretical Perspectives on Moral Development**
•	Cognitive-Development: The idea that a norm of reciprocal respect guides individual behavior. The way we think about a situation guides our behavior.
•	Learning Theory: Moral behavior develops from reinforcement of moral behavior, or through modeling the behavior of others (Ashford et al., 2001).

Research Hypothesis/Question   3.11:
Do people in this country support the practice of parents spanking their children?

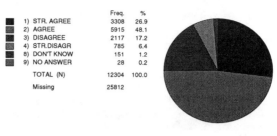

Data File:	**GSS**
Task:	**Univariate**
➤ Primary Variable:	**68) SPANKING**
➤ View:	**Pie**

SPANKING -- Do you strongly agree, agree, disagree, or strongly disagree that it is sometimes necessary to discipline a child with a good, hard spanking? (SPANKING)

		Freq.	%
■	1) STR. AGREE	3308	26.9
▨	2) AGREE	5915	48.1
▨	3) DISAGREE	2117	17.2
▨	4) STR.DISAGR	785	6.4
■	8) DON'T KNOW	151	1.2
▨	9) NO ANSWER	28	0.2
	TOTAL (N)	12304	100.0
	Missing	25812	

[Weight]

Although there has been a great deal of publicity about child physical abuse over the last 25 years, 75% of the people in the United States still believe that it *is sometimes necessary to discipline a child with a good, hard spanking.* To an old social worker, this is hard to comprehend. In the majority of cases of children who are physically abused, according to the abuser, they were just giving the child a "good, hard spanking." Child protection agencies in the United States investigated alleged maltreatment of almost 3 million children in 1997, double the number that was reported in 1980 (Ambrosino et al., 2001).

Foster Care in the United States

The foster care system in the United States is in a state of crisis. The number of children in foster care has almost doubled between 1987 and 1998. The numbers reported below are *point-in-time estimates.* This means that the number of children in foster care reported below is estimated at the end of each year. This estimate does not account for the number of children who experience foster care during a year. This number is substantially greater than *point-in-time estimates.* For instance in 1997, one estimate suggests that approximately 700,000 children were in foster care for some period of time during that year.

National estimates of the numbers of children in foster care between 1987 and 1998:

1987	280,000	1991	404,000	1995	483,000
1988	312,000	1992	417,000	1996	507,000
1989	347,000	1993	430,000	1997	516,000
1990	363,000	1994	455,000	1998	520,000

How Foster Children See the System and Those of Us Who Work in It

Case File: A file where too many people write about you and your life

Foster Care: The black hole for children

Social Worker: A person who drops you off places. The person who tries but cannot understand and is responsible for your life and makes choices for you.

Foster Parent: A face that shifts with each move. Some care, some needed money, some made it clear that I was an outsider while others abused me.

Guardian Ad Litem: A person who is supposed to give you a voice, but never listens to your voice. A person who does not fight for anything in your best interests.

Manipulation: A vague and subjective term used to justify some of the consequences given out by staff.

Privileges: As a foster kid, almost everything that a biological kid can expect becomes a privilege.

Respect:	Something I gave to people who didn't abuse their power over the children.
Abuse:	Something that is unacceptable in biological families but more acceptable from the strangers who are "protecting" you.
Depression:	Not having a permanent family or home to call your own. Being in the system. Knowing you are stuck in it. Hopelessness and the inability to look to the future. Coming to grips with the reality that you have no family. Not feeling loved. Being hurt and betrayed by everyone around you. Fearing that trusting another person will push you over the edge.
Reunification:	When someone in the system decides that it's easier to let you go home rather than struggle to find another placement for you.

You can read more about what foster children think of foster care at www.sos-fosternet.org/define.html.

Indicators of Child Well-Being

Given the less-than-glowing reports on the state of child rearing in the United States today, what are the indicators of child well-being? Indicators typically used to determine the well-being of children in the United States are important to all children in the world. The *2001 KIDS COUNT data book*, a Casey Foundation yearly publication, uses the following as indicators of children's health, safety, and well-being (Annie E. Casey Foundation, 2001).

1. Percent low-birth weight babies
2. Infant mortality rate
3. Child death rate
4. Rate of teen deaths by accident, homicide, and suicide
5. Teen birth rate
6. Percent of teens who are high school dropouts
7. Percent of teens not attending school and not working
8. Percent of children living with parents who do not have full-time, year-round employment
9. Percent of children in poverty
10. Percent of families with children headed by a single parent

End Note: In Chapter 3 you learned how to use basic statistics to tell the story of children. You also saw how a correlational analysis can be used to tell that story. It was clear from the correlation table that countries with high infant mortality rates had higher percentages of child under 15 years of age ($r = .83$, $p < .01$). You also were able to use the *mapping* procedure to test the hypothesis that racial and ethnic groups tend to live in the regions of the United States where their families traditionally lived. Next we will take a look at the lives of older people.

Other Children's Issues

There are a number of issues related to children and the public attitude toward their care and protection that I could not examine in this chapter. However, with the data files provided you can analyze many of these issues on your own. To learn more about other children's issues, enter the following search terms in the InfoTrac College Edition.

Foster care	**Adoption**
International adoption	**Day care**
Child soldiers	**Adolescent drug abuse**
Juvenile delinquency—justice	**Child labor—child slavery**
Teen pregnancy	**Female infanticide**

WORKSHEET

NAME: _____

COURSE: _____

DATE: _____

Workbook exercises and software are copyrighted. Copying is prohibited by law.

Review Questions

Based on the work you've done so far on the issue of family, see how well you do on this short True or False quiz.

Luckily, the United States has the largest population of children 14 years old or younger in the world.	T F
Countries with the largest population of children who are 14 years old and younger are also countries with the lowest levels of economic development.	T F
High rates of infant mortality is one of the indicators that a country's population is living in poverty.	T F
In countries where infant mortality is high, the women tend to be very fertile and have many more children than in countries where infant mortality is low.	T F
In countries with the largest population of children who are 14 years old and younger, spending on education is as dismal as spending on public health.	T F
In the United States, the states with the major pockets of children living in poverty are in the Northwest.	T F
After many years of public education most people in the United States do **not** believe parents should give their children a "good, hard spanking."	T F

MicroCase QUESTIONS

Use the following data files, variables, and analytical approaches to answer the MicroCase questions.

1. Although we have some information about the children of the world, what do you think people of the world believe about children? Based on the data from the **GLOBAL** data file, answer the following.

> ➤ Data File: **GLOBAL**
> ➤ Task: **Mapping**
> ➤ Variable 1: **96) KID OBEY**
> ➤ View: **Map**

a.   Is there a great deal of agreement, in the countries that we have data for, that children should obey their parents?   Yes   No

b.   In the Americas, in what two countries do a majority of people believe that children should be obedient? _____ _____

c.   Japan has many enduring traditions.   Have these traditions effected their belief that children should obey their parents?   Yes   No

2.   Now answer a couple of questions about people who think children should be obedient.

       Data File: **GLOBAL**
      ➢ *Task:*   **Correlation**
  ➢ *Variables:*   **95) KID INDEPN**
               96) KID OBEY

a.   Do people of the world who think children should be obedient also think children should develop independence?   Yes   No

b.   What is the correlation coefficient for the correlation between these two variables?

    $r =$ _____ Is it significant?   Yes   No

3.   Many people think that television has had a negative effect on children and adults.

            Data File: **GLOBAL**
           ➢ *Task:*   **Scatterplot**
  ➢ *Dependent Variable:*   **96) KID OBEY**
 ➢ *Independent Variable:*   **42) TLVSN/CP**
             ➢ *View*   **Reg. Line**

a.   What country has the most television sets in the world? _____

b.   What country has the fewest televisions in the world? _____

c.   What is the Pearson's correlation and level of significance? $r =$ _____, $p <$ _____

    d.   Which statement best describes the relationship between the number of televisions and the belief that children should be obedient?

          1.   There is a weak but statistically significant relationship where more people believe children should be obedient when there are a higher number of televisions in the country.

          2.   There is a strong and statistically significant relationship where fewer people believe children should be obedient when there are a higher number of televisions in the country.

          3.   There is a strong and statistically significant relationship where more people believe children should be obedient when there are a higher number of televisions in the country.

          4.   There is a moderate, but no statistically significant relationship, where fewer people believe children should be obedient when there are a higher number of televisions in the country.

4.   Turning our attention to the United States, one of the primary supports that children need when growing up is adequate housing. Let's see if there are differences among states when it comes to housing. Large apartment buildings are typical in urban areas, but public housing has almost always been constructed in units of 10 apartments or more per unit.

Use the following to determine what percentage of children live in housing units that have 10 or more units and are children of parents who identify themselves as Asian, African American, Hispanic, or white.

➤	*Data File:*	**STATES**
➤	*Task:*	**Mapping**
➤	*Variable 1:*	**14) %ASIAN/P92**
➤	*Subset Variable 1:*	**46) %BIG UNT90**
➤	*Subset Range 1:*	**3.7 – 27.65**
➤	*Subset Variable2:*	**6) %<20 96**
➤	*Subset Range 2:*	**25 – 37**
➤	*View:*	**Map**

HINT: You may want to use the List: Rank feature to answer some of the following questions.

    a.   Which three states have the highest number of large housing units where children 19 and under live with parents who identify themselves as Asian?

_____ _____ _____

b.   What is the Pearson's correlation among children 19 and under whose parents identify as Asian and who live in large apartment buildings? $r =$ _____

c.   List the states among the top 10 states where children 19 and under whose parents identify as Asian, and who live in large apartment buildings, are the same states where Asians have traditionally lived. (See the analysis of states by race/ethnicity and median family income.)

_____

Data File:	**STATES**
Task:	**Mapping**
➢ *Variable 1:*	**13) %BLACKS92**
➢ *Subset Variable 1:*	**46) %BIG UNT90**
➢ *Subset Range 1:*	**3.7 – 27.65**
➢ *Subset Variable2:*	**6) %<20 96**
➢ *Subset Range 2:*	**25 – 37**
➢ *View:*	**Map**

HINT: You may want to use the List: Rank feature to answer some of the following questions.

d.   Which three states have the highest number of large housing units where children 19 and under live with parents who identify themselves as African American?

_____   _____   _____

e.   What are the Pearson's correlation and level of significances among children 19 and under whose parents identify as African American and who live in large apartment buildings?

$r =$ _____, $p <$ _____

f.   How many states where children 19 and under whose parents identify as African American, and who live in large apartment buildings, are the same states where African Americans have traditionally lived? (See the analysis of states by race/ethnicity and median family income.)

_____

Data File:	**STATES**
Task:	**Mapping**
➢ *Variable 1:*	**32) %HISPANIC90**
➢ *Subset Variable 1:*	**46) %BIG UNT90**
➢ *Subset Range 1:*	**3.7 – 27.65**
➢ *Subset Variable 2:*	**6) %<20 96**
➢ *Subset Range 2:*	**25 to 37**
➢ *View:*	**Map**

HINT: **You may want to use the List: Rank feature to answer some of the following questions.**

g. Which three states have the highest number of large housing units where children 19 and under live with parents who identify themselves as Hispanic?

_____   _____   _____

h. What are the Pearson's correlation and level of significances among children 19 and under whose parents identify as Hispanic and who live in large apartment buildings?

$r =$ _____, $p <$ _____

i. How many states where children 19 and under whose parents identify as Hispanic, and who live in large apartment buildings, are the same states where Hispanics have traditionally lived? (See the analysis of states by race/ethnicity and median family income.)

_____

Data File:	**STATES**
Task:	**Mapping**
➤ Variable 1:	**28) %WHITE90**
➤ Subset Variable 1:	**46) %BIG UNT90**
➤ Subset Range 1:	**3.7 − 27.65**
➤ Subset Variable 2:	**6) %<20 96**
➤ Subset Range 2:	**25 − 37**
➤ View:	**Map**

HINT: **You may want to use the List:Rank feature to answer some of the following questions.**

j. Which three states have the highest number of large housing units where children 19 and under live with parents who identify themselves as white?

_____   _____   _____

k. What are the Pearson's correlation and level of significances among children 19 and under whose parents identify themselves as white and who live in large apartment buildings?

$r =$ _____, $p <$ _____

l. How many states where children 19 and under whose parents identify as white, and who live in large apartment buildings, are the same states where most middle-class white families live? (See the analysis of states by race/ethnicity and median family income.)

_____

m. There is a good bit of difference between where children 19 and under from the four major racial and ethnic groups live in the United States. What group has the fewest families living in large apartment buildings? _____

n. Rank the four racial/ethnic groups by the level of the Pearson's correlation.

_____ _____ _____ _____

5. As we saw earlier in this chapter, the General Social Survey (GSS) has a number of interesting responses on numerous questions that influence social welfare. Some of the questions are very controversial. For instance, what do people in the United States think about teenagers having sex? Here are several questions that might be of interest to you.

Use the following in MicroCase to determine any changes in attitudes about teenagers having sexual relations.

>   *Data File:*   **GSS**
> >   *Task:*   **Univariate**
>   *Variable 1:*   **61) TEEN BC 86**
> >   *View:*   **Pie**

a. In 1986, what percentage of people in the United States agreed that "methods of birth control should be available to teenagers between the ages of 14 and 16 if their parents do not approve?" _____

>   *Data File:*   **GSS**
>   *Task:*   **Univariate**
>   *Variable 1:*   **64) TEEN SEX86**
> >   *View:*   **Pie**

b. In 1986, what percentage of people agreed that sex relations were okay for young teens between the ages of 14 and 16? _____

I would like to leave you with the following information: Spina bifida is a neural tube birth defect occurring in the brain or spinal cord (backbone). Spina Bifida means cleft spine, which is an incomplete closure in the spinal column. The organization, Children with Spina Bifida (SBAA) advises women of childbearing age to "not depend on food alone for folic acid." They encourage women to follow the folic acid recommendations of the 1992 report from the U.S. Public Health Service: Women who may become pregnant should take 400 micrograms (mcg) of folic acid through a vitamin. Women whose child is at increased risk for spina bifida should take 4000 micrograms (mcg) of folic acid by prescription for 1 to 3 months before becoming pregnant. Folic acid is a water soluble B-vitamin that helps build healthy cells. The effects of myelomeningocele, the most serious form of spina bifida, may include muscle weakness or paralysis below the area of the spine where the incomplete closure (or cleft) occurs. Approximately four in one hundred thousand births result in the more serious myelomeningocele form of spina bifida.

Retrieved August 9, 2002, from www.waisman.wisc.edu/~rowley/sb-kids/index.htmlx.

Variable Lists Related to Children's Issues

The following is a list of some of the variables that you might find interesting in your study of families. You can examine them as either individual variables or two at a time using the MicroCase approaches you learned in this chapter. To see a list of the variables, the variable descriptions, and the range of values, either select any statistical option in the BASIC STATISTICS menu, or press [F3] at any time to view the variable selection window. Try this with some of the other variables you have already tested.

GLOBAL

4) URBAN %
      1995: PERCENT URBAN (HDR, 1998)
20) SEX RATIO
      NUMBER OF FEMALES PER 100 MALES (HDR, 1994)
43) PRIM.SCH
      1990–1995: PRIMARY SCHOOL ENROLLMENT (IN 1000S) (UNSY, 1997)
44) SEC.SCH
      1990–1995: SECONDARY SCHOOL ENROLLMENT (IN 1000S) (UNSY, 1997)
46) % GO 5TH
      PERCENT OF CHILDREN WHO REACH GRADE 5 BEFORE QUITTING (PON, 1996)

STATES

5) %<5 96
      1996: PERCENT OF POPULATION UNDER 5 YEARS (U.S. BUREAU OF THE CENSUS)
20) %URBAN90
      1990: PERCENT URBAN
21) %RURAL90
      1990: PERCENT RURAL
96) SEX RAT.96
      1996: NUMBER OF MALES PER 100 FEMALES (U.S. BUREAU OF THE CENSUS)

GSS

16) FAM.INCOME
      In which of these groups did your total family income, from all sources, fall last year before taxes?
88) KID TRUANT -- PUBLIC AUTHORITIES INTERVENE:
      The child frequently skips school and the parents don't do anything about it.

Web Pages Related to Children's Issues

If you wish to find a world of resources that are available to you over the Internet, the following list of sites will get you started. Once you visit these Web sites, you will find many interesting links to other useful Web sites.

The Annie E. Casey Foundation
www.aecf.org/kidscount/

The National Information Center for Children
and Youth with Disabilities (NICHCY)
www.nichcy.org/

Stand for Children
www.stand.org/

The David and Lucile Packard Foundation
The Future of Children
www.futureofchildren.org/

References

Annie E. Casey Foundation. (2001). *2001 Kids Count Data Book*. Baltimore, MD: Annie E. Casey Foundation. Retrieved July 25, 2000, from www.AECF.org.

Ambrosino, R., Heffernan, J., Shuttlesworth, G., and Ambrosino, R. (2001). *Social Work and Social Welfare: An Introduction* (4th ed.). Belmont, CA: Wadsworth/Thomson Learning.

Ashford, J. B., Lecory, C. W. and Lortie, K. L. (2001). *Human Behavior in the Social Environment* (2nd ed.). Belmont, CA: Wadsworth/Thomson Learning.

Cherry, A. L. (2000). *A Research Primer for the Helping Professions: Methods Statistics and Writing*. Pacific Grove CA: Brooks/Cole Pub.

Cherry, A. L., Dillon, M. E., and Rugh, D. (eds.) (2001). *Teenage Pregnancy: A Global View*. Westport, CT: Greenwood Pub.

Cherry, A. L., Dillon, M. E., and Rugh, D. (eds.) (2002). *Substance Abuse: A Global View*. Westport, CT: Greenwood Pub.

Jansson, B. S. (2001). *The Reluctant Welfare State* (4th ed.). Belmont, CA: Wadsworth Publishing Company.

Popple, P. R. and Leighnger, L. (2001). *Social Work, Social Welfare, and American Society* (5th ed.). Boston: Allyn and Bacon.

Schriver, J. M. (1998). *Human Behavior and the Social Environment*. Needham Heights, MA: Allyn and Bacon.

Shonkoff, J. P. and Phillips, D. A. (eds.). (2000). *From Neurons to Neighborhoods: The Science of Early Childhood Development*. Washington, DC: National Academy Press.

U.S. Bureau of the Census (2001). *Resident Population Estimates of the United States by Age and Sex: April 1, 1990 to July 1, 1999, with Short-Term Projection to November 1, 2000*. Washington, DC: Population Estimates Program, Population Division, U.S. Census Bureau.

U.S. Bureau of the Census (2000). *America's Children: Key National Indicators of Well-Being, 2000: The Fourth Annual Report to the Nation on the Condition of Our Most Precious Resource, Our Children*. Population Division, U.S. Census Bureau.

WHO (2000). *The World Health Report 2000 Health Systems: Improving Performance*. Geneva: The World Health Organization.

Zastrow, C. (2000). *Introduction to Social Work and Social Welfare* (7th ed.). Belmont, CA: Wadsworth Publishing Company.

Additional Material of Interest

Bolen, R. M. (2001). *Child Sexual Abuse : Its Scope and Our Failure*. New York: Kluwer.

Fraser, M. (ed.) (1997). *Risk and Resilience in Childhood: An Ecological Perspective*. Washington, DC: National Association of Social Press.

Granzow, S. (2000). *Our Dream: A World Free of Poverty*. New York: Published for the World Bank and World Bank Group Staff Association [by] Oxford University Press.

Harkness, S. and Super, C. M. (1996). *Parents' Cultural Belief Systems: Their Origins, Expressions, and Consequences*. New York: Guilford Press.

Klein, P. S. (1996). *Early Intervention: Cross-Cultural Experiences with a Mediational Approach*. New York: Garland Pub.

Martinez, M. L. (2000). *Neighborhood Context and the Development of African American Children*. New York: Garland Pub.

Masten, A. S. (1999). *Cultural Processes in Child Development*. Mahwah, NJ: Lawrence Erlbaum Associates.

Rwomire, A. (2001). *African Women and Children: Crisis and Response*. Westport, CT: Praeger Press. Academic/Plenum Publishers.

Chapter 4

OLDER PEOPLE AND AGING

Tasks: Mapping, Univariate, Scatterplot, Cross-tabulation
Data Files: GLOBAL, STATES, GSS

Overview of Chapter 4

Chapter 4 looks at issues that affect older people. You will first identify countries that have large populations of people over 64 years of age. You will test hypotheses to learn more about the role of the economic environment and work as it affects longevity. Support for euthanasia is another issue that will be examined. Finding out who supports euthanasia and who opposes it should be interesting. Using data from the United States we will identify where older people live and conditions such as obesity and its role in heart disease. We will also see if the number of nursing homes in a given state correlates with the number of older persons living in the state. Public opinion about issues that are important to older people will also be examined. Notice the way the hypotheses are constructed from the literature or conventional knowledge. This chapter will continue to build on what you learned about data analysis in the previous three chapters and introduce you to *cross-tabulation*. You will find *cross-tabs* (as it is often referred to) very useful. You will find that *cross-tabs* are easy to understand and give a great deal of information.

A ging gracefully in the United States is a lost art or an art form that was never developed in this country (Longres, 2000). As suggested in Chapter 1, not only are more people being born but also people are living longer and, consequently, the population of elderly people in the United States and elderly people in almost all countries in the world is increasing. The consequences for social welfare policy and programming are enormous. Who will care for an aging population when elderly people are the majority? Better yet, who will pay for meeting the needs of our elder citizens?

4.1   Ethics of Elder Services

What if a fortune teller told you that you were going to be confined to a wheelchair and that the only living facility available to you will be a nursing home? Your only income will be social security disability and this calamity will happen to you in your mid-60s. What if, by some miracle, 20 years before this was to happen to you, there was a political change and you were in a position to influence legislation on services and the quality of services to nursing home residents in the United States. What kind of nursing home services would you advocate to provide?

As you read in Chapter 1, there are over 6 billion people on the earth today. There has never been this many people on the earth, and we humans continue to increase in numbers, even though the yearly increase has slowed considerably. The number of people reaching old age (defined here as 65 and older) is also greater than ever before in world history. Several reasons have been put forward to explain this increase in longevity. Some are complicated and some are very simple. Without citing the costly major medical miracles like the artificial heart, the primary contributors to longevity for most of the world's older people have been clean water, improved diet, and the most rudimentary medical attention. For those of us in economically developed countries, the modern day miracles of high-blood-pressure medicine, cholesterol medicine, medicine for diabetes, CAT scans, and lifestyle changes have reduced deaths from heart attack, stroke, cancer, and other physical diseases and aliments (United Nations Department of Economic and Social Affairs, 1998).

There are other reasons for longevity that carry a lot of weight in the literature and seem to make sense. The primary forces against longevity in developed countries are the individual's negative attitude about growing old, their loss of market value, and ageism (Ambrosino et al., 2001).

A Global View of Today's Elders

To begin, we need to find out some basic facts about the elders of the world. Are they equally distributed from country to country around the world? Or, do factors beyond their control either condemn them to an early death in their 40s, and 50s because of the country where they live; or, does where the country they were born virtually ensure that they will have a long and relatively happy life?

Based on what we have read and studied, this seems like a reasonable assumption. So let's test it.

Research Hypothesis/Question   4.1:
Who are the elderly people, and where do they live?

> *Data File:* **GLOBAL**
> *Task:* **Mapping**
> *Variable 1:* **22) % OVER 64**
> *View:* **Map**

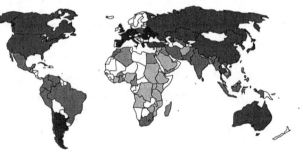

% OVER 64 -- PERCENT OF POPULATION 65 YEARS OLD AND OVER (SAUS, 1998)

Based on the analysis of the number of people in each country over 64 years of age, Italy has the greatest percentage of people over 65 at 17.6% of its population. Italy is followed by Belgium (16.8%), Greece (16.5%), Spain (16.3%), etc. The United States is ranked 15th with 14% of its population made up of people 65 and older.

It looks like Africa has the fewest people over 64 years of age. We might have expected this situation because Africa has so many underdeveloped, poor nations. While 200,000 people died in 1999 because of war and natural disasters, another 2 million died because of AIDS. Among the most tragic consequences of the AIDS epidemic were the children who became orphans because of AIDS. A UNICEF report, entitled *Children Orphaned by AIDS* (1999), stated that since the beginning of the epidemic the number of orphaned children had reached more than 11 million.

Research Hypothesis/Question   4.2:
Are there a lot of people 65 and older living in underdeveloped and developing countries?

Data File:	GLOBAL
Task:	Mapping
Variable 1:	22) % OVER 64
➢ Subset Variable:	24) ECON DEVEL
➢ Subset Category:	Include: 1) LEAST DEV. 2) DEVELOPING
➢ View:	Map

% OVER 64 -- PERCENT OF POPULATION 65 YEARS OLD AND OVER (SAUS, 1998)

[Subset]

Be sure to select the subset variables for this analysis.

Looking at the ranked list of the *Least Developed* nations economically and *Developing* nations, at the top of the list we find Argentina, where 10.2% of their population fall in this age category. At the bottom of the list Sudan, Côte d'Ivoire, and Uganda all have an elder population of only 2.2%.

If you switch back to the map view you can see that if you are 65 years old or older and you live in Central Africa, you are a rare *old person* in your community. From these two comparisons, it is clear that the numbers of older people are not equally distributed throughout the world.

What Contributes to Longevity Among Older People of the World?

Other than being an underdeveloped or developing country, what other conditions in these countries differentiate them from developed countries? One of the conditions or variables mentioned above that made a big difference in longevity for the majority of elderly people in the world is an improved diet. If this does make a real difference, we should find if countries where the caloric intake is high will have more elderly people than countries where caloric intake is low.

Most dietitians recommend that an adult needs between 1,200 and 1,400 calories a day to meet what is called basic metabolic needs, or the number of calories required to keep the heart and internal organs working properly (United Nations Department of Economic and Social Affairs, 1998).

4.2	Estimates of the Number of People over 64 in the Future: 2000–2050	
• 2000	35 million over 64 years old	4 million over 84 years old
• 2010	40 million over 64 years old	5 million over 84 years old
• 2020	52 million over 64 years old	6 million over 84 years old
• 2030	70 million over 64 years old	8 million over 84 years old
• 2030	75 million over 64 years old	13 million over 84 years old
• 2050	80 million over 64 years old	18 million over 84 years old
	(U.S. Bureau of the Census, 2000, 2001; Ambrosino et al., 2001).	

Research Hypothesis/Question   4.3:
How many calories are consumed by people in different countries who are 65 years of age or older?

Data File: **GLOBAL**
Task: **Mapping**
Variable 1: **22) % OVER 64**
➢ Variable 2: **27) CALORIES**
➢ View: **Map**

% OVER 64 -- PERCENT OF POPULATION
65 YEARS OLD AND OVER (SAUS, 1998)

r = 0.822**

CALORIES -- DAILY AVAILABLE
CALORIES PER CAPITA (NBWR, 1991)

This is pretty good evidence ($r = .82$, $p < .01$) that diet is important to longevity. It is a very strong correlation, and it is statistically significant, which means it has a real effect on a great number of the world's people. Likewise, you will note that people living in economically developed countries consume many more calories than people living in India and people living in a number of countries in Africa and Asia. The Pearson's r of .82 suggests that caloric intake explains about 67% ($r^2 = .82 \times .82 = .672$) of the discrepancy in longevity among people of the world.

Caloric intake is an important component involved in longevity; however, another important measure that may help explain long lives is being born in an economically developed country. Elderly people who did not beat the odds to be born in Western Europe, the United States, or Canada often do not have adequate food and medication. It is also important to remember that as a country's economic situation improves, the people of that country change their diet and begin to eat more meat and dairy products. Calories from meat and dairy products are extremely expensive to produce compared to calories from rice and grain (United Nations Department of Economic and Social Affairs, 1998).

To see if those at the United Nations and others who study global consumption are right, let's see if there is a relation between meat consumption and longevity among those 65 or older. If there is, it will drive doctors who are anti red meat crazy.

Research Hypothesis/Question   4.4:
How many calories from meat are consumed by people in different countries who are 65 years old or older?

Data File: **GLOBAL**
Task: **Mapping**
➢ Variable 1: **22) % OVER 64**
➢ Variable 2: **28) MEAT CONS**
➢ View: **Map**

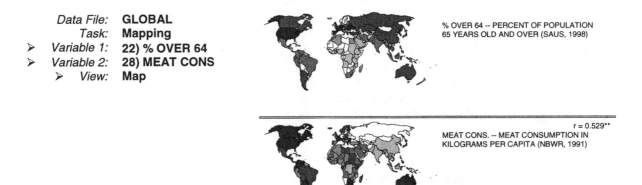

% OVER 64 -- PERCENT OF POPULATION
65 YEARS OLD AND OVER (SAUS, 1998)

r = 0.529**

MEAT CONS. -- MEAT CONSUMPTION IN
KILOGRAMS PER CAPITA (NBWR, 1991)

This is quite interesting. It seems there is a moderate correlation ($r = .53$, $p < .01$) between the amount of meat consumed in a country and the number of people who are 65 years of age and older. It is important, however, to note that this correlation is not nearly as large ($r = .82$, $p < .01$) as the analysis between longevity and calorie consumption from all sources. This relationship suggests that 28% ($r^2 = .53 \times .53 = .28$) of longevity of the world's population can be explained by the amount of meat consumed in a given country.

In light of the high-cholesterol problem that many of us deal with in the economically rich countries, it seems counterintuitive to say that eating meat is the answer to longevity. Eating more meat in the United States could reduce longevity. The difference is that so many people in the world get so few calories from meat that a slight increase in meat consumption by poor elderly people of the world would radically increase the world population of elderly people.

Our Working Elders

One way for elderly people to maintain a diet of 1,200 to 1,400 calories a day is to continue to work, if you are still alive at 65. Most elderly people do work even if they are somewhat disabled by age. If they cannot work at least a little, they typically do not live long. One group of elderly people that might have access to more calories are those elderly workers in agriculture, as opposed to elderly workers in industry—where there would be less access to food products. A good theory, but if the literature on hunger around the world is correct, this logical assumption will *not* be supported by the data (Aiken and LaFollette, 1995).

To test this logical assumption, first we will produce a world map to see where people live who are working in agriculture and are 65 years of age or older. Second, we will generate a scatterplot between the two variables to get a visual picture of the actual relationship between the percentage of people working in each country who are 65 years of age or older, and the type of work they do: agricultural or industrial, to determine the degree to which the two conditions are related.

Research Hypothesis/Question   4.5:
Where do people live who are working in agriculture and are 65 years of age or older?

Data File:	**GLOBAL**
Task:	**Mapping**
➤ *Variable 1:*	**39) % WORK AG**
➤ *Subset Variable:*	**22) % OVER 64**
➤ *Subset Range:*	**2.2 – 17.6**
➤ *View:*	**Map**

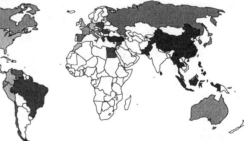

%WORK AG -- 1991-1995: PERCENT OF THE WORK FORCE EMPLOYED IN AGRICULTURE (UNSY, 1997)

[Subset]

Although data on some Africa countries and some South American countries (very large agricultural regions of the world) are missing, we will continue the analysis of the data to see what kinds of work older people in the rest of the world are doing and how it is affecting them. Of course, the missing data are a problem. We will not be able to draw a conclusion about all countries of the world. We can only draw conclusions about the countries on which we have relevant data. Even then, I hesitate to go too far. A lot of missing data can even distort the findings from data we do have on the different countries.

Research Hypothesis/Question   4.6:
In countries where a large percentage of people work in agriculture, are there also higher numbers of people who are over 64 years old?

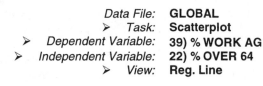

Data File:	**GLOBAL**
➤ *Task:*	**Scatterplot**
➤ *Dependent Variable:*	**39) % WORK AG**
➤ *Independent Variable:*	**22) % OVER 64**
➤ *View:*	**Reg. Line**

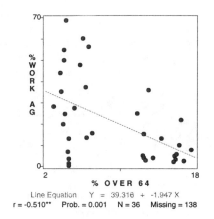

Although it makes sense that those who have access to more food products will also live longer, with the data we have, it does not seem to be the case no matter how logical the assertion my be. Moreover, if this data hold up, and I have no reason to believe that it will not, even with additional data from African and South American countries, longevity will still be associated with caloric intake.

The scatterplot above suggests that a moderate but very significant relationship exists between countries where a large percentage of the people work in agriculture and countries with small percentages of the people who are 65 or over ($r = .51$, $p < .01$). This is another inverse relationship. It suggests that if you visit a country where a large percentage of its people work in agriculture, you will *not* find a large number of people 65 and over. If you have forgotten what an inverse relation means in a correlational analysis, refer back to Box 3.1 in Chapter 3 to refresh your memory.

4.3   Ageism
Ageism is a severe form of institutionalized discrimination against older people that is often subtle but is damaging to the efforts of elderly people to obtain services at all levels. Many professionals, much like the general public—in economically developed nations—have negative attitudes toward elderly people. And their attitudes are reflected in public policies that guide both business and public institutions that they manage and staff.

Moving on, we also want to look at longevity among elderly workers in industrial settings. This will give us some idea about how industrial countries affect the number of elderly workers in those countries. Given the pollutants and dangerous waste from industry, I could logically assume that it would reduce the life expectancy of people living in industrialized countries. At this point, why don't we look at a map of the countries in terms of the percentages of their population that work in industry? Then we will do a scatterplot to see the actual dispersion of countries on these two conditions.

Research Hypothesis/Question   4.7:
Where do people live who are working in industry and are 65 years of age or older?

Data File: **GLOBAL**
➢ Task: **Mapping**
➢ Variable 1: **40) % WORK IN**
➢ Subset Variable 1: **22) % OVER 64**
➢ Subset Range 1: **2.2 – 17.6**
➢ View: **Map**

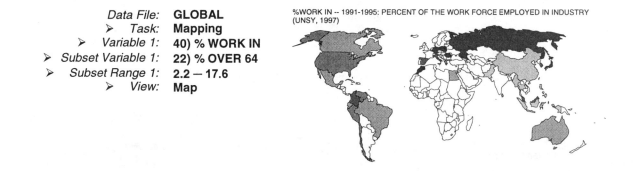

%WORK IN -- 1991-1995: PERCENT OF THE WORK FORCE EMPLOYED IN INDUSTRY (UNSY, 1997)

[Subset]

Again there is not much information on Africa, but we can still look at the relationship among nations of the rest of the world. If you were asked to name the leading industrial nation of the world, I would be willing to wager that you would not have guessed Russia. Click the **[List: Rank]** option while viewing the map in MicroCase to see the rank list of industrial nations of the world. Use the **[List: Alpha]** option to quickly find the rank of countries in alphabetical order. Based on what most of us know about the industrial nations of the world, many of us might have guessed Germany (2nd) and Japan (6th), but who would have guessed that Morocco (3rd) would have such a large percentage of its elderly working in industry? You will notice that the United States is not in the top five nations. The United States is more of a service industry country, providing communications, financial, and consulting services. Out of the 30 countries that we have data for, the United States ranks 16 among industrial nations.

Research Hypothesis/Question   4.8:
In countries where a large percentage of people work in industry, are there also lower percentages of people who are over 64 years of age?

Data File: **GLOBAL**
➢ Task: **Scatterplot**
➢ Dependent Variable: **40) % WORK IN**
➢ Independent Variable: **22) % OVER 64**
➢ View: **Reg. Line**

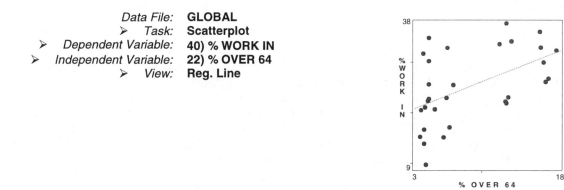

Line Equation   Y = 18.518 + 0.765 X
r = 0.522**   Prob. = 0.002   N = 30   Missing = 144

This is defying logic. The more industrialized a country, the more people there are who are 65 and over. Of course, one of the things I am failing to take into account in this examination is that industrial countries are wealthy countries, and people in wealthy countries can afford a high caloric intake. In the case of the United States and Western Europe, people can afford a caloric intake that is so high it is unhealthy, while people in agricultural countries are so poor, they cannot afford to buy the food they produce. We should not forget that there is also hunger in the industrialized nations. That discussion, however, is for a later examination in the chapter on poverty.

One last test to better understand the dynamics involved in longevity. Given what we know, I believe we can also say that living in an *urban area* will also have longer life expectancy.

Research Hypothesis/Question   4.9:
Do people living in countries with large urban populations have a longer life expectancy?

<table>
<tr><td align="right">Data File:</td><td>GLOBAL</td></tr>
<tr><td align="right">Task:</td><td>Scatterplot</td></tr>
<tr><td align="right">➤ Dependent Variable:</td><td>17) LIFE EXPCT</td></tr>
<tr><td align="right">➤ Independent Variable:</td><td>4) URBAN %</td></tr>
<tr><td align="right">➤ View:</td><td>Reg. Line</td></tr>
</table>

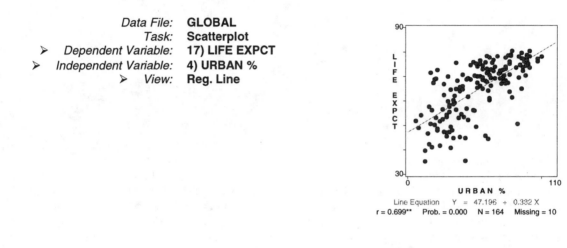

Line Equation   Y = 47.196 + 0.332 X
r = 0.699**   Prob. = 0.000   N = 164   Missing = 10

Given this last scatterplot between countries with large urban populations and countries with large percentages of its population 65 years old or older ($r = .52$, $p = .01$), we can draw some conclusions. Based on the data available to us, it is clear that if you go to an underdeveloped or developing country where the caloric intake is below 1,400 calories a day, there is little meat available for the elderly, people work in agriculture, and many people live in rural communities—you will not find a great many people eligible for the AARP organization.

Euthanasia Is a Divisive Issue Among Our Elders

The attitude toward euthanasia, in many of the developed countries of the world, continues to change in favor of some type of assisted suicide. In the Netherlands, The Royal Dutch Medical Association, which supports the practice of legal euthanasia, continues to refine the procedure as their physicians gain more experience with assisting people to commit suicide. The guidelines are for the protection of the patients as well as the physicians. They instruct doctors to have terminally ill patients administer their own lethal dose of a drug as opposed to the physician administering it. Physicians are also instructed to use an outside consultant who does not have a preexisting or professional relationship with the patient to be with the physician at the time the fatal dose is self-administered by the patient. Although the guidelines do not require a doctor to assist a patient requesting euthanasia, the doctor is required to assist the patient in contacting another physician for assistance (Ashford et al., 2001, pp. 554–555).

Those who oppose euthanasia often point out the warped logic that supports euthanasia. If a doctor refuses to assist in the act of killing another human being, it is considered to be a cruel and unfeeling. Conversely, by the doctor agreeing to kill another person, the doctor is considered compassionate. Some suggest that politicians in the Netherlands adopted euthanasia as a social policy as a way of dealing with a lack of facilities for palliative care, such as hospices, which would reduce the fear of the pain and suffering that lead older people to contemplate and commit suicide (Lang and Dunstain, 1995).

To begin to examine this issue globally, why don't we generate a map to see in what countries people support euthanasia?

Research Hypothesis/Question   4.10:
How do people in different countries feel about euthanasia?

Data File: **GLOBAL**
➢ Task: **Mapping**
➢ Variable 1: **87) EUTHANASIA**
➢ View: **Map**

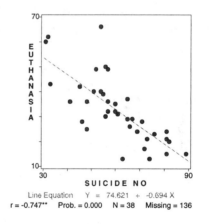

EUTHANASIA -- PERCENT WHO BELIEVE EUTHANASIA IS OK (TERMINATING THE LIFE OF THE INCURABLY SICK) (WVS)

The top four countries that support euthanasia are China, Finland, the Netherlands, and Denmark. Canada and Japan tied for 5th place. It appears from this map that people in the Netherlands who support euthanasia are by themselves. Nonetheless, it seems simplistic to speculate that the only reason people in a country like the Netherlands would support euthanasia is because they do not have adequate palliative care. Even so, let's examine a few more conditions that could help clear up this issue.

Research Hypothesis/Question   4.11:
Do people who oppose suicide also oppose euthanasia?

Data File: **GLOBAL**
➢ Task: **Scatterplot**
➢ Dependent Variable: **87) EUTHANASIA**
➢ Independent Variable: **86) SUICIDE NO**
➢ View: **Reg. Line**

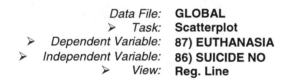

Line Equation   Y = 74.621 + -0.694 X
r = -0.747**   Prob. = 0.000   N = 38   Missing = 136

Although many people would like to think that euthanasia is a liberal West European fad, according to this analysis of global data, people who support euthanasia do not necessarily support a person's right to commit suicide ($r = -.75$, $p. < .01$). What's more, because of the large significant correlation, it may be difficult to find many people who support euthanasia who also support a person's right to commit suicide. How would you explain it?

The next question you might want to answer is: "How much does religion affect peoples' opinions about euthanasia?" In most western religions, as you are probably aware, suicide is prohibited.

Research Hypothesis/Question   4.12:
Does religion reduce a person's support for euthanasia?

Data File:	**GLOBAL**
Task:	**Scatterplot**
Dependent Variable:	**87) EUTHANASIA**
➤ *Independent Variable:*	**67) CH ATTEND**
View:	**Reg. Line**

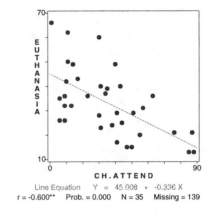

Line Equation   Y = 45.008 + -0.336 X
r = -0.600**   Prob. = 0.000   N = 35   Missing = 139

Per this scatterplot, religion has quite an impact on people's attitudes toward euthanasia. The more religious people in a country are (defined for this analysis as *church attendance*), the more you can expect that they are opposed to euthanasia. Of course, to do this analysis, you must accept the way we are defending religiosity. In fact, most of us would probably agree that church attendance is not the best measure of religiosity, but if it is all you have, it is better than nothing. One more analysis before we leave the subject. Existential philosophy suggests that people who think they will be able to maintain control of their lives up to the end say by being able to request and receive assistance with euthanasia, they will tend to be happier than people who have no control over the end of their lives. We can find out if this is true of people around the world that we have data for using MicroCase.

Research Hypothesis/Question   4.13:
Does being happy reduce the support for euthanasia?

Data File:	**GLOBAL**
Task:	**Scatterplot**
Dependent Variable:	**87) EUTHANASIA**
➤ *Independent Variable:*	**93) VERY HAPPY**
➤ *View:*	**Reg. Line**

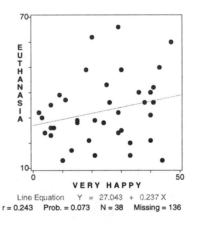

Line Equation   Y = 27.043 + 0.237 X
r = 0.243   Prob. = 0.073   N = 38   Missing = 136

Even though there appears to be a slight positive scatter, based on the plotting of countries it does not reach the level of being statistically significant (*r* = .24, *p* = NS or Not Significant). As such, there is no evidence based on this data that suggests that people in countries who support euthanasia are happier than people in countries who oppose it. The correlation between the two variables is not statistically significant. Now, to satisfy my curiosity, let's do one more scatterplot to see if those who think suicide is always wrong are happier than people who can accept a person's desire to take his or her own life. Among Japanese adolescents who are between 10 to 20 years of age and who become depressed and lose self-esteem, suicide is the most common cause of death, with hanging or leaping from buildings being the most common forms of suicide (Nasuno et al., 1998).

Research Hypothesis/Question   4.14:
Does being happy reduce the support for suicide?

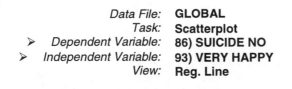

Data File:	**GLOBAL**
Task:	**Scatterplot**
➤ *Dependent Variable:*	**86) SUICIDE NO**
➤ *Independent Variable:*	**93) VERY HAPPY**
View:	**Reg. Line**

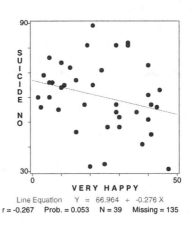

Again, even though there appears to be a slight inverse scatter, based on the plotting of countries ($r = -.27$, $p = $ NS), there is no evidence in this data to suggest that people who think suicide is always wrong are any happier for it.

So, what have we learned from these analyses? One, there are people in many countries, including the Netherlands, who support euthanasia. Two, the people who oppose euthanasia also oppose suicide for any reason. There are two conditions, however, that affect a person's attitude toward euthanasia: living in a country where people tend to live long lives, and living in countries where people tend to be very religious. On your own, you can generate a map of countries that have a high percentage of people who attend church.

Who Are the Elderly People in the United States?

Now that we have taken a serious look at older people around the world, particularly older people that are poor living in underdeveloped or developing countries, we can now examine, by comparison, the older people living in the United States and other economically developed countries. Doing the comparison in this way, we are using the United States to represent all other economically developed nations. Starting with a couple of basic questions will help our understanding of older people and their lives in the United States. Ageism tends to isolate older people. Additionally, to provide a more detailed look at our elders, we will break out those 65 and older into two groups. One map ranks states by the percentage of their population that is 65 to 84 years old. A second map will rank states by the percentage of people that are 85 years old and older. I've categorized the two groups by these ages because they have clearly different life styles and expectations (Kirst-Ashman and Hull, 2001; Longres, 2000; Popple and Leighnger, 2001).

We will organize the data into two age groups or subsets. We will do this by first identifying four variables on age that cover people from 65 to 84 years old, and one variable that identifies people 85 and older. Like all real data, it is not always set up like dummy data—simple, contrived, and undemanding. Real data, in contrast, give us real information on real people, as you have seen in this and previous chapters. It takes a few more points and clicks, but it is genuinely worth the effort. Using these types of subsets, you can learn a great deal.

With this idea in mind, look at the states where older people live. Remember, everything being equal, we expect people in these two groups to be evenly distributed across the United States.

Research Hypothesis/Question   4.15:
What states have the highest percentage of people living in them who are 65 to 84 years old and people who are 85 years old or older?

> *Data File:* **STATES**
> *Task:* **Mapping**
> *Variable 1:* **9) %65—84 96**
> *View:* **List: Rank**

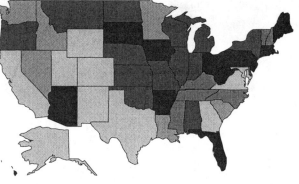

%65-84 96 -- 1996: PERCENT OF THE POPULATION 65 TO 84 YEARS OF AGE (U.S. BUREAU OF THE CENSUS, REPORT ST-96-11)

It appears that the top two retirement states (in the order of their rank) are Florida and West Virginia, with 12 other states sharing the third spot. If you switch back to the map view, you will see there is very little regional pattern to where people retire. While a few warm states are obviously big retirement destinations (Florida, Hawaii, and Arizona), it appears a large number of people do not relocate when they retire.

Now let's see where people 85 years old and older live.

Data File: **STATES**
Task: **Mapping**
> *Variable 1:* **10) %>85 96**
> *View:* **Map**

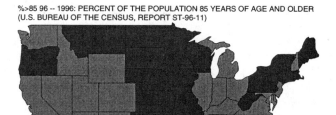

%>85 96 -- 1996: PERCENT OF THE POPULATION 85 YEARS OF AGE AND OLDER (U.S. BUREAU OF THE CENSUS, REPORT ST-96-11)

Interesting, this older group of people are evenly distributed across the United States with the exception of Alaska, which has a very small percentage of people 85 or older. If you look at how these states were ranked, 21 tied for the highest percentage of people 85 and over. This means that a state like Florida, which has a large number of people living there between 65 and 84, has about the same percentage of elderly people living in the state as 21 other states in the first tier of states, in terms of people 85 and over.

California is an exception. California may have the largest percentage of people between 65 and 84 living in a state but not people 85 years old or older. You will find California in the second tier of states for this group. One might speculate that among those who moved to California in the last half of the 20th century many have moved back to the state where they were born. Or, as they approached their mid-80s, they moved back to where they had family, a state other than California. A speculative statement to be sure, but we can do a series of analyses that might help corroborate my explanation.

Most of us know that California has a long history of people moving to the state. The 1849 gold rush was the start. The Okies moved there during the *Dust Bowl* period that preceded the Great Depression. Service men from WWII, Korea, and Vietnam who were stationed there liked it and stayed. So, we would expect that a large number of people in California are people who came from another state. We can see if this tends to be true by looking at a map of domestic migration in the United States.

We use variables that can tell us if there a correlation between states with high levels of domestic migration and states with large populations of people 65 and over. The best variable that we have for measuring domestic migration is the percentages of people who have *not* moved from the state where they were born is the variable **17) %NO MOVE90**.

Research Hypothesis/Question   4.16:
What is the rank of states by the percentage of people who have *not* moved from the state where they were born?

Data File:	**STATES**
Task:	**Mapping**
➤ *Variable 1:*	**17) %NO MOVE90**
➤ *View:*	**Map**

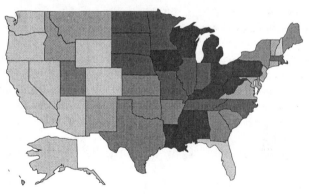

%NO MOVE90 -- 1990: PERCENT BORN IN STATE OF RESIDENCE

As you can see, California stands out as having few people who have *not* moved from the state where they were born. This indicates that most people in California moved there from somewhere else.

Now, we can look at the states in terms of people 65 or over. A scatterplot will be a good visual of how the state populations relate on these two variables.

Research Hypothesis/Question   4.17:
There is a correlation among states with transient residents and states with large populations of people 65 years old and older.

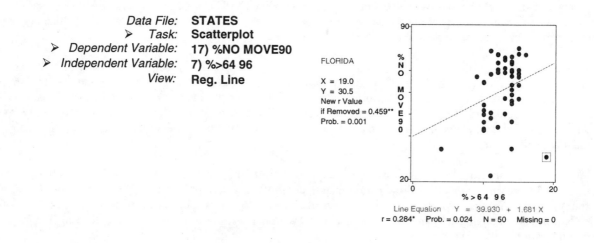

Data File:	**STATES**
➤ *Task:*	**Scatterplot**
➤ *Dependent Variable:*	**17) %NO MOVE90**
➤ *Independent Variable:*	**7) %>64 96**
View:	**Reg. Line**

FLORIDA

X = 19.0
Y = 30.5
New r Value
if Removed = 0.459**
Prob. = 0.001

Line Equation   Y = 39.930 + 1.681 X
r = 0.284*   Prob. = 0.024   N = 50   Missing = 0

As you can see from the scatterplot of states, there will not be much of a correlation between states with a lot of domestic migration and a population of people 65 and over. Then again, if you click on the outlier in the lower right-hand corner of the scatterplot you will find Florida. Interpreting these findings can be a bit tricky because one of the variables (%NO MOVE) measures a negative condition. This requires an interpretation similar to deciphering what a person is saying when using a *double negative* in a sentence.

This scatterplot illustrates how many people in each state have lived in the state since birth and never moved out of state. The state in the United States with the highest percentage of people who are 65 and over, and the state with the lowest percentage of people born in the state who have never moved, is Florida. This finding holds true for me. When my family moved to the Cape Canaveral area of Florida in 1956, when the space program began, there was only one student in my elementary school class who had been born in Florida. Her parents were ranchers.

From these maps and scatterplots, we can tell it was a good idea to break up elderly people into two groups. The two groups have different patterns of lifestyle. The Midwesterners tend to stay put a bit more than the rest of us. It also seems that when we retire from our job, we tend to move to another state to retire. However, if we live into our 80s, which greater and greater numbers of our seniors are doing, a large proportion of them move back to family. This may occur for many reasons: illness, death of a spouse, disability, etc. Whatever the reason, per this data, when people reach their mid-80s they are more evenly spread across the United States than when they are between 65 and 84 years of age.

What Contributes to Longevity in the United States?

Rather than look at caloric intake among people in the United States to see if the elderly people are getting the calories per day for good health, we would learn more about ourselves if we look at the older people in terms of their being overweight (Levkoff, Chee et al., 2001).

Overweight and obesity are found worldwide, and the prevalence of these conditions in the United States ranks high along with other developed nations. Approximately 280,000 adult deaths in the United States each year are attributable to obesity (Allison and Fontaine, 1999). In a study of obesity in 1994, the researchers found 54.9% of Americans overweight and an additional 22.3% to be obese (Flegal et al., 1998).

Research Hypothesis/Question   4.18:
How do states rank on a scale that reflects the weight of the residents of that state?

Data File:	**STATES**
➢ *Task:*	**Mapping**
➢ *Variable 1:*	**66) %FAT 95**
➢ Subset Variable 1:	**7) %<64 96**
➢ Subset Range 1:	**4.0 – 19.0**
➢ *View:*	**Map**

% FAT 95 -- 1995: PERCENT OF POPULATION 18 AND OVER WHO ARE OVERWEIGHT (S.R., 1997)

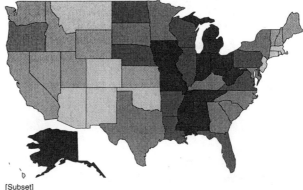

[Subset]

So, Indiana and Missouri have the largest percentage of overweight people who are 65 and older, and Colorado and Hawaii have the greatest percentage of thin people who are 65 and older. Did you check your state to see where it stands in the ranking?

Given this information, we can now look at another indicator of health. We have been told that being overweight leads to heart disease. Let's find out.

Research Hypothesis/Question   4.19:
There is a statistically significant relationship between people who are overweight and people who die from heart disease.

Data File:	**STATES**
➢ *Task:*	**Scatterplot**
➢ *Dependent Variable:*	**65) HEART DD95**
➢ *Independent Variable:*	**66) % FAT 95**
➢ *View:*	**Reg. Line**

Line Equation   Y = 46.579 + 8.102 X
r = 0.410**   Prob. = 0.002   N = 50   Missing = 0

This confirms the relationship. However, it is only a moderate correlation between being overweight and dying of heart disease for the general public ($r = .41$, $p < .01$). The question is, however, do being overweight and being 65 years old or older increase one's chances of dying from heart disease? Logically, if it is a threat to the average person in the United States (average age approximately 34 years), it would surely be a more dangerous condition for people 65 and older. So, let's test our deduction. We believe that because there is a positive statistically significant relationship between people who are overweight and people who have died of heart disease, there will also be an important relationship between those who are 65 or older and people who have died from heart disease.

Research Hypothesis/Question   4.20:
There is a statistically significant relationship between people who die from heart disease and people who are 65 and older.

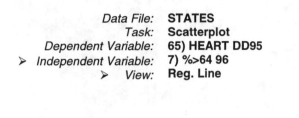

Data File: **STATES**
Task: **Scatterplot**
Dependent Variable: **65) HEART DD95**
➤ Independent Variable: **7) %>64 96**
➤   View: **Reg. Line**

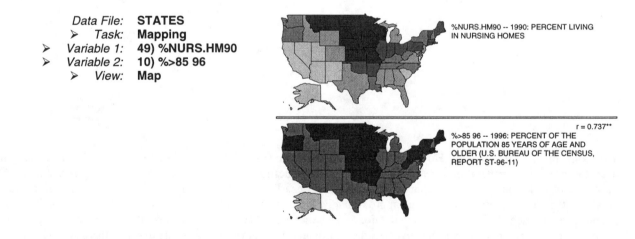

The scatterplot speak for itself in a loud and clear voice. Longevity in the United States favors people who are 65 and over, who are *not* overweight, and who have avoided developing heart disease.

People Living in Nursing Homes

For many, a nursing home will probably be one of our last stopping places. Living a long life means that the possibility of needing a nursing home in your lifetime is highly likely. Let's see which states have the greatest percentage of people living in nursing homes. These states should be similar to states that have the greatest percentages of their population who are 85 and older. Based on the map of people 85 and older, I would surmise that states with the greatest percentage of people living in nursing homes would be in the North-Midwestern states.

Research Hypothesis/Question   4.21:
States with large percentages of people 85 and older will also have a higher percentage of people living in nursing homes.

Data File: **STATES**
➤   Task: **Mapping**
➤   Variable 1:   **49) %NURS.HM90**
➤   Variable 2:   **10) %>85 96**
➤   View: **Map**

%NURS.HM90 -- 1990: PERCENT LIVING IN NURSING HOMES

r = 0.737**

%>85 96 -- 1996: PERCENT OF THE POPULATION 85 YEARS OF AGE AND OLDER (U.S. BUREAU OF THE CENSUS, REPORT ST-96-11)

This is quite a strong positive correlation ($r = 74$, $p < .01$). It clearly shows that states with large percentages of their population living in a nursing home are also the states with large populations of people 85 and older. Select the

[List: Rank] option to see the states that have the most nursing homes. If you look, you will find that South Dakota, Iowa, and North Dakota are the top three states with the largest percentage of people living in nursing homes. If you look at the map of states' rank on the number of people living in a nursing home, you will see that they are also in the tier of states with large percentages of people 85 and over.

Suicide and Elderly People in the United States

Before we close the **STATES** data file, let's look at the suicide rate by state among people 65 years old and over. We would hate to think that elder suicide was the result of people having no other option. After this analysis, we will go to the General Social Survey to see how people 65 and older feel about euthanasia. The assumption I am working on here is that suicide could be an alternative to euthanasia for elderly people in the United States because euthanasia is illegal in every state but Oregon.

Research Hypothesis/Question   4.22:
States with high rates of people who committed suicide will also have a large percentage of their population who are 64 years old and older.

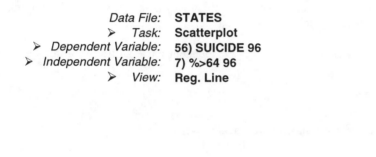

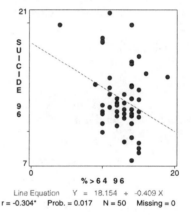

Line Equation   Y = 18.154 + -0.409 X
r = -0.304*   Prob. = 0.017   N = 50   Missing = 0

Counter to my stated hypothesis, the data on suicide by states have a weak, but still significant, inverse relationship with people 65 and over. It appears that states with large percentages of people 65 and older also have lower rates of suicide ($r = -.30$, $p < .05$). While suicide might indeed be an alternative to euthanasia for a few elderly people in the United States, it cannot be detected with the aggregate data we have available to us at this time. Nevertheless, there is no reason to think that elderly people counted for this variable are really that different from those 65 years of age and over who were not included in this variable. The data in the **STATES** data file are fairly accurate and representative of people as a whole in this country.

Before drawing some conclusions, the public view on euthanasia might help fill in some of the missing pieces.

Public Opinion on Euthanasia in the United States

To begin, we will look at how the total sample answered the GSS question about euthanasia. Then, to be a bit more discerning, we will divide the population who responded to this question into three groups: those 64 and under, those 65 to 84, and those 85 and older.

Research Hypothesis/Question   4.23:
What is the public option about euthanasia when a person has an incurable disease?

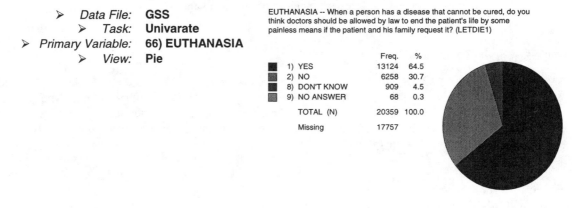

> Data File: **GSS**
> Task: **Univarate**
> Primary Variable: **66) EUTHANASIA**
> View: **Pie**

EUTHANASIA -- When a person has a disease that cannot be cured, do you think doctors should be allowed by law to end the patient's life by some painless means if the patient and his family request it? (LETDIE1)

		Freq.	%
■	1) YES	13124	64.5
▨	2) NO	6258	30.7
■	8) DON'T KNOW	909	4.5
▨	9) NO ANSWER	68	0.3
	TOTAL (N)	20359	100.0
	Missing	17757	

[Weight]

In 1998, 64% of people surveyed in the United States supported a person's right to euthanasia in cases where the person has an incurable disease, and the person and family request euthanasia. Almost 31% did not think a terminally ill person should have the right to request physician-assisted suicide.

Now we will do a couple of analyses to see if the gender and age of the respondent made a difference in their view of euthanasia.

Research Hypothesis/Question   4.24:
In the United States, gender affects one's view of euthanasia if you are under 65.

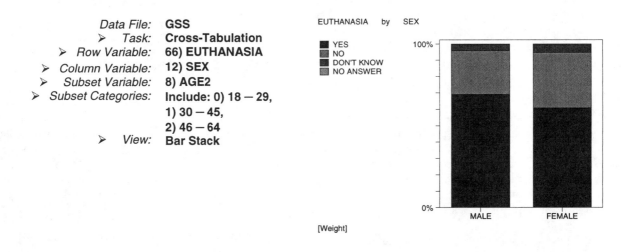

> Data File: **GSS**
> Task: **Cross-Tabulation**
> Row Variable: **66) EUTHANASIA**
> Column Variable: **12) SEX**
> Subset Variable: **8) AGE2**
> Subset Categories: **Include: 0) 18 — 29,**
> **1) 30 — 45,**
> **2) 46 — 64**
> View: **Bar Stack**

EUTHANASIA   by   SEX

- ■ YES
- ▨ NO
- ■ DON'T KNOW
- ▨ NO ANSWER

[Weight]

It is clear from the stack graph, representing those who answered the question and were between the ages of 18 and 64, men are more likely than women to support the idea of euthanasia. Let's do one more analysis to see if people 65 and older have a different view of euthanasia.

Research Hypothesis/Question   4.25:
In the United States, does gender affect one's view of euthanasia if you are over 64?

Data File:	**GSS**
Task:	**Cross-Tabulation**
Row Variable:	**66) EUTHANASIA**
Column Variable:	**12) SEX**
Subset Variable:	**8) AGE2**
➢ *Subset Category:*	**Include: 3) 65 – 97**
➢ *View:*	**Bar Stack**

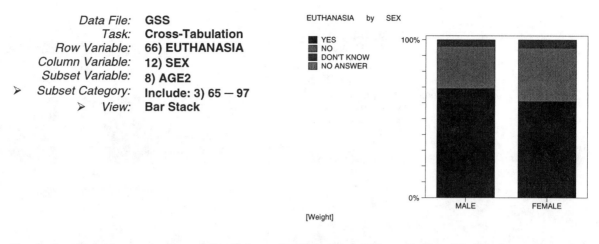

To change the subset category, right-click on the Subset variable and select Modify from the menu that appears. The category selection screen will appear where you can unselect categories 0 – 2, and then select 3) 65 – 97 to continue with this analysis.

This stack bar shows that although men still support euthanasia (60%) more than women (50.2%), the level of support by either men or women over 64 is not as high as for the entire group who answered this question.

Attitudes About Euthanasia Among College Graduates and Nongraduates

When we were examining global data, we found that religion has quite a profound impact on people's attitude toward euthanasia. When looking at an economically developed country, an individual's level of education would tend to shape a lot of his or her thinking. The question is, does education affect one's opinion about euthanasia, and in what way is one's attitude different?

Research Hypothesis/Question   4.26:
How do people with no college view euthanasia as opposed to those with at least one year of college?

Data File:	**GSS**
Task:	**Cross-Tabulation**
➢ *Row Variable:*	**66) EUTHANASIA**
➢ *Column Variable:*	**12) SEX**
➢ *Subset Variable:*	**10) EDUCATION2**
➢ *Subset Categories:*	**Include: 3) Coll 2 yrs,**
	4) Coll 4 yrs,
	5) Coll 6 yrs,
	6) Coll 8 yrs
➢ *View:*	**Bar Stack**

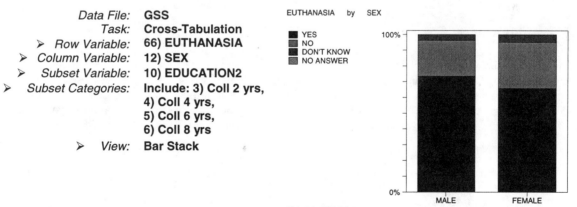

Among people with at least one year of college, 73.21% of men and 65.7% of women support euthanasia. To get these percentages select the **Column %** option.

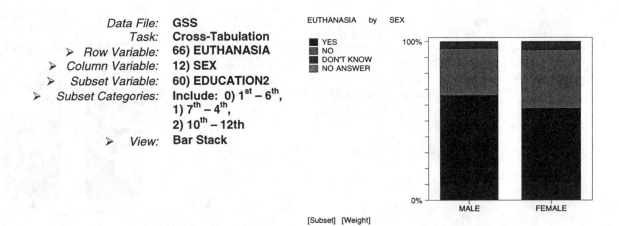

Data File:	**GSS**
Task:	**Cross-Tabulation**
➢ Row Variable:	**66) EUTHANASIA**
➢ Column Variable:	**12) SEX**
➢ Subset Variable:	**60) EDUCATION2**
➢ Subset Categories:	**Include: 0) 1st – 6th, 1) 7th – 4th, 2) 10th – 12th**
➢ View:	**Bar Stack**

[Subset] [Weight]

Among people with *no* college, 66.1% of men (as compared to 73.2% of men with at least some college) and 57.8% of women with no college (as compared to 65.7% of women with at least some college) support euthanasia. To get these percentages, select the **Column %** option.

In this case, those with one year of college or more support euthanasia more than people with no college. If you look closely, you will also notice that both women and men with at least one year of college are approximately 8% more supportive: a 7.3% increase for males and an 8% increase for women. The reactionaries are correct, college does change people's thinking, fortunately something does.

To this point, you have learned a number of analytical procedures in MicroCase that are very useful in analyzing real data sets. These procedures can be used with the variables in Chapters 1 through 3 to do more sophisticated examinations of variables and subgroups than we did in those chapters. Try looking at some of the relations as bar stacks and use subsets with the variables that are of interest to you.

End Note: In this chapter you used the same procedures that you have used in previous chapters to learn more about the world of elderly people. You also began using crosstabs to test bivariate relationships. As you noticed, some findings challenge conventional thinking. That Argentineans have the highest meat consumption in the world and the highest percentage of older citizens is an example of findings that challenge long held beliefs.

Other Aging Issues

There are a number of issues related to aging that I did not examine in this chapter. However, with the data files provided with this book, you can analyze many of these issues on your own. Remember, these are real data about real people like you and me. The following is a partial list of some additional issues important for understanding the plight of families. These issues have been important in the past and continue to be important today. To learn more about other issues related to aging, you can enter the following search terms in the InfoTrac College Edition.

In addition to the issues we have already examined, the following are issues that you can explore using variables from your MicroCase databases.

Elderly persons   **Legal services elderly**
Elderly poor   **Nursing homes**
Frail elderly   **Minority aged**
Abuse aged   **Euthanasia**

WORKSHEET

NAME:

COURSE:

DATE:

Workbook exercises and software are copyrighted. Copying is prohibited by law.

Review Questions

Based on the work you've done so far on the issue of aging, see how well you do on this short True or False quiz.

Elderly people are equally distributed around the world.	T F
Underdeveloped or developing countries need international help to care for the overwhelming numbers of elderly people.	T F
People in countries where there is a lot of agriculture have more access to the calories they need for good health.	T F
People living in industrial countries have a shorter life span than people in agricultural countries because of environmental pollution.	T F
Those 85 and older are fairly well distributed across the United States.	T F
Because people move to California and Florida when they retire, there are more nursing homes in these two states than other states.	T F
Being overweight and being over 64 put one at risk of dying of heart disease.	T F
Euthanasia is a concept that is accepted by a majority of those with some college but rejected by a majority of those with less than one year of college.	T F

MicroCase QUESTIONS

Use the following data files, variables, and analytical approaches to answer the MicroCase questions.

1. One of the questions we did not ask about elderly people in this chapter was about the level of happiness among elderly people of the world.

> Data File: **GLOBAL**
> Task: **Mapping**
> Variable 1: **22) % OVER 64**
> Subset Variable: **93) VERY HAPPY**
> Subset Range **2 – 47**
> View: **Map**

a.   Which 5 countries surveyed had the highest number of people 65 years of age and over responding that they were very happy?

_____   _____   _____   _____   _____

b.   Which 5 countries surveyed had the lowest number of people responding that they are very happy?

_____   _____   _____   _____   _____

c.   Based on the analysis, what do the countries that rank the lowest on happiness have in common?

_____

d.   Do the percentages suggest that most people in the world who are 65 and over are very

happy?   Yes   No

2.   How do those people around the world who consume a lot of calories from meat rate the quality of life in their country?

> Data File: **GLOBAL**
> ➢ Task: **Scatterplot**
> ➢ Dependent Variable: **28) MEAT CONS.**
> ➢ Independent Variable: **26) QUAL. LIFE**
> ➢ View: **Reg. Line**

a.   Would you agree with this statement: There is a very weak but statistically significant relationship between countries where large amounts of meat is consumed and their

population's perception of the quality of life in that country.   Yes   No

b.   What were the correlation and level of significances between the variable that measured meat consumption in a country and the quality of life in that country?

r = _____   p < _____

c.   What country has the highest level of meat consumption and ranks high for quality of life by its people?

_____

3.   Turning our attention to the United States, here are a few questions about people living in this country who are 65 and older.

> ➤   *Data File:*   **STATES**
> >   ➤   *Task:*   **Scatterplot**
> ➤   *Variable 1:*   **7) %>64 96**
> >   ➤   *View:*   **Map**

   a.   Which state has the largest percentage of its population who are 65 and older?

   _____

   b.   Virginia is another state where people like to go to retire.   Yes   No

4.   Next, see what people think about suicide.

> >   ➤   *Data File:*   **GSS**
> >   ➤   *Task:*   **Univariate**
> ➤   *Primary Variable:*   **69) SUIC.ILL**
> >   ➤   *View:*   **Pie**

   a.   What percentage of people agreed that a person has right to end his or her own life if the person has an incurable disease?

   _____

   b.   How many people interviewed say they "didn't know," or would not answer the question?

   _____

5.   Now see if people are excited about their lives.

> >   *Data File:*   **GSS**
> >   *Task:*   **Univariate**
> ➤   *Primary Variable:*   **37) LIFE**
> >   ➤   *View:*   **Pie**

a.   What percentage of people think their life is exciting?

_____

b.   What percentage of people think their life is dull?

_____

6.   Now find out what view of euthanasia is held by people who find life exciting, routine, or dull.

> Data File: **GSS**
> Task: **Cross-Tabulation**
> Row Variable: **37) LIFE**
> Column Variable: **66) EUTHANASIA**
> View: **Reg. Line**

a.   Is there a great deal of difference in views about euthanasia between the people who find their lives exciting and those who find their lives routine?   Yes   No

b.   Are those who think life is dull more supportive of euthanasia?   Yes   No

c.   What do you make of the response of people who think life is dull?

I would like to share with you a Web site where Charlie Fish has posted a number of poems and thoughts on aging and being an elder in the United States: www.charliefish.com/prp1.html

Variable Lists Related to Aging and Elderly People

The following is a partial list of the variables in your data files that you might find interesting in your study of elderly people. You can examine them either as individual variables or two variables at a time using the MicroCase approaches you learned to this point. Try these with the other variables in this chapter.

GLOBAL

6) CITY POP
   1995: % OF TOTAL POPULATION IN CITIES OF MORE THAN 750,000 (HDR, 1998)
41) LITERACY -- 1995: LITERACY RATE. NUMBER OF PEOPLE OVER 15 YEARS OF AGE ABLE TO
   BOTH READ AND WRITE PER 1,000 POPULATION (UNSY, 1997)
84) TRUST KIN?
   PERCENT WHO EXPRESSED COMPLETE TRUST IN THEIR FAMILY

STATES

37) %SNG.MEN90
   1990: PERCENT OF MALES OVER 15 WHO ARE SINGLE
38) %WIDOWR90
   1990: PERCENT OF MALES OVER 15 WHO ARE WIDOWED
39) %SNG.FEM90
   1990: PERCENT OF FEMALES OVER 15 WHO ARE SINGLE
41) MLE HEAD90
   1990: PERCENT OF HOUSEHOLDS THAT ARE MALE-HEADED, NO SPOUSE PRESENT

GSS

6) #CHILDREN
   HOW MANY CHILDREN HAVE YOU EVER HAD?
22) SOC.SEC.$
   SPENDING ON SOCIAL SECURITY
31) AFTERLIFE?
   DO YOU BELIEVE THERE IS A LIFE AFTER DEATH?

Web Pages Related to Aging and Elderly People

If you wish to find a world of resources that are available to you over the Internet, the following list of Web sites will get you started. Once you visit these Web sites, you will find many interesting links to other useful Web sites.

American Society on Aging
www.asaging.org

Administration on Aging, U.S. Govt.
www.aoa.dhhs.gov

National Aging Information Center
www.aoa.gov

U.N. Economic and Social Development
www.un.org/esa

U.S. Senate Special Committee on Aging
www.senate.gov/~aging/

Health Canada: Aging and Seniors
www.hc-sc.gc.ca

References

Aiken, W., and LaFollette, H. (1995). *World Hunger and Mortality.* Englewood Cliffs, NJ: Prentice Hall, Inc.

Allison, D. B. and Fontaine, K. R. (1999). Annual deaths attributable to obesity in the United States. *JAMA, 282*(16), 1530–1538.

Ambrosino, R., Heffernan, J., Shuttlesworth, G., and Ambrosino, R. (2001). *Social Work and Social Welfare: An Introduction* (4th ed.). Belmont, CA: Wadsworth/Thomson Learning.

Ashford, J. B., Lecory, C. W., and Lortie, K. L. (2001). *Human Behavior in the Social Environment* (2nd ed.). Belmont, CA: Wadsworth/Thomson Learning.

Flegal, K. M., Carroll, M. D., Kuczmarski, R. J., and Johnson, C. L. (1998). Overweight and obesity in the United States: Prevalence and Trends, 1960–1994. *International Journal on Obesity, 22,* 39–47.

Kirst-Ashman, K. K., and Hull, G. H. (2001). *Generalist Practice with Organizations & Communities* (2nd ed.). Belmont, CA: Wadsworth Publishing Company.

Lang, R. D. and Dunstain, R. (1995). *Euthanasia: The Debate Continues.* Nanaimo, BC, Canada: Malaspina University-College, The Institute of Practical Philosophy.

Levkoff, S. E., Chee, Y. K. and Noguchi, S. (eds.) (2001). *Aging in Good Health: Multidisciplinary Perspectives.* New York: Springer Pub.

Longres, J. E. (2000). *Human Behavior in the Social Environment* (3rd ed.). Itasca, IL: F. E. Peacock Pub. Inc.

Popple, P. R. and Leighnger, L. (2001). *Social Work, Social Welfare, and American Society* (5th ed.). Boston: Allyn and Bacon.

Nasuno, A., Terayama, M., Kouno, A., and Nakayama, M. (1998). A case report of 101 child unexpected deaths in Osaka prefecture. *Japanese Journal of Pediatrics, 51*(7), 141–146.

UNICEF (1999). *Children Orphaned by AIDS.* The United Nations Children's Fund. Retrieved July 30, 2000, from www.unicef-icdc.org.

U.S. Bureau of the Census (2000). *America's Children: Key National Indicators of Well-Being, 2000: The Fourth Annual Report to the Nation on the Condition of Our Most Precious Resource, Our Children.* Population Division, U.S. Census Bureau.

U.S. Bureau of the Census (2001). *Resident Population Estimates of the United States by Age and Sex: April 1, 1990 to July 1, 1999, with Short-Term Projection to November 1, 2000.* Washington, DC: Population Estimates Program, Population Division, U.S. Census Bureau.

United Nations Department of Economic and Social Affairs (DESA). (1998). *Measuring Changes in Consumption and Production Patterns.* New York: United Nations.

Additional Material That May Be of Interest

Cantor, M. H. (2000). *Social Care of the Elderly: The Effects of Ethnicity, Class, and Culture.* New York: Springer.

Garner, J. D. and Mercer, S. O. (eds.) (2001). *Women as They Age.* (2nd ed.). New York: Haworth Press.

Gornick, M. (2000). *Vulnerable Populations and Medicare Services: Why Do Disparities Exist?* New York: Century Foundation Press.

Hillman, J. L. (2000). *Clinical Perspectives on Elderly Sexuality.* New York: Kluwer Academic/Plenum Publishers.

Koch, T. (2000). *Age Speaks for Itself: Silent Voices of the Elderly.* Westport, CT: Praeger.

Mitchell, D. J. (2000). *Pensions, Politics, and the Elderly: Historic Social Movements and Their Lessons for Our Aging Society.* Armonk, New York: M. E. Sharpe.

Payne, B. K. (2000). *Crime and Elder Abuse: An Integrated Perspective.* Springfield, IL: Charles C. Thomas.

Smith, O. J. (ed.) (2000). *Aging in America.* New York: H. W. Wilson.

Chapter 5

HEALTH CARE

Tasks: Mapping, Univariate, Scatterplot, Correlations, Cross-tabulation, ANOVA, Regression, Historical Trends

Data Files: STATES, GLOBAL, GSS, US TRENDS

Overview of Chapter 5

Chapter 5 deals with a few questions about health care both globally and nationally. While trying to answer questions about health care, take notice of the systematic approach that is used to arrive at the answers. Using both the literature and statistical findings, we will methodically work through the variables until we have the best answer given the data available to us. This is an exercise that will help you develop or improve your critical thinking skills. This approach is explained in some detail in the section in this chapter called *Learning a Logical Approach to Data Analysis Can Help Build Your Critical Thinking Skills*. This chapter begins with the ethics of providing health care to all. As you are aware by this point, these are ethical challenges that ask you to put yourself in a situation and then decide on what ethical level you would support. After the ethics exercise, we start by taking a look at public health in countries around the world. We will try to find out what determines a country's spending on public health. Is it as important as military spending? How do expenditures on public health affect infant mortality? Building on what you have already learned, ANOVA and regression analytical procedures will be introduced. You will also use a fourth database that will give us information of statistical trends over time. I think you will find the trend data intriguing.

H eart disease, stroke, and cancer remain the three leading causes of death in the United States. In 1997, almost a third of people who died in the United States died from diseases of the heart. Deaths from cancer have continued to rise even as some interventions have prolonged the life of people with cancer. Increasingly, different types of cancer are linked to environmental factors. Cancer kills about a third of those who die each year. The rates of breast cancer continue to increase despite aggressive interventions. Even though progress continues to be made on many medical fronts, most of the people around the world will never access these medical advancements (Ambrosino et al., 2001). The resources devoted to health systems around the world are very unequally distributed. Low-and middle-income countries account for only 18% of world income and 11% of global health spending ($250 billion or 4% of GDP in those countries). Yet, 84% of the world's population lives in these countries, and they bear 93% of the world's disease burden (WHO, 2000a).

With the beginning of the new millennium, people in the United States began to say that the health-care system in this country is in a serious state of crisis. During this period, as health-care costs soared upward (Health Care Financing Administration, 2000), ever-increasing numbers of people found themselves without health insurance and without access to health care. "Health care statistics show that more infants are dying at birth and other people are experiencing serious health problems that are often treatable" (Ambrosino et al., 2001). We will return to the statement about an increase in infant deaths later in this chapter to test the veracity of the statement.

| 5.1 | Ethics of Health Care |

5.1   Ethics of Health Care

Suppose for a moment that you were taking a cross-country trip. While taking a side trip to see a historic site in an unfamiliar city, you become lost. Seeing a young man standing on the corner of the isolated rundown neighborhood, you pull over to ask directions. Then, the guy you thought would help you instead pulls a gun and hijacks you and your car. After a brief struggle, he shoots you and you go into a coma. When you are found, you are naked with no identification. Despite the fact that the hospital administration alerts the local police, there is no missing person's report on you because your family and friends have no idea you are missing. After a week, the cost for your care is mounting rapidly, putting the hospital administrators in a position where they must make a decision on the type of care you should receive. The doctors could not be sure that you would ever wake from the coma, but they also agreed you could come out of it tomorrow. They feared you could not live without life-support equipment at that moment. Of course, because you had a union job, you had a great Health Maintenance Organization (HMO) plan, but you had never been fingerprinted, so there was no way for the authorities to trace your identity. In this state of anonymity, totally dependent on the indigent health-care system of the United States, as it is defined at the most basic level of care for an individual, what kind of health-care policies and basic services would you want to be available for you and others who are totally dependent on the indigent health-care system?

Even though no country on earth spends more money on health care than the United States, our health-care system is not the best in the world. It is not even ranked in the top 10 countries, or the top 15 countries, with good health care (Ambrosino et al., 2001). Nevertheless, before examining the health-care system in the United States, why don't we look at other countries and their health-care systems. It will give us a broader perspective on the issues when we do turn our attention to the health-care system in the United States.

A Global View of Health Care

On the world stage, the World Health Organization (WHO) is an important player. WHO aims to stimulate a vigorous debate about better ways of measuring health system performance and thus finding a successful new direction for health systems to follow. Developing a way of measuring health performance could be useful in many ways but for sure, it would give a country an indication of how its health-care system stood up to other health-care systems. It could also increase our understanding of how health systems behave. WHO also tries to help policy-makers weigh the many complex issues involved, examine their options, and make wise choices (WHO, 2000a). Let us begin with a look at the money individual countries spend on public health.

Research Hypothesis/Question   5.1:
What do different countries spend on health care around the world, as a percentage of GDP?

> *Data File:* **GLOBAL**
> *Task:* **Mapping**
> *Variable 1:* **32) PUB HEALTH**
> *View:* **Map**

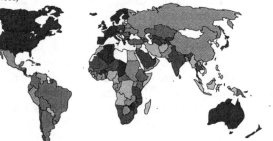

PUB HEALTH -- 1991: TOTAL EXPENDITURE ON HEALTH AS PERCENTAGE OF GDP
(HDR, 1998)

After you have studied the map, select **[List: Rank]** to see how the countries compare on the amount they spend on public health.

As you will see from the ranking of the countries, there are a few surprises in this list. The bottom 10 ranked countries are expected, but a couple of the top 10 countries are unexpected. Of course, we expected the United States to be the in the top 10 and it is number 1, but did you expect the United Arab Emirates (5) and Nicaragua (9) to be in the top 10? Remember, this measure is the percent of Gross Domestic Product (GDP) spending on public health.

5.2   Global Health Systems
Enormous gaps remain between the potential of health systems and their actual performance, and there is far too much variation in outcomes among countries that seem to have the same resources and possibilities (WHO, 2000a).

Research Hypothesis/Question   5.2:
The number of doctors will also vary from country to country.

> *Data File:* **GLOBAL**
> *Task:* **Mapping**
> ➢ *Variable 1:* **30) DOCTORS**
> ➢ *View:* **Map**

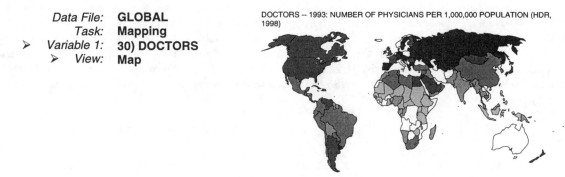

DOCTORS -- 1993: NUMBER OF PHYSICIANS PER 1,000,000 POPULATION (HDR, 1998)

Select the **[List: Rank]** option to see a list of the countries by rank. Now this list is sure to raise a few eyebrows in disbelief and distain in the exile Cuban community around the world. If you are looking for the United States to be in the top 10, you will be disappointed. Keep going down the list, and you will find the United States ranks 36th.

In this section, I will only examine the issue of spending on public health. Later you will be asked to do a similar analysis to identify government spending priorities that influence the number of doctors per country.

What Determines a Country's Spending on Public Health

What is different about countries that spend a great deal on public health and countries that spend very little on public health? Is it a decision determined by government spending priorities?

The next step is to pick several variables that we think can explain the difference in a country's spending on public health. Again, we can use our current knowledge and common sense to identify several related political characteristics of countries that explain the variation in spending around the world. The variable THREEWORLD will be used to separate the countries into three groups: First World, Second World, and Third World countries. Michael Le Roy (personal communication, March 2, 2002), a political scientist, defines First World countries as "democratic-capitalist nations." Second World nations are defined as "countries that were in the communist sphere of influence." And he defines Third World countries as the remainder "of all of the rest of the countries in the world."

Research Hypothesis/Question   5.3:
(1) The variation in the rank of countries as a First World, Second World, or Third World country; (2) the amount of the national income taken by the rich; (3) the variations in the total national government expenditure; and (4) the variations in expenditures on national defense will be related to the difference in the portion of its GDP a country spends for public health (the dependent variable).

This hypothesis looks more complicated than it is. Basically, we are using four variables that we believe are correlated with a country's spending on public health.

In other words, I believe, when spending on public health is high in a country, the country will be ranked as a First World country; the country will also restrict the total amount of the national income taken by the rich. The country will also spend larger amounts per capita on all government services; and the government will spend less on military defense. The statement sounds logical.

Using a correlation analysis to test these relationships is an efficient approach to test the relationship between the five variables I selected. A statistically significant correlation between the dependent variable (public health expenditures) and any of the independent variables will tell me if the variables are as important as I thought they were. **This is important to remember: if there are independent variables that do not correlate with the dependent variable in a bivariate analysis, it is a waste of time to use them in a more sophisticated, multivariate analysis. They will not be correlated to the dependent variable in a multivariate, either. We drop these from future analyses.**

		Correlation Coefficients Table			
	PUB HEALTH	THREE WORLD	$ RICH 10%	EXPND/CP	DEFNS/CP
PUB HEALTH	1.000 ($n = 145$)	-0.648** ($n = 145$)	-0.514** ($n = 7$)	0.556** ($n = 126$)	0.385** ($n = 119$)
THREE WORLD	-0.648** ($n = 145$)	1.000 ($n = 174$)	0.677** ($n = 80$)	-0.696** ($n = 150$)	-0.425** ($n = 138$)
$ RICH 10%	-0.514** ($n = 75$)	0.677** ($n = 80$)	1.000 ($n = 80$)	-0.563** ($n = 76$)	-0.502** ($n = 76$)
EXPND /CP	0.556** ($n = 126$)	-0.696** ($n = 150$)	-0.563** ($n = 76$)	1.000 ($n = 150$)	0.702** ($n = 133$)
DEFNS /CP	0.384** ($n = 119$)	-0.425** ($n = 138$)	-0.502** ($n = 76$)	0.702** ($n = 133$)	1.000 ($n = 138$)

Data File: **GLOBAL**
➤ Task: **Correlation**
➤ Variables: **32) PUB HEALTH**
  25) THREEWORLD
  33) $ RICH 10%
  36) EXPND/CP
  65) DEFNS/CP
➤ Deletion: **Pairwise**
➤ Test: **2-tailed**

PAIRWISE deletion (2-tailed test)   Significance Levels: * =.05, ** =.01

Now that we have four variables that are statistically related to a country's expenditure on public health, next we will examine these four independent variables in a series of bivariate analyses with the dependent variable, public health spending, to see what they tell us. This will also give us an easy-to-understand visual picture of the interplay between the four independent variables and the percentage of a country's GDP spent on public health, the dependent variable.

Research Hypothesis/Question   5.4:
There is a strong relationship between a country's total government expenditures and spending on public health.

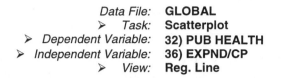

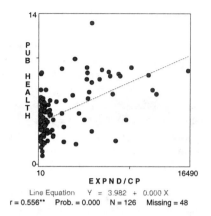

Data File:	**GLOBAL**
Task:	**Scatterplot**
Dependent Variable:	**32) PUB HEALTH**
Independent Variable:	**36) EXPND/CP**
View:	**Reg. Line**

This scatterplot indicates that all else being equal, spending on public health tends to rise and fall when overall government spending for all services rises and falls ($r = .556$, $p < .01$).

Research Hypothesis/Question   5.5:
There is a strong relationship between a country's ranking as a Third World country and reduced spending on public health.

For this next analysis, we will need to learn a new type of analysis, analysis of variance (ANOVA), which is designed specifically for when you have one nominal- or rank-order variable with a limited set of categories (e.g., THREEWORLD) and another interval/ratio variable with a wide range of values that go from low to high (PUBHEALTH). You will find ANOVA on the BASIC STATISTICS menu.

Data File:	**GLOBAL**
Task:	**ANOVA**
Dependent Variable:	**32) PUB HEALTH**
Independent Variable:	**25)THREEWORLD**
View:	**Summary**

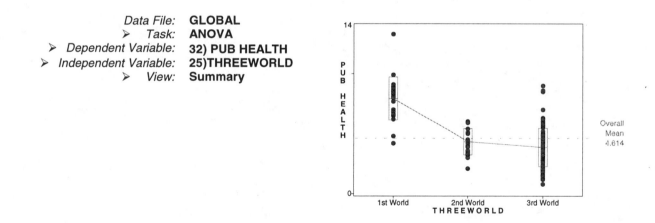

This bar-and-whiskers graph looks a bit different from a scatterplot; however, like a scatterplot, each nation is represented by one of the dots on the graph. The location of a nation on the graph is based on the percentage of GDP expenditure on public health and its Three Worlds classification. First, the dot is placed horizontally according to its category. You will notice that on the bottom of the graph, each category in the Three Worlds classification is represented. Then, the dot is placed vertically according to its expenditure on public health.

The rectangle shown for each category of the independent variable (THREEWORLD) indicates the high and low range in which most countries are located. While some countries will be located outside this range, the majority (around 70%) will be found within the range of this rectangle.

When you read an ANOVA graphic, focus on the means in this graphic (the average expenditure on public health) for each category of the independent variable. The location of the mean is shown with a flat line in the center of each rectangle. Your task is to compare the mean for one category against the means for the other categories. It's fairly easy to see whether a mean for one category is higher or lower than a mean for another category because there is a line that connects each of these mean points. The flatter the lines between the means, the less difference there is between the categories. We can now easily compare the different types of nations. In this graph you can easily see that expenditures for First World nations are much higher than expenditures for either Second or Third World nations. Second World nations have higher expenditures than Third World nations. You can also look at the mean expenditures for each group of countries in the form of a table.

	Data File:	**GLOBAL**
	Task:	**ANOVA**
Dependent Variable:		**32) PUB HEALTH**
Independent Variable:		**25)THREEWORLD**
➢	View:	**Means**

Means, Standard Deviations and Number of Cases of Depended Var: PUB HEALTH by Categories of Independent Var: THREEWORLD.

Difference of means across groups is statistically different (Prob. 0.000).

	N	Mean	Std. Dev.
1st World	24	7.933	1.788
2nd World	22	4.345	1.087
3rd World	99	3.870	1.584

This table shows the actual average (mean) percentage of GDP that is spent on health care for each category of THREEWORLD. As we can see, First World countries have the highest percentage of GDP going to health care (7.933). Second World countries have the next highest expenditure (4.345), and the Third World has the lowest (3.870). We can see from the line above the table that probability = 0.000. There is a test of statistical significance for ANOVA as well. For this we need to switch to the ANOVA view.

	Data File:	**GLOBAL**
	Task:	**ANOVA**
Dependent Variable:		**32) PUB HEALTH**
Independent Variable:		**25)THREEWORLD**
➢	View:	**ANOVA**

Analysis of Variance
Dependent Variable: PUB HEALTH
Independent Variable: THREEWORLD   N: 145
Missing: 29

ETA Square: 0.483

TEST FOR NONLINEARITY:
R Square = 0.420   F = 17.110   Prob. = 0.000

Source	Sum of Squares	DF	Mean Squares	F	Prob
Between	320.863	2	160.431	66.202	0.000
Between	344.117	142	2.423		
TOTAL	664.980	144			

Focus in on the F column in the table. The "*F*" or, as it is known, the "F Ratio" is used to test for the significance of differences between three or more means. Here, *F* = 66.2, which signifies a large difference between First and Third World countries on their expenditures on public health.

Research Hypothesis/Question   5.6:
The larger the proportion of a nation's income taken by the rich, the smaller the amount available to spend on public health.

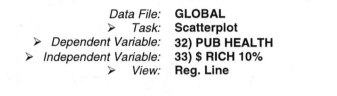

Data File:	**GLOBAL**
➤ *Task:*	**Scatterplot**
➤ *Dependent Variable:*	**32) PUB HEALTH**
➤ *Independent Variable:*	**33) $ RICH 10%**
➤ *View:*	**Reg. Line**

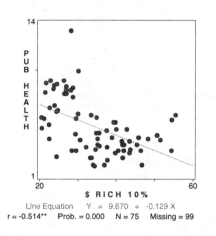

Obviously, there is a relationship between the amount of a country's income taken by the rich and the money available for public health (*r* = -.514, *p* < .000). Then again, it may not be as much the amount of the national income taken by the rich, but the mindset of the political leaders that allows the rich to take a large portion of the country's income. It would be unusual for a country's leaders to enact policies giving large sums to the rich and at the same time spending large sums on public health. Now let's see how defense spending affects public health spending.

Research Hypothesis/Question   5.7:
High levels of defense spending by a country will reduce the expenditures on public health in that country.

Data File:	**GLOBAL**
➤ *Task:*	**Scatterplot**
➤ *Dependent Variable:*	**32) PUB HEALTH**
➤ *Independent Variable:*	**65) DEFNS/CP**
➤ *View:*	**Reg. Line**

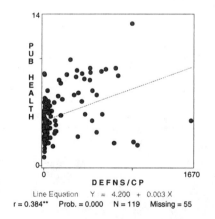

Oddly enough, our hypothesis that defense spending would reduce public health spending, as you can see from the scatterplot, did not hold up. The more spent on defense, the more spent on public health ($r = .38$, $p < .01$). It is a weak correlation, but it is still a statistically significant relationship.

5.3   Three Health-Care System Reforms

During the 20th century, there have been three overlapping generations of health-care system reforms. The three health-care systems were created because of perceived failures in health care, and because health-care providers were trying to develop a system that would provide greater efficiency, fairness, and responsiveness to the expectations of the people that the health-care systems serve. The first generation saw the founding of the national health-care systems and the expansion of these systems into poorer countries in the 1950s and 1960s. By the late 1960s, many of the health-care systems were under great financial strain. Health-care costs were rising as the volume and intensity of hospital-based care increased in developed and developing countries alike. Among health-care systems, health services still are used more heavily by the better-off, and efforts to reach the poor have often been incomplete and have had little effect. Too many people continued to depend on their own resources to pay for health care, and could often get only ineffective or poor-quality health care (WHO, 2000a).

Now we can see if the spending policies we identified contribute to the explanation of public health spending or if only one or two of the spending policies (predictor variables) can explain the difference in spending on public health. The best approach to use in this case is a multiple regression procedure.

Research Hypothesis/Question   5.8:
(1) A country's Third World ranking, (2) the amount the rich take from the national income, (3) the amount the government spends for all purposes, and (4) the amount spent on national defense will explain a large part of the difference in what a country spends for public health.

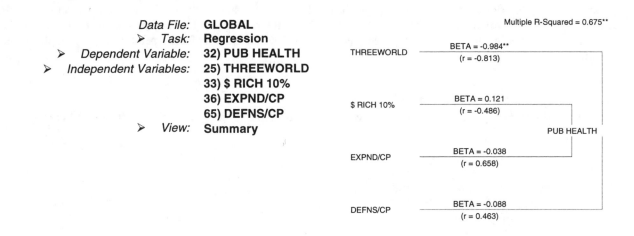

Data File:	**GLOBAL**
➤ Task:	**Regression**
➤ Dependent Variable:	**32) PUB HEALTH**
➤ Independent Variables:	**25) THREEWORLD**
	33) $ RICH 10%
	36) EXPND/CP
	65) DEFNS/CP
➤ View:	**Summary**

In the upper right-hand corner, the screen reads: Multiple R-Squared = 0.675**. This stands for R^2, which is a measure of the combined effects of the four independent variables on the dependent variable. Simply explained, this means that the variables reflecting the country's nation type, amount of wealth held by the richest 10%, amount of expenditure on all services, and expenditures on defense together account for 67.5% percent of the variation in expenditure on public health.

But that's not all we can see with this graphic. Beneath each of the horizontal lines is the value of *r*, which is the Pearson's correlation coefficient. These are, of course, the same values as those shown in the set of correlations we have already examined. Above each line is the word **beta**, followed by a numerical value. This stands for the standardized Beta, which estimates **the independent effect of each independent variable on the dependent variable**.

The independent variables in this analysis are correlated with one another as well as with the dependent variable. What regression does is sort out the independent contributions of these four variables. Reading from the top of the graphic down, what we first discover is that only the THREEWORLD variable has a significant Beta (significance is represented by **), which signifies that a small amount of GDP spending on public health is directly impacted by a country meeting Third World classification. This is good information, but what policies in these Third World countries result in different spending from country to country?

In this case we are lucky, there is a category on the variable **25) THREEWORLD** that groups nations identified as Third World countries together. Because spending can be identified as different by these nation groups, we can take another step in our examination to see how government spending policies in these countries influence spending on public health. We can look at a subset of these countries identified as Third World countries to see how, as a group of similar nations, public spending affects public health.

Research Hypothesis/Question   5.9:
(1) The amount the rich take from the national income, (2) the amount the government spends for all purposes, and (3) the amount spent on national defense will explain a large part of the difference in the portion a Third World country spends for public health.

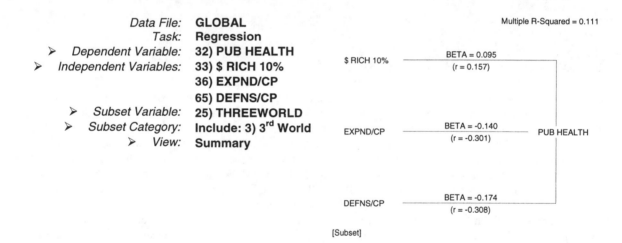

Data File:	**GLOBAL**
Task:	**Regression**
➤ *Dependent Variable:*	**32) PUB HEALTH**
➤ *Independent Variables:*	**33) $ RICH 10%**
	36) EXPND/CP
	65) DEFNS/CP
➤ *Subset Variable:*	**25) THREEWORLD**
➤ *Subset Category:*	**Include: 3) 3ʳᵈ World**
➤ *View:*	**Summary**

Multiple R-Squared = 0.111

$ RICH 10% — BETA = 0.095 (r = 0.157)

EXPND/CP — BETA = -0.140 (r = -0.301)

DEFNS/CP — BETA = -0.174 (r = -0.308)

PUB HEALTH

[Subset]

Real-world data strike again. Even though one would think that these spending policies in Third World countries are based on the data, they explain *nothing* about the difference in spending from country to country. This suggests that if the World Health Organization is hoping that Third World countries will make better spending decisions based on logical and social priorities, they may be waiting a long time.

I hope that you will continue to examine the global health issue. If you do, I suspect you will find the difference in public health spending among Third World countries will be more predictable using political, historical, and cultural data as predictor variables.

The AIDS Pandemic

A major health issue challenging the nations of the world is the AIDS pandemic. We would be remiss if we did not see if any of the spending choices made by Third World countries affected the number of AIDS deaths in those countries.

Research Hypothesis/Question   5.10:
Status as a Third World country, expenditures on public health, the percentage of the national income taken by the rich, per capita spending by Third World countries for goods and services, and defense spending will explain a great deal of the differences in AIDS deaths from country to country.

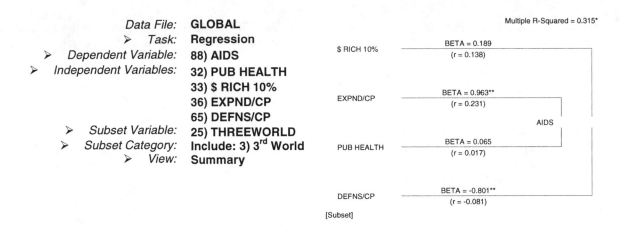

Data File:	**GLOBAL**
➤ *Task:*	**Regression**
➤ *Dependent Variable:*	**88) AIDS**
➤ *Independent Variables:*	**32) PUB HEALTH**
	33) $ RICH 10%
	36) EXPND/CP
	65) DEFNS/CP
➤ *Subset Variable:*	**25) THREEWORLD**
➤ *Subset Category:*	**Include: 3) 3rd World**
➤ *View:*	**Summary**

Multiple R-Squared = 0.315*

$ RICH 10%   BETA = 0.189   (r = 0.138)

EXPND/CP   BETA = 0.963**   (r = 0.231)

AIDS

PUB HEALTH   BETA = 0.065   (r = 0.017)

DEFNS/CP   BETA = -0.801**   (r = -0.081)

[Subset]

This makes a little more sense. At least a small percentage of the difference in government spending for AIDS can explain higher or lower death rates from AIDS in Third World countries (R^2 = .315, p < .05). If you look even closer, or look at the ANOVA statistics by selecting ANOVA in the statistics box, you will find that only *government spending* and *defense spending* explained even the small change in the number of deaths from AIDS. These *small changes,* as I put it, turn out to be thousands of people who will die from AIDS depending on the spending decisions made by a country's politicians. Again, make sure to note the direction of total government expenditures and defense spending in relationship to the number of deaths from AIDS in a particular Third World country. What the findings suggest is that when you find a Third World country where per capita government expenditures on services are high, death from AIDS will be high. Furthermore, in Third World countries where you find spending on defense to be high, you will find the deaths from AIDS to be low. Again, the explanation for the difference in deaths from AIDS from country to country is partly political, historical, cultural, and partly caused by spending decisions. By the year 2000, 50 million people had been infected. Consequently, many children have become orphans. In 2001, 25.3 million people worldwide were infected with the virus. About 95% of AIDS orphans lived in Sub-Saharan Africa. Over the six-year period of World War II, 183,000 children became orphans. In Sub-Saharan Africa, 180,000 children become orphans each month (UNICEF/UN-AIDS, 1999).

Learning a Logical Approach to Data Analysis Can Help Build Your Critical Thinking Skills

Have you ever said, "Give me a few minutes to think about it. I am trying to weigh all of the facts before making a decision"? If you said this or something similar, you could have said with a great deal of accuracy, "Give me a few minutes. I am doing a multiple regression equation in my head."

The problem-solving approach I used to analyze global health is an approach that can help build your critical thinking skills. As you move through this examination of global health, you are using an approach for gathering information that can help you in many ways other than when doing research. For one, it is an approach for gathering and organizing information that may be critical for making good decisions in your work in the helping professions. The added development of your critical thinking skills comes from learning to break a problem up into manageable parts, and having an idea of how to start looking closely at a new problem or phenomenon. The analysis that I do in this chapter is an example of using this critical thinking skill.

In the case of global health, I first made the decision to use two variables on which I had data and that seemed to be good indicators of the health of a country's people. I picked two variables that I thought would be applicable to all countries around the world. They were (1) the amount a country spends on public health, and (2) the number of doctors per person in the country. Starting with these two *dependent variables,* I mapped out the countries by rank of how much they spend on public health and how many doctors they had in their country. Using these two dependent measures of health gives me the triangulation, as I mentioned earlier in Chapter 2. This map, as a visual representation of the difference in spending by country, is very useful for getting a sense of the degree of variation from country to country. If there is no difference (no variation) between the countries in the amount spent on public health, and the number of doctors in each country—we will not be able to use these two measures (variables) to look at differences in health among nations. When I did the univariate analysis, using the mapping procedure, as expected there was a great deal of difference from country to country. Once I knew that there were differences among countries, the next step was to try to explain why there was this observable difference in spending on a service that is so vital to people and ergo the country itself.

To find out why some countries spend more on public health than other countries, I reviewed the literature for an explanation of the difference in public health spending. The literature had a number of possible explanations, but the one I thought had the best chance of explaining the difference was based on the spending decisions of political leaders. Leaders in some countries place spending on public health somewhere low on their list of spending priorities (World Health Organization, 2000b). Then using my best judgment, based on all I could find out, I selected four variables that I thought would explain *a good bit* of the difference (*a good bit* = my unscientific term for relationships that are statistically significant). After selecting the four independent variables (predictor variables), I used the Pearson's correlation procedure to determine the strength of each variable with the dependent variable *spending on public health*. The strength of the relationship is indicated in the correlation table by one or two asterisks. When I look at a correlation table, I am looking for these statistically significant correlations. What's more, the correlations tell me the direction of the significant relationship. If you recall, I said when spending is high on national defense, spending in that country on public health services would be low. When spending on defense goes up, I said spending on public health will go in the other direction—it will go down. As it turned out, I was wrong; in this case my hypothesis was not supported. Even so, in this analysis I learned something unexpected. It will make my final explanation more accurate.

Next, I set about looking at the relationship between the dependent variable and each of the predictor variables (independent variables) in a bivariate analysis. This gives me a lot of information about each of the independent variables and how they impact spending, on public health. This is when I realized that defense spending was not correlated with lower public spending, but it was correlated with higher public health spending. Once I had this more complete picture, it was obvious that there was overlap in what the predictor variables were measuring. The four independent variables cannot account for over 100% of the variance in the dependent variable. This means that some of the variables are correlated with *public health spending*; they change at a similar time, but they do not cause all the changes in public health spending. Using an analogy, when you take a computer class to learn a new computer program like PowerPoint, only part of the skills you use to produce a PowerPoint presentation will be learned in class. Even though you had never used PowerPoint, you already knew a lot about how to use it because you were familiar with Windows-based programs.

To see which independent variables have a *causal effect* and can possibly make changes in spending on public health, and to identify those independent variables that are not causing a change in public health spending, we will use the multiple regression analysis technique. This analysis selected the independent variables that cause a change and then tells us how much of the change in the dependent variable is caused by the independent variables.

The analysis done in this way produced strong evidence that you can use to predict that low levels of spending on public health will be found in countries classified as Third World countries. "So what is new?" you may ask. "What government spending policies in the Third World explain public health expenditures?" To answer this question, I need to do the same multiple regression analysis with the same variables. This time, however, I will analyze the data from only Third World countries.

This systematic approach, which we have been using, increases my chances of finding real answers to real problems. Here, it helps identify the difference in public health spending from one country to another. It can be used to study other phenomena, as well as to improve your practice skills.

Health Care in the United States

When we try to look at the social welfare issues in the United States, it often helps to start out with a little reality check. In 1998, the United States ranked 17th in life expectancy and 14th in infant mortality among 20 industrialized countries with a population of 6 million or more (Ambrosino et al., 2001).

This is a good place to start our examination of the health-care system in the United States. Using our **GLOBAL** data file, we can see where the United States ranks on these two indicators of national health. I will start with infant mortality and let you examine life expectancy at a later time. In our database, it will be unlikely to find the United States is 14th among nations in our database. Our database covers 174 countries. The list mentioned above was made up of only 20 industrial nations with populations of 6 million or more. Why would you do this anyway? Because, we might learn something from countries that have an infant mortality rate lower than the United States.

Research Hypothesis/Question   5.11:
How does the United States rank on infant mortality among the nations of the world for which we have data?

> *Data File:* **GLOBAL**
> *Task:* **Mapping**
> *Variable 1:* **12) INF.MORTL**
> *View:* **Map**

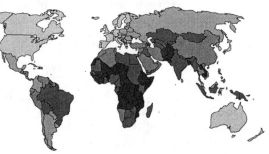

INF. MORTL -- NUMBER OF INFANT DEATHS PER 1,000 BIRTHS (TWF, 1997)

The United States ranks 156 out of 174. It is important to note that this variable is set up to show the number of infant deaths per 1,000 live births. Therefore, a lower number on this variable is a good thing. If you switch to the **[List: Rank]** view, you will find that 21 countries have a lower infant mortality rate than the United States. You will also find that Canada ranks 163, higher than 11 other countries, and Singapore and Japan have the lowest rates of infant mortality. If you map out life expectancy [17) LIFE EXPCT], you will find that the United States ranks 26 out of 174 countries, with the Japanese enjoying the longest life expectancy. What do you think they are doing right with health care in Iceland?

Health Spending and Health Outcomes in the United States

To try to understand how the United States can spend more money than any country in the world on public health, and still rank below 20 other nations on these health indicators, let's map out the number of doctors and hospitals available to people in the United States.

Research Hypothesis/Question   5.12:
There will be a lot of variation from state to state on the number of doctors and hospital beds available to provide health care.

> *Data File:* **STATES**
> *Task:* **Mapping**
> *Variable 1:* **68) DR.RATE96**
> *View:* **Map**
> *Display:* **Legend**

DR.RATE96 -- 1996: ACTIVE NONFEDERAL PHYSICIANS PER 100,000 POPULATION

Values			N
145	To	180	(9)
185	To	200	(11)
203	To	222	(9)
223	To	241	(11)
244	To	393	(10)
Missing Data			

There is not a lot of pattern to this map, but generally the largest concentration of doctors is found in states with higher urban populations, and lower concentrations are found in states with higher rural populations. Now take a look at the distribution of hospital beds.

> *Data File:* **STATES**
> *Task:* **Mapping**
> *Variable 1:* **70) HSP.B RT94**
> *View:* **Map**
> *Display:* **Legend**

HSP.B RT94 -- 1994: COMMUNITY HOSPITAL BEDS PER 100,000 POPULATION (AHA

Values			N
214	To	254	(10)
258	To	327	(10)
328	To	368	(10)
374	To	435	(10)
436	To	689	(10)
Missing Data			

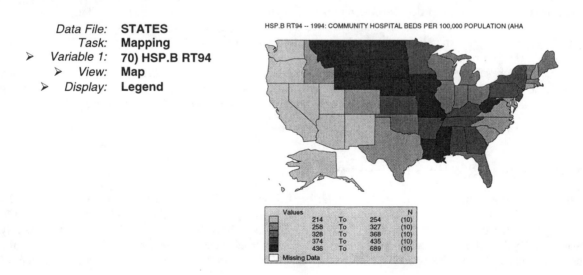

If, like me, you were thinking that the states with more doctors would also be the same states with a large number of hospital beds, which seems logical, like me, you were wrong. The patterns of dark and light states tell the story. All the same, our hypothesis that there would be an unequal distribution of doctors and hospital beds from state to state was supported by the two maps. We got it wrong by thinking somehow the two would be related. Just out of curiosity, why don't we see if the more doctors a state has predicts that the state will have more hospital beds.

5.4   Rural Hospitals

In 1946, the Hill-Burton Act funded construction of numerous rural hospitals. This improved health nationally. Nonetheless, to this day, living in extremely rural areas or crowded urban areas puts one at more risk for having health problems. In the 1980s and 1990s, many hospitals in rural areas went out of business because of the high cost of providing health care to the poor (Ambrosino et al., 2001; Findley and Miller, 1999).

Research Hypothesis/Question   5.13:
States with large numbers of doctors will also have large numbers of hospital beds.

Data File:	**STATES**
➤ *Task:*	**Scatterplot**
➤ *Dependent Variable:*	**70) HSP.B RT94**
➤ *Independent Variable:*	**68) DR.RATE96**
➤ *View:*	**Reg. Line**

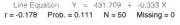

Line Equation   Y = 431.709 + -0.333 X
r = -0.178   Prob. = 0.111   N = 50   Missing = 0

Here we go again. Real life continues to defy logic. Why would states with more doctors not have more hospital beds, and vice versa? You would expect that as the number of doctors increase so would the number of hospital beds, but this is not the case ($r = -.18$, $p = $ NS). The *NS* means the relationship is not statistically significant. This implies that there is no relationship between the number of doctors and hospital beds in the United States. As in many cases where we analyze real data, the findings leave us with more questions than we started with. Why is it that the number of doctors in a state has nothing whatsoever to do with the number of hospital beds? That would be similar to finding that the number of automobiles per person in a state exceeded the number of licensed drivers. It would not make much sense. However, there is always the exception. In Florida, there are far more cars than residents with driver's licenses. The reason is simple: tourism. So, what could explain the lack of a relationship between doctors and the number of hospital beds? I am guessing now, but perhaps if you have many doctors in a community, you do not need as many hospital beds, and vice versa.

Accessing Health Care in the United States.

It really does not matter how many doctors or hospital beds there are if you cannot access them. Access to the health-care system is a major problem in this country for many working people and their families, often referred to as the *working poor*. Many people work full-time, but the company they work for does not offer them or their family health insurance. By far, "the vast number of people in the United States access the *health care industry* through the health insurance plan carried by their employer (Budetti et al., 1999). If I am making a true statement, the number of people per capita who have health insurance will vary from state to state because the types of employment varies from state to state and the ability or willingness of those employers to provide health coverage for employees and their family will also vary. First we will map out the states by the number of residents who have health insurance.

Research Hypothesis/Question   5.14:
What is the rank of states on the number of people who have health insurance in the state?

> Data File: **STATES**
> ➤ Task: **Mapping**
> ➤ Variable 1: **69) HLTH INS96**
> ➤ View: **Map**

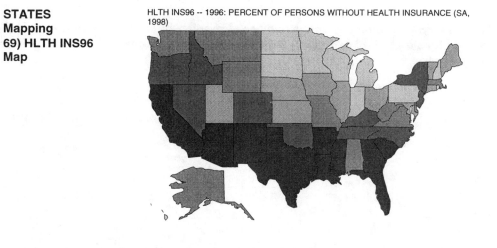

HLTH INS96 -- 1996: PERCENT OF PERSONS WITHOUT HEALTH INSURANCE (SA, 1998)

As we predicted, there is a lot of variation among states in the number of people who have health insurance. All things being equal, this would be unexpected in a country as rich in wealth and talent as the United States. But, you and I know there are scores of people without health insurance in this country and we really do not know why. For example, why is a single mother working full-time for a convenience store in Massachusetts, earning slightly above minimum wage, provided health insurance, where a mother in Florida in the same circumstances is not provided health insurance? Rather than dismiss these variations as politics or caused by greed for higher corporate profits, let's see if we can learn anything about other situations in a state that could cause fewer people to be covered by health insurance.

Here is where you put your critical thinking skills into high gear. Review the literature in your introduction to social work, social welfare, human behavior text, etc. to see what might influence this phenomenon that we can test with real data.

If you start your literature review with the question about problems with access to health care, you will find several reasons mentioned by the authors of most texts that discuss this issue. These reasons will probably include poverty, female-headed families, living in a rural versus an urban area, family income, and different levels of health spending by local and state governments (e.g., Ambrosino et. al., 2001; Budetti et al., 1999; Jansson, 1999, 2001; Trenholm and Kung, 2000; Zastrow, 2000). Of course, there are a number of other possible explanations for people and families not having health insurance, but these seem to be very important per the literature, given the plethora of possible explanations.

Staying with our logical approach to examining a complicated issue like health care in the United States, I next ran a correlation with the variable *percent of people without health insurance*, thinking of it as the dependent variable. I included six independent variables or predictor variables in the correlation that came as close as possible to six of the causes for people not having health insurance cited in the professional literature. Rather than take up space here with the independent variables that were not significantly related to whether or not people had health insurance, I will list them and then do a correlation with only the variables that may have the power of prediction.

Of the seven variables I predicted to explain why people do not have health insurance, two were not statistically significantly related to people without health insurance. They were **21) %RURAL90** and **97) HLTH$/CP94** (the amount the state spends per capita for health services and hospitals). The remaining five variables were to some degree related to the cause for the difference in people without health insurance in different states. However, they are also somewhat related to each other, which means there will probably be some overlap in measurement.

Research Hypothesis/Question   5.15:

What is the relationship between the number of people who have health insurance in a given state and the number of families headed by women, the percent of poor in that state, and local government expenditures on health and hospitals?

Data File: **STATES**
➢   Task: **Correlation**
➢   Variables: **69) HLTH INS96**
        43) F HEAD/C90
        74) %POOR 96
        75) MED.FAM$96
        94) HEALTH $87
➢   Deletion: **Pairwise**
➢   Test: **2-tailed**

Correlation Coefficients Table

	HLTH INS96	F HEAD/ C90	%POOR 96	MED FAM $96	HEALTH $87
HLTH INS96	1.000 (n = 50)	0.475** (n = 50)	0.714 (n = 75)	-0.370** (n = 126)	0.355 ** (n = 50)
F HEAD/ C90	0.475** (n = 50)	1.000 (n = 50)	0.503** (n = 50)	-0.145** (n = 50)	0.528** (n = 50)
%POOR 96	0.714 (n = 50)	0.503** (n = 50)	1.000 (n = 50)	-0.665** (n = 50)	0.311* (n = 50)
MED FAM $96	-0.370** (n = 50)	-0.145** (n = 50)	-0.665** (n = 50)	1.000 (n = 50)	-0.426** (n = 133)
HEALTH $87	0.355* (n = 50)	0.528** (n = 50)	0.311** (n = 50)	-0.416** (n = 50)	1.000 (n = 50)

Pairwise deletion (2-tailed)   Significance Levels: ** =.01, * =.05

Although I studied the scatterplot of each bivariate relationship in this correlation matrix, I will examine only one bivariate relationship here because of space considerations. You can take a look at the rest of the possible independent variables by repeating the same bivariate procedure I use below with each of the variables in the matrix that I do not present here.

Research Hypothesis/Question   5.16:

There is a relationship between states with large numbers of female-headed families and families without health insurance.

Data File: **STATES**
➢   Task: **Scatterplot**
➢   Dependent Variable: **69) HLTH INS96**
➢   Independent Variable: **43) F HEAD/C90**
➢   View: **Reg. Line**

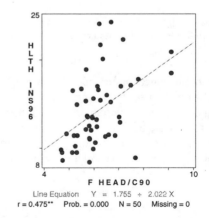

Line Equation   Y = 1.755 ÷ 2.022 X
r = 0.475**   Prob. = 0.000   N = 50   Missing = 0

This clearly shows that female-headed households tend to be without health insurance or at risk of not having health insurance for herself and her children. This could be eliminated as a problem by expanding Medicaid to include female-headed households that are not at 125% of the poverty level. In 1965, President Lyndon Johnson signed into law an amendment to the Social Security Act that created the Medicare and Medicaid programs that provide hospital insurance to the elderly, along with supplementary medical insurance for other medical costs. Medicare is the health-care program for the elderly. Medicaid is the health-care program for poor individuals and families. In 1996, Medicare was funded at a cost of $203.1 billion and served 38.1 million elderly and disabled persons. Medicare does not provide nursing home care or the costs of special wheelchairs. Medicare pays for less than 50% of the total costs of health care for the elderly (U.S. Census Bureau, 1999; Ambrosino et al., 2001).

Research Hypothesis/Question   5.17:
(1) A state with sizeable numbers of female-headed families, (2) a sizeable population of poor residents, and (3) a lower-than-average family income will explain a large part of the difference in the portion a state spends for public health.

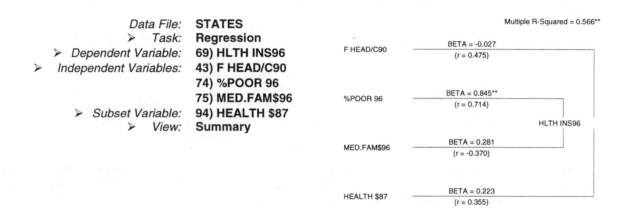

Data File:	**STATES**
➤ *Task:*	**Regression**
➤ *Dependent Variable:*	**69) HLTH INS96**
➤ *Independent Variables:*	**43) F HEAD/C90**
	74) %POOR 96
	75) MED.FAM$96
➤ *Subset Variable:*	**94) HEALTH $87**
➤ *View:*	**Summary**

Now, when we look at the independent effect of each independent variable on the dependent variable (HLTH INS96), these results are different from what we have seen previously. Here, only the percent poor (beta = 0.845**) has a statistically significant relationship with the percent of persons without health insurance. However, living in a female-headed household (beta = -0.027), the median family income (beta = 0.281), and percent of local expenditures spent on health care (beta = 0.223) do not have statistically significant impacts on the percent of persons without health insurance. Together, these variables account for 56.6% percent of the variation in the percent of people without health insurance (Multiple $R^2 = 0.566$, $p < 0.01$).

5.5   Comparing Health-Care Coverage in the U.S. with That of Sweden

In the United States, public assistance grants provide an income well below the poverty level. It is intended to motivate women to work. Public assistance offers nothing to parents who keep just above the poverty line. Health-care coverage is not provided to children of indigent parents who are not on public assistance. Medicaid covers about half the cost of health care. By contrast, Sweden's payments to single mothers include day care, subsidized housing, and health insurance, and it provides a modestly decent standard of living. Swedish policy is designed to support a large female labor force by continuing benefits at a generous level when women return to work after giving birth. Even so, the married mother with a working husband remains far better off. What the policy does is avert destitution for single mothers (Cherry et al., 2001).

As we saw in the correlation matrix earlier, the three remaining independent variables are all related to poverty. We next will repeat this analysis, without the independent variable %POOR 96, so that we can better see how these three variables affect the percentage of people without health insurance. Did you know better than 32% of the poor in this country did not have health insurance in 1998 and 1999 (U.S. Census Bureau, 2000)?

Research Hypothesis/Question   5.18:
(1) A state with sizeable numbers of female-headed families, (2) a lower-than-average family income, and (3) where the local government spends little on health and hospitals will have fewer people with health insurance.

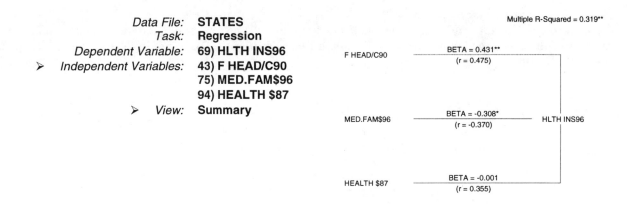

Data File:	**STATES**
Task:	**Regression**
Dependent Variable:	**69) HLTH INS96**
➤ *Independent Variables:*	**43) F HEAD/C90**
	75) MED.FAM$96
	94) HEALTH $87
➤ *View:*	**Summary**

Multiple R-Squared = 0.319**

F HEAD/C90   BETA = 0.431**
                  (r = 0.475)

MED.FAM$96   BETA = -0.308*   HLTH INS96
                  (r = -0.370)

HEALTH $87   BETA = -0.001
                  (r = 0.355)

Once the independent variable %POOR 96 is removed from the analysis, the most important variable that explains why some families have no health insurance is that they are households headed by a female. These three variables, however, explain less of the variance of why some families do not have health insurance ($R^2 = 0.319$, $p < 0.01$).

Explaining a third of the variance in whether or not people have health insurance may not seem like a lot at first, but because this is real data about real people and women running families on a tight budget, we are talking about millions of women with children, some of whom you probably know. If politicians really wanted to increase the number of people with health insurance, they could focus on women with children and make sure they were covered. They could also increase the minimum wage, which would increase the median family income. Because poverty in general is the major reason people do not have health insurance, politicians could pass legislation to develop a program that would provide individuals and families with health insurance on a sliding scale.

Of course, this assumes the politicians really want to reduce the numbers of people in their state who have no health insurance. You have seen the numbers; using a few simple strategies based on hard evidence, a state could increase the number of residents with health insurance by as much as 50%.

The Differences Between States on Rates of Infant Mortality

Trying to put these sad events in the context of a mechanistic category, *infant mortality* seems cold, but in many ways, I know for some of us, it is a way of trying to reduce the visual pictures that a term like *baby deaths* brings to one's mind. It can never do justice to the grief of the parents and those touched by the experience. We can even read about the death of a child and it can weigh heavily on our minds for some time.

Infant mortality is also a stinging measure of a state's quality and equality of health care. In this examination, we will use the same four variables that we found to be good predictors of people without health care. In this next situation, we will see if these variables can predict the rate of infant mortality in a particular state. Because poverty is such a catch-all condition, I will drop it from this analysis and propose a similar hypothesis to the last one.

Research Hypothesis/Question 5.19:
(1) A state with sizeable numbers of female-headed families, (2) a lower-than-average family income, and (3) where the local community spends little for health and hospitals will have higher rates of infant mortality.

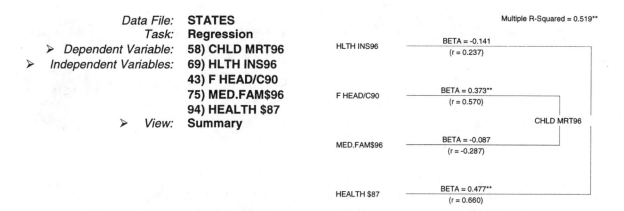

Data File:	**STATES**
Task:	**Regression**
➤ *Dependent Variable:*	**58) CHLD MRT96**
➤ *Independent Variables:*	**69) HLTH INS96**
	43) F HEAD/C90
	75) MED.FAM$96
	94) HEALTH $87
➤ *View:*	**Summary**

The results of this analysis are troubling. The variation in infant mortality from state to state is strongly predicated on the percent of households headed by a female (beta = 0.373**) and by the percent of local expenditures that go to health care (beta = 0.477**). This makes the strongest case yet for focusing on access to health care. States with a higher percent of expenditures going to health care, and states with a lower percent of female-headed households, all have lower infant mortality rates. The combined influence of all four variables explains half the variation in infant mortality rates by state (Multiple R^2 = 0.519, p < 0.01). This makes a strong case for increased spending on health care in communities with large numbers of single moms, especially in the area of prenatal care. If your agency provides prenatal care, your clients who are pregnant and single moms are at a higher risk of their child dying in the first year of life. Yet, even with health insurance, it may be a hard choice between spending money for the co-payment for medicines a mom needs to take during pregnancy and whether or not the oldest child gets a cheap pair of tennis shoes. It has been my experience that single moms must choose how to spend too little money for too many mouths.

Do People Think HMOs Are the Cause of the Health-Care Crisis in the United States?

Let's turn our attention to another pressing national issue that affects almost everyone in the country: accessing health care in a Health Maintenance Organization (HMO) environment. Are HMOs responsible for the United States having a lower life expectancy than people in 25 other countries and a higher rate of infant mortality than 21 other nations? We outspend the rest of the world per capita for health care; what is going on? There were several questions asked during the GSS interview about HMOs that might give us a sense of how people feel about HMOs.

5.6 Managed Care

The *managed-care* revolution began in the 1990s. It was a national health-care industries' response to double-digit annual increases in cost. Before the advent of managed care, physicians set their own prices and were reimbursed by insurance companies or patients; no questions asked. As costs took off in the 1990s, as a way of establishing limits on these fees, HMOs were developed and set rates and fees they would pay physicians and hospitals (Jansson, 1999). This reduced the costs of health care, but the savings were somewhat offset by the

---

marketing costs, the profit motive, and huge executive salaries.

Research Hypothesis/Question 5.20:
A statistically significant number of people will report that they think HMOs prevent patients from receiving needed medical care.

> *Data File:* **GSS**
> *Task:* **Univariate**
> *Variable 1:* **86) HMO4**
> *View:* **Pie**

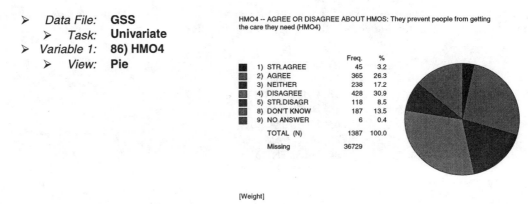

HMO4 -- AGREE OR DISAGREE ABOUT HMOS: They prevent people from getting the care they need (HMO4)

		Freq.	%
■	1) STR.AGREE	45	3.2
■	2) AGREE	365	26.3
■	3) NEITHER	238	17.2
▨	4) DISAGREE	428	30.9
■	5) STR.DISAGR	118	8.5
▨	8) DON'T KNOW	187	13.5
■	9) NO ANSWER	6	0.4
	TOTAL (N)	1387	100.0
	Missing	36729	

[Weight]

This is interesting; with as much as people, politicians, and patient advocates complain, I thought more people would agree with this negative statement. Anyway, the data are the data. Less than a third of those interviewed thought HMOs restricted patient care. Therefore, if the majority of people feel HMOs are not trying to restrict health care to patients, then let's see how they feel about HMOs serving the main purpose for their existence—to save on medical costs. Do people believe that HMOs are at least saving money so we get more medical service for our dollar?

"Medicare generally does not cover outpatient prescription drugs. Most Medicare beneficiaries have some form of public or private supplemental insurance to help pay for prescription drugs. These sources of supplemental coverage include employer-sponsored retiree health plans, Medicaid, Medigap, and Medicare HMOs" (The Henry J. Kaiser Family Foundation, 2001).

The High Cost of Health Care

A number of reasons are given for the accelerating cost of health care in this country. The major reason is that the provision of health care is profit-driven. The health-care industry is not operating in a free market where people can choose health care or choose to do without it. Thus, health care, unlike other commodities (e.g., cars, houses, and clothes), does not contend with free-market pressures to provide better medical services or work for better medical outcomes. Medical research focuses on developing expensive treatments that leave little funding for prevention research and initiatives. Prevention programs and lifestyle education programs, some critics point out, will not produce fat corporate profits that the expensive medical treatments will (Zastrow, 2001). Over the years, health care has increased from 5.1% of GDP in 1960 to 13% in 1999 (U.S. Census Bureau, 2000). Increases in health-care costs have also been needed to offset the cost of new technology and skilled medical personnel that have saved lives and improved the quality of life for so many more. Furthermore, third-party payments have increased costs. When the cost of a procedure is paid for by someone other than the patient, it is thought that physicians will order diagnostic and treatment procedures to protect themselves as opposed to being necessary for patient recovery (Zastrow, 2001).

Research Hypothesis/Question 5.21:
Over 50% of people who feel HMOs are not restricting care will also strongly agree, or agree, that HMOs are saving money.

[Weight]

> ➢ *Data File:* **GSS**
> ➢ *Task:* **Cross-tabulation**
> ➢ *Row Variable:* **85) HMO3**
> ➢ *Column Variable:* **86) HMO4**
> ➢ *View:* **Bar Stack**

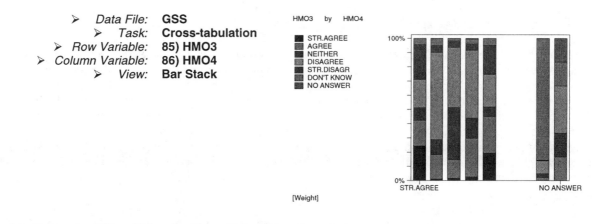

Collapsing Categories When Using the Cross-Tabulation Procedure

This bar chart is very difficult to read with all the categories in each variable. When you run a cross-tabulation that includes this many categories, one thing you can do is combine (collapse) similar categories or drop unneeded categories–dropping categories adds this data into the *Missing* data category that is excluded from our analysis. We will collapse and drop categories here. MicroCase allows you to collapse or drop categories temporarily. Once you select new variables, or leave this task, these variables will again have the original number of categories.

For this example, we want to make two columns and rows for each variable. To begin, you first need to return to the table view. You can do this by selecting **Column%** from the left of your screen. To begin removing categories you then click on the following row headings: *NEITHER, DON'T KNOW,* and *NO ANSWER.* You will notice that these rows are now highlighted in green to show they have been selected. Next, click on the [Collapse] button on the left of the screen. In the window that appears, select the second option, "Convert to Missing Data (Drop)." These two rows have now disappeared. Repeat this exact same process for the columns with the same names. Now we want to collapse some rows and columns so we are left with two rows and two columns. Select the two rows named *STR.AGREE* and *AGREE.* Then click the [Collapse] button. In the window that appears, name the new row *YES-Sav.* Repeat this process for the two rows named *DISAGREE* and *STR.DISAGR,* except name this new row *NO-Sav.* You next need to repeat this process for the identically named columns. This ability to collapse rows and columns will come in handy in the remaining chapters. Now switch back to the Bar Stack view.

> *Data File:* **GSS**
> *Task:* **Cross-tabulation**
> ➢ *Row Variable 1:* **85) HMO3**
> ➢ *Column Variable 2:* **86) HMO4**
> ➢ *View:* **Bar Stack**

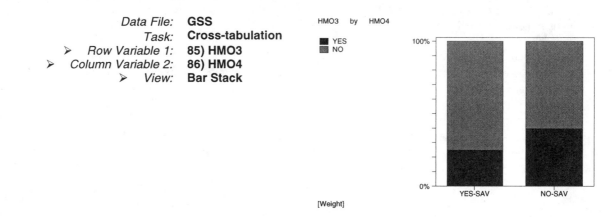

[Weight]

This bar graft is a lot easier to read and understand. The two attitudes about HMOs are inversely related. The majority of people who think HMOs save money do not agree that they restrict patient care, and vice versa. There is a sizeable group in this country, provided this GSS data are representative of people in this country, who have an opinion about these issues and who believe that HMOs restrict care and do not save money (approximately 40%).

A Historical Anomaly: The Swine Flu Epidemic

While teaching at a college in Scranton, Pennsylvania, I often jogged through the Scranton Cemetery. It was quiet and cars were no problem. During my runs, I noticed a number of peculiar headstones and mausoleums. In spite of these gaudy monuments, what slowly caught my attention were a number of small brass plaques about 8 inches by 4 inches, each with a number. I had seen them before but I suddenly realized there were hundreds of them. At first I thought they were markers for "potter's graves" or criminals. Being curious, I asked the grounds keeper about the brass plaques. Apparently, I wasn't the first to ask. He said during the Swine flu epidemic, in 1919, people were dying so quickly that headstones could not made fast enough, so plaques were used instead. The thinking was that when the epidemic was over, families of those who died would place a headstone on the grave. After the epidemic, however, there was no one left to put a more personal memento on many of the graves; entire families had been wiped out.

Research Hypothesis/Question   5.22:
Life expectancy in the United States has increased significantly and steadily over the last 100 years.

> *Data File:* **US TRENDS**
>   *Task:* **Historical Trends**
> *Variable:* **6) LIFE EXP**

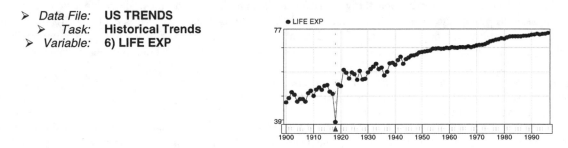

During the Swine flu epidemic in the United States, *550,000 people died out of a population of 105 million people* and 20 million died worldwide. It was spread across the United States in large part by soldiers returning home from World War I. My grandmother recalled the Swine flu hitting her little southern town after a solider returned home from the war. When she recovered from the flu-induced delirium, she found several members of her family and many friends in her community had died.

End Note: This chapter was important because it shows that logical thinking and the literature are at least as important as a knowledge of statistical procedures. It will continue to form the backbone of the following chapters.

Other Health-Care Issues

Due to the rapid advancements in biological research, we are confronted with ethical and economical dilemmas. Who should receive the expensive medical care that will save a person's life? Should we clone humans to have replacement body parts? What about manufacturing embryos for stem cell research? To learn more about other issues related to health care, you can enter the following search terms in the InfoTrac College Edition.

Individual Health Issues

Catastrophic illnesses   HMO
Genetics   Developmental disabilities
Mental health   Health environment
Health   Occupational hazards—Gun laws

WORKSHEET

NAME: _____

COURSE: _____

DATE: _____

Workbook exercises and software are copyrighted. Copying is prohibited by law.

EXERCISE

5

Review Questions

Based on the work you've done so far on issues related to health, see how well you do on this short True or False quiz.

Countries that spend large sums of their GDP on defense, based on the GLOBAL data file, spend small amounts on public health.	T	F
Third World countries, for whatever reasons, tend to be the countries that spend the least per capita on public health.	T	F
In Third World countries where government spending per capita for public health is high, the number of deaths from AIDS tends to be high.	T	F
The United States is exceptional because it has one of the five lowest rates of infant mortality in the world.	T	F
Only a small percentage of poor people in the United States, less than 5%, do not have some form of health insurance.	T	F
Only 30% of people in the United States who answered the GSS survey question said they believe HMOs prevent people from getting the health care they need.	T	F

MicroCase QUESTIONS

If you have any difficulties using the software to obtain the appropriate information, or if you want to learn additional features of the ANOVA or Regression tasks, use the online help (F1).

Use the following data files, variables, and analytical approaches to answer the MicroCase questions about health care.

1. For your first exercise, use the variables that we used to test public heath spending to see if they affect the number of doctors in a country. Again, first map out the number of doctors per million in countries around the world.

> ➤ Data File: **GLOBAL**
> ➤ Task: **Mapping**
> ➤ Variable 1: **30) DOCTORS**
> ➤ View: **Map**

    a.   Based on the map, what region of the world has the fewest doctors per million people?

_____

    b.   Again, based on the map, what region has the highest number of doctors per million people?

_____

2.   Now I want you to do a series of bivariate analyses with the dependent variable **30) DOCTORS**. In this first analysis, run an ANOVA with the independent variable **25) THREEWORLD**, and then fill in the table and answer the following questions.

> Data File: **GLOBAL**
> Task: **ANOVA**
> ➤ Dependent Variable: **30) DOCTORS**
> ➤ Independent Variable: **25) THREEWORLD**
> ➤ View: **Means**

    a. $p <$ _____

	Mean
1st World	
2nd World	
3rd World	

    b.   Can we use 25) THREEWORLD as a subset variable?   Yes   No

    c.   For which type of country is there a significant difference in the number of doctors?

        FIRST WORLD   SECOND WORLD   THIRD WORLD

3.   Let's continue the bivariate analyses using the independent variables **32) PUB HEALTH, 33) $ RICH 10%, 36) EXPND/CP**, and **65) DEFNS/CP**. For each of these variables, generate a scatterplot using **30) DOCTORS** as the dependent variable. For each analysis, enter the information in the following table. Then answer the questions that follow.

> Data File: **GLOBAL**
> ➤ Task: **Scatterplot**
> ➤ Dependent Variable: **30) DOCTORS**
> ➤ Independent Variables: **32) PUB HEALTH**
> **33) $ RICH 10%**
> **36) EXPND/CP**
> **65) DEFNS/CP**
> ➤ View: **Reg. Line**

Data File:	**GLOBAL**
➤ *Task:*	**Scatterplot**
➤ *Dependent Variable:*	**30) DOCTORS**
➤ *Independent Variables:*	**32) PUB HEALTH**
	33) $ RICH 10%
	36) EXPND/CP
	65) DEFNS/CP
➤ *View:*	**Reg. Line**

Fill in the table below.

	$r =$	$p =$
32) PUB HEALTH		
33) $ RICH 10%	_____	_____
36) EXPND/CP	_____	_____
65) DEFNS/CP	_____	_____
	_____	_____

a.   Which independent variable was related the strongest to the rate of doctors in a nation?
_____

b.   Briefly summarize your findings in the above table.

4.   Now do a multiple regression analysis of the four independent variables with the dependent variable **30) DOCTORS** to determine what, if any, role they may play in explaining the number of doctors in a country. Then fill in the following table and answer the following questions.

Data File:	**GLOBAL**
➤ *Task:*	**Regression**
➤ *Dependent Variable:*	**30) DOCTORS**
➤ *Independent Variables:*	**25) THREEWORLD**
	32) PUB HEALTH
	33) $ RICH 10%
	36) EXPND/CP
	65) DEFNS/CP

Fill in the table below.

	$r =$	beta =	Statistically Significant?	
25) THREEWORLD	_____	_____	Yes	No
32) PUB HEALTH	_____	_____	Yes	No
33) $ RICH 10%	_____	_____	Yes	No
36) EXPND/CP	_____	_____	Yes	No
65) DEFNS/CP	_____	_____	Yes	No

a. What is the Multiple R-Squared? $R^2 =$ _____

b. Which variables have the greatest impact on the rate of doctors in a state? (Circle all that apply.)

THREEWORLD   PUB HEALTH $ RICH 10%   EXPND/CP   DEFNS/CP

5. Turning our attention to the United States, I would like you to examine other factors that may be related to the number of doctors per 100,000 people. Use the STATES data file to perform a series of scatterplots to examine the bivariate relationships between the doctor rate and a selection of other health variables. For each independent variable you need to fill in the information specified for each scatterplot in the appropriate row.

> ➢ Data File: **STATES**
> ➢ Task: **Scatterplots**
> ➢ Dependent Variable: **68) DR.RATE96**
> ➢ Independent Variables: **58) CHLD MRT96**
> **75) MED.FAM$96**
> **86) %HLTH EM90**
> **94) HEALTH $87**
> ➢ View: **Reg. Line**

5.7   They Come in Billions

Even though we talk about gigahertz (1 billion) when describing computer speed, a billion is still so large there is not much to compare it with in our personal world. This was not as hard for the Chief Executive Officer of the Coca-Cola Company. "A billion hours ago, human life appeared on Earth. A billion minutes ago, Christianity emerged. A billion seconds ago, the Beatles changed music forever. A billion Coca-Colas ago was yesterday morning" (Golzueta, 1997).

Fill in the table below.

	r =	p =	Hypothesis supported?	
58) CHLD MRT96 HYPOTHESIS: Where the rate of doctors is higher, the infant mortality rate will be lower.	_____	_____	Yes	No
75) MED.FAM$96 HYPOTHESIS: Where the median family income is higher, there will be a higher rate of doctors.	_____	_____	Yes	No
86) %HLTH EM90 HYPOTHESIS: Where there is a higher percent of the population employed in health care, there will be a higher rate of doctors.	_____	_____	Yes	No
94) HEALTH $87 HYPOTHESIS: Where more money is spent on health care, there will be more doctors.	_____	_____	Yes	No

a.   Which independent variable was related the strongest to the rate of doctors in a state?
_____

b.   Briefly summarize your findings in the above table.

6.   Now use the regression task with this same selection of health variables to see if the correlations you found above hold true when all the variables are considered together. Then fill in the table and answer the questions.

Data File:	**STATES**
➢ *Task:*	**Regression**
➢ *Dependent Variable:*	**68) DR.RATE96**
➢ *Independent Variables:*	**58) CHLD MRT96**
	75) MED.FAM$96
	86) %HLTH EM90
	94) HEALTH $87

Fill in the table below.

	r =	beta =	Statistically Significant?
58) CHLD MRT96	_____	_____	Yes No
75) MED.FAM$96	_____	_____	Yes No
86) %HLTH EM90	_____	_____	Yes No
94) HEALTH $87	_____	_____	Yes No

a.   What is the Multiple R-Squared? R^2 = _____

b.   Which variables does the regression show have the greatest impact on the rate of doctors in a state?

CHLD MRT96   MED.FAM$96   %HLTH EM90   HEALTH $87

c.   Thinking back to the regression you examined in the chapter to explain infant mortality rates, what explanations can you provide for the findings in doctor rates?

I would leave you with this thought. In the year 2001, "The United States is investing substantially in financing health programs, even so, it faces significant health care and public health challenges. Some 42 million Americans—nearly 18% of the total non-elderly population—do not have health insurance. About one-third of all people age 65 and over do not have insurance coverage for prescription drugs, even as costs are forecast to increase at least 13% a year. Public health threats such as HIV/AIDS continue to challenge the nation's ability to respond, with more people living with AIDS in the U.S. than ever before and 40,000 new HIV infections occurring in the U.S. each year" (The Henry J. Kaiser Family Foundation, 2001).

Variable Lists Related to Health-Care Issues

The following is a partial list of the variables in your data files that you might find interesting in your study of health care. You can examine them using the MicroCase approaches you learned in the last five chapters. Try using some of these variables with the other variables you have already tested.

GLOBAL

29) %UNDRWGHT
    PERCENT OF CHILDREN BELOW AGE 5 WHO ARE UNDERWEIGHT (PON, 1996)
34) GDP GROWTH
    ANNUAL GROSS DOMESTIC PRODUCT GROWTH RATE (TWF, 1997)
53) FEM POWER
    GENDER EMPOWERMENT MEASURE (GEM) (HDR, 1998)
66) ARMY/DOCTR
    1987: ARMED FORCES PER DOCTOR

STATES

89) HLTH.SV$87
    1987: RECEIPTS OF HEALTH SERVICES ESTABLISHMENTS PER PERSON
95) SS DSAB$94
    1994: AVERAGE MONTHLY SOCIAL SECURITY PAYMENT TO DISABLED WORKERS

GSS

36) HEALTH
    Would you say your own health, in general, is excellent, good, fair, or poor?
84) HMO1
    The health-care system is changing rapidly with more and more people being treated in Health Maintenance Organizations (or HMOs) and in managed-care plans. How much do you agree with how the HMOs and managed-care plans are working? Do they improve the quality of care?

Web Pages Related to Health-Care Issues

If you wish to find a world of resources that are available to you over the Internet, the following list of Web sites will get you started. Once you visit these Web sites, you will find many interesting links to other useful Web sites.

American Association for World Health
www.aawhworldhealth.org/

Harvard World Health News
www.worldhealthnews.harvard.edu/

World Health Organization
www.who.int/home-page/

U.S. Dept. of Health and Human Services
www.hhs.gov/

U.S. Public Health Services
www.os.dhhs.gov/phs/

Occupational Safety and Health Adm. (OSHA)
www.osha.gov/

National Inst. on Disability and Rehab. Research
www.ed.gov/offices/OSERS/NIDRR/

The Disability Rights Activist
www.disrights.org/

References

Ambrosino, R., Heffernan, J., Shuttlesworth, G., and Ambrosino, R. (2001). *Social Work and Social Welfare: An Introduction* (4th ed.). Belmont, CA: Wadsworth/Thomson Learning

Budetti, J., Duchon, L., Schoen, C., and Shikles, J. (1999). *Can't afford to get sick: A reality for millions of working Americans, the Commonwealth Fund 1999 national survey of workers' health insurance.* New York: The Commonwealth Fund. (Posted 10/22/1999). Retrieved 8/11/01 from www.abtassoc.com/reports/health-economics/commfund.pdf.

Cherry, A. L., Dillon, M. E., and Rugh, D. (eds.). (2001). *Teenage Pregnancy: A Global View.* Westport, CT: Greenwood Pub.

Findley, S., and Miller, J. (1999). *Down a Dangerous Path: The Erosion of Health Insurance Coverage in the United States.* Washington, DC: National Coalition on Health Care. (Posted 06/18/1999). Retrieved 8/16/01 from www.nchc.org/1999PolicyStudies/1999policystudies.

Golzueta, R. C. (1997). *Coca-Cola's 1997 Annual Report.* Atlanta, GA.

Health Care Financing Administration. (2000). *1999 Nation Health Expenditures.* Washington, DC: Health Care Financing Administration, Office of the Actuary: National Health Statistics Group; U.S. Department of Commerce, Bureau of Economic Analysis; and U.S. Bureau of the Census.

Jansson, B. S. (1999). *Becoming an Effective Policy Advocate: From Policy Practice to Social Justice.* Pacific Grove, CA: Brooks/Cole Publishing Company.

Jansson, B. S. (2001). *The Reluctant Welfare State* (4th ed.). Belmont, CA: Wadsworth Publishing Company.

The Henry J. Kaiser Family Foundation. (2001). *Federal Budget Chart Book 2001.* Menlo Park, CA: Author.

Trenholm, C., and Kung, S. (2000). *Disparities in state health coverage: A matter of policy or fortune?* Washington, DC: Mathematica Policy Research, Inc., (Posted 03/21/2001). Retrieved 8/16/01 from www.mathematica-mpr.com/press%20releases/disparitiesrel.htm.

UNICEF/UN-AIDS. (1999). *Press briefing: World AIDS day – 1999.* Joint United Nations Programme on HIV/AIDS (UN-AIDS). December. Retrieved September 15, 2001, from www.un.org/english/.

U.S. Bureau of the Census (2000). *America's Children: Key National Indicators of Well-Being, 2000: The Fourth Annual Report to the Nation on the Condition of Our Most Precious Resource, Our Children.* Population Division, U.S. Bureau of the Census.

U.S. Bureau of the Census. (1999). *Statistical Abstracts of the United States, 1999.* 119th ed. Washington, DC: U.S. Government Office.

WHO. (2000a). *The world health report 2000.* Geneva, Switzerland: The World Health Organization.

WHO. (2000b). *The World Health Report 2000 Health Systems: Improving performance.* Geneva, Switzerland: The World Health Organization.

Zastrow, C. (2000). *Introduction to Social Work and Social Welfare.* (7th ed.). Belmont, CA: Wadsworth Publishing Company

Additional Material that may be of Interest

Andrew, T., and Smith, P. (eds.). (2001). *Plagues and Politics: Infectious Disease and International policy.* New York: Palgrave.

Collins, T. W., and Wingard, J. D. (Eds.). (2000). *Communities and Capital: Local Struggles Against Corporate Power and Privatization.* Athens, GA: University of Georgia Press.

Garrett, L. (2000). *Betrayal of Trust: The Collapse of Global Public Health.* New York: Hyperion.

Koop, C. E., Pearson, C., and Schwarz, M. R. (2001). *Critical Issues in Global Health.* San Francisco: Jossey-Bass.

Whiteford, L. M., and Manderson, L. (eds.). (2000). *Global Health Policy, Local Realities: The Fallacy of the Level Playing Field.* Boulder, CO: Lynne Rienner.

Chapter 6

SUBSTANCE ABUSE

Tasks: Univariate, Mapping, Cross-tabulation, Scatterplot, Correlation, t Test, ANOVA, Regression, Logistic Regression, Historical Trends

Data Files: GLOBAL, STATES, GSS, US TRENDS

Overview of Chapter 6

Chapter 6 deals with substance abuse and the different forms it takes around the world. The most used and abused drug in the world and the United States is, of course, alcohol. It is legal and accessible in all countries with the exception of countries that follow fairly strict Islamic law. Other substances, however, are used and abused. Some are legal such as tobacco and some are not legal such as cocaine. As we identify countries that consume these substances, you will find that some countries have high levels of drug consumption and some have low levels of drug consumption. Even so, you will find that drug consumption is not randomly distributed. This suggests that the environment in these countries and states in the United States plays a role in the consumption of these substances. We will also look at the consequences of substance abuse such as cirrhosis, a chronic disease of the liver, and suicide. You will continue to use statistical procedures such as *Mapping, Scatterplot,* etc., which you are surely familiar with by now. A new statistical procedure will also be introduced called *Logistic Regression*. It is much like *Multiple Regression* except that it is designed to use a nominal-level variable such as a question that is answered as *Yes* or *No* as a dependent variable. Much of the data collected by organizations are nominal-level. This makes *Logistic Regression* a useful tool. So let's see what we can learn about substance use and abuse.

A critical issue affecting, in one way or another, nearly every person in our society is chemical substance use and abuse. Nearly everyone has one or more relatives or friends who are abusing alcohol or another drug. Some of the readers of this text may be personally struggling with this issue (Zastrow and Kirst-Ashman, 2001). Drugs have become part of our daily lives. We use drugs to relax, to increase our pleasure, to feel less inhibited, to get rid of unwanted emotions, to keep awake, and to fall asleep. Practically all Americans use drugs of one kind or another. People have coffee in the morning, soda (which has caffeine) during the day, cocktails before dinner, and aspirin or something stronger to relieve any pains before going to bed (Zastrow and Kirst-Ashman).

Humans, at least for the past 10,000 years, have been actively producing and consuming some type of mind-altering drug. And although humans are not the only drug-taking animals on earth, drug use is more widespread among humans than other animals. Others in the animal kingdom who imbibe on occasion include the Florida Mocking Bird. This bird has been known to tie one on when the dates from the Date Palms swell with water and ferment. We know they are eating the dates for the alcohol because the birds eat far more than they need to. They get so drunk they cannot fly and wind up staggering around on the ground. Elephants have been known to eat fermented fruit to get drunk. When you have a nasty drunk in the form of a 2,000-pound elephant, you have a real problem.

The definition of a *drug* is usually broad and encompassing. The most common use of the word is to describe either a medication that you take for some medical reason or a chemical compound used and misused to get high. In the latter case, the chemical compound known as a *drug* suppresses the external stimuli by depressing the sensitivity of the central nervous system. These drugs are often addicting, but they do not have to be addicting. Indeed, lysergic acid diethylamide (LSD) probably alters the mind more than any drug ever used, but it is not addicting. Typically, after experiencing one or two *trips* on LSD, people never use it again.

Ethical Foundation for Substance Abuse Treatment

To examine the impact of drug use addiction, and treatment, both globally and in the United States, we need to have a rationale for treating those who become addicted. All too often, to justify paying for treatment for those who are severely addicted, politicians and lobbyists talk about how much it will cost to withhold treatment. Of the 2 million plus people in jails and prisons in the United States in 2001, almost 1 million were in jail with a drug charge. Among these inmates, so many were addicted that in the late 1990s, many states began to operate substance abuse treatment centers within the prisons themselves. One of the reasons addiction treatment is so controversial is that, up until the early 1900s, addiction was thought to be a character issue. At the time, it was—and still is to some extent — believed that a man or a woman of "strong will could stop if he or she tried hard enough" (Brecher, 1972).

Moreover, compared to the United States and England in the 19th century, drug use in the United States today is a mere shadow of what it was after the Civil War, when opium and heroin were sold over-the-counter to people of all ages. One of the most famous drug drinks was Godfrey's Cordial, "a mixture of opium, molasses for sweetening, and sassafras for flavoring." The drink was especially popular in England. Dr. C. Fraser Brockington reports that in mid-19th century Coventry England, 10 gallons of Godfrey's Cordial (enough for 12,000 doses) were sold weekly and were administered to 3,000 infants under two years of age (Brecher, 1972). "There was not a laborer's house in which the bottle of opium was not to be seen, and not a child, but who got it in some form." Wholesale druggists reported the sale of immense quantities of opium; "a retail druggist dispensed up to 200 pounds a year — in pills and penny sticks or as Godfrey's Cordial" (Brecher). The nonmedical use of opiates, while legal in both the United States and England, was not considered respectable and even considered immoral. An anonymous but perceptive writer in the *Catholic World,* September 1881, describes attempts to quit using opiates. "Suddenly his eyes are open to his folly and he realizes the startling fact that he is in the toils of a serpent as merciless as the boa-constrictor and as relentless as fate" (Brecher). Treatment has changed a great deal over the last 120 years for the addict. Addictive drugs (with the exception of alcohol, tobacco, caffeine, and other socially acceptable drugs) are illegal. But, if one does become addicted, treatment is available. Even so, the addict's experience with the cravings, and the physical and mental anguish during withdrawal are the same today as they were for the addict in the 19th century.

6.1   Ethics and Substance Abuse Treatment

Many people are injured and suffer unrelenting pain. It is often devastating to the person and his or her family. Life as the person knew it before the injury is never the same. Imagine, for a moment, that you were in a rollover accident in a Ford Explorer with Firestone tires. You injured your back and you had been living with the excruciating pain for about six months. The pain was so bad you were considering suicide. Fortunately, just in time, a new drug for pain came on the market. It really helped your pain. For minutes at a time you could even forget the pain. You fell in love with the drug; it was your salvation. Then after several months on the drug, you are told that the drug is very addictive and your prescription was being stopped. When you ask your doctor what other medication could relieve your pain, you are told nothing else would work as well as Oxycontin. Resigning yourself to pain, you finished off the last of the prescription. You had no problems being on the drug, but after the prescription ran out, in the middle of the night, you woke up in a cool sweat, sick to your stomach, and desperate for just one more 20-mg Oxycontin tablet. You called your doctor, but all you got was the answering service. Then you remembered an acquaintance that also had taken Oxycontin. At 3 A.M., you call her up and ask if she had a pill until you can get to your doctor. She told you her prescription had also been canceled and she had none to share. Even though she would not give you her Oxycontin, she told you that she knew someone who would sell you some. A meeting with her and the drug dealer was set for the next day. To make it through the night and to reduce the agonizing cramps, nausea, and anxiety associated with

---

addiction, you took codeine and drank rum until daylight. After meeting the drug dealer, things went okay for a while, but as time passed, things went from bad to worse. The number of Oxycontin tablets you took each day increased to 25 a day. The cost of a 20-mg tablet was between $3 and $4. Your pills were costing you as much as a hundred dollars a day. You were afraid to tell your doctor that you were addicted. You knew he would want you to stop using the drug. The pain from the injury and the withdrawal from Oxycontin were too much. You became so addicted that even when sleeping, you awakened every hour or so and you would need to take another pill before you could go back to sleep. The last straw was being arrested while buying the drug from your dealer. You have now been labeled a drug addict and felon. Given your situation after the arrest, the chronic pain, and the severe addiction, what course of action would you want the court to take in your case, and what social services and treatment options would you want available to you and others in a similar predicament?

Medications that are developed to help pain, insomnia, anxiety, etc. have often been found to be very addictive. They often become drugs used and abused by people. The lives of many of the patients who were treated with these drugs were destroyed. This has occurred numerous times in our history. In the United States, there were so many Civil War soldiers addicted to morphine while being treated for injuries and wounds that the addiction became known as the "Soldier's Disease." Similar events to that described in this vignette occurred when Valium was introduced. During its heyday, Valium was the world's most prescribed drug. Many people became severely addicted to Valium. Treatment takes time and it is very difficult for the Valium or benzodiazepine addict to "kick the habit." The first addicted client I lost after becoming a social worker overdosed on Valium and alcohol.

A Global View of Substance Abuse

About the only place on earth where alcohol was not used in antiquity was among the people living in the arctic regions of Canada and Alaska. This region is too cold for active fermentation most of the year. The Aleut and Eskimo did not make or consume alcohol until the mid-1700s when ships visited the arctic area to trade for furs. In several cases, the Aleut traded their winter food supplies and entire villages starved to death (Cherry et al., 2002).

With the exception of the Arctic and Antarctica regions, the natural process of fermentation makes alcohol whenever it is warm enough and sugar, yeast, and water come together. Alcohol also is always present in human blood. It is created naturally as part of normal digestion.

Another issue that needs to be mentioned is the cultural aspect of substance use. Religion, access to a certain drug, the drug's capacity for addicting the user, and legal sanctions determine drug use more than individual predilection for a specific drug. Religious law prohibits a Muslim from drinking alcohol. Mormon teachings forbid alcohol and all drinks with caffeine such as coffee and most sodas. Where alcohol is banned in many Muslim-controlled countries, smoking and eating hash may be acceptable. In countries where wine is a major source of income, drinking and even getting *a little drunk* is a socially accepted behavior. Acting like a drunk is still considered a good way for a comedian to get a few laughs.

Based on this thumbnail sketch of the global use of alcohol, one would guess that religious and secular laws would result in people in one country consuming alcohol and people in another country not drinking alcoholic drinks. To test this construct, we will use the **Global** data file.

Research Hypothesis/Question   6.1:
How many countries report alcohol consumption?

➢ *Data File:*   **GLOBAL**
➢ *Task:*   **Mapping**
➢ *Variable:*   **89) ALCOHOL**
➢ *View:*   **Map**

ALCOHOL -- NET ANNUAL ALCOHOL CONSUMPTION PER CAPITA, IN LITRES (IP)

To see how many countries reported their net annual alcohol consumption, while viewing the map select **[List: Rank]**. This will give you the list of the countries reporting alcohol consumption and a value representing the country's consumption. In this case, only 48 out of 174 countries reported yearly alcohol consumption. Examining the map shows that no alcohol consumption was reported by countries in Africa and Asia. Given my experience in the United States in bars and taverns, I do not know how I would act in a bar in India where they sold only milk. I suspect that after a couple of tall glasses of buttermilk, seeing I never could stand buttermilk, I would get sick to my stomach and throw it up like I have done when I drank too much booze.

Nevertheless, the map confirms our expectation: a number of countries did not report the alcohol consumption of their people. For whatever reason, 126 countries did not report any alcohol consumption. Among the countries that did report, I will wager you would have never guessed that Luxembourg led the world in alcohol consumption. If you turn your attention to the countries on the list that report the least alcohol consumption, you will see that they are countries that have large Muslim populations (e.g., Algeria, Morocco, Turkey).

Among the many problems an individual may have with heavy alcohol consumption is a medical condition known as *cirrhosis of the liver*. This is a chronic disease of the liver resulting in swelling and scarring that cause a loss of function. After a while the liver becomes more fibrous, loses its suppleness, and becomes rigid. Cirrhosis can also result from a nutritional deficit or infection, particularly from the hepatitis virus. Given this information, we can hypothesize that there will be a strong correlation between alcohol consumption and cirrhosis of the liver.

Research Hypothesis/Question   6.2:
There is a strong correlation between countries with high alcohol consumption and the number of deaths from cirrhosis in those countries.

Data File: **GLOBAL**
Task: **Mapping**
Variable 1:   **89) ALCOHOL**
➢ *Variable 2:*   **85) CIRRHOSIS**
➢ *View:*   **Map**

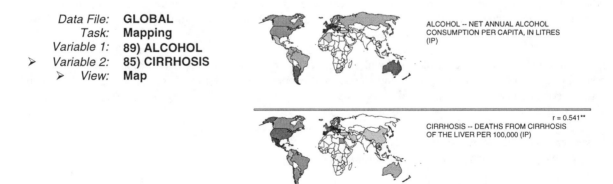

ALCOHOL -- NET ANNUAL ALCOHOL CONSUMPTION PER CAPITA, IN LITRES (IP)

r = 0.541**

CIRRHOSIS -- DEATHS FROM CIRRHOSIS OF THE LIVER PER 100,000 (IP)

This confirms that there is a moderate relationship between heavy alcohol consumption and cirrhosis ($r = .54$, $p <$ .01), but it is not as strong as I thought it would be. A *plausible explanation* for the lack of a stronger correlation between alcohol consumption and cirrhosis is that heavy alcohol use is not the only way to develop cirrhosis of the liver. Poor diet can also cause cirrhosis, as well as eating contaminated shellfish. This may explain the high rate of cirrhosis among the poor of Chile. Look at Russia on the map of cirrhosis. White indicates that no official number exists for those who die from cirrhosis. It does not mean that people are not dying from cirrhosis in Russia. In fact, due in large part to the heavy consumption of vodka, the life expectancy of Russians dropped to the mid-50s after the breakup of the Soviet Union and the shift to a market economy (Cherry et al., 2002). One study of the alcohol problem in Russia found that between 1987 and 1992 the annual per capita consumption of alcohol rose from about 11 liters of pure alcohol to 14 liters in 1992. Consumption in the late 1990s was estimated to be 15 liters of pure alcohol per Russian. The World Health Organization standards suggest that over 8 liters of pure alcohol per person per year is likely to cause major medical problems. In 1994, about 53,000 Russians died of alcohol poisoning, an increase of about 36,000 over the number of deaths in 1991 (Bureau of European Affairs, 2000).

If this is true, a poor diet and contagious diseases that run rabid in poor countries with inadequate public health systems also cause cirrhosis, so there should be differences in countries that are identified as First World, Second World, and Third World countries.

Research Hypothesis/Question   6.3:
Third World countries report significantly more deaths from cirrhosis than First or Second World countries.

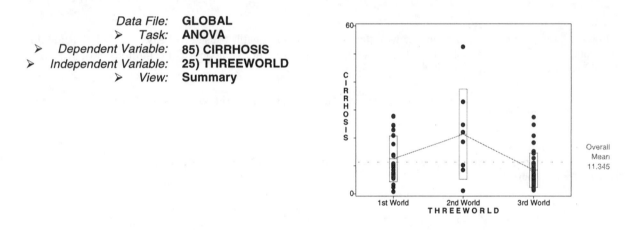

Data File:	**GLOBAL**
➢ *Task:*	**ANOVA**
➢ *Dependent Variable:*	**85) CIRRHOSIS**
➢ *Independent Variable:*	**25) THREEWORLD**
➢ *View:*	**Summary**

Just looking at the graph, Third World countries appear to have fewer deaths from cirrhosis than I expected. The means (First World: mean = 12.50, Second World: mean = 21.33, Third World: mean = 8.50), and the ANOVA statistics verify our visual assessment ($F = 11.57$, $p < .001$). To see the number of countries analyzed in each group (*N*) and the standard deviations (Std. Dev.), click the *means* in the Statistics box on the left of the screen. To view the ANOVA statistics, click ANOVA in the same box on the left of the screen.

This is where good critical thinking skills can be used to improve the test of this hypothesis. First, we revisit our hypothesis. The objective is to identify the impact of heavy alcohol consumption on the number of deaths by cirrhosis. We do not want to know how many deaths are caused by a combination of poverty and alcohol consumption. We need a group of countries with different levels of alcohol consumption; countries where people have a good diet, and countries where there are good public health programs to reduce contagious disease. The result will be a group of nations where deaths from cirrhosis will be more attributable to alcohol consumption. With a group of countries that meet this protocol, we will have fewer problems with diet and disease causing a sizable number of deaths from cirrhosis. The protocol I described for a group of countries that would better test my hypothesis can be operationalized by using the subgroup of First World countries. The reasoning goes something like this: if a First World country consumes large quantities of alcohol and it also has a high rate of death from cirrhosis, there is more of a chance that the cirrhosis was caused by heavy alcohol consumption than by poor diet or disease. Try the following to verify the assumption.

Research Hypothesis/Question   6.4:
There is a strong correlation between First World countries with high levels of alcohol consumption and deaths from cirrhosis.

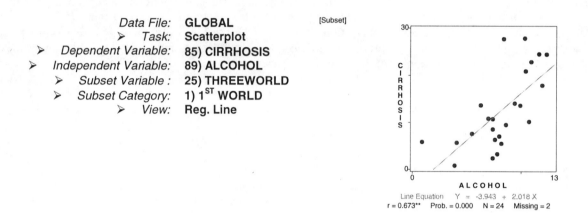

Data File:	**GLOBAL**
➤ *Task:*	**Scatterplot**
➤ *Dependent Variable:*	**85) CIRRHOSIS**
➤ *Independent Variable:*	**89) ALCOHOL**
➤ *Subset Variable :*	**25) THREEWORLD**
➤ *Subset Category:*	**1) 1ST WORLD**
➤ *View:*	**Reg. Line**

This correlation is probably more in line with the real numbers of deaths caused by heavy alcohol consumptions. At any rate, there is a substantial correlation between the two conditions: alcohol consumption and cirrhosis in First World countries ($r = .67, p < .000$).

Let us look at the correlation between these two variables with Third World countries.

Research Hypothesis/Question   6.5:
There is a strong correlation between Third World countries with high levels of alcohol consumption and deaths from cirrhosis.

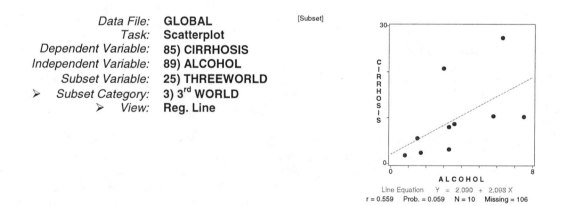

Data File:	**GLOBAL**
Task:	**Scatterplot**
Dependent Variable:	**85) CIRRHOSIS**
Independent Variable:	**89) ALCOHOL**
Subset Variable:	**25) THREEWORLD**
➤ *Subset Category:*	**3) 3rd WORLD**
➤ *View:*	**Reg. Line**

The correlation is fairly large, but it is not large enough to be significant at the .05 level because only 10 Third World nations in the sample reported both alcohol consumption and cirrhosis. For the correlation to be significant using a sample of only 10 Third World countries, the correlation would need to be in the .70 range. In spite of this, you will find that Chile has the highest rate of cirrhosis among Third World countries.

Custom, Laws, and Religion Shape National Alcohol Consumption Patterns

Alcohol use and even abuse are regulated as much by environmental forces as they are regulated by an individual's wish to get intoxicated. In this analysis, we will look at the effect of social change on drinking levels. Much like the impact of *anomie* on the rate of suicide in a country, as demonstrated by Emile Durkheim (1897), heavy alcohol use is also affected by change in a society.

A social change that has been especially difficult for males to deal with has been the changing role of women in society (Cherry et al., 2001). Even though the role of women has not changed as much for women in the developing countries as it has for women in the developed countries, after more than 10,000 years of remaining much the same, in the 20th century the role and expectations of women changed for all women on the earth. At times, religious governments try to turn back the clock on women's rights, but the genie is out of the bottle, so to speak. For both men and women, the changing expectations have left them unsure of their role and unsure about how to treat and be treated by the opposite sex.

Given this perspective, we would expect that in countries where alcohol consumption is high, (1) gender equality would be high. In these countries, there is less tradition to guide behavior, creating more anxiety. Alcohol is a quick way to relieve anxiety. We would also expect alcohol use to be higher in countries where (2) there are more women than men. This condition will require women to make a life without the option of a traditional marriage. There are 117 women for every 100 men in the Ukraine. It is quite the opposite in the United Arab Emirates where there are only 48 women for every 100 males. Beyond culture is the increase in the number of people drinking when women are not constrained by traditional roles that discourage women drinking alcohol. Alcohol use would also be higher in countries where (3) women work and (4) where women use contraceptives in large numbers. These behaviors free women from the traditional roles and place them in an environment where drinking alcohol is accepted. People in countries with (5) a higher quality of life will also use more alcohol. In contrast, we would expect people in countries where (6) church attendance is high, where (7) the fertility rate is high, and where (8) large families were the norm will have lower rates of alcohol consumption. Large families can and often do provide support and stability.

6.2	An Easy Way to Remember the Levels of Measurement

- *Ratio-level* is a continuous measure where the value of that measure can be divided and multiplied. Ratio is the highest level of measurement.
- *Interval-level* is simply a ratio variable that has been divided into equal intervals. We know where each interval begins and ends.
- *Rank/Ordinal-level* has intervals, but we do not know exactly where the intervals begin and end.
- *Nominal-level* has no mathematical value; it is simply a number that represents a name. Any number could be used to represent "Single," as a value of marital status (Cherry, 2000).

After examining each variable using a univariate analysis, I ran a set of correlations between alcohol consumption and eight variables that best represent the above characteristics. From this analysis, *church attendance* was not significantly related to alcohol use ($r = .01$, $p = $ NS), so I dropped it. *Fertility* and the *use of contraceptives* had a high inverse correlation ($r = -.924$, $p < .01$). I dropped fertility because contraceptive use was a variable that gave women more say in their lives. The remaining five variables were analyzed in a set of bivariate correlations with the dependent variable *alcohol consumption*.

Research Hypothesis/Question   6.6:
Alcohol consumption will be higher in countries where more women work, use contraception, and outnumber men; in countries with high levels of quality of life; and where gender equality is high.

Data File: **GLOBAL**
➤ Task: **Correlation**
➤ Variables: **89) ALCOHOL**
13) CONTRCEPT
20) SEX RATIO
26) QUAL. LIFE
50) %WKR WOMEN
52)GENDER EQ
➤ Deletion: **Pairwise**
➤ Test: **2 tailed**

Correlation Coefficients Table

	ALCOHOL	CONTR-CEPT	SEX RATIO	QUAL. LIFE	%WKR WOMEN	GENDER EQ
ALCOHOL	1.000 ($n = 48$)	0.604 ** ($n = 38$)	0.651 ** ($n = 48$)	0.760 ** ($n = 39$)	0.47988 ($n = 48$)	0.631 ** ($n = 48$)
CONTR-CEPT	0.604 ** ($n = 38$)	1.000 ($n = 121$)	0.106 ($n = 119$)	0.882 ** ($n = 89$)	0.081 ($n = 121$)	0.884 ** ($n = 121$)
SEX RATIO	0.651 ** ($n = 48$)	0.106 ($n = 119$)	1.000 ($n = 160$)	0.064 ($n = 110$)	0.629 ** ($n = 155$)	0.015 ($n = 155$)
QUAL. LIFE	0.760 ** ($n = 39$)	0.882 ** ($n = 89$)	0.064 ($n = 110$)	1.000 ($n = 111$)	-0.034 ($n = 106$)	0.950 ** ($n = 106$)
%WKR WOMEN	0.497** ($n = 48$)	0.081 ($n = 121$)	0.629 ** ($n = 155$)	-0.034 ($n = 106$)	1.000 ($n = 161$)	-0.067 ($n = 161$)
GENDER EQ	0.631 ** ($n = 48$)	0.884 ** ($n = 121$)	0.015 ($n = 155$)	0.950 ** ($n = 106$)	-0.067 ($n = 161$)	1.000 ($n = 162$)

Pairwise deletion (2-tailed test)   Significance Levels: ** =.01, * =.05

This correlation matrix has a good example of two variables measuring almost the same thing. If you look at the correlation between the two independent variables, *quality of life* and *gender equality* you will see that they correlate at an $r = .95$. This is almost a perfect correlation. This indicates that, to a great degree, the quality of life depends on the level of gender equality. This also indicates the existence of what is called *multicollinearity*. In other words, *quality of life* and *gender equality* may be a measure of the same condition. See Box 6.3 for a detailed explanation of multicollinearity. There are also other large correlations between the independent variables. This makes it impossible to find the important independent variables. Regression analysis, however, can address this problem. So, let's try to explain how these variables interact to produce high levels of alcohol consumption.

Research Hypothesis/Question   6.7:
The variation in alcohol consumption can be accounted for by variations in (1) the percentage of women who work in a country, (2) the percentage of women using contraception, (3) the number of women to men, (4) the quality of life, and (5) the level of gender equality in the country.

Data File: **GLOBAL**
➤ Task: **Regression**
➤ Dependent Variable: **89) ALCOHOL**
➤ Independent Variables: **13) CONTRCEPT**
20) SEX RATIO
26) QUAL. LIFE
50) %WKR WOMEN
52) GENDER EQ
➤ View: **Summary**

Multiple R-Squared = 0.812**

CONTRACEPT	BETA = 0.014 (r = 0.604)
SEX RATIO	BETA = 0.559** (r = 0.833)
QUAL. LIFE	BETA = 0.486 (r = 0.786)
%WKR WOMEN	BETA = -0.004 (r = 0.663)
GENDER EQ	BETA = -0.056 (r = 0.735)

ALCOHOL

These variables explain a great deal of the variation in alcohol consumption from one country to another ($R^2 = .812$, $p < .000$). This means that the five variables in this analysis can explain 81% of the difference between countries with low levels and countries with high levels of alcohol consumption. In spite of accounting for a high percentage of the variation of alcohol consumption, these five variables do not contribute equally to the sum of the R Square. If you look closely, you will see that in fact only two variables really contribute to the R Square, *sex ratio* and *quality of life*. So let's see if these two variables explain the same amount of variance as did the five variables as a group.

Research Hypothesis/Question   6.8:
The variation in alcohol consumption can be accounted for by variations in (1) the number of women to men, and (2) the quality of life in the country.

Data File:	**GLOBAL**
Task:	**Regression**
Dependent Variable:	**89) ALCOHOL**
➤ *Independent Variables:*	**20) SEX RATIO**
	26) QUAL. LIFE
➤ *View:*	**Summary**

Well, the R^2 is not .81, it is .79. Even so, the parsimony of using two variables to explain almost 80% of the variation in alcohol consumption is important. Notwithstanding other variables that might explain the variation in alcohol consumption, I would say that if you find a country with more women than men and the country has a high quality of life, you can expect that if they consume alcohol in any form, it will be at higher levels than in countries where there are fewer women than men and where the quality of life is poor.

6.3   Multicollinearity

The issue of multicollinearity is relevant when using multiple regression, MANOVA, discriminate analysis, etc. or any of the multivariate statistical procedures based on linear algebra. Multicollinearity must be considered when making a statement about the relationship among variables. The question is: How do two independent variables affect each other and the dependent variable? The two independent variables must not account for the same variance. In other words, the two independent variables should not be measuring the same thing about the dependent variable at the same time in your regression equation (Cohen and Cohen, 1975).

For example, let us say you are interested in the effect of "self-esteem" and "self-concept" on grade point average (GPA) of junior high school students. Both of these concepts, "self-esteem" and "self-concept," tend to measure the same thing in junior high students. If the "self-esteem" scale can help predict GPA, then the "self-concept" will predict GPA with about the same accuracy because they both measure the same "one" dimension, "feelings about self." However, if you put the values of the two scales measuring "self-esteem" and "self-concept" into one multivariate analysis, you will induce multicollinearity into the statistical results. In this case, if you did not know that the two scales measured virtually the same dimension, as a result of reading the inflated regression results, you would be led to conclude that these two variables explained a great deal more about GPA than they really did.

Perfect collinearity: This is a condition where one of the independent variables (X) has a perfect linear relationship with one or more of the other independent variables (X).

Near-collinearity: This is a condition where there is a linear relationship between two or more of the independent variables (X), but it is *not a perfect linear relationship*.

Multicollinearity is a problem in nonexperimental or quasi-experimental research because it is difficult to control all the influences that affect the independent variables or to be precise as to what a scale is measuring in any particular group of people. We hope we are measuring what we think we are measuring (internal validity), but we have no empirical way of completely testing this assumption. Consequently, you may be measuring the same dimension with what seems to be two different scales (i.e., self-esteem and self-concept).

INDICATORS OF MULTICOLLINEARITY

Although there are a number of indicators, some of the most obvious are
1. In your statistical results, the F-test for all of the independent variables in the regression equation is significant; however, none of the individual independent variable regression coefficients are significant.
2. In your statistical results, the standardized betas "blow up." You will see betas with coefficients that are greater than the value of 1, and these coefficients will have the opposite positive or negative sign from betas of similar values.
3. In your statistical results, the correlation matrix of the "estimates" of the independent variables will contain large correlations.
4. You use the same variables with two different samples and you get very different regression coefficients.

MANAGING MULTICOLLINEARITY

There are several ways to prevent or manage multicollinearity:
1. Increase the size of your sample.
2. Eliminate from the equation one of the independent variables or scales that tends to be measuring the same domain.
3. Combine independent variables that are suspected of being redundant, making them into one independent variable.
4. You can use "principal component" regression to reduce the effect of multicollinearity on the results of the data analysis (Cherry, 2000).

The Global Use of Beer, Wine, and Cigarettes

The two forms of alcohol drinks *beer* and *wine* are widely used in many countries around the globe. Additionally, nicotine (from cigarettes) is an addictive drug that kills many people every year. Yet, there is general acceptance of tobacco use in most societies around the world. We will take a look at where these drugs are used globally before turning our attention to the drug problem in the United States.

Research Hypothesis/Question   6.9:
How many countries report beer consumption?

Data File:	**GLOBAL**
➤ *Task:*	**Mapping**
➤ *Variable 1:*	**90) BEER DRINK**
➤ *View:*	**Map**

BEER DRINK -- BEER CONSUMPTION IN GALLONS PER CAPITA (NBWR, 1991)

As you can see, more nations reported beer consumption than reported alcohol consumption. Only 48 countries reported alcohol consumption, while 104 reported beer consumption. This is a good sample.

6.4   Operation Intercept

President Nixon's first drug war effort was an offensive against Mexico that included searching one in three vehicles crossing the border. This spurred an increase in prescription drug use, and traffickers switched to boats and planes. The Mexican effort also expanded the Southeast Asian drug markets, which were already making inroads thanks to the Vietnam War. The border searches disrupted commerce and therefore could not be sustained. Thus the result was increased use of prescription drugs, expanded Southeast Asian supplies, and Mexican traffickers having not only land routes, but also sea and air routes (Zeese, 2000).

Now, we will compare the influence of the same variables used to explain alcohol consumption to see how well they explain beer consumption. After performing a correlational analysis with these five independent variables, we found that with the exception of percentage of women working (%WKR WOMEN), the other variables were correlated with beer drinking: CONTRACEPT ($r = .555$, $p < .01$), SEX RATIO ($r = .318$, $p < .01$), QUAL. LIFE ($r = .572$, $p < .01$), %WKR WOMEN ($r = .189$, $p < $ NS), GENDER EQ ($r = .604$, $p < .01$). At this point, we are ready to do a multiple regression analysis. The variable that represents the percentage of women working will be dropped from the regression analysis. So, let's see if these four variables can explain the variance in beer consumption as well as they explained alcohol consumption.

Research Hypothesis/Question   6.10:
The variation in beer consumption can be explained by variations in (1) the percentage of women using contraception, (2) the number of women to men, (3) the quality of life, and (4) the level of gender equality in the country.

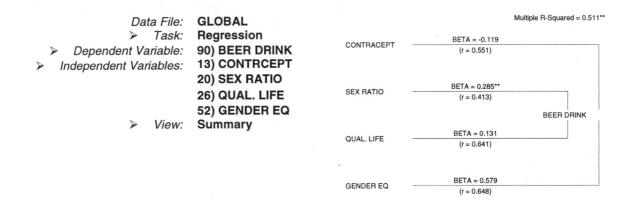

These four variables do not account for as much in the differences in beer consumption from country to country ($R^2 = .511$, $p < .01$), as they did in explaining alcohol consumption ($R^2 = .80$, $p < .01$). In spite of this, these variables still explained over half the variation in beer drinking from one country to another. Next, we will take a look at wine consumption.

Research Hypothesis/Question   6.11:
How many countries report wine consumption?

Data File:	**GLOBAL**
➤ Task:	**Mapping**
➤ Variable 1:	**91) WINE DRINK**
➤ View:	**Map**

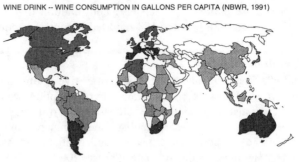

More nations reported wine consumption (86) than alcohol consumption (48), but this number is less than the number of nations reporting beer consumption (104). Nevertheless, as you can see, wine consumption has widespread acceptance. Now let us see how many countries report cigarette consumption.

Research Hypothesis/Question 6.12:
How many countries report cigarette consumption?

Data File:	**GLOBAL**
Task:	**Mapping**
➤ Variable 1:	**92) CIGARETTES**
➤ View:	**Map**

Among the 93 nations reporting cigarette consumption, the top five consuming nations are a mixed bag of countries having few things in common other than high cigarette use. They are Albania, Greece, Japan, the United States, and Canada. I suspect (I have never tried to test it) that the advertising of cigarettes over the last 75 years in the United States and Canada is the cause for high cigarette consumption in North America. I really have not a clue as to why so many people smoke in the other countries.

One of the most common combinations of the drugs we have examined to this point is an alcoholic drink and a cigarette. Many people have tried to quite smoking only to give in while drinking a beer, a glass of wine, or a cocktail.

To see if our observations about booze and cigarettes go together, we will do a correlation among the four drugs.

Research Hypothesis/Question 6.13:
There is a strong correlation between cigarette use and the use of alcohol, beer, and wine.

Data File:	**GLOBAL**
➤ Task:	**Correlation**
➤ Variables:	**89) ALCOHOL**
	90) BEER DRINK
	91) WINE DRINK
	92) CIGARETTES
➤ Deletion:	**Pairwise**
➤ Test:	**2 tailed**

Correlation Coefficients Table

	ALCOHOL	BEER DRINK	WINE DRINK	CIGARETTES
ALCOHOL	1.000 (48)	0.632 ** (40)	0.696 ** (39)	0.574 ** (39)
BEER DRINK	0.632 ** (40)	1.000 (104)	0.311 ** (84)	0.527 ** (90)
WINE DRINK	0.696 ** (39)	0.311 ** (84)	1.000 (86)	0.428 ** (76)
CIGARETTES	0.574 ** (39)	0.527 ** (90)	0.428 ** (76)	1.000 (93)

Pairwise deletion (2-tailed test)   Significance Levels: ** =.01, * =.05

This confirms our observation that cigarettes are indeed used in large quantities in countries where alcoholic drinks, beer, and/or wine are consumed in large quantities. Then again, of the three alcohol drinks, wine and cigarettes seems to be the least common ($r = .428$, $p < .01$).

At this point, let's turn our attention to drug use in the United States.

Substance Abuse in the United States

The Global analysis helped ground our thinking about drug use in the United States. We found that people in the United States are major consumers of all alcohol drinks and cigarettes.

This time, I will start by selecting seven variables, and then do a univariate analysis to answer several basic questions about each variable of interest. I selected *alcohol consumption* as my primary variable of interest. Then, I picked seven other variables that would help explain some of the areas that are associated with alcohol abuse and addiction: *cocaine use, beer consumption, wine consumption, AIDS, suicide, heart disease*, and the amount of money spent on *school-based drug education*. The reason I selected these variables is that these conditions (related to the environment) and characteristics (related to individuals and groups) often occur together. I selected *alcohol consumption* because alcohol has widespread use in this country. Additionally, in states where people are heavy users of alcohol, many suffer serious problems that affect both his or her family, and the community as a whole (Zastrow, 2000). I picked *cocaine use* because it is an illegal drug that we hear a great deal about. *Beer* and *wine consumption* are in the mix to provide a triangulation view. As I mentioned earlier, when relationships hold up in several different ways, it is better; it is supporting evidence. *AIDS, suicide,* and *heart disease* were selected because they are often associated with alcohol and drug use. Finally, I chose state expenditures on *school-based drug education*. This will tell me if the states with the more serious drug problems are spending more on school-based drug education. I call it an *acid test*. Using this variable, we will be able to see if people are *putting their money where their mouth is*.

Means, Standard Deviation, and Sample Size

Before we move into another analysis, there are a few definitions you need to know. The most common statistical term used in research is *mean*. However, all we are talking about is an *average*. Using the *mean*, we can find the *average* score, the *average* person, the *average* perception, the *average* attitude, and so on. The three most commonly used measures of *central tendency* are the *mean/arithmetic average, median*, and *mode*. These summary statistics tell us the average response to a specific question. These measures of *central tendency* work best with *Ratio-levels* of measure. The *mean, median,* and *mode* all have the same value on a *normal curve* or in a *normally distributed population* (Cherry, 2001).

Research Hypothesis/Question   6.14:
What is the level of measure, the central tendency, and the sample size of alcohol consumption, cocaine addicts, AIDS deaths, and school funds spent on drug education in the United States?

> *Data File:* **STATES**
> *Task:* **Univariate**
> *Primary Variable:* **63) ALCOHOL 89**
> *View:* **Summary**

ALCOHOL 89 – 1989: GALLONS OF ALCOHOLIC BEVERAGES CONSUMED PER PERSON 16 AND OVER (HCSR, 1993)		
Mean: 35.003	Std. Dev.: 6.496	N: 50
Median: 34.020	Variance: 42.192	Missing: 0

Where the *mean* score gives us an idea of the average or typical response, *range, variance* and *standard deviation* tell us the extent individual scores depart from the *mean* score. The *median* score tells us the cut off score where 50% of the scores are below the median and 50% of scores are above the median. The median score from the *Alcohol Beverage Consumption* variable is 34.02. In this case 50% of the states had a population that consumes more than 34.02 gallons of alcohol beverages in 1989 and 50% of states had populations that consume fewer than 34.02 gallons of alcohol beverages that year.

The simplest measure of dispersion is *range. Range* tells us the highest and lowest values of a variable in a data set. For the variable *Alcohol Beverage Consumption* (click on the *summary* view), the range goes from a low of 21.4 gallons to a high of 60.76 gallons consumed over a year. The range tells us that, on average, people in Utah consume 21.4 gallons a year and people in Nevada consume 60.69 gallons of alcoholic beverages a year. The highest-consuming state consumes about three times the volume of alcohol as the state with the lowest consumption.

The measure of *standard deviation* is the most important and commonly utilized measure of variability in research in the helping professions. Based on the *mean* as a point of reference, *standard deviation* is computed by determining the average distance of each score from the *mean.* Using *standard deviation,* we can determine if the scores cluster around the *mean* or are scattered widely above and below the *mean* (Cherry, 2001). The *standard deviation* for the *alcohol* variable above indicates that in a normal distribution, 68% of people fall within *one standard deviation* of the mean or average *gallons of alcoholic beverages consumed per person 16 and over in the United States* (35.003 gallons). In this example (presuming a normal distribution of the data) with a standard deviation of 6.496 gallons, 68% of people in the United States consume between 28.5 gallons and 41.5 gallons of alcohol a year. Additionally, 95% of people fall within two *standard deviation* of the mean. In this case, 95% of the people consume between 22.011 and 47.995 gallons of alcoholic beverages a year.

An easy way to visualize *standard deviation* is to remember that a "small" *standard deviation* would indicate that the scores of the people in a study were "very similar." They had close to the same score. Likewise, a "large" *standard deviation* would indicate that the scores of the people in a study were "very different." The people had scores that were very different from the average score. A "small" *standard deviation* would indicate a *homogeneous* population. The scores would cluster closely around the *mean.* Similarly, a "large" *standard deviation* would indicate that the scores do *not* cluster closely around the *mean;* the population is *heterogeneous.* In a large *standard deviation*, the scores are spread out away from the *mean.*

The *variance* reported in the table is a measure of the variation or dispersion around the mean of the scores obtained on the variable *alcohol beverage consumption.* Variance is the *average squared deviation score* around the mean.

The squared deviation scores (differences in gallons consumed by a state's population and the mean for all states squared) are added together and the average becomes the variance coefficient. To turn this variance coefficient into a more useful number, we can find the square root of the variance, which is the standard deviation. This is important because the standard deviation is in the same units of measurement as the variable. In this case, one standard deviation is equal to one gallon of alcohol. The *variance* coefficient for the alcohol consumption variable is 42.192 (see the table above). The square root of 42.192 is 6.496, the standard deviation for that variable.

Data File:	**STATES**	COKEUSER90 -- 1990: COCAINE ADDICTS PER 1,000 POPULATION (SENATE JUDICIARY COMMITTEE, USA TODAY:8/6/90)
Task:	**Univariate**	
➤ Primary Variable:	**60) COKEUSER90**	Mean: 7.230 Std. Dev.: 4.769 Median: 6.60
➤ View	**Summary**	N: 50 Missing: 0 Variance: 22.74

The univariate analysis above tells us that on average there were 7.230 addicts per 1,000 people in the United States in 1990. It also tells us that in 68% of the states (1 standard deviations from the mean) the number of people who were addicted to cocaine went from a low of 2.461 to a high of 11.999 per 1,000 people in 1990.

Data File:	**STATES**	AIDS 95 – 1995: AIDS/HIV DEATHS PER 100,000 (SA, 1998)
Task:	**Univariate**	
➤ Primary Variable:	**64) AIDS 95**	Mean: 12.660 Std. Dev.: 8.402 N: 42
➤ View	**Summary**	Median: 10.20 Variance: 70.602 Missing: 8

The univariate analysis above indicates that on average 12.660 people per 100,000 people in the United States died from HIV/AIDS in 1995. It also tells us that in 68% of the states (1 standard deviations from the mean) the number of people who died from HIV/AIDS ranged from a low of 4.258 to a high of 21.08 deaths per 100,000 in 1995.

Data File:	**STATES**	SUICIDE 96 -- 1996: SUICIDES PER 100,000 (SA,1996)
Task:	**Univariate**	
➤ Primary Variable:	**56) SUICIDE 96**	Mean: 12.964 Std. Dev.: 3.214 N: 50
➤ View:	**Summary**	Median: 12.40 Variance: 10.327 Missing: 0

This univariate analysis of the suicide variable tells us that on average 12.964 people per 100,000 people in the United States committed suicide in 1996. It also tells us that in 68% of the states (1 standard deviations from the mean) the number of people who committed suicide in 1996 went from a low of 9.750 to a high of 16.178 suicides per 100,000 people per year.

Data File:	**STATES**	DRUG ED 90 – 1990: SCHOOL FUNDS PER STUDENT SPENT ON DRUG EDUCATION IN DOLLARS (SENATE JUDICIARY COMMITTEE, USA TODAY, 9/6/90)
Task:	**Univariate**	
➤ Primary Variable:	**88) DRUG ED 90**	Mean: 8.242 Std. Dev.: 3.813 N: 50
➤ View:	**Summary**	Median: 6.67 Variance: 14.538 Missing: 0

This univariate analysis of the variable *funds per student spent on drug education* tells us that on average the states spent an average of $8.24 per student for drug education in 1990. However, among 68% of the states, some spent as little as $4.429 and as much as $12.055 per student in 1990.

We used the variable *heart diseases* in the last chapter. We know it is a ratio-level measure and there is no missing data. We will not do the univariate analysis again. Based on the univariate analyses, all the variables are ratio variables. The variable that measures *AIDS deaths* is the only one with missing data. We do not have data for eight states regarding the number of AIDS deaths in these states.

Negative Consequences of Alcohol Consumption

If you ask a person who drinks alcoholic beverages why he or she drinks, you will hear any number of individual reasons for drinking. The reasons will vary from "to get drunk" or "to feel good" to reasons such as "to be sociable or "because everyone else is drinking." Aside from these individual explanations, the more influential factors regulating individual alcohol consumption include socioeconomic circumstances, gender, age, religion, urban-rural environment, and geographic region (Doweiko, 2002). The negative consequences of excessive alcohol use include jeopardizing relationships with others, harming the user's health, or endangering society (Doweiko, 2002).

The negative consequences from drinking alcoholic beverages that we will examine are AIDS related deaths, cocaine addiction, and suicide rates. To determine the type of statistical tests to use with these variables, we first need to find out the level of measure of the variable. Once we know the level of measure, then we can select the most appropriate statistical tests. The variables I picked for this examination of the consequences of alcohol and drug use are all *ratio-level* measures. This means that we can use correlation and regression statistical procedures with the six variables I selected to see how they relate to each other in the aggregate from state to state.

The majority of people who drink alcoholic beverages do so with few consequences, other than perhaps suffering the pain from a hangover and making a fool of one's self. For others, however, it can ruin their lives, and it is associated with driving accidents, domestic violence, birth defects, violence, suicide, and numerous health problems (Doweiko, 2002). The three major areas of concern are excessive alcohol use, alcohol dependency, and other alcohol-related problems. Even though excessive alcohol use causes a lot of problems for society, the focus is usually on those who are addicted and who do great harm to themselves, their family, and their friends.

Research Hypothesis/Question   6.15:
Which states have the highest rate of alcohol consumption per person 16 years of age or older?

Data File: **STATES**
➢ Task: **Mapping**
➢ Variable 1: **63) ALCOHOL 89**
➢ View: **Map**

ALCOHOL 89 -- 1989: GALLONS OF ALCOHOLIC BEVERAGES CONSUMED PER PERSON 16 AND OVER (HCSR, 1993)

Based on the map, the highest levels of alcohol consumption are in the southwest United States, with the exception of Alaska, Montana, Wisconsin, New Hampshire, and Connecticut. What is even more interesting is that Nevada (ranked 1st in consumption) is west of Utah (ranked 50th) and Arizona (ranked 4th). This clearly demonstrates that alcohol use can vary widely from one state to another. This also makes a good variable to use in a statistical analysis.

The problems associated with alcohol misuse in our society are numerous and interrelated. To study a social problem such as suicide, for instance, without recognizing the role that alcohol plays in the behavior will yield an incomplete picture at best and a misleading picture at worst.

People with mild to severe psychiatric problems such as depression, anxiety, obsessive-compulsive disorders, anti-social personality disorders, and even schizophrenia often use alcohol and other illegal drugs to treat their disorder. Some who become depressed or violent after heavy drinking will overdose on prescription drugs. This is a familiar situation to those who work in mental health and substance abuse fields (Swan, 1996). Let's see if the relationship that we notice so often in the helping professions is strong enough to show in national data.

Because we have three variables that measure alcohol consumption, and a variable that gives us the percentage of cocaine addicts in a given state, why don't we do a correlation with all the drug measures and the variable that provides a count of the number of suicides per 100,000 in a given state? In this analysis, I am looking at several predictor variables from a single dimension—alcoholic beverages.

Research Hypothesis/Question   6.16:
The higher the consumption of alcohol in a given state, the higher the rate of suicide will be in that state.

Data List: **STATES**
➤ *Task:* **Correlation**
➤ *Variables:* **56) SUICIDE 96**
60) COKEUSER90
61) BEER 95
62) WINE 95
63) ALCOHOL 89
➤ *Deletion:* **Pairwise**
➤ *Test:* **2-tailed test**

Correlation Coefficients Table

	SUICIDE 96	COKE USER90	BEER 95	WINE 95	ALCO-HOL 89
SUICIDE 96	1.000 ($n = 50$)	0.018 ($n = 50$)	0.484 ** ($n = 50$)	-0.046 ($n = 50$)	0.316 * ($n = 50$)
COKE USER90	0.018 ($n = 50$)	1.000 ($n = 50$)	0.207 ($n = 50$)	0.354 * ($n = 50$)	0.378 ** ($n = 50$)
BEER 95	0.484 ** ($n = 50$)	0.207 ($n = 50$)	1.000 ($n = 50$)	0.223 ($n = 50$)	0.850 ** ($n = 50$)
WINE 95	-0.046 ($n = 50$)	0.354 * ($n = 50$)	0.223 ($n = 50$)	1.000 ($n = 50$)	0.635 ** ($n = 50$)
ALCO-HOL 89	0.316 * ($n = 50$)	0.378 ** ($n = 50$)	0.850 ** ($n = 50$)	0.635 ** ($n = 50$)	1.000 ($n = 50$)

Pairwise deletion (2-tailed test)   Significance Levels: ** =.01, * =.05

To a regrettable degree, it appears that suicide is correlated to beer ($r = .484$, $p < .01$) and alcohol consumption ($r = .316$, $p < .05$). Interestingly, the more wine consumed, the fewer the suicides. It is also notable that in states with higher rates of cocaine addicts, there are not higher rates of suicide. The state with the highest beer consumption is also the state with the highest number of suicides per 100,000.

The culpability of beer consumption is a little surprising. I had expected it to be higher in states with high alcohol consumption. High rates of alcohol consumption are significant in increasing suicide rates, but it does not increase suicide rates like the heavy consumption of beer does. This could be because a measure of alcohol consumption includes all alcohol, including beer and wine. Wine is associated with reduced suicide rates, when combined in a measure with beer (which increased suicide rates) wine tends to reduce the effect of alcohol as a predictor of suicide.

AIDS/HIV and Alcohol and Drugs

As a consequence of being intoxicated and participating in risky sexual behavior, a number of people have become HIV-infected and have later died from AIDS complications. Sexually transmitted diseases (STDs) are recognized as a major public health problem in most of the industrialized world. The World Health Organization (WHO) estimates that in the mid-1990s, 30 million curable sexually transmitted infections (syphilis, gonorrhea, chlamydia, and trichomoniasis) occurred every year in North America and Western Europe. An additional 18 million cases occurred in Eastern Europe and Central Asia (Renton and Whitaker, 1997). If intoxication puts you at risk for becoming infected with HIV or other STDs, we should find that in states with higher levels of alcohol and drug consumption (in this case cocaine), there will be higher rates of AIDS-related deaths.

Research Hypothesis/Question   6.17:
The higher the consumption of alcohol and cocaine in a given state, the higher the rate of AIDS deaths will be.

	Data File	STATES
	Task:	Correlation
➤	Variables:	64) AIDS 95
		60) COKEUSER90
		61) BEER 95
		62) WINE 95
		63) ALCOHOL 89
➤	Deletion:	Pairwise
➤	Test:	2 tailed

Correlation Coefficients Table

	AIDS 95	COKE USER90	BEER 95	WINE 95	ALCO-HOL 89
AIDS 95	1.000 ($n = 42$)	0.435 ** ($n = 42$)	-0.160 ($n = 42$)	0.328 * ($n = 42$)	-0.002 ($n = 42$)
COKE USER90	0.435 ** ($n = 42$)	1.000 ($n = 50$)	0.207 ($n = 50$)	0.354 * ($n = 50$)	0.378 ** ($n = 50$)
BEER 95	-0.160 ($n = 42$)	0.207 ($n = 50$)	1.000 ($n = 50$)	0.223 ($n = 50$)	0.850 ** ($n = 50$)
WINE 95	0.328 * ($n = 42$)	0.354 * ($n = 50$)	0.223 ($n = 50$)	1.000 ($n = 50$)	0.635 ** ($n = 50$)
ALCO-HOL 89	-0.002 ($n = 42$)	0.378 ** ($n = 50$)	0.850 ** ($n = 50$)	0.635 ** ($n = 50$)	1.000 ($n = 50$)

Pairwise deletion (2-tailed test)   Significance Levels: ** =.01, * =.05

This analysis suggests that the more cocaine addicts in a state and the more people in a state who are high wine consumers are also states with higher numbers of people dying from complications related to AIDS. What do you make of these associations?

Alcohol, Cocaine, and Heart Disease

Conventional wisdom would suggest that alcohol, cocaine, and heart disease go together like a *hand in a glove*. Maybe, but there are conditions that may reduce heart disease. We have all heard that a glass or two of red wine will reduce heart disease. If this is true, we should be able to see it in our data.

Research Hypothesis/Question   6.18:
The higher the consumption of alcohol and cocaine in a given state, the higher the rate of heart disease will be.

	Data File:	STATES
	Task:	Correlation
➤	Variables:	65) HEART DD 95
		60) COKEUSER90
		61) BEER 95
		62) WINE 95
		63) ALCOHOL 89
➤	Deletion:	Pairwise
➤	Test	2-tailed

Correlation Coefficients Table

	HEART DD 95	COKEUSER90	BEER 95	WINE 95	ALCOHOL 89
HEART DD 95	1.000 (*n* = 50)	-0.086 (*n* = 50)	-0.208 (*n* = 50)	-0.281 (*n* = 50)	-0.317 * (*n* = 50)
COKEUSER90	-0.086 (*n* = 50)	1.000 (*n* = 50)	0.207 (*n* = 50)	0.354 * (*n* = 50)	0.378 ** (*n* = 50)
BEER 95	-0.208 (*n* = 50)	0.207 (*n* = 50)	1.000 (*n* = 50)	0.223 (*n* = 50)	0.850 ** (*n* = 50)
WINE 95	-0.281 (*n* = 50)	0.354 * (*n* = 50)	0.223 (*n* = 50)	1.000 (*n* = 50)	0.635 ** (*n* = 50)
ALCOHOL 89	-0.317 * (*n* = 50)	0.378 ** (*n* = 50)	0.850 ** (*n* = 50)	0.635 ** (*n* = 50)	1.000 (*n* = 50)

Pairwise deletion (2-tailed test)   Significance Levels: ** =.01, * =.05

Well, we can say one thing for sure. When looking at a national data set by states, with a measure on the number of cocaine addicts and the amount of alcohol and wine they consume, you don't have to worry about cocaine abuse causing heart disease. Cocaine abuse is not related at all to heart disease ($r = -.086$, $p = NS$). You also do not have to be concerned with alcohol and wine contributing to heart disease, as we hypothesized; in states where alcohol consumption was high, heart disease was low ($r = -.317$, $p < .05$). Now on your own, try generating a map of states by the amount of alcohol they consume and another map of states with heart disease. States whose residents consume the most alcohol per person are also the states with the least heart disease.

Alcohol Consumption Rank	Heart Disease Rank	Name Of State
1	33	Nevada
2	32	New Hampshire
3	25	Wisconsin
4	34	Arizona
5	50	Alaska
6	46	New Mexico
7	41	Texas
8	47	Hawaii
9	39	Montana
10	27	Vermont

Okay, let's see if people are really as concerned about the problem of alcohol and drugs as they say they are. Do the states that have the most alcohol and cocaine addicts spend more money on school-based drug education?

Research Hypothesis/Question   6.19:
States with high levels of alcohol consumption and cocaine will spend more on school drug education.

To save space, I will let you run the correlations between expenditures on school-based drug education [88] DRUG ED 90], with cocaine use [60] COKEUSER90], and beer [61] BEER 95], wine [62] WINE 95] and alcohol [63] alcohol 89] consumption. Be sure to select *Pairwise deletion* and the *2-tailed test.* You will find that the only drug use that correlated by state with *school-based drug education* is a higher level of wine consumption ($r = .321$, $p < .05$). Before we turn our attention to the General Social Survey and look at the effects of alcohol and drugs on the individual, take a look at a scatterplot of states with higher levels of wine consumption and states that spend more on school-based drug education. Find out where your state stands. I live in Florida; it ranks 16th in wine consumption and 24th in spending for school-based drug education.

Attitudes and the Effect of Alcohol and Drugs on the Individual

The General Social Survey (GSS) is a survey that is currently conducted every two years. Thousands of people are interviewed and asked hundreds of questions. Using these data, we will attempt to find individual characteristics that are associated with the differences in alcohol use.

A question on the GSS asks people if *on occasion they drink more than they think they should.* This is a good question, because many people who drink, drink more than they intended to on occasion. This is a nominal-level measure, so we will only be able to use Crosstabs or t-Tests to do the bivariate analysis, but we will use a logistic regression to look at the combined effect of several variables that might help us better understand people who admit that they sometimes drink more than they should.

To begin, I would like to know the number of people who answered this question. It could be that everyone refused to answer this question, although I doubt it. I suspect that the question about overdrinking occasionally was answered by some people and others refused to answer the question.

Research Hypothesis/Question   6.20:
How many people answered the question that asked: Do you sometimes drink more than you think you should?

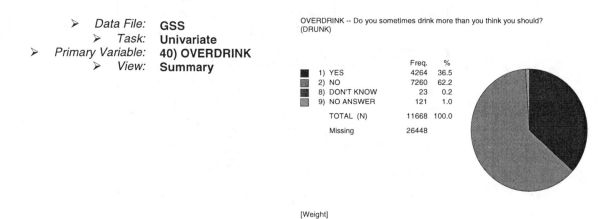

➤ *Data File:* **GSS**
➤ *Task:* **Univariate**
➤ *Primary Variable:* **40) OVERDRINK**
➤ *View:* **Summary**

OVERDRINK -- Do you sometimes drink more than you think you should? (DRUNK)

		Freq.	%
■	1) YES	4264	36.5
▨	2) NO	7260	62.2
▨	8) DON'T KNOW	23	0.2
▨	9) NO ANSWER	121	1.0
	TOTAL (N)	11668	100.0
	Missing	26448	

[Weight]

In this case, we have a good size sample. Some 11,524 people answered the question either *yes* or *no*. We need a large sample to do a multivariate analysis because most variables in our GSS data file have missing data. These are questions that the people who were interviewed did not answer. The reason so many people did not answer the question is not known. I am sure there were many reasons for people not answering the question; however, missing data is a problem in a multivariate analysis. I will explain why at the end of the bivariate analysis.

My next concern is that these questions are *self-report* variables. They are referred to as *self-report* variables to signify that the person reported his or her drinking behavior and that the veracity of the answer was not verified by another source.

A Theoretical Conception That Can Partially Explain the Differences in Alcohol Uses

In this examination, I want to explain the differences in alcohol use, by selecting questions that fit a particular theoretical protocol. I would like to use Hirschi's (1969) conceptualization of *control theory* to see how much, if any, it can explain of the differences in alcohol use. This theory proposes that there are four components that control deviant behavior: (1) attachment; (2) commitment; (3) involvement; and (4) belief. Attachment refers to the psychological and emotional connection of the individual toward other people or groups, to the extent these persons' or groups' opinions affect the individual. Commitment is the investment in conventional norms. In the case of alcohol use, control theory would suggest that gender, religion, family, and work will act as controls on an individual's drinking behavior.

To get the maximum benefit out of quantitative research methods, use theoretical conceptualizations as the basis for selecting and explaining how your choice of variables will predict changes in the dependent variable. I think you are at the point in your understanding of research where you can appreciate using a theory to explain human behavior. Shall we see if control theory can explain any part of this particular drinking behavior?

To begin, we need to do a series of bivariate analyses to examine the strength and direction of the variables that tend to control drinking. Why don't we start with gender? It is common knowledge that it is socially acceptable for men to drink more than women. We should find it to be true in the GSS data.

Research Hypothesis/Question 6.21:
There is a statistically significant difference between males and females who self-report drinking too much on occasion.

The two variables we will use in this analysis are nominal-level variables, so we will have to use a statistical test that can analyze nominal level-variables. The *Cross-Tabulation* procedure allows us to examine the joint distribution of two or more nominal or categorical variables. The variables used with a cross-tabulation are typically either nominal or ordinal. The resulting table may be in percentages by row, by column, or by the total. Expected frequencies and chi-square results are shown in the summary statistics. First let's look at a bar graph using these two variables.

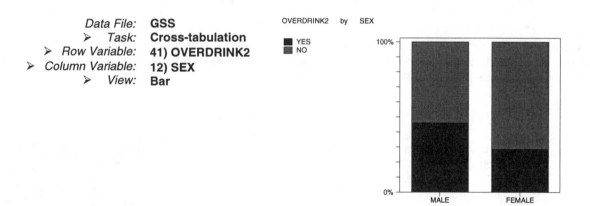

Data File:	**GSS**
➤ *Task:*	**Cross-tabulation**
➤ *Row Variable:*	**41) OVERDRINK2**
➤ *Column Variable:*	**12) SEX**
➤ *View:*	**Bar**

The stack bar graph is a good visual picture of the significant difference between men and women who self-report that they drink too much on occasion. However, the chi-square statistic in the *Statistic Summary* tells us if the association is statistically significant or not. In this case the chi-square statistic ($\chi^2 = 385.583$, df $= 1$, $p < .000$) tells us that the association between the two variables (overdrinking and sex) that we observed in this sample is similar to the association that exists in the total population sampled. Indeed, if you look at the summary analysis, you will see the Cramer's *V* is .18. The Cramer's *V*, as you may remember, is a measure of association between two nominal variables much like the Pearson's *r* is a measure of correlation between two ratio variables. Both coefficients give us a measure of relatedness. In this case, it is a weak association, but because the sample is very large and the trend is consistent throughout the sample, it is a significant association. I would guess that religion would also be a strong deterrent or control on drinking too much on occasion. With a little apprehension, I will propose that in this country there will be a moderate to strong association with overdrinking and religion.

Research Hypothesis/Question   6.22:
In the United States, religious beliefs often act as a control on one's drinking behavior.

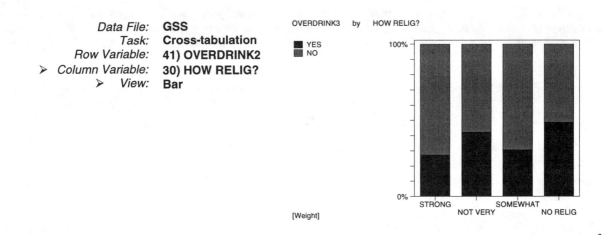

Data File:	**GSS**
Task:	**Cross-tabulation**
Row Variable:	**41) OVERDRINK2**
➢ *Column Variable:*	**30) HOW RELIG?**
➢ *View:*	**Bar**

In this analysis, religious beliefs do appear to be acting to reduce the number of times a person drinks to excess (χ^2 = 288.027, df = 3, *p* < .000). The Cramer's *V* was .16, even less than gender. Then again, if you look at the responses *not very* and *somewhat*, they are backward to what I would have expected. Those who answered *somewhat* reported overdrinking less than those who responded *not very*. I am concerned that respondents may have been confused about the difference between the two. To see the statistics, select *summary*. To deal with the possibility of this confusion, I will collapse the two values into a response called *somewhat* and redo the analysis.

Research Hypothesis/Question   6.23:
There will be a moderate association between those who report overdrinking on occasion and those who report being less than strongly religious.

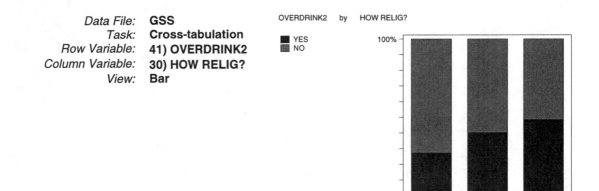

Data File:	**GSS**
Task:	**Cross-tabulation**
Row Variable:	**41) OVERDRINK2**
Column Variable:	**30) HOW RELIG?**
View:	**Bar**

MicroCase allows you to temporarily collapse columns and rows in a cross-tabulation. To collapse (combine) the two columns NOT VERY and SOMEWHAT; you will first need to select [Column %] from the menu on the left. You will now be looking at the table view. Then click on the column headings NOT VERY and SOMEWHAT; the columns will turn blue. Now click the [Collapse] button on the left menu. A box will appear. Type in SOMEWHAT as the new category label and click [OK]. You now have three columns for your HOW RELIG? variable. Click [Bar] to return to the Bar view.

This stack bar clearly shows that this variable is a rank-order level measure. In this case, it is significant ($\chi^2 = 230.88$, df = 2, $p < 000$). As well, given it is a rank-order level of measure, we can use the Gamma statistics for our measure of association (Gamma = -.274, $p < .000$). This is still a weak correlation, even though it increased the association around a third in strength. It is more predictive, however, than gender for determining when a person will report *not* overdrinking.

6.5   From the 'Burbs to the 'Hood

This is a school-based drug abuse prevention program based on a program called Life Skills Training that has been shown to lower drug use among white middle-class adolescents and also reduces drug use among minority youths, according to soon-to-be-published results from a NIDA-funded study. The study indicates that the intervention had preventive effects on African American and Hispanic American youths' use of tobacco, marijuana, and alcohol and lowered their intentions to use drugs in the future (Mathias, 1997).

Now, if we use the variable that tells us the number of children a person is responsible for, we have a good variable to see if people who have more children to care for tend to overdrink less than people without the responsibility of caring for children. The number of children is a ratio variable and the *overdrink* variable we will use is a two category nominal variable, so we will use a t-Test, a type of analysis of variance, to look at the bivariate relationship.

The t-Test and ANOVA statistical procedures are both used to test whether the values of an ordinal or ratio variable vary across the levels of a nominal or categorical variable. We use the t-Test when the independent variable has only two categories. We use the ANOVA procedure when the independent variable has more than two categories. You can use the t-Test e.g. that compares the means of the groups to examine the effect of overdrinking on occasion and the number of live children the respondents reported having in their lifetime.

Research Hypothesis/Question   6.24:
People who report overdrinking occasionally will as a group tend to have significantly fewer children.

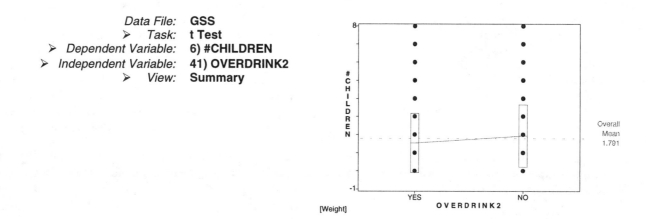

Data File: **GSS**
➤ Task: **t Test**
➤ Dependent Variable: **6) #CHILDREN**
➤ Independent Variable: **41) OVERDRINK2**
➤ View: **Summary**

This association is also statistically significant. If you select the ANOVA statistic, you will see that the *means* of the two groups are significantly different ($t = 12.052$, $p < .000$). To see the means, select *mean* in the statistic box.

Another variable that could help explain differences in drinking behavior is work. A question that will give us a broad view of how work might effect drinking is a question that determines a person's occupational prestige. My thinking here is that control theory (Hirschi, 1969) would suggest that as a group fewer people with prestigious jobs would risk them by overdrinking.

Research Hypothesis/Question   6.25:
People who report overdrinking occasionally will as a group tend to have less prestigious jobs than those who do not overdrink.

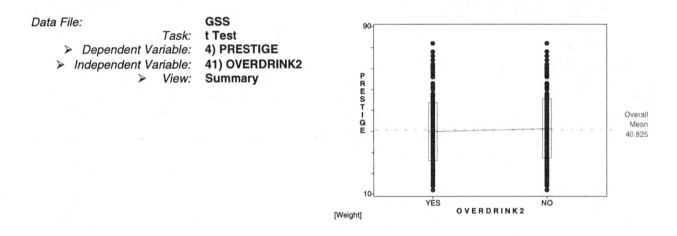

Data File:	**GSS**
Task:	**t Test**
➢ *Dependent Variable:*	**4) PRESTIGE**
➢ *Independent Variable:*	**41) OVERDRINK2**
➢ *View:*	**Summary**

This bivariate relationship is also statistically significant. This means that prestige might also help explain the differences between those who self-report drinking too much on occasion and those who do not. Among the 9,265 people who answered both of these questions, there was a significant difference between those who overdrink and those who reported they did not overdrink ($t = .46$, $p < .000$).

Sample-Size Problems in Multivariate Analyses

A problem occurs when people do not answer all the questions in a survey. Take, for instance, the question about over-drinking; some people will not answer a question like this. They may think the question is insulting or inappropriate, so they will not answer it. Some 9,265 people out of 38,116 people who participated in the GSS survey did answer the question. This means 76% of the 38,116 people did not answer this question or were not asked this question. Taken to the next step, the second question, say, *religion,* is answered by only 50% of the people who answered the question about overdrinking. In a bivariate analysis with these two questions, your sample size would drop to 4,632 people. Now add a third question that a lot of people did not answer, say the *number of children they have;* let's say another 75% of the people who answered the overdrinking question would not answer the question on the *number of children* in their family. Your sample is now down to 1,158 people. Of these another 75% did not answer the question about *occupational prestige,* your sample drop to 290 people. It would be hard for any of us to believe that these 290 people, even though they are from all over the United States, are really representative of those of us who overdrink occasionally and those of us who report that we never overdrink. This can happen a great deal more often than you think in a multivariate analysis, even with a sample that starts out with 38,000 participants.

Control Theory as a Partial Explanation of the Differences in Alcohol Use

Now that we have several variables that could help show us if control theory can explain the variations in alcohol use, we need to look at them in a multivariate way to see which ones are truly important and which help explain the variance in alcohol use. Remember, the dependent variable, *overdrinking*, is a nominal-level measure (yes or no); this means that we will need to use the *logistic regression* procedure to do the multivariate analysis. Logistic regression has only one condition for the nominal-level dependent variable; it must have only two outcomes. This is the case with *overdrink*, as the respondent can answer only yes or no.

Research Hypothesis/Question   6.26:
People who report overdrinking occasionally will as a group tend to be less religious, hold less prestigious jobs, have fewer children, and have less family income.

Data File:	GSS		Beta Coef	Std. Err	Prob.	Odds Ratio
➢ Task:	**Logistic Regression**					
➢ Dependent Variable:	**41) OVERDRINK2**					
➢ Independent Variables:	**30) HOW RELIG?**	CONSTANT	0.122	0.080	0.065	
	4) PRESTIGE					
	6) # CHILDREN	HOW RELIG?	-0.221	0.025	0.000	0.802 -20%
	16) FAM.INCOME					
➢ View:	**Regression**	PRESTIGE	0.008	0.002	0.000	1.008 0.8%
		# CHILDREN	0.122	0.013	0.000	1.138 14%
		FAM INC	0.004	0.004	0.002	1.004 0.4%

Logistic Regression can be found on the ADVANCED STATISTICS menu.

This analysis suggests that for every increase in a unit of religion (0 = strongly religious to 3 = no religion) there will be a 20% decrease in people who, on occasion, drink too much (0 = yes overdrinks and 1 = no overdrinking). For every unit increase in occupational prestige, there is negligible decrease of 0.8% among people who overdrink. Likewise, for every unit increase in family income, there will be a negligible 0.4% decrease in overdrinkers. The number of children, however, reduced overdrinking. For each additional child a person is responsible for in his or her family, there is a 14% decrease in those who occasionally overdrink. This accounts for approximately 20% of the difference in alcohol use among people in the United States between 18 and 90+ years of age.

It is not a big deal to be able to explain 20% of why a person overdrinks on occasion, but it does suggest that these four simple *control* variables explained a fifth of the difference in people who overdrink on occasion and people who do not. Now if you add a few more control variables to the ones we have identified here that cover different dimensions of control, you might be able to explain even more of the difference in alcohol use.

A Historical Look at Cirrhosis

Cirrhosis, a disease of the liver, can be caused by any number of conditions. A precursor to cirrhosis is a liver inflammation that causes the liver to swell. The swelling can be caused by chemicals, poisons, drugs, numerous medications, bacteria, and parasites. The bacteria and parasites are often found in food products that are prepared in less than sanitary situations. Seafood, such as clams and oysters, can carry such parasites. If the swelling of the liver (hepatitis) becomes chronic, it can lead to cirrhosis. Most often, however, in the developed countries where bacteria and parasites are better controlled, cirrhosis is caused by excessive alcohol consumption. If this is true, then we should be able to see a good deal of variation in the number of cases of cirrhosis over the years as the amount of alcohol consumed varies. So let's try it as an analysis.

Research Hypothesis/Question 6.27:
Cirrhosis in the United States has varied substantially over the last 100 years.

> *Data File:* **US TRENDS**
> > *Task:* **Historical Trends**
> *Variable:* **17) CIRRHOSIS**

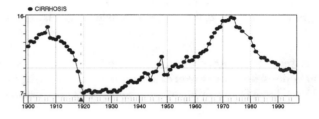

There is no doubt there has been a great deal of variation in the number of cases of cirrhosis over the years. The two years with the most cases of cirrhosis reported were in 1907 and in 1973. What is also interesting is that the number of cases of cirrhosis dropped to its lowest point in the last 100 years in 1920. This was the year that the 18th Amendment prohibiting the sale and consumption of alcohol was ratified. The drop in the number of cases of cirrhosis can hardly be attributed to the ratification of the 18th Amendment, however, because the number of cases had been dropping since 1910. I suspect that the drop in the number of cases of cirrhosis and the ratification of the 18th Amendment were in large part caused by the influence of such organizations such as the American Temperance Society, the National Prohibition party, and the Anti-Saloon League. These organizations and others like them had large memberships and were politically strong and influential by 1910 (Ray, 1978). They were often led by women, many of whom were instrumental in the passage of the 19th Amendment in 1920, which gave women the right to vote.

End Note: In this chapter, you were asked to do some very sophisticated analyses while examining global and national issues related to the use and abuse of substances. As you noticed, however, even the most sophisticated analysis moves through a systematic and logical step-by-step process. This process is often called model building. The effort is to develop the best model or explanation from the variables on which you have data. The analyses that we did strongly suggest that there are both positive and negative health consequences from using alcohol drinks. Low consumption levels of alcoholic drinks can reduce health problems such as heart disease; however, abuse can result in numerous health problems like cirrhosis. You have heard all this before, I am sure. Even so, I would wager that you have never seen it demonstrated with real data on real people right in front of your eyes. To work with real data is to truly experience discovery.

Other Issues Related to Substance Abuse

There are a number of issues related to substance abuse that I could not examine in this chapter. However, with the data files provided with this book, you can analyze many of these issues on your own. To learn more about other issues related to substance abuse you can enter the following search terms in the InfoTrac College Edition.

Substance abuse	Codependency suffers
Dual diagnosis	Sexual addiction
Detoxification	Delinquency substance abuse
Drug treatment centers	Fetal Alcohol Syndrome
Drunk driving	Minority substance abuse
Other addictions	Relationship addiction

Exploring Global Social Welfare

Workbook exercises and software are copyrighted. Copying is prohibited by law.

WORKSHEET

NAME:

COURSE:

DATE:

EXERCISE

Review Questions

Based on the work you've done so far on the issue of substance abuse see how well you do on this short True or False quiz.

For the most part, it is acceptable to be a little drunk in societies where alcohol is legally used.	T F
There was a substantial correlation between nations around the world with high levels of alcohol consumption and cirrhosis of the liver.	T F
Fortunately, people living in Third World countries have not been affected by alcohol abuse nor drug abuse.	T F
In the United States, where wine consumption is high, people have lower rates of heart disease than people who live in states where less wine is consumed.	T F
The United States ranks in the lower half of countries in terms of cigarette consumption.	T F
Among drugs associated with high rates of suicide in the United States, cocaine is among the worse.	T F
Control-type variables such as religion have no influence on the amount of alcohol consumed by people in the United States.	T F

MicroCase QUESTIONS

If you want to learn additional information about the LOGISTIC REGRESSION task in MicroCase, use the online help (F1).

Use the following data files, variables, and analytical approaches to answer the MicroCase questions.

1. When we tested variables that explained alcohol consumption, we found that the number of men to women and the quality of life in a country could explain about 80% of alcohol use. How much variance in beer consumption can be explained by these two variables?

> *Data File:* **GLOBAL**
> *Task:* **Regression**
> *Dependent Variable:* **90) BEER DRINK**
> *Independent Variables:* **20) SEX RATIO**
> **26) QUAL. LIFE**
> *View:* **Summary**

a.   Sex ratio explained _____% of the variance in beer-drinking countries, while the quality of life in these countries explained an additional _____% of the variance in beer drinking. The Standardized Betas of each independent variable tell us the percentage of variance that each variable explains when analyzed together.

b.   The total amount of variance explained by these two variables is _____%.

2.   We looked at the association between AIDS deaths and substance use in the United States, using the correlation analysis. Why don't you finish the analysis using the regression procedure to analyze AIDS deaths in relationship to the drug use variables we used in the correlation matrix. There is no need to look at the effect of beer and alcohol consumption in a regression analysis, because they were not associated with AIDS deaths in the correlational analysis.

> *Data File:* **STATES**
> *Task:* **Regression**
> *Dependent Variable:* **64) AIDS 95**
> *Independent Variables:* **60) COKEUSER90**
> **62) WINE 95**
> *View:* **Summary**

a.   Would you agree with the statement: higher levels of cocaine use and wine consumption explain over 20% of the difference in AIDS deaths from state to state.

Yes   No

b.   Of the two independent variables in your analysis, which one was the most important in explaining the differences in AIDS deaths from state to state? _____

3.   Addiction is one of those conditions that support a number of other situations such as the treatment community, people who treat addiction. What is the effect on the number of psychiatrists in a given state by high levels of substance use?

>   Data File: **STATES**
>   Task: **Regression**
> ➤ Dependent Variable: **71) SHRINKS 90**
>   ➤ Independent **60) COKEUSER90**
>   Variables: **61) BEER 95**
>   **62) WINE 95**
>   **63) ALCOHOL 89**
>   ➤   View **Summary**

a.   Were you surprised at how much cocaine use contributed to the explanation of the number of psychiatrists in a given state?

   Yes   No

b.   What was the most important variable in this analysis? _____

c.   What was the contribution of beer drinking to the number of psychiatrists in a given state?
   _____%

d.   If the effect of heavy beer consumption in a state holds true to the findings in your regression analysis, do you think that if everybody drank more beer, we would need fewer psychiatrists?

   Yes   No

e.   The state of New York has a lot of psychiatrists. How would you expect it to rank among beer-drinking states?

   High   Low

4.   Now drop beer consumption from the analysis to see how much the other substances contribute to the number of psychiatrists in a given state.

>   Data File: **STATES**
>   Task: **Regression**
>   Dependent Variable: **71) SHRINKS 90**
> ➤ Independent Variables: **60) COKEUSER90**
>   **62) WINE 95**
>   **63) ALCOHOL 89**
>   ➤   View: **Summary**

a.   What happened to alcohol use as a predictive variable in this analysis?

   i. It decreased in importance.

   ii. It was the most important variable in the analysis because it had the largest positive Standardized Beta.

   iii. It now reflects the influence of the missing beer variable and now has an inverse relationship with the number of psychiatrists per state.

b.   How much of the total variance of psychiatrists from state to state did these three variables explain?

   _____%

5.   In the GSS data file, a question asks if the respondent thought marijuana should be legal. I would like you to interpret that statistical analysis to determine what the independent variables tell us is different about those who think grass should be legal and those who think it should not be legal.

   a.   Calculate in the odds ratio percentage for each independent variable below. [Hint: the ratio is calculated using the formula (100 * (Odds Ratio – 1).] The first one is calculated for you.

	Odds Ratio
GRASS? 2	.602
	_39.8____%
HOW RELIG?	_____
	_____%
PRESTIGE	_____
	_____%
# CHILDREN	_____
	_____%
FAM.INCOME	_____
	_____%

   b.   Which variable is the most important in this analysis? _____

   c.   How much of the total variance in people's opinions regarding legalizing marijuana did these four variables explain? (Hint: Add the odds ratio percentages.)

   _____%

I would leave you with this thought: The global drug problem has three major themes that are clearly discernible in most of the countries around the world. (1) There is a major concern about young people and drugs. (2) There is a major concern about addiction. (3) There is broad concern over the effect of the illegal production, trafficking, and selling of drugs. To deal with these three primary concerns about drug use, two major policy and programming approaches are used. They are (1) the criminal justice model is utilized to stop or control drug use, and (2) the public health model based on harm reduction is utilized to reduce health problems among drug users from drugs they use. The criminal justice model has failed. The harm reduction is effective in reducing drug use (Cherry et al., 2002).

Variable Lists Related to Substance Abuse

The following is a partial list of the variables in your data files that you might find interesting in your study of families. You can examine them as individual variables or several variables at a time using the approaches you learned in this chapter. To see a list of all of the variables, the question the variable asks, and the range of values, press [F3] to open the variable list window from anywhere in the software. Try using some of the variables below with the variables you have already tested.

GLOBAL

38) UNEMPLYRT
    ANNUAL UNEMPLOYMENT RATE (TWF, 1997)
58) CIVIL LIBL
    EXTENT OF INDIVIDUAL CIVIL LIBERTIES: 1 = LEAST FREE, 7 = MOST FREE (FITW, 1997)
67) CH.ATTEND
    PERCENT WHO ATTEND RELIGIOUS SERVICES ONCE A MONTH OR MORE (WVS)

STATES

57) MA <20 93
    PERCENTAGE OF BIRTHS TO MOTHERS UNDER 20 YEARS OLD (SA,1996)
59) RITALIN
    METHYLPHENIDATE (RITALIN) USE PER 10,000 (DEA, 1996)
67) SYPHILIS 91
    REPORTED CASES OF SYPHILIS PER 100,000 (MMWR,1/3/92)

GSS

5) MARITAL
    Are you currently married, widowed, divorced, separated, or have you never been married?
28) CRIME IMP?
    How important is the crime issue to you—would you say it is one of the most important, important, not very important, or not important at all?
43) TRY QUIT?
    Have you ever tried to give up smoking?

Web Pages Related to Substance Abuse

If you wish to find a world of resources that are available to you over the Internet, the following list of Web sites will get you started. Once you visit these Web sites, you will find many interesting links to other useful Web sites.

The national Center on Addiction and
Substance Abuse at Columbia University
www.casacolumbia.org/

National Institute on Alcohol and Alcoholism
www.niaaa.nih.gov/

Center for Substance Abuse Prevention (ASAP)
www.samhsa.gov/centers/

eurocare: Adovacy for the Prevention of
Alcohol Related Harm in Europe
www.eurocare.org/profiles/

DRCNet – The Drug Reform Coordination Network
www.drcnet.org/

Recreational Drugs Information Home Page
www.a1b2c3.com/drugs/

References

Brecher, E. M. (1972). *Licit & Illicit drugs.* Boston, MA: Little, Brown and Company.

Bureau of European Affairs. (May 2000). *Background Notes: Germany.* Washington DC: U.S. Department of State.

Cherry, A. L. (2000). *A Research Primer for the Helping Professions: Methods Statistics and Writing.* Belmont, CA: Brooks/Cole Pub.

Cherry, A. L., Dillon, M. E., and Rugh, D. (eds.). (2001). *Teenage Pregnancy: A Global View.* Westport, CT: Greenwood Pub.

Cherry, A. L., Rugh, D. and Dillon, M. E., (eds.). (2002). *Substance Abuse: A Global View.* Westport, CT: Greenwood Pub.

Cohen, J. and Cohen, P. (1975). *Applied Multiple Regression/Correlation Analysis for the Behavioral Sciences.* Hillsdale, NJ: Lawrence Erlbaum Asso., Pub.

Doweiko, H. E. (2002). *Concepts of Chemical Dependency* (5th ed.). Belmont, CA: Brooks/Cole Pub.

Durkheim, E. (1951). *Suicide.* (J. A. Spaulding and G. Simpson, eds.). New York: Free Press. (Original work published in 1897.)

Hirschi, T. (1969). *Causes of Delinquency.* Los Angeles, CA: University of California Press.

Mathias, R. (1997). From the 'Burbs to the 'Hood. *Prevention Research*, 12(2). Retrieved on May 15, 2001, from 165.112.78.61/NIDA_Notes/NNVol12N2/Students.html.

Ray, O. (1978). *Drugs, Society, and Human Behavior.* Saint Louis, MO: The C. V. Mosby Co.

Renton, A. and Whitaker, L. (1997). Using STD occurrence to monitor AIDS prevention: Final report of the working group on STD surveillance—EC concerted action on assessment of AIDS/HIV prevention Strategies. Lausanne, Switzerland: Institut Universitaire de Médecine Sociale et Préventive.

Swan, N. (1996). Type A and B? Classification may help in treating Cocaine abuse. *NIDA Notes: Treatment Advance, 11*(4), 1–4.

Zastrow, C. (2000). *Introduction to Social Work and Social Welfare.* (7th ed.). Belmont, CA: Wadsworth Publishing Company.

Zastrow, C., and Kirst-Ashman, K. K. (2001). *Understanding Human Behavior in the Social Environment* (5th ed.). Belmont, CA: Wadsworth Publishing Company.

Zeese, K. B. (2000, March 29). Ignoring lessons of drug wars past. *The Progressive Response. 4*(13). Retrieved on October 17, 2000, from www.foreignpolicy-infocus.org/progresp/volume4/v4n13.html#ignoring.

Additional Material That May Be of Interest

Abbott, A. A. (ed.). (2000). *Alcohol, Tobacco, and Other Drugs: Challenging Myths, Assessing Theories, Individualizing Interventions.* Washington, DC: NASW Press.

Miller, W. R. and Rollnick, S. (1991). *Motivational Interviewing: Preparing People to Change Addictive Behavior.* New York: Guilford Press.

Monti, P. M., Colby, S. M., and O'Leary; T. A. (eds.). (2001). *Adolescents, Alcohol, and Substance Abuse: Reaching Teens Through Brief Interventions.* New York: Guilford Press.

National Treatment Plan Initiative. (2000). Changing the conversation: Improving substance abuse treatment: The National Treatment Plan Initiative: Panel reports, public hearings, and participant acknowledgements. Rockville, MD: U.S. Dept. of Health and Human Services, Substance Abuse and Mental Health Services Administration, Center for Substance Abuse Treatment.

Chapter 7

GENDER EQUALITY

Tasks: Mapping, Cross-tabulation, Scatterplot, Correlation, t-Test, Regression, Logistic Regression
Data Files: STATES, GLOBAL, US TRENDS

Overview of Chapter 7

Our focus in Chapter 7 deals with a number of gender issues that are important to gender equality both globally and nationally. The chapter begins by mapping the nations of the world on their level of gender equality. Then we will look at the role that education plays in gender equality and fertility. Other conditions that tend to be involved in promoting gender equality such as women legislators in a country, women working at the top levels of government, and women in the workforce will be examined to determine their influence on gender equality. We will also look at conditions that tend to suppress gender equality in a country such as rape and murder. Once we have identified the most important global variables related to gender equality, then these variables will be appraised by regions of the world to see if and how differently they play out in different regions of the world. Gender equality is fairly high in the United States, although it can and surely will improve. Nevertheless, as we saw when looking at families headed by women, the rate of poverty was higher than for families headed by males. This chapter will continue to investigate and try to identify some of the variables that will help explain a part of this discrepancy. Then using historical trend data we will look at marriage rates, divorce rates, and mothers in the workforce over the last century. To do these analyses, we will use the same logical approach we have been using and the same analyses you have used in previous chapters. So, let's see what we can learn about gender equality globally, nationally, and how it has changed over the last century.

T he term *gender equality* is composed of a sociological and legal term. *Gender* is roughly defined as the social and cultural role expectation of males and females (Barkan, 1998). The biological term *sex* indicates physical differences. *Equality* refers to privileges and rights being the same for all, especially—*equality before the law*. As you might guess, these terms, although being simple in definition, are extremely controversial.

How can *gender* be controversial? When it is tied to rights and privileges, it can be very controversial. How can *equality* be controversial? In most cases, moving to a condition of *equality* means moving from a condition where some people have special rights or privileges and others do not. In many groups, a discussion of the idea that men, women, gays, the untouchables, in other words *all people* are *equal,* is so divisive even among women that there seems no end to the possibilities for discord. To better understand the controversy, and hopefully in the future to help right the wrong, it is helpful to become more familiar with the manifestations of the inequality between men and women around the world.

Social and Economic Justice: Women

Women have been the victims of inequality, gender discrimination, and sexism throughout recorded history. Historically, in almost all societies women were viewed as inferior to men, and women had fewer rights than men and fewer opportunities than men. Even though there have been advances toward equality in most countries, women are still discriminated against and they are victims of life events (i.e., rape and domestic violence) that do not often happen to men—with the exception of men in prison (Zastrow and Kirst-Ashman, 2001).

At the beginning of the 21st century, despite the best efforts of many women over the last 100 years, most women around the world continue to experience gender discrimination or worse. In many areas of daily life sexism is so institutionalized it would be invisible but for its powerful impact on women. This impact can be demonstrated in many ways and particularly with accurate data on how men and women differ.

Ethical Foundation for Gender Equality

It seems strange to me to propose that there is an ethical foundation for gender equality. Gender equality should be an axiom; it should be a basic principle of life among humans, but it is not. In actual truth, gender equality is closer to being a reality today than it was 100 or even 50 years ago. This movement to gender equality for women, however, is not happening in a uniform way. In different countries around the world gender equality is moving forward at a fast pace. In other countries, particularly Third World countries and countries with large traditional populations, gender equality is moving forward but at a slower pace than, say, in Europe or the United States, but it is moving forward (Cherry, et al., 2001).

Gender inequality when supported by society or government is wrong and unethical because it is unfair. It breaches the social contract. In the 17th and 18th centuries, philosophers needed a democratic principle that could oppose the theory of the divine right of kings. The social contract was the democratic principle that emerged. This is a voluntary contract among all parties and lays out the obligations and conditions between individuals and their governments. In the current political and economic environment, women are not treated equally to men. I also believe this phenomenon will be observable in current data collected on different countries around the world. It is unlikely that women would agree to a social contract that would make them second-class citizens. If they do not agree to be second-class citizens, but the data show they are in fact treated less than equally, it is an unethical political and economic arrangement.

7.1   Ethics and Gender Equality
What if you were born a boy, but during circumcision, an accident left you with a severely damaged penis. This is a possibility when a male baby is being circumcised. It has happened many times in the past. After consulting with several specialists, your doctor recommended that a surgeon take what was left of your penis and surgically fold it into a constructed vagina. At least, the doctors believed, you would be able to experience a sexual relationship. If you were to experience this type of accident, how would you want women and men to be treated? As they are treated today, or would you insist on equal rights for all adults?

A Global View of Gender Equality

The first step in the examination of gender equality is to *operationalize* the term *gender equality*. In this case, we can use the *gender-related development index*. It is a variable in the GLOBAL data file. Once we have selected this index as our variable of primary interest, the next step is to do a univariate analysis of this variable to see if the sample size of countries that we have information on is large enough to use in this analysis. This is important because some countries may not report or allow the reporting of such information because it could be embarrassing or because it would be in conflict with religious and/or political positions and aims.

7.2   Nigerian Women Want Fewer Children Than Men Do
Women in Nigeria want, on average, eight children. Nigerian men want, on average, 13 children. Among educated women in Nigeria, the rate is much lower (Metz, 1991).

Research Hypothesis/Question   7.1:
How many countries report on the measure of gender equality?

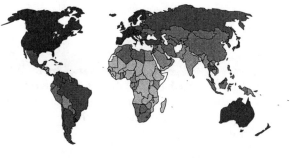

➢ *Data File:*   **GLOBAL**
  ➢ *Task:*   **Mapping**
➢ *Variable 1:*   **52) GENDER EQ**
  ➢ *View:*   **Map**

GENDER EQ -- 1995: GENDER-RELATED DEVELOPMENT INDEX (GDI) (HDR, 1998)

We have a measure of gender equality on 162 countries out of a possible 174 countries. This is a good size sample. Remember, if we start the analysis with a variable with a great deal of missing data, when we add another variable to the analysis with missing data, the sample can be greatly reduced, as I explained in Chapter 6.

Before we move forward, view the countries by rank order of their scores on the *Gender-related development index*. This will show you what countries have high scores and what countries have low scores. How about Canada? Would you have guessed that Canada would rank first in the world on this index on gender equality? Check the rank of the United States.

7.3   Social Justice and Fairness

Barusch (2002) offers what may seem to be a simple definition of social justice but it has profound implications in society: social justice is "the fair allocation of cost and benefits of group membership." The problems occur when defining "fair allocation" and "group membership." Even so, this definition is based on four historical positions on social justice.

Oligarchy: To each according to his or her status in the group.

Libertarianism: Each person has the right to make his or her own decisions in life. If a person chooses to take a job for less pay because he or she likes being outdoors, or if he or she chooses be poor, no one has the right to force him or her to make a different decision.

Liberalism: "Economic liberty and political equality for all" (Barusch).

Socialism: "From each according to his or her ability to each according to his or her need" (Barusch).

Deontologists (people who study the theory of moral obligations and ethics) attempt to deal with the ethical dilemmas that arise in the provision of social justice and when trying to determine fairness, by first identifying the ethical principles that are relevant to the ethical dilemma. "Then, they decide on balance, which choices or actions best satisfy the ethical principles involved." "When ethical principles conflict—that is, point to different choices—seek a compromise solution that satisfies each to some degree" (Jansson, 1999).

At this point, in a typical examination of a complex issue such as gender equality, we will select a theoretical concept to organize our thinking and to guide us in selecting variables. The best theory available to study the global plight of women is more of a perspective on theory than a formal theory, but it is especially applicable in this examination. I will use the *feminist perspective* on theory to organize and select the variables we will analyze. At the same time, the protocol will restrict variables to those that are prevalent, severe, and relevant to the global struggle of women going on around the world today.

Our overarching hypothesis is that there are characteristics found among nations of the world that are predictive of gender equality. Remember this is a hypothesis. In fact, there is no reason for such characteristics to exist if gender equality exists in all the nations of the world.

The world map analysis gives us information on individual nations; it shows that gender equality varies a great deal from country to country and that there are data on this condition for almost all the nations of the world. This will be a good primary variable with which to conduct our study.

The map also shows us that gender equality varies by region of the world. This suggests that we will need to use a *multivariate analysis* procedure to find what characteristics separate the regions of the world on gender equality. We will know a lot if we can explain a few differences from country to country, but we will know a great deal more when we identify a few characteristics that are so powerful that they influence social behavior in an entire region of the world.

The areas of ***education, fertility,*** and ***work*** are issues that have a great impact on the lives of women around the world. These broad dimensions can be broken down into groups of questions or measures on which we have data. To start, most of us would agree that without education equality, there will never be lasting gender equality. Let's survey the world in terms of the average number of years females spend in school compared to their male counterparts.

Research Hypothesis/Question   7.2:
In what countries do women have the same average years of schooling as men?

      Data File: **GLOBAL**
          Task: **Mapping**
➤ *Variable 1:*   **51) M/F EDUC.**
     ➤ *View:*   **Map**

M/F EDUC. -- AVERAGE FEMALE YEARS OF SCHOOLING AS A PERCENTAGE OF AVERAGE MALE YEARS (CALCULATED)

On this measure, we have information from 147 countries; this is less than the 162 on the measure of gender equality. In spite of the smaller sample size, it still represents 85% of the total sample of 174 nations. This is still a large *n* (*n* = the number of cases or countries in the study). Nonetheless, we will need to keep an eye on the *n* in each bivariate and multivariate analysis we use, to guard against having too much missing data in our statistical analysis.

The map shows the average number of years females spend in school compared to males in most countries with the exception of countries in what was once the Soviet Union. As I mentioned earlier, these countries are still trying to recover from the economic shift to a market economy. As a result, many of the social indicators in these countries are sadly as low or lower than in many Third World countries. This map clearly shows that the Americas, Europe, and Australia provide the most equal educational opportunity for its male and female citizens.

                                        Exploring Global Social Welfare

It also shows that countries in Africa and Asia provide fewer educational opportunities for females. These regions of the world are also known for their male-dominated societies.

The next step is to see if the two conditions are correlated. My guess from previous study is that these two conditions will be highly correlated. What is your guess?

Research Hypothesis/Question   7.3:
Countries where gender equality is high will be countries where men and women have equal educations.

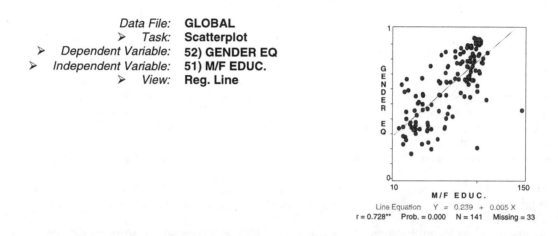

Data File:	**GLOBAL**
➤ *Task:*	**Scatterplot**
➤ *Dependent Variable:*	**52) GENDER EQ**
➤ *Independent Variable:*	**51) M/F EDUC.**
➤ *View:*	**Reg. Line**

Line Equation   Y = 0.239 + 0.005 X
r = 0.728**   Prob. = 0.000   N = 141   Missing = 33

This is a strong correlation (*r* = .728, *p* < .000) and shows the essential role that education plays in equal rights for women. This suggests, as well, that the steady yearly increase in the number of women going to college will continue to increase the level of gender equality in their home country and around the world.

This is a good bivariate correlation to show you how an *outlier* can affect a correlation. The same applies to multivariate analyses. While viewing the scatterplot, select the Outlier option in the Find box on the left side of the screen. This represents the country of Lesotho. By dropping this country from the analysis, the correction will go from *r* = .728 to *r* = .764. Now select the next outlier in the same way. The next outlier is Burkina Faso. With these two outliers dropped from the analysis, the correlation increased 6.5% (from *r* = .728 to *r* = .793) in the degree of correlation. This change occurred because the scatter of the nations that remain in the analysis now forms a tighter scatter than they did with the other two countries in the analysis, thus a higher correlation. A more in-depth discussion of *outliers* and their effect on bivariate and multivariate analyses is presented in Chapter 2.

7.4   Breast-Feeding Inequity
A National Family Health Survey in India found that girls were breast-fed for shorter periods of time than boys. Girls are less likely to be vaccinated or to receive treatment for diseases such as diarrhea, fever, and acute respiratory infections. Child mortality in the 0 to 4 age group is 43% higher for females (at 42 per 1,000) than for males (29 per 1,000) (Sen, 1994).

Another situation or national policy that women need in place to be able to obtain equal rights with men is the right to control their reproductive lives.

Research Hypothesis/Question   7.4:
There will be a strong association between countries where fertility is high and countries where gender equality is low.

Data File: **GLOBAL**
Task: **Scatterplot**
Dependent Variable: **52) GENDER EQ**
➤ Independent Variable: **10) FERTILITY**
➤ View: **Reg. Line**

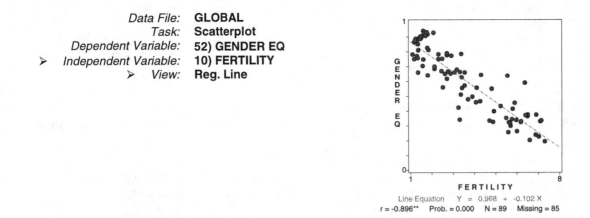

Line Equation   Y = 0.968 + -0.102 X
r = -0.896**   Prob. = 0.000   N = 89   Missing = 85

This is a very compelling scatterplot. It makes a strong case for people in countries who want to improve gender equality in their country ($r = .896$, $p < .000$). Giving women control of their reproductive lives enables them to obtain the education available to them, and to eventually obtain equal rights with men. Or is this Western thinking and not applicable to regions like Asia or Africa? This is a good reason to do a multivariate study comparing regions of the world on the variables that we find are significantly related to gender equality.

You will also note that the *cases* (which are countries in this analysis) are grouped close to the regression line. This strong inverse relationship is what a correlation between two highly correlated variables should look like.

To continue our investigation of global gender equality, let's look at where women work in different countries around the world. I will look at the percentage of women working in the parliaments of different countries. I will also examine the percentage of women at the government ministerial level of each country. Lastly, I will see how the percentage of women to men in the workforce affects gender equality. We can use a simple correlation to look at all of these variables at once because they are all ratio-level measures. They are represented as percentages, and percentages are ratio-level mathematical expressions.

Research Hypothesis/Question   7.5:
When we find a greater percentage of women in the national legislature, a greater percentage of women working at the top level of government, and a greater percentage of women in the workforce, the country will have a higher level of gender equality than a country where smaller percentages of women are found in these work positions.

Data File: **GLOBAL**
➤ Task: **Correlation**
➤ Variables: **52) GENDER EQ**
48) %FEM.LEGIS
49 %FEM.HEADS
50) %WKR WOMEN
➤ Deletion: **Pairwise**
➤ Test: **2-tailed**

Correlation Coefficients Table

	GENDER EQ	%FEM. LEGIS	%FEM. HEADS	%WKR WOMEN
GENDER EQ	1.000 (162)	0.452 ** (102)	0.265 ** (157)	-0.067 (161)
%FEM. LEGIS	0.452 ** (102)	1.000 (102)	0.701 ** (101)	0.350 ** (102)
%FEM. HEADS	0.265 ** (157)	0.701 ** (101)	1.000 (161)	0.256 ** (157)
%WKR WOMEN	-0.067 (161)	0.350 ** (102)	0.256 ** (157)	1.000 (161)

Pairwise deletion (2-tailed t-test)   Significance Levels: ** =.01, * =.05

Of the three, the percentage of women in a country's legislature is more important than the other two by a magnitude of approximately two. In this case, we can eliminate the percentage of women in the workforce as a variable that will help explain gender equality. It was not significantly correlated with gender equality. I will also drop the variable that measures the percentage of women working at the top levels of government in a country. This variable has a smaller correlation with gender equality than the other variables and is highly correlated with the percentage of women legislators. In fact, it is more correlated to the number of women in the legislature ($r = .70$, $p < .01$) than it is to a country's level of gender equality ($r = .265$, $p < .01$). This suggests that in some countries, there are large numbers of women working at the top levels of government but gender equality is still low. Given this circumstance and the fact that there will be very unique information contributed by this variable that the measure on the *percentage of women legislators* will not pick up, I will also drop this measure from the final analysis.

Now let's move to the dimension of crime and violence against women around the world. Using the GLOBAL data file, we can look at crime and the difference in crime between countries where there are differences in gender equality. Crime, particularly violence against women, has been used and is still being used to suppress women and to maintain gender *inequality*. In court, when a defense attorney is allowed to attack a woman who was raped as if she were the guilty party, it puts a chill on women's efforts to see that rapist and batterers are brought to justice. Thus, this results in more violence or the continuation of violence at the current levels. Males will not as easily give up the strategy of using violence to suppress women without the threat of some type of castigation if they use violence.

I will do another correlation using three variables that measure *rape, murder,* and *assault*. I believe the rape variable will be highly and inversely correlated with countries where gender equality is high. This does not have to be the case. Although the rate of teenage pregnancy is low, the number of rapes of teenagers by teenagers has increased in Germany and other European countries (Cherry al et., 2001). During the 1990s, the number of teenagers charged with serious sex crimes rose in some countries across Europe by over 100%. Part of this increase was the result of teenage girls being more willing to report sex offenses. According to some researchers, another cause for this increase in teenage rape is that when German, and most Western European teens meet, they are very assertive in declaring their sexual motives. This leaves little room for flirting. If flirting is involved, a casual meeting can take on a "vulgar and sometimes violent tone" (Daruvalla et al., 1999).

Research Hypothesis/Question   7.6:
In countries where there are higher numbers of rapes per person, there will also be higher numbers of murders and assaults per person, and lower levels of gender equality.

Data File: **GLOBAL**
Task: **Correlation**
➤ *Variables:* **52) GENDER EQ**
68) ASSUALT
69) MURDER
70) RAPE
➤ *Deletion:* **Pairwise**
Test: **2-tailed**

Correlation Coefficients Table

	GENDER EQ	ASSAULT 90	MURDER 90	RAPE 90
GENDER EQ	1.000 (162)	0.167 (50)	-0.147 (52)	0.181 (54)
ASSAULT 90	0.167 (50)	1.000 (51)	0.486 ** (47)	0.667 ** (49)
MURDER 90	-0.147 (52)	0.486 ** (47)	1.000 (53)	0.505 ** (51)
RAPE 90	0.181 (54)	0.667 ** (49)	0.505 ** (51)	1.000 (55)

Pairwise deletion (2-tailed t-test)   Significance Levels: ** =.01, * =.05

Well, I believe this makes a compelling augment for why crime, particularly violent crime, is a pervasive force for suppressing women. It has been in the past and it continues to be used at many different levels. In fact, however, these three forms of crime and violence do not increase or reduce gender equality in countries on the global level. They are not correlated to gender equality. The most important thing to notice about this analysis is that the *n* (the number of countries on which we have data) is very small considering that we have gender equality information on 162 nations. This indicates there are a number of countries that we do not have data on, in terms of the other three remaining variables.

Now, we will use the multiple regression procedure. We can use the multiple regression procedure because the measures in this analysis are all ratio level.

Research Hypothesis/Question 7.7:
Fertility, the percentage of women in a country's legislature, and the ratio of men's educational level to women's will explain a significant amount of the variance among nations who report gender equality.

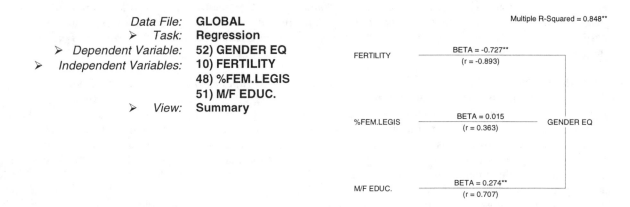

Data File: **GLOBAL**
➤ Task: **Regression**
➤ Dependent Variable: **52) GENDER EQ**
➤ Independent Variables: **10) FERTILITY**
48) %FEM.LEGIS
51) M/F EDUC.
➤ View: **Summary**

Multiple R-Squared = 0.848**

FERTILITY — BETA = -0.727** (r = -0.893)

%FEM.LEGIS — BETA = 0.015 (r = 0.363) — GENDER EQ

M/F EDUC. — BETA = 0.274** (r = 0.707)

Worldwide, these three variables are extremely important. As a set, they explain 85% (R^2 = .848, $p < .000$) of the difference in countries with high levels of gender equality and in countries with low levels of gender equality. Of the three, the most important is fertility. It contributes about three times (Beta = -.727) of the explanation of the variance in gender equality from country to country than does the ratio of male to female education (Beta = .274). Notice here that fertility is inversely correlated to gender equality—the higher the fertility in a country, the greater the degree of gender *inequality* in that country. This suggests that in most countries gender equality increases when the fertility among the women of that country drops.

This is strong evidence that the more control women have over their reproductive lives, and the greater the equality of educational opportunity for both male and females, the greater the gender equality will be in that country.

Given this finding, however, I must reiterate that even though these three variables are important on the world stage, they will be different for different regions of the world (Cherry et al., 2001). Let's start by seeing how these three variables describe Europe.

Research Hypothesis/Question 7.8:
Fertility, the percentage of women in a country's legislature, and the ratio of men's educational level to women's will explain a significant amount of the variance among the nations of Europe who report gender equality.

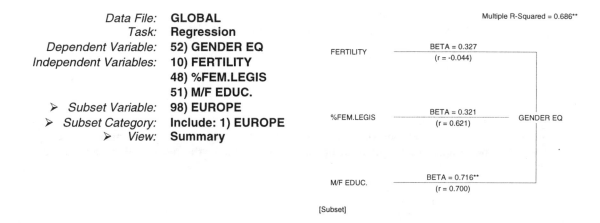

Data File: **GLOBAL**
Task: **Regression**
Dependent Variable: **52) GENDER EQ**
Independent Variables: **10) FERTILITY**
48) %FEM.LEGIS
51) M/F EDUC.
➢ Subset Variable: **98) EUROPE**
➢ Subset Category: **Include: 1) EUROPE**
➢ View: **Summary**

Multiple R-Squared = 0.686**

FERTILITY — BETA = 0.327 (r = -0.044)

%FEM.LEGIS — BETA = 0.321 (r = 0.621) — GENDER EQ

M/F EDUC. — BETA = 0.716** (r = 0.700)

[Subset]

The most important variable in Europe is the education of females. It has twice the impact (Beta = .716) on gender equality than *fertility* (Beta = .321) and *Female Legislators* (Beta = .327). The most interesting finding here is that gender equality is tied to a slightly increased fertility among women in European countries. This finding is consistent with other reports.

7.5   European Fertility Rates

Although the replacement rate for a nation's people is 2.1 children per woman, in Europe the fertility rate has dropped to 1.42 children per woman. Spain has the lowest birth rate in the world, 1.15 children per woman. At this rate Europe will lose 100 million people by the year 2050 (NCPA, 2001).

Europe is different from the rest of the world in terms of the role played by fertility rates. All together, these three variables account for better than two-thirds of the difference in gender equality in the 38 nations of Europe. These three variables do not account for as much of the differences between the countries of Europe as they do for the entire world, but they are still very important for explaining the variation in gender equality among the nations of Europe (R^2 = .686, p < .000). Now we will use the same three variables to see their importance among the countries of Asia.

Research Hypothesis/Question   7.9:
Fertility, the percentage of women in a country's legislature, and the ratio of men's educational level to women's will explain a significant amount of the variance among the nations of Asia who report gender equality.

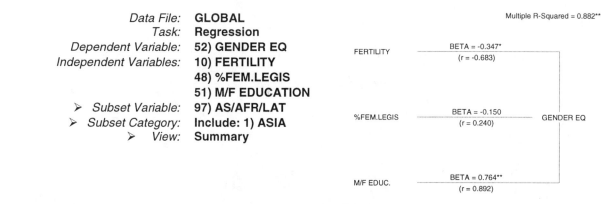

Data File: **GLOBAL**
Task: **Regression**
Dependent Variable: **52) GENDER EQ**
Independent Variables: **10) FERTILITY**
48) %FEM.LEGIS
51) M/F EDUCATION
➢ Subset Variable: **97) AS/AFR/LAT**
➢ Subset Category: **Include: 1) ASIA**
➢ View: **Summary**

Multiple R-Squared = 0.882**

FERTILITY — BETA = -0.347* (r = -0.683)

%FEM.LEGIS — BETA = -0.150 (r = 0.240) — GENDER EQ

M/F EDUC. — BETA = 0.764** (r = 0.892)

[Subset]

Among these three variables, in Asia, the two important ones are *female education* (Beta = .764) and *fertility* (Beta = -.347). Again, notice that fertility is inversely related to gender equality in Asia. Altogether, the three variables account for more three-quarters of the variation (R^2 = .882, p < .000). In this case, *female education* has over twice the magnitude of impact of *fertility* and five times the influence of the *number of female legislators*. It could be that there are too few women legislators to have a great impact.

Research Hypothesis/Question   7.10:
Fertility, the percentage of women in a country's legislature, and the ratio of men's educational level to women's will explain a significant amount of the variance among the nations of Africa who report gender equality.

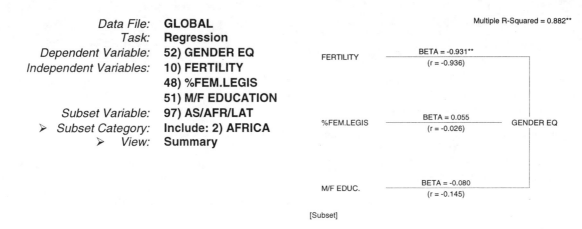

In Africa, of the three conditions or variables, the most important one is *fertility* (Beta = -.93, p < .000). The other two variables do not contribute very much to our understanding of gender equality. This Beta tends to suggest that the first major step to increasing gender equality in Africa is for women to gain more control over their reproductive lives.

Research Hypothesis/Question   7.11:
Fertility, percentage of women in a country's legislature, and the ratio of men's educational level to women's educational level will explain a significant amount of the variance among the nations of Latin America who report gender equality.

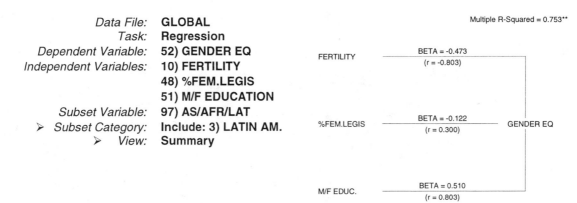

In Latin America, like Africa, the major characteristic that distinguishes nations with high and low levels of gender equality is the level of fertility (R^2 = .753, p < .000). You will notice that the R Square for Latin America is smaller in magnitude than the R Square for Africa. This means that *fertility* is very important to gender equality in Latin America, but it is 20% more important for explaining gender equality on the continent of Africa. The more women are able to control their reproductive life in Latin America, the greater the gender equality in their country.

Any number of variables might help explain gender equality in different countries around the world, but the three we have used here are quite powerful. They also help explain some of the most salient features of gender equality. In countries where poverty, illiteracy, and birth control are not promoted and/or are not available, the most important first step is to help women gain control of their reproductive lives by educating women about birth control, both medical and natural methods.

7.6   A Woman Giving Birth as a Teenager Has Double the Number of Children

In the developing countries of Africa, Asia, and Central and South America, women who have their first child before they are 18 years old have an average of seven children throughout their lives, double the number for women who have their first child after they are 25 years old. In most of the world, the majority of young women become sexually active during their teenage years (Cherry et al., 2000).

These findings suggest that women in different countries around the world (with the exception of women in Europe) must keep their fertility rates low to be able to take advantage of educational opportunities and to develop a cadre of women legislators in their respective countries. In Europe, on the other hand, the fertility rate is so low that to increase the gender equality in their respective countries, women must slightly increase their fertility rate. This will increase their value and give more weight to their demands for equality. At this point, let's turn our attention to women and issues important to gender equality in the United States.

Gender Equality in the United States

One of the overriding issues for women in the United States is the *feminization of poverty*. Jansson (1999) points out that "So many women have become mired in poverty when they must raise children single-handed that terms such as *feminization of poverty* have evolved." The economic poverty that women experience is a result of being paid less than a man for the same work and having fewer opportunities to acquire jobs usually occupied by men that pay higher salaries. For example, Kirst-Ashman and Hull (2001) report that nearly 59% of all women worked outside the home (including those with young children), but women working full-time earned 74.6% of what men earned working full-time.

One reason for this disparity, often given, is that women and men tend to be clustered in different kinds of occupations. This is true; however, even within the same occupation, women tend to earn less. To learn more about women and poverty we can use two variables in the STATES data file. The variable %FEMALE96 measures the percentage of women to men in a given state. The variable POV.LINE measures the percentage of people in each state who are living below the poverty line as determined by the United States Commerce Department. My thinking is that, if as a group, women tend to be paid less and tend to be the single head of their family, they will probably be living in poverty. It follows that states with a large percentage of women will be states that have more people living below the poverty line. Let's see if the hypothesis is supported by the data.

Research Hypothesis/Question   7.12:
States with a large percentage of women will be states that have a larger percentage of people living below the poverty line.

> Data File: **STATES**
>> Task: **Mapping**
> Variable 1: **27) %FEMALE96**
> Variable 2: **78) POV. LINE**
>> View: **Map**

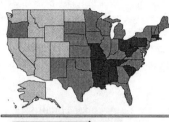

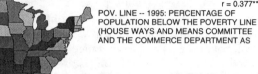

%FEMALE96 -- Collapsed from
%FEMALE 96: 1996: PERCENT OF
POPULATION WHO ARE FEMALE (U.S.
BUREAU OF THE CENSUS, REPORT

r = 0.377**
POV. LINE -- 1995: PERCENTAGE OF
POPULATION BELOW THE POVERTY LINE
(HOUSE WAYS AND MEANS COMMITTEE
AND THE COMMERCE DEPARTMENT AS

It is a weak correlation ($r = .377$, $p < .01$) but statistically significant. This means that states with a higher percentage of females to males have more individuals living below the poverty line than states with more males. I would also expect more people to be on welfare in states with a greater percentage of women.

It is crucial to incorporate gender into efforts to understand racism and intolerance of others. Including gender discrimination in our assessment of bigotry (and all form of oppression) will make intolerance more visible and more responsible for the disadvantages experienced by so many around the world.

Research Hypothesis/Question   7.13:
States with a large percentage of women are states that derive a larger percentage of state revenues from welfare grants.

Data File: **STATES**
Task: **Mapping**
Variable 1: **27) %FEMALE96**
> Variable 2: **77) WELFARE**
> View: **Map**

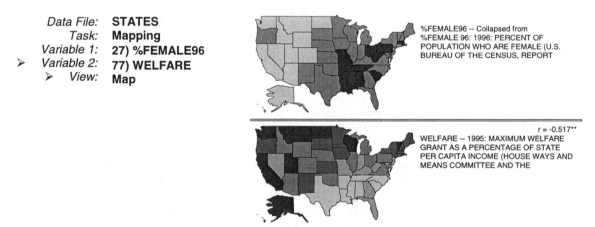

%FEMALE96 -- Collapsed from
%FEMALE 96: 1996: PERCENT OF
POPULATION WHO ARE FEMALE (U.S.
BUREAU OF THE CENSUS, REPORT

r = -0.517**
WELFARE -- 1995: MAXIMUM WELFARE
GRANT AS A PERCENTAGE OF STATE
PER CAPITA INCOME (HOUSE WAYS AND
MEANS COMMITTEE AND THE

This is a higher correlation ($r = -.517$, $p < .01$) than the variable that measured people living below the poverty line. Moreover, it is an inverse correlation. To determine what this correlation means, I will go back to the question to determine in which direction the variable WELFARE measures the percentage of a state's per capita income. In fact, the darker the state, the higher the percentage of the state's per capita incomes comes from welfare.

Exploring Global Social Welfare

My error in logic is apparent. I expected that the more women in a state, which indicates more people living in poverty, would also result in more state revenue coming from welfare grants. As you can see, however, states with a larger percentage of women are states that receive less revenue from welfare grants. In other words, the higher the percentage of women in a state, the smaller welfare grants in that state.

7.7   Education's Role as a Contraceptive

Nearly 1 billion of the 6 billon people on earth cannot read nor write. More than half of those denied an education are girls. The rates of illiteracy are high in growth countries such as India, Bangladesh, and Pakistan. In Brazil, women with less than a secondary education have an average of 6.5 children. Women of Brazil with a secondary education have an average of 2.5 children (NCPA, 2001). If developing countries wish to reduce the fertility rate, one intervention would be to educate the girls.

Research Hypothesis/Question   7.14:
The higher the percentage of women to men in a state, the more households in that state will receive food stamps.

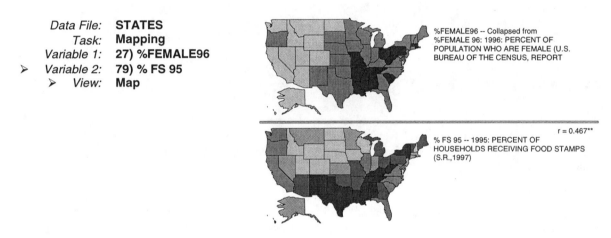

Data File: **STATES**
Task: **Mapping**
Variable 1:   **27) %FEMALE96**
➢   Variable 2:   **79) % FS 95**
➢   View: **Map**

%FEMALE96 -- Collapsed from %FEMALE 96: 1996: PERCENT OF POPULATION WHO ARE FEMALE (U.S. BUREAU OF THE CENSUS, REPORT

r = 0.467**

% FS 95 -- 1995: PERCENT OF HOUSEHOLDS RECEIVING FOOD STAMPS (S.R.,1997)

This is another important variable for explaining the difference in gender equality in the United States. States with a greater percentage of women to men tend to be states that have greater numbers of households receiving food stamps ($r = .467, p < .01$). These states may give small welfare grants, but at least food is not withheld from these needy families. Of course, the food stamp program is a federal program, while state welfare grants are made up of federal grants that require a state match. For poor states, it is often difficult for them to come up with the entire match needed; as a result, their welfare payments are typically smaller than other states.

Are states distinguishable on these variables? A multiple regression will tell us the answer. Using the percentage of females to males in a state as the dependent variable, the per capita of state income from welfare grants, the percentage of those living below the poverty level, and those who receive food stamps will account for a significant amount of difference among states.

Research Hypothesis/Question   7.15:
States with lower per capita state income from welfare, with higher percentages living below the poverty line, and with high percentages of households receiving food stamps will be those states with a greater percentage of women to men.

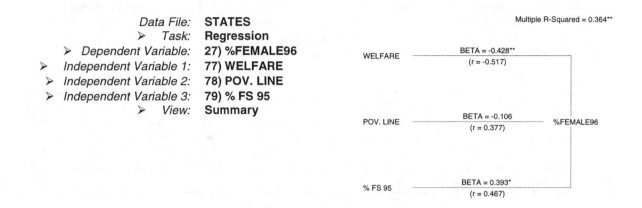

Data File: **STATES**
➢ Task: **Regression**
➢ Dependent Variable: **27) %FEMALE96**
➢ Independent Variable 1: **77) WELFARE**
➢ Independent Variable 2: **78) POV. LINE**
➢ Independent Variable 3: **79) % FS 95**
➢ View: **Summary**

Multiple R-Squared = 0.364**

WELFARE — BETA = -0.428** (r = -0.517)

POV. LINE — BETA = -0.106 (r = 0.377) — %FEMALE96

% FS 95 — BETA = 0.393* (r = 0.467)

I have not explained a great deal of variance between states $(R^2 = .384, p < .01)$, based on these poverty indicators or variables, but it is pretty amazing that I can explain any of the differences between males and females on poverty indicators. It is also interesting that the most distinguishing features of this inequality are states with low welfare payments that have the highest percentage of food stamp recipients. These findings support what others have found, and they clearly suggest that gender equality is still a goal that has not yet become a reality in the United States.

WOMEN AND WORK

The *principle of comparable worth* is another issue of major importance to women around the world, but especially important in First World countries, where the types of work people do is vast and seems to defy definition. *Comparable worth* is often defined as "equal pay for males and females doing work requiring comparable skills, effort, and responsibility under similar work conditions" (Bellak, 1984). Comparable worth helps deal with the old argument of comparing *apples to oranges*. It helps us compare jobs that are not identical, but are similar. Take, for example, a deliveryperson and an administrative assistant working for the same company. Both jobs take about equal levels of skill and training; however, the delivery job is traditionally a male job and the administrative assistant job, of course, is traditionally a female job.

Given this information, which of the two do you hypothesize is traditionally paid less (Zastrow and Kirst-Ashman, 2001)? The concept of *comparable worth* helps balance the playing field for women and men alike. Zastrow and Kirst-Ashman (2001) offer these examples from estimates put out by the Unites States Bureau of the Census in 1998. In the United States, female computer programmers earned 80% of the average male computer programmer. Female cooks earned 76% of what male cooks earned. A female bookkeeper earned 73% of that earned by her male counterpart. Even female office managers were only paid 61% of what male office managers were paid. And, female salespersons earned only 58% of what male salespersons earned (Zastrow and Kirst-Ashman, 2001). These are not my personal opinions but statistical findings that in a court of law can be used as *prima facie* evidence.

To begin our examination of the issues around *comparable worth*, let us look at those people who are working full-time, part time, and who are unemployed. In this analysis, we will be using the GSS data file. The responses to these questions are from real people who were employed either full-time or, part-time, or were unemployed at the time that they were interviewed by a GSS researcher. In this sample of people, we are excluding people who were retired, keeping house, and going to school. I dropped these groups because they are not predominantly made up of people who must work for a living for themselves and a family. First, I did a univariate analysis to check the number of people who answered both questions. Then, because both variables had a decent sample size, the next step is to check the distribution of the measure.

Exploring Global Social Welfare

Research Hypothesis/Question   7.16:
There is a significant difference between males and females who are working full-time, part-time, and who are unemployed.

> *Data File:* **GSS**
> *Task:* **Cross-tabulation**
> *Row Variable:* **12) SEX**
> *Column Variable:* **3) WORKING?2**
> *Graph:* **Bar Stack**

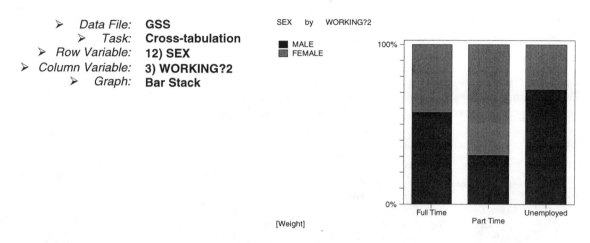

This is a good example of why we need to check the distribution of values on the variables we intend to use in an analysis. The data from a variable need to be normally distributed. The variable WORKING2 cannot be assumed to be normally distributed. As is observable from the stack bar graph above, the data on this variable, WORKING2, do not fit the model of the normal curve. This means that we will need to use nonparametric statistics to analyze the differences in work between men and women. Nonparametric statistical analytical procedures like cross-tabulation do not use linear math to calculate coefficients and level of probability.

7.8   Women in Politics

As of September, 1, 2001, 61 of the 435 representatives in the U.S. House of Representatives and 13 of the 100 U.S. senators were women. Among the governors of the states, only 3 of 50 were women (Longley, 2001). The average for both the Senate and House is about 14%. This disparity is also present in professions that are thought of as female-dominated; often men hold the leadership positions.

Research Hypothesis/Question   7.17:
Family income reported by men and women will be significantly different, with women reporting less family income.

> *Data File:* **GSS**
> *Task:* **t Test**
> *Dependent Variable* **17) FAM INCOM2**
> *Independent Variable* **12) SEX**
> *View:* **Graph**

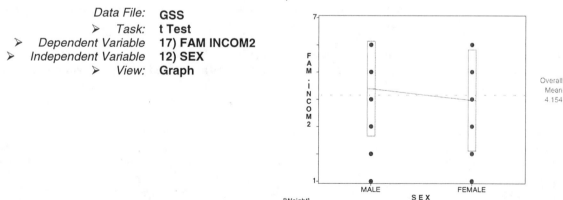

Based on the t-Test there is a major difference between what the 12,650 men who answered this question earned as compared to what the 10,896 women who answered this question earned ($t = 21.283$, $p < .000$). If we select those people, however, who were interviewed for the GSS survey and who were divorced, separated, or widowed (men and women) with children, we will be able to see if being a single mother is more or less difficult than being a single dad. Family income is an important variable in our society. You also would agree, I am sure, that women who are divorced, separated, or widowed tend to have less family income than their male counterparts.

Research Hypothesis/Question   7.18:
Family income of divorced, separated, and widowed men and women with children will be significantly higher for divorced, separated, and widowed men with children.

			<9,999	10K–19,999	20K & UP	Missing	TOTAL
Data File:	**GSS**	MALE	520	451	877	223	1847
➤ *Task:*	**Cross-tabulation**		28.1%	24.4%	47.5%		100.0%
➤ *Row Variable:*	**12) SEX**	FEMALE	2341	1271	1285	831	4897
➤ *Column Variable:*	**17) FAM.INCOM2**		47.8%	26%	26.2%		100.0%
➤ *Subset Variable:*	**6) # CHILDREN**	TOTAL	2861	1722	2161	1055	6744
➤ *Subset Categories:*	**Exclude 0) NONE**		42.4%	25.5%	32%		

Additional settings listed:
Subset Variable: **5) MARITAL**
Subset Categories: **Include: 1) WIDOWED, 2) DIVORCED, 3) SEPARATED**
➤ *View:* **Tables**
➤ *Display* **Row %**

> **To temporarily collapse the columns as shown in the table above, first click on the headings for columns < 4,999 and 5,000–9,999. The columns will turn blue. Then click the [Collapse] button. Enter < 9,999 as the New Category Label. Do the same for the columns 10K–14,999 and 15K–19,999, renaming this new category 10K–19,999, and finally collapse 20K–24,999 and 25K & UP and rename this 20K & UP.**

The difference here is observable and it is a statistically significantly different ($\chi^2 = 312.132$, df = 2; $p < .000$). This analysis suggests that women as a group have a higher percentage of jobs that pay under $10,000 a year (women = 48%, men = 28%). Women also hold fewer jobs that pay over $20,000 a year (women = 26%, men = 47.5%). This is an inverse relationship. As the number of men who earn high wages increases, in this data the numbers of women who earn high wages go down. The color of gender inequality in this case is the color of money.

We found that education was important to gender equality in Europe. Shall we see if it is also important to the plight of women in the United States?

To access the influence of education on women's income in the United States, we will first look at men and women without a high school education. Using the same variables as we used above, we will produce a table for women and men without a high school education.

Research Hypothesis/Question   7.19:
A lack of a high school education will put more women who are divorced, separated, and widowed with children in the lower income group than men who are divorced, separated, and widowed with children.

		<9,999	10K-19,999	20K & UP	Missing	TOTAL
MALE		336	155	123	99	614
		54.7%	25.3%	20%		100.0%
FEMALE		1318	309	131	393	1758
		75%	17.6%	7.5%		100.0%
TOTAL		1653	464	254	492	2372
		69.7%	19.6%	10.7%		

Data File: **GSS**
Task: **Cross-tabulation**
Row Variable: **12) SEX**
Column Variable: **17) FAM.INCOM2**
➤ Control Variable: **11) DEGREE**
➤ Subset Categories: **6) # CHILDREN**
➤ Subset Variable: **Exclude 0) NONE**
➤ Subset Categories: **5) MARITAL Include 1) WIDOWED, 2) DIVORCED, 3) SEPARATED**
➤ View: **Tables (NOT H.S.)**
➤ Display: **Row %**

The control variable can be selected from the same screen as the other variables. When a control variable is selected, an individual table is created for each category of the control variable. You will again need to collapse the FAM.INCOM2 categories as explained in the previous example.

In this cross-tabulation analysis, women without a high school degree are certainly at a disadvantage compared to their male counterparts. In this analysis, 75% of women without a high school degree earned under $10,000 a year compared to 54.7% of men without a high school degree.

Now, while viewing the above table in MicroCase, click the *control* arrow to move through the control categories to control group number 5 (GRAD. EDUC.). This will give you a sample of men and women who have graduate degrees to test the following hypothesis.

Research Hypothesis/Question   7.20:
A graduate degree will help level the playing field between men and women, with children, who are divorced, separated, and widowed, in that women will have incomes that are more equal to men with children who are divorced, separated, and widowed.

Data File: **GSS**
Task: **Cross-tabulation**
Row Variable: **12) SEX**
Column Variable: **17) FAM.INCOM2**
Control Variable: **11) DEGREE**
Subset Categories: **6) # CHILDREN**
Subset Variable: **Exclude 0) NONE**
Subset Categories: **5) MARITAL Include 1) WIDOWED, 2) DIVORCED, 3) SEPARATED**
➤ View: **Tables (GRAD. DEG.)**
➤ Display: **Row %**

		<9,999	10K-19,999	20K & UP	Missing	TOTAL
MALE		16	10	81	7	107
		15.0%	9.3%	75.7%		100.0%
FEMALE		8	31	116	14	155
		5.2%	20.0%	74.8%		100.0%
TOTAL		24	41	197	21	262
		9.2%	15.6%	75.2%		

The disparity in the percentage of women working at high-end jobs as compared to men who work at top-paying jobs does not become equal until women reach the graduate level of education. At this level of education, although the numbers of our sample are small, the number of men and women who earn over $20,000 a year is about equal (women = 74.9%, men = 76.2%). We have now tested five variables that seem to be important in explaining the difference between men and women in the United States. To see which of these are the most important, we can use the logistic regression approach. It is designed to allow us to use a nominal variable such as *sex* as a dependent variables.

Research Hypothesis/Question   7.21:
The number of children, the educational level, family income, and employment will be significantly different for women than it is for men.

		Beta Coef.	Std. Err.	Prob.	Odds Ratio
	CONSTANT	1.536	0.144	0.000	
	# CHILDREN	0.085	0.020	0.000	1.025
	DEGREE	0.110	0.031	0.000	1.054
	FAM.INCOM2	-0.238	0.021	0.000	0.933
	WORKING?2	-0.248	0.062	0.000	1.273

Data File: **GSS**
➢   Task: **Logistic Regression**
➢   Dependent Variable: **12) SEX**
➢   Independent Variables: **6) #CHILDREN**
                11) DEGREE
                17) FAM.INCOM2
                3) WORKING?2
➢   View: **Regression**

This last analysis adds a great deal of support to the claim of women that they are discriminated against in many areas of life in the United States. Given this finding, in the real world, I expect that women as a group will be caring for more children than men as a group (odds ratio = 1.025, $p < .000$). Women as a group will be better educated than men (odds ratio = 1.054, $p < .000$). Women will have less family income (odds ratio = .993, $p < .000$), in part because significantly more women than men work part-time (odds ratio = 1.273, $p < .000$).

The *principle of comparable worth* is a concept that gives us a concrete example of the harm that *gender inequality* has on women in the United States. It goes deeper, however, than income. As President Nelson Mandela said on May 24, 1994, at the opening of South Africa's first democratically elected parliament, "It is vitally important that all the structures of Government, including the President should understand fully that freedom cannot be achieved unless women have been emancipated from all forms of oppression." Gender equality is necessary for the United States to continue to be a leader in the world. Gender equality is necessary for civilization to move to the next philosophical level, that is, equality for all *adults*. The qualifier is adult. Do we grant our children equality? Do we mean equality for our infirm elders? Does our definition include those who struggle with a mental health problem or disability? These are tough questions; they truly present us with an ethical dilemma. Even so, when almost half of the adult population of the world, *women,* are denied equality with adult men, it is a gross violation of the inalienable rights of all humans no matter where they live in this world.

Historical Trend: Marriage, Divorce, Birth Rate, and Working Moms

Much of the data we work with are data from one point in time, such as the percentage of people who married in 1998. With historical data, the percentages of those who marry over many years are organized in a time series so that we can better see the ebb and flow in these percentages over many years. To see changes over time we can use the US TRENDS data file and the Historical Trends analytical procedure found on the Basic Statistics screen.

Research Hypothesis/Question   7.22:
The number of marriages has decreased and the number of divorces has increased during the last 80 years.

> _Data File:_ **US TRENDS**
> _Task:_ **Historical Trends**
> _Variables:_ **3) MAR. RATE**
> **4) DIV RATE**

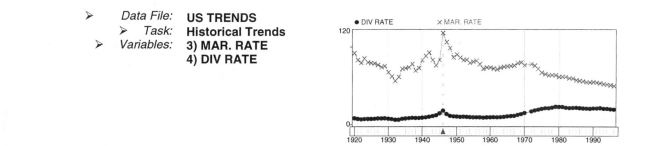

I do not know what one thing has to do with the other, but the peak in marriages in this country occurred the year mainframe computers became important. The peak in marriages in this country occurred in 1946, the year after World War II ended. It was also the beginning of the _baby boom_ generation.

At times, it may seem as if everyone is getting divorced, but the data show that a greater number of people are getting married than are getting divorced, and it has been like this since the 1920s. True, the numbers are different today than they were in the 1920s. Every year since 1950 fewer people have married than they did the year before and each year more people get a divorce than they did the previous year. Now let's see how all four conditions have varied over time.

Research Hypothesis/Question   7.23:
The number of marriages has decreased, the number of divorces has increased, the number of births has decreased, and the number of women with children under 5 who are working has increased during the last 80 years.

Data File: **US TRENDS**
Task: **Historical Trends**
> _Variables:_ **3) MAR. RATE**
4) DIV RATE
5) BIRTH RATE
25) MOM LAB

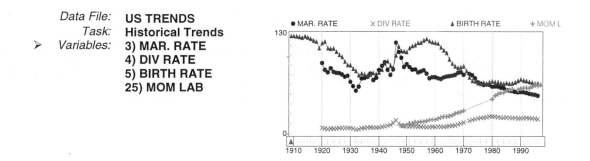

This is a clear and disturbing picture and one that will impact the future of today's children. Although the number of children born since the baby boom generation (1944 through the mid-1960s) has dropped significantly, the number of women with children under 6 who are in the workforce has increased exponentially since 1950.

Is there gender inequity around the world? Based on our analysis, and the preponderance of evidence both qualitative and quantitative from around the world, the answer is a resounding "yes!" Is there gender inequality in the United States? Given this analysis, and the evidence that we are faced with everyday, the answer is a resounding "yes!" Now, what are you going to do about it?

7.9   Women's Suffrage in the United States

The struggle for women's suffrage in the United States was long and difficult. There were many setbacks before the 19th Amendment finally became law in 1920. The fight for the vote began in the early 1800s when women won partial suffrage in Kentucky in 1838. *Partial suffrage* gave certain classes of women the right to vote in some elections but not in others. In some states, women could only vote in municipal or school board elections, and on tax or bond propositions.

- Women won partial suffrage in 19 states between 1838 and 1890.

- Women won partial suffrage in the Utah territory in 1870, but lost the right to vote in the state of Utah in 1887. Then, they won full suffrage in Utah in 1896.

- In 1890, Wyoming was the first state where women won full suffrage.

- In 1893, women won full suffrage in a second state, Colorado.

- Between 1838 and 1890, women won partial suffrage in 19 states.

- Women won partial suffrage in New Jersey in 1887 only to lose it in 1894.

- Before 1910, women had won full suffrage in only four states.

- In 1917, women won partial suffrage in Indiana, but the law was ruled unconstitutional in the same year.

- Between 1910 and 1919, women won full suffrage in 17 more states.

- In eight states, women never won even partial suffrage before the 19th Amendment was ratified. These states were Alabama, Florida, Georgia, Maryland, North Carolina, South Carolina, and Virginia.

- There were 10 states that did not ratify the 19th Amendment.

- Before the 19th Amendment was ratified, women had won full suffrage in 12 states and partial suffrage in 28 states.

This information was compiled from the Library of Congress (www.loc.gov/) and its American Memory Web site at www.memory.loc.gov/.

End Note: Again, this chapter examined an issue that is current and relevant to social policy and research. We demonstrated a straightforward approach to looking at gender inequality. The statistics were sophisticated toward the end as we moved through the development of each model, but the results do have the feel of tapping into reality. This is typically what you experience when working with real data from real people. Using real quantitative data and statistical procedures to analyze the data, you slowly sketch a description of reality.

Other Issues Related to Gender Equality

There are a number of issues related to poverty and the distribution of wealth that I could not examine in this chapter. However, with the data files provided with this book, you can analyze many of these issues on your own. To learn more about other issues related to gender equality poverty, you can enter the following search terms in the InfoTrac College Edition.

Gender discrimination	**Family violence**
Gender identity	**Female offenders**
Violence against women	**Female studies**
Abortion	**Affirmative action**
Gender justice	**Female infanticide**

NAME:

COURSE:

DATE:

Workbook exercises and software are copyrighted. Copying is prohibited by law.

Review Questions

Based on the work you've done so far on the issue of gender equality, see how well you do on this short True or False quiz.

Based on the measure *gender-related development index,* women in North America and Europe enjoy the highest levels of gender equality in the world.　　　　　T　F

Educational opportunities for girls and women are more important in Europe than in Africa in determining the level of gender equality.　　　　　T　F

Fertility rates, because they reflect the degree to which women have control over their reproductive lives, is extremely important on the world stage as an indicator of gender equality.　　　　　T　F

The number of female legislators in each country around the world averages about 40%.　　　　　T　F

In the United States, the percentage of female legislators is approximately 25%.　　　　　T　F

There is a statistically significant correlation between a country's score on the gender development index and the number of females the country will have among its legislators.　　　　　T　F

Although a lot has changed over the last 100 years, one of the most profound changes has been in the number of women with children under the age of 6 who are in the workforce in the United States.　　　　　T　F

MicroCase QUESTIONS

If you want to learn additional information about any of the tasks used in this chapter, use the online help (F1).

Use the following data files, variables, and analytical approaches to answer the MicroCase questions.

1.　　When we mapped out gender equality around the world, we found that gender equality varied by region of the world. Use the following to see if gender equality is correlated with countries identified as Third World countries.

> ➤ *Data File:*　**GLOBAL**
> ➤ *Task:*　**Mapping**
> ➤ *Variable 1:*　**52) GENDER EQ**
> ➤ *Variable 2:*　**25) THIRDWORLD**
> ➤ *View:*　**Summary**

a.   The correlation between gender equality and Third World counties is $r =$ _____, which is a(n) _____ (positive or inverse) correlation?

b.   The correlation between gender equality and Third World countries is larger than the correlation between gender equality and fertility.   True   False

2.   Now, using the same database and the following variables, examine the correlations between these variables and gender equality.

> Data File: **GLOBAL**
> ➤ Task: **Correlation**
> ➤ Variables: **52) GENDER EQ**
>   **25) THIRDWORLD**
>   **49) %FEM.HEADS**
>   **50) %WKR WOMEN**

a. Fill in the blanks for the GENDER EQ row.

	THIRDWORLD	%FEM.HEADS	%WKR WOMEN
GENDER EQ	$r =$ _____ Prob. < _____	$r =$ _____ Prob. < _____	$r =$ _____ Prob. < _____

b.   Which variable correlates the strongest with GENDER EQ?   _____

c.   Which variable does not correlate with GENDER EQ?   _____

3.   Now, using the same database and the same variables, identify the contribution of the independent variables in explaining the difference among countries in terms of gender equality.

> Data File: **GLOBAL**
> ➤ Task: **Regression**
> ➤ Dependent Variable: **52) GENDER EQ**
> ➤ Independent Variables: **25) THIRDWORLD**
>   **49) %FEM.HEADS**
>   **50) %WKR WOMEN**
> ➤ View: **Summary**

a.   How much of the total variance do these three variables account for in terms of gender equality around the world? $R^2 =$ _____

b.   Which variable is the most important independent variable in this set? _____

c.   Of the three independent variables in your analysis, which one is the least important independent variable? _____

d.   What is the direction of the effect of the variable representing Third World countries and their score on gender equality? _____ .

e.   What does the direction tell us about the relationship between gender equality and Third World status? _____

4.   These analyses continue to support the assertion that there is great inequity between men and women around the world. Gender inequality may not be as bad in the United States, but it is still harmful. The following may add to the depth of our understanding of gender inequality in the United States. Use the STATES data file to answer the following questions.

> Data File: **STATES**
> Task: **Correlation**
> Variables: **27) %FEMALE96**
> **60) COKEUSER90**
> **61) BEER 95**
> **62) WINE 95**

a.   Which of the drugs in this analysis is significantly related to higher percentages of women in a state? _____

b.   Describe the relationship between the significant bivariate relationship(s). Your determination of the direction of the relationship: _____ .

c.   What is the correlation between wine consumption and states with higher percentages of women?

$r = $ _____ $p < $ _____

5.   There are several other variables that could be important to our study of gender equality in the United States. Use the following problem-oriented independent variables to see how they are related to states with larger percentages of women.

> Data File: **STATES**
> > Task: **REGRESSION**
> > Dependent Variable: **27) %FEMALE96**
> > Independent Variables: **56) SUICIDE96**
> > **59) RITALIN**
> > **82) FEM UNE 96**

a. As a set of variables, what is the R^2 for these three independent variables?

$R^2 = .$_____ $p < .$_____

b. The variable that measures the rate of suicide has an interesting role in this multivariate analysis. Explain how the variable suicide relates to states with higher percentages of females. _____

_____

6. In this exercise you will need to use the US TRENDS data file. As mentioned before, one way to reduce fertility among women is to increase the chances that their children will live. This seems reasonable in Third World countries, but has it had a similar effect in the United States? Use the variables *BIRTH RATE* and *LIFE EXPECTANCY* to see if, over time, birth rate changes as life expectancy changes.

> > Data File: **US TRENDS**
> > Task: **Historical Trends**
> > Variables: **5) BIRTH RATE**
> > **6) LIFE EXP**

a. What happened to life expectancy in the United States during the last hundred years?

_____

b. Describe the change in birth rate and its relationship with the life expectancy variable.

_____

I would like to leave you with this observation. Women in Kuwait do not have the right to vote or the right to run for public office. In the United Arab Emirates, where the members of Parliament are appointed, neither men nor women have the right to vote.

Variable Lists Related to Gender Equality

The following is a partial list of the variables in your data files. To see a list of all of the variables, the question the variable asks, and the range of values, press [F3] to open the variable list window from anywhere in the software. Try using some of the variables below with the variables you have already tested.

GLOBAL

47) FEM.PROF.
WOMEN PER 100 MEN IN PROFESSIONAL AND TECHNICAL OCCUPATIONS (TWW, 1995)

53) FEM POWER
GENDER EMPOWERMENT MEASURE (GEM) (HDR, 1998)

54) SEX MUTIL
PERCENT OF WOMEN WHO HAVE BEEN SEXUALLY MUTILATED (ALL EXTERNAL SEXUAL ORGANS CUT AWAY) (PON, 1996)

STATES

5) %<5 96
PERCENTAGE OF POPULATION UNDER 5 YEARS

47) HOUSE $90
MEDIAN VALUE OF OWNER-OCCUPIED NONCONDOMINIUM HOUSING UNITS

73) BUS90
PERCENT WHO TAKE BUS OR TROLLEY TO WORK

GSS

15) HH SIZE
NUMBER OF HOUSEHOLD MEMBERS (HOMPOP)

49) LIKE JOB?
On the whole, how satisfied are you with the work you do–would you say you are very satisfied, moderately satisfied, a little dissatisfied, or very dissatisfied?

52) $ RANK
Compared with American families in general, would you say your family income is far below average, below average, average, above average, or far above average? (FINRELA)

Web Pages Related to Gender Equality

If you wish to find a world of resources that are available to you over the Internet, the following list of Web sites will get you started. Once you visit these Web sites, you will find links to other useful Web sites.

Commission on Gender Equality
www.cge.org.za/

United Nations Development Fund for Women
www.undp.org/unifem/

Women in National Parliments
www.ipu.org/wmn-e/world.htm

The Status of Women in Finland
virtual.finland.fi/finfo/english/women/naiseng.html

Women's International Net
www.winmagazine.org/

The United States Agency for International Development
www.usaid.gov/

Human Rights Watch
www.hrw.org/

Face to Face International: Equality for All Women
www.facecampaign.org/main.html

References

Barkan, R. L. (1998). *The Social Work Dictionary* (4th ed.) Washington, DC: NASW Press.

Barusch, A. S. (2002). *Foundations of Social Policy: Social Justice, Public Programs, and the Social Work Profession*. Itasca, IL: F. E. Peacock Publishers, Inc.

Bellak, A. O. (1984). Comparable worth: A practitioner's view. In *Comparable Worth: Issues for the 80's*. Washington DC: U.S. Commission on Civil Rights.

Cherry, A. L., Dillon, M. E., and Rugh, D. (eds.). (2001). *Teenage Pregnancy: A Global View*. Westport, CT: Greenwood Pub.

Daruvalla, A., Kaplar, Z., Labi, A., Landry, K., and Penner, M. (1999). Rebels without a cause, Today's cool teenagers in Europe show more mature attitudes to sex than did the '60s "revolutionaries." *Time International*, Aug. 16.

Goodkind D. and Thuc Anh, P. (1997). *Reasons for Rising Condom Use in Vietnam*. New York: The Alan Guttmacher Institute.

Jansson, B. S. (1999). *Becoming an Effective Policy Advocate: From Policy Practice to Social Justice*. Pacific Grove, CA: Brooks/Cole Publishing Company.

Knodel, J., Chamratrithiron, A., and Devabalya, N. (1987). *Thailand's Reproductive Revolution: Rapid Fertility Decline in a Third-World Setting*. Madison WI: University of Wisconsin Press.

Kirst-Ashman, K. K. and Hull, G. H. (2001). *Generalist Practice with Organizations & Communities* (2nd ed.). Belmont, CA: Wadsworth Publishing Company.

Longley, R. (2001). *Women in the U.S. Congress*. Retrieved September 18, 2001, from www.autoweb.com/researchused/.

Metz, H. C. (1991). *Nigeria, A Country Study*: Library of Congress, Federal Research Division. Retrieved August 2, 2000, from lcweb2.loc.gov/frd/cs/ngtoc.html.

NCPA. (2001). *International Issues: The world's Declining Fertility Rate*. Dallas, TX: National Center for Policy Analysis.

Sen, A. (1994). Population Policy: Authoritarianism versus co-operation. *Social Change*. 24(3–4), 20–35.

Women in National Parliaments. (2001). *World and regional averages: Situation as of 1 July 2001*. Retrieved September 15, 2001, from www.ipu.org/wmn-e/world.htm.

Zastrow, C. and Kirst-Ashman, K. K. (2001). *Understanding Human Behavior in the Social Environment* (5th ed.). Belmont, CA: Wadsworth Publishing Company.

Additional Material that may be of Interest

Ben-Arieh, A and Gal, J. (eds.). (2001). *Into the Promised Land: Issues Facing the Welfare State*. Westport, CT: Praeger Press.

Cashin, E. J. and Eskew, G. T. (2001). *Paternalism in a Southern City: Race, Religion, and Gender in Augusta, Georgia*. Athens, GA: University of Georgia Press.

Cole, M. (ed.). (2000). *Education, Equality and Human Rights: Issues of Gender, Race, Sexuality, Special Needs and Social Class*. New York: Routledge/Falmer Press.

González, V. and Kampwirth, K. (eds.). (2001). *Radical Women in Latin America: Left and Right*. University Park, PA: Pennsylvania State University Press.

Walter, L. (ed.). (2001). *Women's Rights: A Global View*. Westport, CT: Greenwood Press.

Chapter 8

Racial and Ethnic Diversity

Tasks: Mapping, Univariate, Scatterplot, Correlation, Multiple Regression, ANOVA, Logistic Regression, Factor Analysis
Data Files: STATES, GLOBAL, GSS, COUNTIES, US TRENDS

Overview of Chapter 8

The focus of Chapter 8 is on diversity, particularly racial and ethnic diversity. This seems like an old concept that is well established, but it was not long ago that people coming to the United States were expected to assimilate; they were to become *Americans*. This meant that immigrants were to put aside their cultural heritage and take up the cultural norms of *Americans*. Today, in the United States, most people recognize and appreciate the cultural heritage found among the people in this country. It has also become evident that cultural pluralism strengthens our society. To learn more about racial and ethnic diversity, we will first look at the degree of multiculturalism found in different nations around the world. Then we will see what effect multiculturalism has on the population in these countries. For instance, how does the level of multiculturalism affect human development and other social indicators in a country? Does it affect a country's economy? What role does it play in cultural conflicts? Then we will use a new database that has information on race and ethnicity of people living in each county in the United States. You will test the hypotheses in this chapter with statistical procedures you have used before, and you will be introduced to a new statistical procedure called *factor analysis*. I believe you will find the county database very interesting.

T he attributes or characteristics that one group of people use to discriminate against another group of people has always both amazed and puzzled me. Some of the ways that people are separated for discriminatory treatment is quite imaginative, and, to the outsider, it can seem a bit silly. In spite of what may seem trivial and stupid to us, it can be deadly serious and for many it has meant death. Several years back there were a number of exchange students visiting the university where I was teaching. Due to my ignorance of the characteristics that were used by the Northern Irish Catholics and the Northern Irish Protestants to distinguish one group from another, I asked the students how did they know another Irish person was Catholic or Protestant. In other words, how did they know whom to discriminate against? My thought was that they would not know another Irish person was Catholic or Protestant unless they observed a religious behavior or the other person told them he or she was Catholic or Protestant. The students quickly assured me that it was the way Protestants or Catholics walked and talked that made them easy to recognize.

People who are different from the dominant group are often singled out and treated unequally or worse. A person's race is a common characteristic that is often used to identify people who can be mistreated or discriminated against without fear of sanction or reprisal from the dominant group. *Ethnicity*, a cluster of behaviors and characteristics that are developed within a culture, is another set of identifiers that is often used to distinguish people who can be discriminated against by members of the dominant group. Gender as shown in Chapter 7 is another attribute that is used around the world to suppress one of the world's largest groups of people—girls and women.

Assimilation Versus Cultural Pluralism

A major debate over the last 20 years has been the debate between *assimilation* and *cultural pluralism.* *Assimilation* describes a process where members of the nondominant group adopt the values and behaviors of the dominant group. Supposedly, as the person assimilates, discrimination and prejudice will fade. This happens only in theory. In the real world, people continue to use sexual and racial features to identify individuals for unequal treatment. The difficulty is that a person of a different race or one who is female has enormous difficulty assimilating because of the features of his or her race and gender. These features cannot be changed (Ambrosino et al., 2001). For advocates of *cultural pluralism,* cultural diversity enriches our culture and lives. As an alternative to assimilation, cultural pluralism supports the coexistence of all ethnic and racial groups. In a world of cultural pluralism, cultural differences are respected and valued as being equal to the culture of the dominant group (Ambrosino et al.).

Without a doubt, multiculturalism is becoming more widespread and, given the ease of transportation from one country to another, it will only increase. Multiculturalism is already increasing in the vast majority of countries. There are countries, however, such as North Korea, that are almost inaccessible to other racial and ethnic groups. You can see for yourself the countries that restrict immigration by examining the map of the degree of multi-cultural populations in the countries around the world.

In the Americas, immigrant groups have been arriving since Columbus stumbled on a small Caribbean island. Even so, new immigrants meet with hostility and conditions restricting their opportunities as set by the dominant group. Without a doubt, most immigrant groups experience prejudice and open discrimination by the dominant group. At times in the United States and other nations, discrimination and prejudice are so ingrained in the minds of the dominant group, in public policy, and in the law, that they become institutionalized. Institutional racism and sexism are extremely harmful to minorities, other out groups, and in truth, they are harmful to the people in the dominant group. In the United States, the dominant group continues to be the white male. This is a group, however, that also excludes the majority of their own kind from the special opportunities that are available to the upper class. Exclusive educational opportunities have been the purview of the wealthy for hundreds of years, but women, the poor, and minorities have penetrated even these barriers. As such, the experience of women, American Indians, and African Americans, and the experiences of immigrant groups such as Hispanics, Asians, and subgroups such as, the Irish and Italians—in the United States—have been one of learning to cope with differential treatment and limited opportunities.

Racial and Ethnic Social and Economic Justice

As shown in Chapter 7, economic justice is far from a reality. The wage gap between women and men in the United States is even greater when research accounts for race and ethnicity. Women of color are far more disadvantaged than white women. Hispanic women earn less than African American women do, and both groups earn less than white women do. All races of women earn significantly less than men at every educational level, with the exception of women with graduate degrees in modern countries. Women with a bachelor's degree earn 65% of what men with a college education do. Similarly, women with a high school education make 67% of what men do with a similar degree (Zastrow and Kirst-Ashman, 2001).

In this chapter, we will use our data files to examine multiculturalism and other conditions unique to countries with high and low levels of multiculturalism.

Ethical Foundation for Racial and Ethnic Equality

The lack of tolerance for differences, a common human characteristic, is repeatedly exploited by political and religious leaders to advance their own, often narrow, agenda. It is much easier to incite people to strike out against those that are different than to help a multicultural group of people learn to respect and appreciate each others' differences.

> **8.1**   **Ethics and Racial and Ethnic Equality**
>
> Suppose that you are a white person who developed a pigment disorder that turned your skin color from white (or pink) to a dark brown. How would you expect strangers to treat you? Would they recognize that your features were Caucasian, or do you think a lot of white people and even other people of color would treat you differently? If you were suddenly a person of color, what rights and treatment would you want people of color to have to ensure equal access to resources and opportunity? A good book, that was also produced as a movie with the same title, that hopefully is still in your library, is *Black Like Me*, by John Howard Griffin, published in 1961, by the New American Library. You can probably rent it at your local video store.

A Global View of Racial and Ethnic Equality

The first step in the examination of *racial* and *ethnic* equality is to *operationalize* the terms. In this case, a variable, MULTI-CULT, measures the degree of multiculturalism. This variable provides us with a score for each country that represents the odds that any two people will differ in their race, religion, ethnicity, or language. An odds ratio measure is a good way to determine multiculturalism in a country. It does not fall victim to dominant groups and culturally based prejudices.

Research Hypothesis/Question   8.1:
How many countries do we have with a score on multicultural diversity?

> ➢   *Data File:*   **GLOBAL**
> ➢   *Task:*   **Mapping**
> ➢   *Variable 1:*   **61) MULTI-CULT**
> ➢   *View:*   **Map**

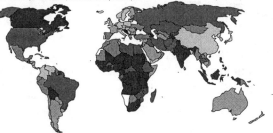

MULTI-CULT -- MULTI-CULTURALISM:ODDS THAT ANY 2 PERSONS WILL DIFFER IN THEIR RACE, RELIGION, ETHNICITY (TRIBE),OR LANGUAGE GROUP (STARK)

This variable provides a measure of multicultural differences for 169 of the 174 nations in our data file. It looks like there is a great deal of cultural diversity in most countries. In an age where global travel is commonplace, the level of diversity can only increase in all countries of the world. While viewing the map of multicultural diversity, click on the **[List: Rank]** button to see the countries with the most diversity and the countries with the least diversity. Did you think India, the Congo, and Bolivia were some of the most diverse countries on earth? How about North Korea, Japan, Portugal, and Haiti being the least diverse countries in the world? Remember, this variable measures the odds that any two people have a different race or ethnicity.

Next, we will try to identify a few general characteristics and attributes that vary with the degree of multi-culturalism in a given country. The overarching research question will break down characteristics and attributes into domains of influence. It can be stated as: "What characteristic in the following domains is associated with multicultural countries: *economic, education, environment, and political?*" After an in-depth study of the variables and the characteristics that they measured, and a check to see if the sample of countries responding on each question or variable was reasonably large (considering I might use a multivariate analysis to complete the analyses), I selected one variable from the GLOBAL data file to represent each domain I intend to study. The five variables are:

Dependent Variable: 61) MULTI-CULT—Multiculturalism: odds that any two persons will differ in their race, religion, ethnicity (tribe), or language group. This is a ratio measure.
Independent Variable 1: (Representing education) —23) HUMAN DEV.—Human development index. Higher score = more developed. This is a ratio measure.
Independent Variable 2: (Representing environment)—36) THREEWORLD—Classification of countries into three worlds model: 1 = First World, 2 = Second World, 3 = Third World. This is a rank-order variable. Even though it appears like an interval variable, we do not know exactly where the intervals begin and end (Cherry, 2000).
Independent Variable 3: (Representing economic) —35) GDP/CAP—Gross domestic product per capita in U.S. dollars. This is a ratio measure.
Independent Variable 4: (Representing the political environment)—62) C.CONFLICT—Index of cultural conflict: 0 = None; 1 = Limited to political means; 2 = Violence (terrorism and/or violent repression); 3 = Armed conflict. This is again a rank-order variable; even though it has intervals, we do not know exactly where the intervals begin and end.

As a set, these variables represent the four domains that I selected to study in relationship to multiculturalism. There are many other variables that could be employed in this analysis. You will find some of them at the end of this chapter. Nevertheless, using my best judgment, I selected the variables above.

These variables are also a mix of *ratio-* and *rank/ordinal*-level measures. The dependent variable will be MULTI-CULT. It is a ratio-level variable. Remember, the level of measure dictates what statistical procedure we will need to use to analyze sets and groups of variables. In this case, we use analytical procedures such as correlation and multiple regression to determine the unique contribution that each of the four independent variables makes in describing multicultural diversity.

Research Hypothesis/Question   8.2:
Countries that have high scores on multicultural diversity will have high scores on the human development index.

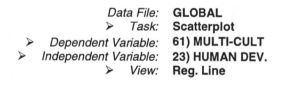

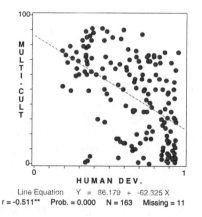

I used a scatterplot because both variables are ratio-level and the scatterplot is one of the best ways to visually display a bivariate relationship between two ratio variables. There is a correlation between the *multicultural*

measure and countries with high levels of human development; however, it is an inverse relationship, not a positive relationship. This correlation suggests that countries with high levels of multiculturalism tend to have low levels of human development ($r = -.511$, $p < .000$). This may be a bit surprising, but let's continue to look at the bivariate relationships. Did you realize that the simple direction of a variable could be so important? It turned my bivariate hypothesis on its proverbial head. See if you agree with my next hypothesis. In this case, do a correlation with the variables that represent the three worlds model. In this case, three variables can be used to represent each grouping of nations. This is similar to using dummy variables. The variable THREEWORLD has been broken into three variables: FIRSTWORLD, SECONDWORLD, and THIRDWORLD. These variables have values of 0 and 1. In this case, all nations that are not identified as First, Second, or Third World nations in each variable are represented by a value of 0. All nations represented by a value of 1 are the type of nation specified by the variable. This allows us to use these variables as an interval level-variable.

Research Hypothesis/Question   8.3:
Countries identified as having high scores on multicultural diversity will be countries identified as Third World countries.

Data File:	**GLOBAL**
➤ *Task:*	**Correlation**
➤ *Dependent Variable:*	**61) MULTI-CULT**
➤ *Independent Variables:*	**102) FIRSTWORLD**
	103) SECONDWORLD
	101) THIRDWORLD
➤ *Deletion:*	**Pairwise**
➤ *Test:*	**2-tailed**

Correlation Coefficients Table

	MULTI-CULT	FIRST WORLD	SECOND WORLD	THIRD WORLD
MULTI-CULT	1.000 (169)	-0.317 ** (169)	-0.137 ** (169)	0.349 ** (169)
FIRST WORLD	-0.317 ** (169)	1.000 (174)	-0.199 ** (174)	-0.593 ** (102)
SECOND WORLD	-0.137 ** (169)	-0.199 ** (174)	1.000 (174)	-0.671 ** (174)
THIRD WORLD	0.349 ** (169)	-0.593 ** (174)	-0.671 ** (174)	1.000 (174)

Pairwise deletion (2-tailed t-test) Significance Levels: ** =.01, * =.05

Although the procedure provides correlations between all these variables, the most important correlations are between the MULTI-CULT variable and the variables FIRSTWORLD, SECONDWORLD, and THIRDWORLD. These correlations suggest that the only group of nations that correlates with high levels of multicultural diversity are nations identified as Third World countries ($r = .349$, $p < .01$). The correlations between multicultural diversity and First and Second World nations are inverse or negative correlations. This suggests Second World countries are less multiculturally diverse ($r = -.137$, $p < 01$) than Third World countries, and First World countries are less multiculturally diverse than Second or Third World countries. These three bivariate relationships are a convincing argument for the importance of the direction of a statistically significant relationship.

8.2   The Destruction of the World Trade Center

In the midst of completing this chapter, the two World Trade Center towers were destroyed along with a section of the Pentagon. Over 3,000 people, both on the ground and in the four passenger planes, lost their lives. Everyone in the United States was traumatized at some level. Likewise, most of the people around the world will also experience secondary trauma. One of the world's symbols of strength, prosperity, and hope—the United States—was viciously attacked and wounded. This shook the world's people to their core. If people in the United States are not safe, then no one, no matter where they live or hide, is safe from racial, ethnic, and religious hate groups. The people in the United States and people around the world will experience and suffer the symptoms of post-traumatic stress. Some will try to dismiss the symptoms. Even the enemies of the United States will tremble at the destruction and the sense that no one is safe. The only outcome will be more blood shed. Where it will stop is anyone's guess. What is observable is that race, ethnicity, and religion are being used to identify the *enemy*. President George W. Bush put it, the people who conspired to attack the World Trade Center and the Pentagon are not just the enemies of the United States; they are the enemies of the "civilized world." As Osama bin Laden is supposed to have said in a call for a Jihad against Israel and the United States, "By God's leave, we call on every Muslim to kill the Americans and plunder their possessions." What is obvious is that human differences are again being used to incite more racial and ethnic prejudice and hate on all sides. One step that could help is to make hate crimes a special category of international crime, punishable under international law (Lewis, 2001).

Research Hypothesis/Question   8.4:
Countries with high scores on multicultural diversity will have lower GDP per capita.

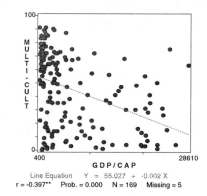

Data File:	**GLOBAL**
➤ *Task:*	**Scatterplot**
➤ *Dependent Variable:*	**61) MULTI-CULT**
➤ *Independent Variable:*	**35) GDP/CAP**
➤ *View:*	**Reg. Line**

Again, this is a weak correlation, but it is significant ($r = -.397$, $p < .000$). It suggests that countries that have high scores on cultural diversity have a slight tendency to have a lower GDP per capita than countries with lower levels of cultural diversity.

Research Hypothesis/Question   8.5:
Countries that have high scores on multicultural diversity will have a higher level of cultural conflict.

Data File:	**GLOBAL**
➤ *Task:*	**Mapping**
➤ *Variable 1:*	**61) MULTI-CULT**
➤ *Variable 2:*	**99) C.CONFLIC2**
➤ *View:*	**Map**

MULTI-CULT --
MULTI-CULTURALISM:ODDS THAT ANY 2 PERSONS WILL DIFFER IN THEIR RACE, RELIGION, ETHNICITY (TRIBE),OR

r = 0.655**

C.CONFLIC2 -- Collapsed from C.CONFLICT: INDEX OF CULTURAL CONFLICT:0=NONE;1=LIMITED TO POLITICAL MEANS;2=VIOLENCE

Wow! This is quite disturbing. There is a strong correlation between countries with a high level of cultural diversity and countries that are experiencing cultural conflict at some level. This belies our hopes, at least in the short run, that people living in a multicultural society believe that a diverse society can enhance the culture of the dominant society.

Now we are ready to use all of the independent variables in a multivariate analysis to determine how much unique variance that the four independent variables can account for in terms of predicting a country's score on the multicultural scale.

Research Hypothesis/Question   8.6:
A country's Human Development Index score, its position as a Third World country, its GDP per capita, and the presence of cultural conflict will be useful for predicting an individual country's score on the Multicultural Index.

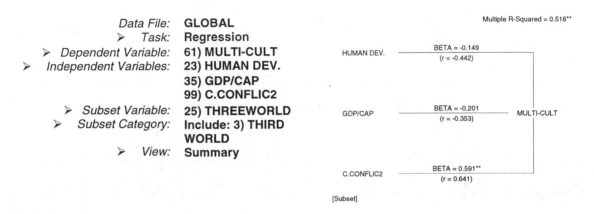

Data File: **GLOBAL**
➤ Task: **Regression**
➤ Dependent Variable: **61) MULTI-CULT**
➤ Independent Variables: **23) HUMAN DEV.**
                         35) GDP/CAP
                         99) C.CONFLIC2
➤ Subset Variable: **25) THREEWORLD**
➤ Subset Category: **Include: 3) THIRD WORLD**
➤ View: **Summary**

This set of variables explains about 52% of unique variance in the dependent variable, multiculturalism. This is a substantial amount of variance to be able to account for in a dependent variable. If you look a little closer, you will see that the most important variable for predicting whether a country is culturally diverse is the level of cultural conflict in a country ($R^2 = .516$, $p < .000$).

Given this last analysis, if I find a group of countries with elevated scores on the *Cultural Conflict Index,* I would also expect to find that the same group of countries will have elevated scores on the *Multicultural Index.* In other words, Third World countries with high levels of *multiculturalism* will be experiencing an ongoing struggle between groups that have drawn a mythical line between opposing cultural beliefs and behaviors.

This was an important finding. It suggests that cultural conflict is not just occurring in the First World countries like the United States, England, and Germany, where minority groups often hold protest rallies to air their grievances. These clashes are also going on in Third World counties around the world. This finding should dispel any ideas that the only places experiencing cultural conflict are modern countries like the United States, England, Germany, France, etc.

For me, one of the more remarkable findings in this analysis was the statistically significant relationship between cultural diversity and cultural conflict ($r = .655$, $p < .000$). Given this relationship, let's look at a summary graph that will give us a visual picture of the relationship. I will use the ANOVA procedure to produce the graph.

Research Hypothesis/Question   8.7:
There is a strong relationship between countries with multicultural populations and countries in the midst of some level of cultural conflict.

Data File:	**GLOBAL**
➤ Task:	**ANOVA**
➤ Dependent Variable:	**61) MULTI-CULT**
➤ Independent Variable :	**62) C.CONFLICT**
➤ View:	**Summary**

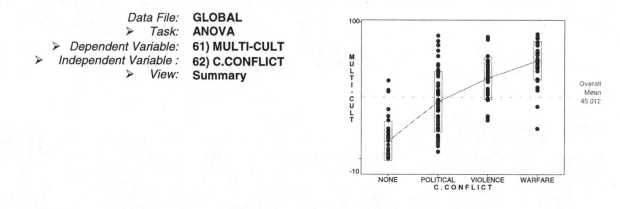

The graph shows a sad but statistically significant relationship ($F = 81.652$, df = 3, $p < .000$). The more a country tends to have a multicultural population, the higher the expectation that the country will be involved in some type of cultural conflict.

8.3	**Landmines**
•	There are an estimated 110 million landmines buried underground in 68 countries.
•	There were 255 United Nation and NATO troops wounded, and 29 killed by mines in Bosnia.
•	Almost 90% of those killed and maimed by landmines are civilians – primarily women and children.
•	A landmine costs as little as $3 to make, and $300+ to clear from the land (CARE, 2001).

Now let's try to identify variables that are predictive of different levels of *cultural conflict*.

Cultural Conflict and Related Conditions

Conflict is loosely defined as a state of disharmony between people who have diametrically opposing ideas, interests, or in this case cultures. To the outsider, it may seem difficult to understand the concept of the *untouchables* as it relates to a class of people in India. To those who grew up in that system of segregation, it is hard to imagine changing that system. If people from another country, say the United States, migrated to India in large numbers with ideas of freedom, I suspect there would be quite a cultural clash as we tried to elevate the status of the *untouchables* to that of the Brahmans. We would not be the first to try to improve the plight of the untouchables; Mahatma Gandhi tried and failed. Of course, this class system has a religious base—Hindu; and this religion has existed in India for about 3,500 years.

As we have seen first hand in New York, cultural and religious conflicts are typically extremely destructive. The question is, however, what characteristics or conditions are found in countries where cultural conflict is high?

To address this question, we must change the direction of our inquiry from looking at the characteristics in countries with high levels of cultural diversity to looking at characteristics and conditions of countries with high levels of cultural conflict. In many ways, the process of this inquiry starts again from scratch. We start by first examining variables in our database that might be used to represent characteristics or conditions that we think will be associated with countries with different levels of cultural conflict. We are not totally without some direction because we have seen that there is a strong correlation between a country's level of *multiculturalism* and *cultural conflict*. This means that the variables that were found to be correlated with *multicultural* will more than likely be associated with *cultural conflict*.

Exploring Global Social Welfare

Sets of Variables or Dimensions

There is another approach to help organize our search for characteristics related to culture. We can think in terms of sets of variables that measure different *dimensions* such as an *economic dimension,* an *environmental dimension,* a *political dimension,* a *religious dimension,* and other dimensions that are best measured with a set of variables. Then we can ask and answer questions such as, "How much does the political dimension explain about cultural conflict?" In the following analysis, I will examine the part that a political dimension plays in countries with varying levels of cultural conflict.

If you carefully examine the variables in the GLOBAL database, you will find a number of variables that may measure a political and an environmental dimension. As I went down the list, eight variables stand out that would possibly measure a political dimension. They were (1) life expectancy, (2) economic development, (3) expenditures on public education, (4) expenditures on public health, (5) the percentage of population that completed the 5th grade in each country, (6) the score on the gender equality index, (7) the score on a freedom index, and (8) the country's position on capital punishment.

I selected life expectancy because a stable country would tend to have an increased life expectancy. Economic development, expenditures on public health and public education will probably be lower in countries with high levels of cultural conflict. This is speculation on my part, based on the assumptions that the dominant group will limit public expenditures that may provide resources to groups that are not in political power. As the percentage of a country's population who completed the 5th grade increases, the more tolerant I expect the population to be of those who are different. The gender equality measure and the freedom measure are both expected to be low in countries with high levels of cultural conflict. The final variable may seem a little far afield, but it does suggest a particular political mindset. Capital punishment is used in countries around the world to control political, cultural, and religious dominance by one group over another.

Now that we have selected our variables, based on the belief that these variables measure unique characteristics of the political landscape among nations of the world, we need to determine their level of measure and the number of countries on which data are available on each variable. In part, the protocol I used to select variables was based on the number of countries on which data were collected. If a variable reported on less than 75% of countries or under 130 countries, I rejected the variable. As demonstrated earlier, too much missing data is a serious threat to the analysis and can produce misleading information.

Among the nine variables selected, three are rank-order-level measures. The *economic development* variable, the *capital punishment* variable, and the *cultural measure* are rank-order variables.

One assumption, when using a multivariate approach, is that the data on each variable under equal conditions are normally distributed. By their nature, ratio- and interval-level measures typically meet this assumption; although most of us still check them to be sure they have a normal distribution. An exception would be a situation where everyone in a study was the same age.

Rank-order data, however, need to be checked carefully. If the sample is over 100 cases and the rank-order data are normally distributed, then an accurate mean and standard deviation can be calculated and used with interval and ratio variables. When you look at a bar graph of data such as on the variable ECON DEVEL, the distribution of values should look similar to a *bell shape*, and in this case, it does. A *normal curve* in statistics is often referred to as a *bell curve* because of its bell-like appearance. If you want to learn additional information about any of the tasks or terms used in this or other chapters, while in MicroCase, click on the **help** button at the top of your screen or press (*F1*) to select the Help Topics window.

To determine if the variables we selected can be used in a multivariate analysis, we need to examine each variable to see if the data have variance and if the sample size is sufficiently large to use in a multivariate analysis (Cherry, 2000). We will do three separate univariate analyses with these rank-order variables.

Research Hypothesis/Question   8.8:
The three rank-order variables ECON DEVEL, CAP PUNISH, and C.CONFLICT meet the assumption of normalcy.

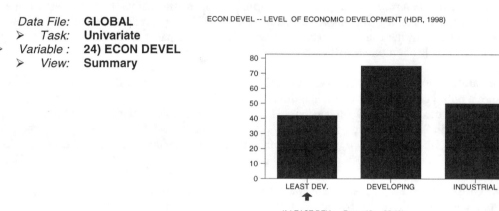

Data File:	**GLOBAL**
➤ *Task:*	**Univariate**
➤ *Variable :*	**24) ECON DEVEL**
➤ *View:*	**Summary**

ECON DEVEL -- LEVEL OF ECONOMIC DEVELOPMENT (HDR, 1998)

1) LEAST DEV.   Freq.: 42   25.1%

This is a very good normal distribution. Although it is a rank-order variable, because it has a normal distribution, I might consider using it like an interval-level measure. If you click on the summary view, you will also see it is only missing data on seven countries. This is a good variable to use in a multivariate analysis.

8.4	**Parametric Tests Have Strict Assumptions About the Data**

These tests of statistical significance require that at least one variable be an interval- or ratio-level measure. The sample distribution of the interval or ratio variable(s) must be normally distributed. If you are comparing different groups, the members should be randomly assigned to each group to meet the assumption that group members are independent of one another. The t-Test, analysis of variance, and Pearson's product-moment correlation are examples of parametric tests (Cherry, 2000).

Data File:	**GLOBAL**
➤ *Task:*	**Univariate**
➤ *Variable :*	**9) FREEDOM**
➤ *View:*	**Summary**

Mean: 4.190   Std.Dev.: 2.011   N: 171
Median: 4.500   Variance: 4.045   Missing: 3
99% confidence interval +/- mean: 3.793 to 4.587
95% confidence interval +/- mean: 3.888 to 4.492

Range	Freq.	%	Cum.%	Z-Score
1.0 - 1.0	17	9.9	9.9	-1.586
1.5 - 1.5	11	6.4	16.4	-1.338
2.0 - 2.0	13	7.6	24.0	-1.089
2.5 - 2.5	12	7.0	31.0	-0.840
3.0 - 3.0	6	3.5	34.5	-0.592
3.5 - 3.5	11	6.4	40.9	-0.343
4.0 - 4.0	13	7.6	48.5	-0.095
4.5 - 4.5	13	7.6	56.1	0.154
5.0 - 5.0	14	8.2	64.3	0.403
5.5 - 5.5	11	6.4	70.8	0.651
6.0 - 6.0	10	5.8	76.6	0.900
6.5 - 6.5	21	12.3	88.9	1.149
7.0 - 7.0	19	11.1	100.0	1.397

This variable has a good distribution across all seven levels on this freedom index variable. We will need to watch the direction of any relationships, however, because 1 = *most free* and 7 = *least free*. There are only three countries with no score.

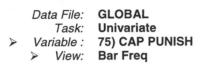

Data File: **GLOBAL**
Task: **Univariate**
➤ Variable : **75) CAP PUNISH**
➤ View: **Bar Freq**

CAP PUNISH -- 1=ABOLISHED, 2=RETAINED FOR CRIMES AGAINST STATE OR SPECIAL CIRCUMSTANCES, 3=RETAINED, BUT NO RECENT EXECUTIONS, 4=USED FOR ORDINARY CRIMES (KIDRON & SEGAL, 1995)

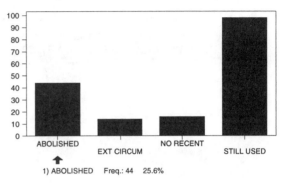

1) ABOLISHED   Freq.: 44   25.6%

This is not a good variable to use in a multivariate analysis because the variance is not normal. If you look at the summary view, you will see that this variable is only missing information on two countries; however, because of the lack of the *bell shape*, we will drop it from the set of variables. While viewing the *Bar Freq* graph, you can see what each bar represents by pointing and clicking on the bar. In the view above, I clicked on the first bar.

8.5   Capital Punishment Around the World

More than **30** additional countries and territories abolished the death penalty between 1990 and 2001. They include countries in **Africa** (i.e., Angola, Côte d'Ivoire, Mauritius, Mozambique, South Africa), the **Americas** (Canada, Paraguay), **Asia** (Hong Kong, Nepal), and **Europe** (Azerbaijan, Bulgaria, Estonia, Georgia, Lithuania, Poland, Turkmenistan, Ukraine). During 2000, some **1,457** prisoners were executed in **27** countries. Another **3,058** people were sentenced to death in **65** countries. These figures only include reported cases. In 2000, **88%** of all known executions took place in China, Iran, Saudi Arabia, and the United States. In 2000, China executed at least **1,000 people.** Saudi Arabia reported executing **123** people, but the total may have been much higher. In 2000, **85** people were executed in the United States. At least **75** executions were carried out in Iran. In addition, hundreds of executions were reported in Iraq, but many of them may have been extrajudicial (Amnesty International, 2001).

To finish the analysis of the rank-order variables, let's look at the variable representing cultural conflict.

Data File: **GLOBAL**
Task: **Univariate**
➤ Variable : **62 C.CONFLICT**
➤ View: **Bar Freq**

C.CONFLICT -- INDEX OF CULTURAL CONFLICT:0=NONE;1=LIMITED TO POLITICAL MEANS;2=VIOLENCE (TERRORISM AND/OR VIOLENT REPRESSION); 3=ARMED CONFLICT (STARK, 1996)

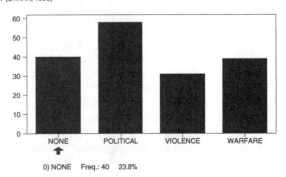

0) NONE   Freq.: 40   23.8%

This is an interesting distribution. While viewing the above graph in MicroCase, if you point and click on the bar representing *warfare*, you will see that 23.2% of those countries we have data for are experiencing cultural conflict that involves warfare. To improve the distribution, we can collapse the bars *Political* and *Violence*. This will give us the ranks that are normally distributed. I have collapsed the two values, and now it appears very different from the distribution above.

Data File: **GLOBAL**
➢   Task: **Univariate**
➢ Variable : **100) C.CONFLIC3**
➢   View: **Bar Freq**

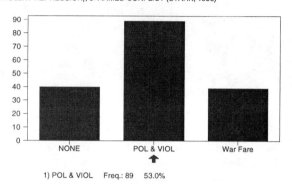

C.CONFLIC3 -- Collapsed from C.CONFLICT: INDEX OF CULTURAL
CONFLICT:0=NONE;1=LIMITED TO POLITICAL MEANS;2=VIOLENCE (TERRORISM
AND/OR VIOLENT REPRESSION); 3=ARMED CONFLICT (STARK, 1996)

1) POL & VIOL   Freq.: 89   53.0%

This distribution of the data looks a great deal better. Approximately 25% of the countries have no cultural conflict. Approximately 25% of the countries are involved in warfare caused by cultural conflict, and about 50% of the nations are having some problems with cultural conflict.

8.6   Immigration 1990–2000

Approximately 44% of the total immigrant population in the United States, approximately 30.5 million, arrived in the 1990s. Among immigrant children, 7 in 10 spoke Spanish at home. Some 78% of the foreign-born immigrants from Mexico were not citizens, compared with 50% of immigrants from Asia and 45% from Europe who were not citizens (U.S. Bureau of the Census, 2000).

To save space, I will not show you the univariate analysis I conducted on the remaining ratio-level variables (you can do that on your own). It is important that you always do the frequency analysis on all the variables you use in any statistical analysis. After completing the univariate analysis of all eight variables that may be used in the analysis, the next step is to see if the remaining seven independent variables are correlated with the dependent variable, *cultural conflict*. Remember, we dropped the CAP PUNISH variable.

Data File: **GLOBAL**
➢   Task: **Correlation**
➢ Variables: **100) C.CONFLIC3**
              17) LIFE EXPCT
              24) ECON DEVEL
              31) PUB EDUCAT
              32) PUB HEALTH
              46) % GO 5TH
              52) GENDER EQ
              59) FREEDOM
➢ Deletion: **Pairwise**
➢   Test: **2-tailed**

	C. CONFLC3	LIFE EXPCT	ECON DEVEL	PUB EDUCAT	PUB HEALTH	% GO 5TH	GENDER EQ	FREEDOM
C.CONFLI-C3	1.000 (168)	-0.435 ** (168)	-0.242 ** (164)	-0.177 (121)	-0.297 ** (142)	-0.345 ** (137)	-0.399 ** (159)	-0.428 ** (168)
LIFE EXPCT	-0.435 ** (168)	1.000 (174)	0.717 ** (167)	0.106 (123)	0.380 ** (145)	0.789 ** (140)	0.886 ** (162)	0.473 ** (171)
ECON DEVEL	-0.242 ** (164)	0.717 ** (167)	1.000 (167)	0.314 ** (123)	0.466 ** (145)	0.768 ** (140)	0.785 ** (162)	0.467 ** (167)
PUB EDUCAT	-0.177 (121)	0.106 (123)	0.314 ** (123)	1.000 (123)	0.275 ** (108)	0.364 ** (105)	0.274 ** (123)	0.208 * (123)
PUB HEALTH	-0.297 ** (142)	0.380 ** (145)	0.466 ** (145)	0.275 ** (108)	1.000 (145)	0.291 ** (125)	0.427 ** (141)	0.492 ** (145)
% GO 5TH	-0.345 ** (137)	0.789 ** (140)	0.768 ** (140)	0.364 ** (105)	0.291 ** (125)	1.000 (140)	0.859 ** (136)	0.411 ** (140)
GENDER EQ	-0.399 ** (159)	0.886 ** (162)	0.785 ** (162)	0.274 ** (123)	0.427 ** (141)	0.859 ** (136)	1.000 (162)	0.557 ** (162)
FREEDOM	-0.428 ** (168)	0.473 ** (171)	0.467 ** (167)	0.208 * (123)	0.492 ** (145)	0.411 ** (140)	0.557 ** (162)	1.000 (171)

When you examine this correlation table, you will find that the only variable that does not correlate with C.CONFLICT is the variable PUB EDUCAT ($r = -.177$, $p = $ NS). This is probably the same effect at play as it was in the earlier chapter when we found public expenditures on education were not as vulnerable to political influences as other public spending. In any case, we will drop the variable PUB EDUCAT from our analysis.

Confirming a Political Dimension

The proposal that there is a political dimension is really a hypothesis. In other words, I am operationally defining the set of six variables as a political dimension. This is a good way to organize our thinking and our variables. However, are these eight variables truly from a single political dimension or are two or more dimensions represented by these eight variables? We can use the *factor analysis* procedure to test our hypothesis about the variables representing a single dimension. Factor analysis is not a new method. It has been widely studied by statisticians and methodologists and has wide applications. It produces a set of equations that describe and predict behavior (NoruŚis, 1990). Let's use all six variables we selected to see what happens to *public education expenditures*. Remember, unlike the other seven independent variables, it was not correlated with cultural conflict.

Research Hypothesis/Question 8.9:
The eight variables selected to define a political dimension will form a single factor.

> Data File: **GLOBAL**
> Task: **Factor Analysis**
> Variables: **17) LIFE EXPCT**
> **24) ECON DEVEL**
> **32) PUB HEALTH**
> **46) % GO 5TH**
> **52) GENDER EQ**
> **59) FREEDOM**
> **Final Factors:**
> View: **Rotated**

Principal Axis -- After VARIMAX rotation
Number of iterations: 2

	Factor 1
LIFE EXPCT	0.881
ECON DEVEL	0.845
PUB HEALTH	0.479
% GO 5TH	0.854
GENDER EQ	0.973
FREEDOM	0.571
Contribution	3.722
% Tot.Var	62.026

The Factor Analysis task can be found on the ADVANCED STATISTICS menu. Select the six variables listed and click [OK]. The Rotated view will be selected automatically.

As was hypothesized, these variables form a single dimension. To define what a factor is measuring (it is a creative process), take your direction from the highest factor loadings. In this factor, the country's *score on gender equality, life expectancy,* the *percentage of a country's population that completed the 5th grade,* and *economic development* have the highest loadings. This could be called a *political measure* of the *quality of life* in a country. You may have a different interpretation or name you would give this factor.

Shall we test this factor or set of variables that measure a country's *quality of life* to see how well it explains the variation of culture conflict from one country to the next?

Research Hypothesis/Question   8.10:
The set of variables that make up the dimension, called a *political measure* of the *quality of life* in a country, will explain a significant amount of the cultural conflict from country to country.

Data File	**GLOBAL**
➤ *Task:*	**Regression**
➤ *Dependent Variable:*	**100) C.CONFLIC3**
➤ *Independent Variables:*	**17) LIFE EXPCT**
	24) ECON DEVEL
	32) PUB HEALTH
	46) %GO 5TH
	52) GENDER EQ
	59) FREEDOM
➤ *View:*	**Summary**

Multiple R-Squared = 0.238**

LIFE EXPCT — BETA = -0.374* (r = -0.417)

ECON DEVEL — BETA = 0.243 (r = -0.281)

PUB HEALTH — BETA = -0.095 (r = -0.264)

C.CONFLIC3

% GO 5TH — BETA = -0.017 (r = -0.307)

GENDER EQ — BETA = -0.078 (r = -0.399)

FREEDOM — BETA = -0.237* (r = -0.375)

This dimension derived from the factor analysis explained a small but statistically significant amount of the variation in cultural conflict from country to country (R^2 = .238, p < .000), or about 25% of differences among the countries on which we have data. Not all of the variables, however, contribute to an explanation of cultural conflict. Only two of the independent variables are statistically significant. They are *life expectancy* (Beta = -.374, p < .05) and *freedom* (Beta = -.237, p < .05). Note that the Beta of both *life expectancy* and *freedom* is inverse, or negative. These negative Betas suggest that in countries where *life expectancy* is high and people have high levels of *freedom,* there are lower levels of cultural conflict. The remaining four variables are all correlated with the dependent variable *cultural conflict,* but they do not help explain differences in *cultural conflict* when in an equation with *life expectancy* and *freedom.*

Comparing Logistic Regression and Multiple Regression

We are fortunate; the distribution of the new *cultural conflict* variable tends to be normally distributed. This has allowed us to use a multiple regression procedure to tell us how much variance the independent variables can explain about the differences in cultural conflict (R^2 = .238, p < .000). We also have the opportunity to make this variable (cultural conflict) into a nominal variable by collapsing all the conflict categories into one category and leaving the zero category as it is. This will make an excellent dependent variable to use with the *logistic regression* procedure. This will allow you to look at the difference in output between these two similar statistical approaches. Using C.CONFLIC2 as a dependent variable in the logistic regression analysis, I will test the hypothesis that the independent variable, *freedom*, will tell us the odds that an increase in cultural conflict will occur when there is a unit increase in *freedom*.

Research Hypothesis/Question   8.11:
The set of variables that make up the dimension, called a *political measure* of the *quality of life* in a country, will be significantly related to cultural conflict. A unit increase in the independent variables will significantly increase or decrease the odds of causing a unit change in cultural conflict.

		Beta Coef.	Std. Err.	Prob.	Odds Ratio
Data File: **GLOBAL**	CONSTANT	9.196	2.925	0.001	
➤ *Task:* **Logistic Regression**	LIFE EXPCT	-0.140	0.067	0.018	0.869
➤ *Dependent Variable :* **99) C.CONFLIC2**	ECON DEVEL	1.213	0.789	0.062	3.365
➤ *Independent Variables:* **17) LIFE EXPCT**	PUB HEALTH	-0.154	0.130	0.118	0.857
24) ECON DEVEL **32) PUB HEALTH** **46) %GO 5TH**	%GO 5TH	0.010	0.023	0.325	1.010
52) GENDER EQ **59) FREEDOM**	GENDER EQ	1.222	4.192	0.385	3.396
➤ *View:* **Regression**	FREEDOM	-0.383	0.198	0.027	0.682

A *logistic regression* analysis tells us the odds of a dependent variable changing when there is a unit increase in the independent variables. As in the multiple regression analysis on the preceding page, there are only two statistically significant variables in this logistic regression analysis. They are *life expectancy* ($p < .018$) and freedom ($p < .027$). These are the only two odds ratio that can be used to predict changes in dependent variable, *cultural conflict*. Other independent variables such as the measures for *gender equality* and *economic development* have large odds ratios, but they are not statistically significant, which indicates that they cannot predict change in cultural conflict. In this logistic regression analysis, as *life expectancy* increases by one unit there is a decrease of .131, or 13%, in *cultural conflict*. There is even a larger decrease in cultural conflict when there is a one-unit increase in freedom. A one-unit increase in *freedom* will result in a .318, or 31%, decrease in *cultural conflict*.

With logistic regression, we can tell if our independent variables are significantly related to the dependent variable. We can also find out what the odds are that changes will take place in the dependent variable when the independent variables change. The multiple regression procedure can also tell us if our independent variables are significantly related to the dependent variable; in addition, it tells us how much of the variance in the dependent variable can be explained by the independent variables.

In this comparison, both procedures found that among the six variables that we identified as possibly being important for reducing cultural conflict, only two were statistically significant, *life expectancy* and *freedom*. So, why do they use different ways to describe the relationships? The difference is in the nature of the dependent variable. With ratio-level variables, the relationship between the two can be more precise. We do not have to allow all that much for statistical error. It is the opposite when using a dichotomous or nominal-level measure for a dependent variable. Because of the lack of precision in a nominal variable, there is more chance for error; thus the relationships must be greater to be statistically significant when using logistic regression. Interestingly, as you can see from comparing the two statistical procedures, both procedures are effective for identifying the most important independent variables in an equation.

Racial and Ethnic Diversity in the United States

The United States was once thought of as a *melting pot*. This is another term for *assimilation*. The question is, however, do the major ethnic and racial groups live together in the same community? We tend to see an integrated society, but does this extend to the places we call home? If we compare the racial and ethnic groups by their place of residence and those residences are fully integrated, we would expect there to be no correlation between, say, states where *whites* tend to live and states where *blacks* tend to live. Although using terms such as *white* and *black* to describe people have little meaning outside the United States and Europe, data on populations in the United States have been collected using these categories since the states were colonies. In this examination, we will look at the populations who are identified as *white, black, Hispanic,* and *Asian* or *Pacific Islander*. This will not be a complicated analysis. In this analysis, we will do a simple Pearson's correlation between states where these racial and ethnic groups live. This analysis will help us see if there are any significant differences in states with different racial and ethnic groups. For this analysis, we will use the COUNTIES data file.

Research Hypothesis/Question   8.12:
States with large percentages of people who identify themselves as white will be inversely correlated with states with large populations of people who identify themselves as blacks.

> *Data File:* **COUNTIES**
> *Task:* **Mapping**
> *Variable 1:* **2) %WHITE90**
> *Variable 2:* **3) %BLACK90**
> *View:* **Map**

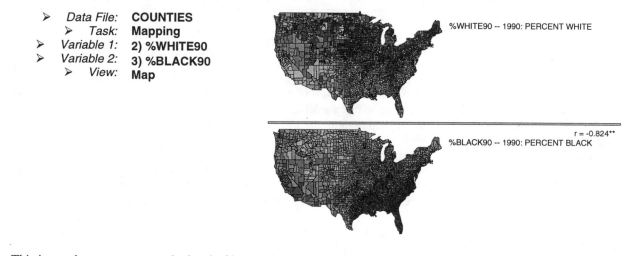

This is a sad commentary on the level of integration between people who identify themselves as white and people who identify themselves as black. The inverse relationship is very strong ($r = -.824$, $p < .01$). This suggests that where a county has a large white population, the same county will almost surely have a smaller population of people who identify themselves as black. If there were no statistically significant relationship, it would suggest that the races are integrated. What about whites and Hispanic groups? Given this outcome, do you think the same pattern will emerge?

8.7	Racial and Ethnic Diversity in the United States Facts
•	In 2000, 63% of Hispanics selected white as their race compared to 48% who selected white in 1990.
•	In 2000, American Indians and Alaska Natives made up 0.9% of the total U.S. population.
•	In 2000, Asian persons accounted for 3.6% of the total U.S. population.
•	In 2000, African Americans made up 12.3% of the total U.S. population.
•	In 2000, Hispanics made up 12.5% of the total U.S. population.
•	In 2000, white non-Hispanics made up 69.1% of the total U.S. population.
•	Some 2.4 % of people in the U.S. report two or more races (U.S. Bureau of the Census, 2001).

Research Hypothesis/Question   8.13:
States with a large percentage of people who identify themselves as white will be negatively correlated to states with large populations of people who are of Hispanic origins.

Data File:	**COUNTIES**
Task:	**Mapping**
Variable 1:	**28) %WHITE90**
➢ *Variable 2:*	**32) %HISPANC90**
➢ *View:*	**Map**

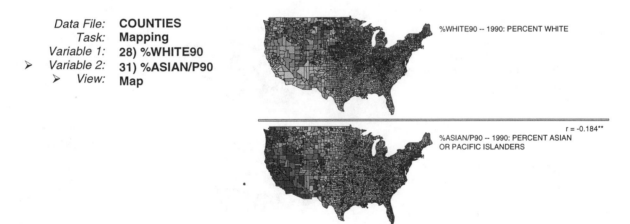

In this test, there is a small inverse relationship between counties that have large white populations and counties that have large Hispanic populations ($r = -.163$, $p < .01$). This tells us that whites and Hispanics are more integrated in our country than African Americans and whites. How do you think the hypothesis predicting segregation will hold up when we look at whites and Asians or Pacific Islanders?

Research Hypothesis/Question   8.14:
States with a large percentage of people who identify themselves as white will be negatively correlated to states with large populations of people who are Asian or from the Pacific Islands.

Data File:	**COUNTIES**
Task:	**Mapping**
Variable 1:	**28) %WHITE90**
➢ *Variable 2:*	**31) %ASIAN/P90**
➢ *View:*	**Map**

The analysis continues to show a pattern of segregation, although it is weak between whites and Asian and Pacific Islanders. There is about the same level of separation between these two groups ($r = -.184$, $p < .01$) as there was between Hispanics and whites. Now let's look at the correlations between African Americans, Hispanics, and Asians or Pacific Islanders. This will tell us if this pattern also exists among the three minority groups in the United States.

Research Hypothesis/Question   8.15:
States with a large percentages of people who identify themselves as black will be inversely correlated with states with large populations of people who identify themselves as Hispanic.

Data File: **COUNTIES**
Task: **Mapping**
➢ Variable 1: **29) %BLACK90**
➢ Variable 2: **32) %HISPANC90**
➢ View: **Map**

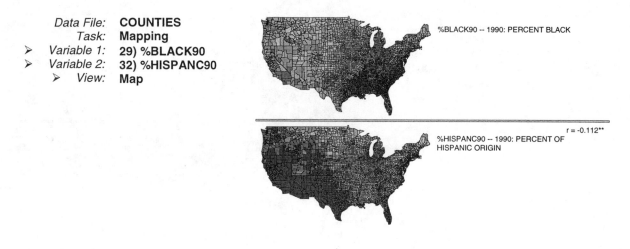

The pattern of separation between African Americans and Hispanics is small, but it is still statistically significant ($r = -.112$, $p < .01$). This indicates there is a small but clear separation between African Americans and Hispanics. If African Americans and Hispanics are slightly segregated, is there segregation between African Americans and Asians or Pacific Islanders?

Research Hypothesis/Question   8.16:
States with a large percentages of people who identify themselves as blacks will be inversely correlated with states with large populations of people who identify themselves as Asian or from the Pacific Islands.

Data File: **COUNTIES**
Task: **Mapping**
Variable 1: **29) %BLACK90**
➢ Variable 2: **31) %ASIAN/P90**
➢ View: **Map**

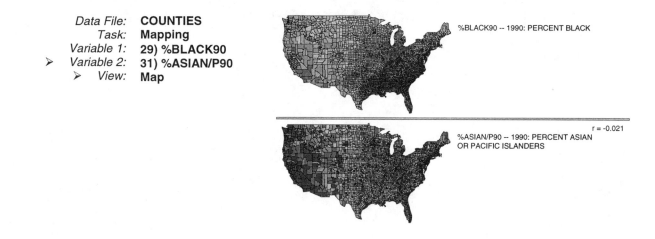

Finally, there is no correlation between counties with large African American populations and counties with large Asian and Pacific Islander populations ($r = -.021$, $p = $ NS). There is little or no segregation between African Americans and Asians and Pacific Islanders.

Do you think the same pattern of little or no segregation will hold true between Hispanics and Asians and Pacific Islanders?

Research Hypothesis/Question   8.17:
States with a large percentages of people who identify themselves as Hispanic will be inversely correlated with states with large populations of people who identify themselves as Asian or Pacific Islanders.

Data File: **USCOUNTIES**
Task: **Mapping**
➢ Variable 1: **32) %HISPANC90**
➢ Variable 2: **31) %ASIAN/P90**
➢ View: **Map**

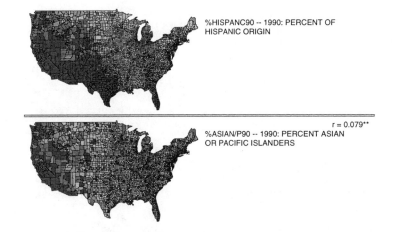

%HISPANC90 -- 1990: PERCENT OF HISPANIC ORIGIN

$r = 0.079^{**}$

%ASIAN/P90 -- 1990: PERCENT ASIAN OR PACIFIC ISLANDERS

This is a very different relationship than the ones we have seen previously. The correlation ($r = .079$, $p < .01$) is very small, but it is statistically significant and positive. This suggests there is a weak trend between counties that have large Hispanic populations and counties with large Asian or Pacific Islander populations. Could it be that these two groups are found in large numbers in the same counties because many in these two groups are immigrants to the United States and live in communities with high immigrant populations? That is another hypothesis you will see again in the exercises for this chapter.

Together, these correlations suggest that in the United States, African American, Hispanic, and Asians and Pacific Islanders continue to live in communities that are, for all intents and purposes, segregated. Has segregation increased or decreased in the United States? This is another question you can expect to see in the exercises at the end of this chapter.

Historical Trends: Racial and Ethnic Diversity

Several historical measures in our US TRENDS data file reveal changes in the levels of discrimination and inequality over the last hundred years. One variable measures the change in the percentage of people over the years that would vote for a woman or for an African American for president. Another condition that tends to reduce discrimination and inequality has been the education level of the population.

Let's see how these variables play out over time. As you can see, records have been kept since 1910 on the number of people completing high school in the United States. Data have been kept since the mid-1930s on the percent of people who would vote for a woman for president. No data were collected until 1972 on the percent of people who would vote for an African American for president of the United States.

Research Hypothesis/Question   8.18:
As the number of people in the United States who finish high school increases, the number of people who are willing to vote for a woman or an African American for president will increase.

> Data File: **US TRENDS**
> > Task: **Historical Trends**
> Variable 1: **14) %HS**
> Variable 2: **27) %BLK PRES**
> Variable 3: **28) %F F.PRES**

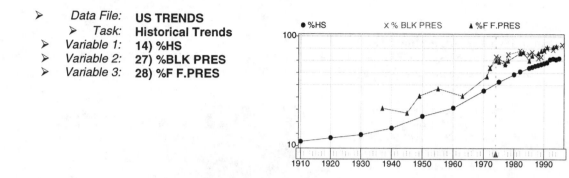

As you can see, as the education level increased among the people of the United States, they became more open to voting for a woman or an African American for president. The interest in women and African Americans first peaked during the Watergate Senate hearings and after President Nixon resigned in disgrace.

End Note: In this chapter we tried to look at variables or conditions that influence cultural conflict. What we learned is that although we might have wanted to use certain variables to test our hypotheses about cultural conflict, if the data on the variables were not *normally distributed*, we could not use them in the multivariate analysis. The results in all likelihood would be inaccurate. This, of course, limited the variables we could use. You also saw how the factor analysis procedure can be used to verify that certain variables, although measuring different conditions, can form a single dimension. The methodical examination of each variable to be sure it meets the assumption of normalcy paid off when we compared the findings from the *multiple regression* procedure to the findings of the *logistic regression* procedure. Both procedures identified the same two variables as being significantly related to cultural conflict. Like they say about computers, "garbage in, garbage out." The same goes for statistical analyses, garbage variable in, garbage variables out.

Other Racial and Ethnic Diversity Issues

There are a number of issues related to poverty and the distribution of wealth that I could not examine in this chapter. However, with the data files provided with this book, you can analyze many of these issues on your own. To learn more about other issues related to racial and ethnic diversity, you can enter the following search terms in the InfoTrac College Edition.

Ethnic disparities	**Race relations**
Ethnic health	**Death penalty**
Ethnicity children	**Racial discrimination**
Emigration, immigration	**Racial profiling**
Multiculturalism	**Interracial marriages**
Welfare	**Native Americans**
Cross-cultural	**Racial identity**
Antislavery	**Ethnocentrism**

WORKSHEET

NAME:

COURSE:

DATE:

Workbook exercises and software are copyrighted. Copying is prohibited by law.

EXERCISE

8

Review Questions

Based on the work you've done so far on the issue of racial and ethnic diversity, see how well you do on this short True or False quiz.

Based on the analysis of the variables MULTI-CULT and GDP/CAP, there is a positive correlation between these two variables.   T   F

Based on the analysis of the variables MULTI-CULT and GDP/CAP, the correlation between these two variables is very high.   T   F

Based on the analysis of the variables MULTI-CULT and GDP/CAP, the correlation between these two variables is statistically significant.   T   F

Based on the analysis of the variables %WHITE and %BLACK, in the United States the correlation suggests that where you find large numbers of white residents in a community, you will find large numbers of African Americans – the communities in which these two racial groups live are highly integrated.   T   F

Based on the analysis of the variables %BLACK and %ASIAN/P, there was no correlation between the two racial groups, positive or negative. This suggests that in the United States African Americans and Asian Americans are not integrated nor segregated.   T   F

One problem we have to be concerned about is the number of missing cases on each variable. The more variables with missing data we use in a multivariate analysis, the more likely the number of missing cases will increase.   T   F

The univariate analysis was performed on each variable selected for inclusion in the examination of the issue of cultural conflict to make sure there was variation among the responses, to check the statistical assumption that the data on the variable was normally distributed, and to make sure that there was not a great deal of missing data on each variable.   T   F

In this chapter, factor analysis was used to help identify an underlying dimension related to cultural conflict.   T   F

Over the years in the United States, the increase in those completing high school has paralleled the number of people who are willing to vote for a woman or an African American for president.   T   F

MicroCase QUESTIONS

Use the following data files, variables, and analytical approaches to answer the MicroCase questions.

1. To examine discrimination around the world, use the following variables and analysis to see if racism is correlated with antisemitism.

    > Data File: **GLOBAL**
    > Task: **Scatterplot**
    > Dependent Variable: **76) ANTI-SEM.**
    > Independent Variable: **79) RACISM**
    > View   **Reg. Line**

    a. Fill in the blank and circle the correct answer. The correlation between antisemitism and racism is very strong ($r =$ _____ $p <$ _____), and it is a (<u>positive</u> / <u>inverse</u>) correlation.

    b. The correlation between antisemitism and racism suggests that where you find antisemitism you will often find that the same countries have (<u>high</u> / <u>low</u> / <u>no</u>) correlation with the index of racism.

2. Now, using the same variable, antisemitism, see if there is a correlation between antisemitism and education.

    Data File: **GLOBAL**
    Task: **Scatterplot**
    Dependent Variable: **76) ANTI-SEM.**
    > Independent Variable: **45) SEC/CP**
    > View   **Reg. Line**

    a. Does education act as a moderator of antisemitism? In other words, the higher the educational level of people in a specific country, the lower the expressions of antisemitism by the people of that country?   Yes   No

    The correlation and the level of significance 2. is $r =$ _____, and the probability is

    _____.

    b. How many missing cases do you have when using these two variables in a correlational analysis? There are _____ missing cases.

    c.   Is the number of missing cases in this analysis a problem?

          Yes   No

    d.   Why would the number of missing cases in this analysis be a problem?

        _____

        _____

3.   Another good measure of racism in a community is the attitude about racial intermarriages. Use the following database and variables to do two analyses to answer the following questions on attitudes toward racial intermarriages in the United States.

> ➤   _Data File:_   **GSS**
> ➤   _Task:_   **Univariate**
> ➤   _Primary Variable:_   **32) INTERMAR72**
> ➤   _View_   **Pie**

    a.   What was the percentage of people who thought there should be laws against marriages between African Americans and whites in 1972? _____%

>   _Data File:_   **GSS**
>   _Task:_   **Univariate**
> ➤   _Primary Variable:_   **33) INTERMAR98**
> ➤   _View_   **Pie**

    b.   What was the percentage of people who thought there should be laws againstmarriages between African Americans and whites in 1998? _____%

    c.   What was the percentage change over the 26 years between 1972 and 1998?

         _____%

    d.   Do you think interracial marriages are more acceptable today than in 1972?

         Yes   No

4.   Now let's see what might have modified people's opinions about interracial marriages. Use the following database, variables, and bivariate analyses to answer the following questions about attitudes toward racial intermarriages in the United States.

> Data File: **GSS**
> ➢ Task: **ANOVA**
> ➢ Dependent Variable: **33) INTERMAR98**
> ➢ Independent Variable: **10) EDUCATION2**
> View   **Summary**

a.   Did an increase in education among this group of people result in a decrease in the attitude that there should be laws against marriages between African Americans and whites?   Yes   No

b.   What was the mean for people who had a 6th grade education or less?
Mean = _____. What was the level of significance? $p <$ _____

5.   Let's see if the person's age might have modified people's opinions about interracial marriages.

> Data File: **GSS**
> Task: **ANOVA**
> Dependent Variable: **33) INTERMAR98**
> ➢ Independent Variable: **8) AGE2**
> View   **Summary**

a.   Did an increase in age among this group of people result in a decrease in the attitude that there should be laws against marriages between African Americans and whites?
Yes   No

b.   What was the mean for people 18–29? Mean = _____.

c.   What was the mean for people 65–97? Mean = _____.

d.   What was the level of significance? $p <$ _____

e.   Do you think it is possible to reduce the discrimination against African Americans and other minorities?   Yes   No

I would leave you with these facts.

1859: The last slave ship carrying slaves, the _Clothilde_, arrived in Mobile Bay, Alabama.

1865: The 13th Amendment was ratified, outlawing slavery in the United States.

1866: Frederick Douglass met with President Andrew Johnson at the White House to advocate for suffrage for black men. The president opposed suffrage for black American men.

1870: The 15th Amendment to the Constitution was ratified, giving black American men the right to vote.

1875: The Civil Rights Act of 1875, guaranteeing equal rights to blacks Americans in public accommodations and jury duty, was invalidated by the Supreme Court in 1883.

This information was compiled from the Library of Congress (www.loc.gov/) and its American Memory Web site at www.memory.loc.gov/ammem/aap/timeline.html.

Variable Lists Related to Racial and Ethnic Diversity

The following is a partial list of the variables in your data files. You can examine them as individual variables or several variables at a time using the approaches you learned in this chapter. To see a list of all of the variables, the question the variable asks, and the range of values, press [F3] to open the variable list window from anywhere in the software. Try using some of the variables below with the variables you have already tested.

GLOBAL

77) ANTI-FORGN
> PERCENT WHO WOULD NOT WANT FOREIGNERS AS NEIGHBORS

78) ANTI-MUSLM
> PERCENT WHO WOULD NOT WANT MUSLIMS AS NEIGHBORS (WVS)

81) HOME LIFE?
> PERCENT WHO SAID THEY WERE "VERY SATISFIED" WITH THEIR HOME LIFE (WVS)

STATES

16) %NON-ENG90
> 1990: PERCENT OF THOSE OVER 5 SPEAKING LANGUAGE OTHER THAN ENGLISH

54) %EMERG.90
> 1990: PERCENT LIVING IN EMERGENCY SHELTERS FOR HOMELESS

72) PUB.TRNS90
> 1990: PERCENT WHO USE PUBLIC TRANSPORTATION (BUS, STREETCAR, SUBWAY, ELEVATED, RAILROAD, FERRYBOAT, TAXICAB)

GSS

14) PAR. BORN
> Were both your parents born in this country? (PARBORN)

20) IF:WHO 92?
> IF DID NOT VOTE OR INELIGIBLE: Who would you have voted for president if you had voted?

26) LIVE WELL
> All in all, one can live well in America.

Web Pages Related to Race and Ethnic Equality

If you wish to find a world of resources that are available over the Internet, the following list of Web sites will get you started. Once you visit these Web sites, you will find many interesting links to other useful Web sites.

Amnesty International
www.amnesty.org/

Dreams in USA
www.dreamsinusa.com/ENGLISH/index.htm

OneWorld.Net
www.oneworld.net/

Migrations
www.migrations.com/

Irish Center for Migration Studies
migration.ucc.ie/

Human Rights Watch
www.hrw.org/

Institute for Foreign Policy Analysis (IFPA)
www.ifpa.org/

International Organization for Migration (IOM)
www.iom.int/

CAIR – Council of American-Islamic Relations
www.cair-net.org

SOROS Foundation Network
www.soros.org/

References

Ambrosino, R., Heffernan, J., Shuttlesworth, G. and Ambrosino, R. (2001). *Social Work and Social Welfare: An Introduction* (4th ed.). Belmont, CA: Wadsworth/Thomson Learning.

Amnesty International. (2001). *Death Penalty Library*. Retrieved September 2, 2000, from www.amnesty.org/.

CARE (2001). Landmine info center. GA: Atlanta, Retrieved September 15, 2001, from www.care.org/index.cfm.

Cherry, A. L. (2000). *A Research Primer for the Helping Professions: Methods Statistics and Writing*. Belmont, CA: Brooks/Cole Pub.

Lewis, B. (2001). A manifesto for war. Miami, FL: *The Miami Herald*. September 22, 1L–6L.

NoruŚis, M. J. (1990). *SPSS Advanced Statistics Student Guide*. Chicago: SPSS, Inc.

U.S. Bureau of the Census. (2000). *America's Children: Key National Indicators of Well-Being, 2000: The Fourth Annual Report to the Nation on the Condition of Our Most Precious Resource, Our Children*. Population Division, U.S. Census Bureau.

Zastrow, C., and Kirst-Ashman, K. K. (2001). *Understanding Human Behavior in the Social Environment* (5th ed.). Belmont, CA: Wadsworth Publishing Company.

Additional Material That May Be of Interest

RACE:

Hollandsworth, J. G. (2001). *An Absolute Massacre: The New Orleans Race Riot of July 30, 1866*. Baton Rouge, LA: Louisiana State University Press.

Buckley, G. L. (2001). *American Patriots: The Story of Blacks in the Military from the Revolution to Desert Storm*. New York : Random House.

Smelser, N. J., Wilson, W. J., and Faith Mitchell, F. (eds). *America Becoming: Racial Trends and Their Consequences*. Washington, DC: National Academy Press.

Burguière, A. and Grew, R. (eds.) (2001). *The Construction of Minorities: Cases for Comparison Across Time and Around the World*. Ann Arbor, MI: University of Michigan Press.

ETHNICITY:

Ghai, Y. (ed) (2000). *Autonomy and Ethnicity: Negotiating Competing Claims in Multi-Ethnic States*. Cambridge, U.K. New York: Cambridge University Press.

Volkan, V. D. (1997). *Bloodlines: From Ethnic Pride to Ethnic Terrorism*. New York: Farrar, Straus and Giroux.

Touraine, A. (2000). *Can We Live Together? Equality and Difference* (David Macey, Trans.). Stanford, CA: Stanford University Press.

McAll, C. (1990). *Class, Ethnicity, and Social Inequality*. Montreal Canada: McGill-Queen's University Press.

Chapter 9

Poverty and the Distribution of Wealth

Tasks:	Mapping, Univariate, Scatterplot, Correlation, MANOVA
Data Files:	GLOBAL, STATES, COUNTIES, GSS

Overview of Chapter 9

Chapter 9 deals with a problem that has been a part of human existence for thousands of years, poverty and the distribution of wealth. Especially since the beginning of the Industrial Revolution, it has been the center of many heated debates. It continues to be a political *hot potato* in most countries around the world, including the United States. The nexus of the debate, however, is the perspective of the people who are poor. If one believes that poverty is the result of the individual's decisions or behavior, poverty is *not* viewed as unjust. If poverty is viewed as resulting from inequity of opportunity, it is viewed as unjust. In this chapter we will examine the problem of poverty around the world and in the United States. Using the *global* database, we will look at poverty in First World, Second World, and Third World countries. We will also test the idea that a relationship exists between poverty and revolution. Using the *counties* database, we will look at poverty rates among American Indians, African Americans, the urban poor and the effect that poverty has on the education of adolescents living in poverty. Finally, we will study the opinions of the U.S. public to try to understand why there is a lack of commitment by the public and politicians to deal with poverty in the United States. You will use the same critical thinking skills and analytical procedures you have used in the previous chapters. In addition, you will learn about the role that residuals play in linear analyses such as correlations and regression analyses. This will give you a visual picture to help your understanding of how these procedures determine relationships between variables.

P overty is one of the world's major problems. There are many organizations in the United States and around the world that are interested in helping to *balance the playing field* for disadvantaged people and countries. In this effort, we need to have reliable and valid ways (methodologies) to identify injustice and inequality that harm all members of society. The most important *health issue* facing the world today is poverty. The greatest threat to world stability is poverty. Eliminating poverty around the world would not solve all human problems, but it would put an end to a man-made problem (Paxman, 2001).

Poverty as I see it is not a naturally occurring human condition. Historically, people in tribes, basically large and extended families, shared their provisions. If, for one reason or another, the food supply was interrupted, the whole tribe went hungry and in many cases starved to death. There are numerous historical records of entire tribes starving to death. This commonly shared destiny changed over time when humans organized themselves into large settlements. Once these social groups moved away from everyone being related to everyone else, there was no longer the motivation to share provisions equally. Human tribes have always viewed those from other tribes with suspicion. Humans have also never felt kinship with humans who are different from themselves.

Early in human history this was an advantage because while some tribes may have died out others were able to survive and propagate the species (Cherry, 1994).

This early survival strategy took on several forms as human society grew. Quarantines, segregation, and isolation were the first approaches used to dealing with contagious diseases that were a threat to the whole tribe. Leper colonies, a way to quarantine lepers, were established before recorded history. Even today, although leprosy is a treatable disease using modern medicines, in a few Third World countries leper colonies are still being used. When I was studying for my master's degree, I had a professor who had collected qualitative data on several leper colonies located on different islands in the Caribbean for his dissertation. He did his research in the early 1970s. The point I am trying to make is that this type of behavior, ostracizing others who are different, allows one to *blame the victim* and reject any responsibility for the condition of these being ostracized (Cherry).

Quarantining one group in a *ghetto* or segregating people to the *other side of the tracks* has been used through the ages to protect people with a disproportionate amount of resources from people who have a great deal less. When it is used to separate *us* from *them,* it can be vary harmful to both groups' case with worldwide poverty.

Another point that needs to be made: just because a country lacks material wealth does not mean that the people of that country are deprived. A country that has great material wealth but where a large group of its people struggles to survive is a country where people are deprived. Generally, the term *developed country* means a country where the living standards are such that all people have enough food, water, and clothing. It is a country with a stable social environment, with equitable ownership of land, basic rights and freedom, and where all people have a fair chance for a decent life (Paxman, 2001).

Nature could never devise a system that would result in such abject poverty among a majority of the world's people. To do so, in the early developmental stages of humans, would have doomed us from the start. Humans could only survive as families, or in collectives. Only man could systematize a scheme that feeds on it own when it is unnecessary for survival. This common behavior known as cannibalism is pervasive in human history. As a strategy, in today's world, it is only acceptable when cannibalism is identified as a metaphoric condition. This is the case with *poverty.* No matter what we call it, it is still a condition that results from one group unfairly prospering while other groups are left impoverished, suffering and dying unnecessarily (Cherry, 1994).

A critical problem that has perpetuated global poverty is the concentration of wealth in a few countries. This concentration of wealth results in a concentration of political power, and political power has historically been used to divert resources from one country to another. All too often, the diverted resources are needed to meet domestic needs in the politically weak and poor country. This problem has left 1.3 billion people around the world living in severe poverty (UNDP, 2001).

Is poverty harmful? Not only is it harmful to those without, it damages those of us who must try to ignore the plight of so many of the world's population.

9.1   World's Sanitation and Food Requirements

It would take about $13 billion to meet the basic sanitation and food requirements of the world's impoverished peoples who are living without these provisions. This is about the same amount of money that people in the United States and the European Union spend on perfume each year (Paxman, 2001).

Ethical Foundation for Redistributing the Wealth

How can such global inequities be *right*? They are not *right,* they are *wrong.* And, it is up to each of us to change it. This will not happen overnight, and it may never happen in my or your lifetime; however, as responsible citizens of the world, we need to know that these injustices exist and that they are indeed *injustices*. Without the knowledge of these circumstances, there is no hope for change. To find the true impact of poverty and decide how you think it should be handled by the larger society, consider the ethics of providing for people where poverty, as a condition, could strike at any time and anyone.

9.2   Ethics, Poverty, and the Distribution of Wealth

Suppose, for a moment, that a year or so before you were planning to retire there was a worldwide depression and suddenly you found yourself penniless. Overnight, the stocks in which you invested your life savings and the major portion of your retirement savings (at the urging of the federal government) became worthless. Shortly thereafter, you lose your job because of the *economic downturn*. (This happened to millions of people in the 1930 depression. It also happened after the terrorist attack on the World Trade Center in 2001, and the stock market crash of July, 2002.) Because of the economic crisis congress begins to debate the best approach to deal with the economic depression. One group of congresspersons wants to give large grants to the military industry and the wealthy so they can invest in businesses. The other group argues that something must be done for people who lost their life savings and retirement funds in the stock market crash. Besides, they argue, if economic relief is given to those in need of financial aid, all the money would be spent to buy necessities and pay overdue bills to companies. If the money is given to the rich, they point out, a large portion of it would be saved and a portion of what was invested would have to be set aside for debt service to the rich. If it were in your power to influence national policy, which side would you be on?

A Global View of Poverty and the Distribution of Wealth

The facts and figures on global poverty are not hard to find. In the section at the end of this chapter, a number of Web sites give examples of the impact of global poverty. For instance, many sites will give the number of people (1.3 billion) around the world who live in severe poverty. They also break the numbers down. Of the 1.3 billion people living in severe poverty, 800 million do not get enough food, and the remaining 500 million people are chronically malnourished (UNDP, 2001). Poverty is also a problem in industrial countries. The United Nations Development Programme estimated that in industrial countries 100 million people are living below the poverty line, 5 million are homeless, and another 37 million are jobless (UNDP, 2001).

Even though those in possession of resources vigorously insist that they are honest and productive and fulfill a social need, given the available facts that suggest that poverty is a condition that the poor have no control over, how do people feel about the poor in their country?

Research Hypothesis/Question   9.1:
Do people in different countries differ in their attitude toward people who are poor?

➢   *Data File:*   **GLOBAL**
➢   *Task:*   **Mapping**
➢   *Variable 1:*   **83) INJUSTICE**
➢   *View:*   **Map**

INJUSTICE -- PERCENT WHO SAID THAT PEOPLE ARE POOR BECAUSE "THERE IS INJUSTICE IN OUR SOCIETY" (WVS)

The darkest color identifies those countries with the highest percentage of people responding that they feel people are poor because of injustices. Interestingly, people in the United States, China, and India tend to believe that in their societies there is little injustice. Let's now look at a similar variable that asks if the poor are impoverished because they are lazy. If you believe a person is poor because he or she is lazy, you might view helping the person as enabling that person to remain lazy and poor. You surely would not see your actions as a pattern of inequality caused by a powerful entity subjugating the poor and keeping them dependent; an interesting dichotomy, but there may be no real difference between the two positions. But it is a debate with implications for international peace. In 1948, George Kennan (a U.S. Cold War planner) observed that "We [the United States] have 50% of the world's wealth, but only 6.3% of its population. In this situation, our real job in the coming period is to devise a pattern of relationships which permit us to maintain this position of disparity. To do so, we have to dispense with all sentimentality. We should cease thinking about human rights, the raising of living standards and democratization" (Pilger, 1998).

9.3   The Trap of Unequal Trades

"The powerful and cunning had learned to plunder by trade centuries ago and societies ever since have been caught in the trap of those unequal trades. Once unequal trades were in place, restructuring to equal trade would mean the severing of arteries of commerce which provide the higher standard of living for the dominant society and collapse of those living standards would almost certainly trigger open revolt. The world is trapped in that pattern of unequal trades yet today" (Smith, 1994).

Research Hypothesis/Question   9.2:
Do people in different countries think that the poor are lazy?

Data File:	**GLOBAL**
Task:	**Mapping**
➤ *Variable 1:*	**82) POOR LAZY**
➤ *View:*	**Map**

POOR LAZY -- PERCENT WHO SAID THE MOST IMPORTANT REASON THAT PEOPLE IN THEIR COUNTRY ARE POOR IS "LAZINESS AND LACK OF WILL POWER" (WVS)

Well, people in the United States are consistent. We tend to believe that injustice does not explain poverty but being lazy does. Public opinion in the United States, as in most affluent countries, has changed since the Great Depression. We have forgotten the lessons and hardships of that period. In 1933, when Franklin Roosevelt took office as president of the United States, unemployment had increased exponentially. There were some 15 million people or about 20% of the U.S. population who did not have a job. Very few people during the Depression thought the poor were poor because they were lazy. Jobs for even the most hard-working man or woman were not available during the Depression.

Taking into consideration that we in the Unites States have forgotten the hard lessons of the Depression, do you think that globally among people who believe that, there will be a correlation between these two variables? In other words, if a people believe that the poor are poor because of injustice, do you think that they will also believe that the poor are also lazy? If this is the case, we will not find a correlation between the two variables. Let's use a scatterplot to give us both a visual picture and a correlation to help determine the degree of the relationship between these two variables.

Research Hypothesis/Question   9.3:
People in countries who think that the poor are lazy do not think that the people are poor because there are injustices in society.

Data File: **GLOBAL**
➢   Task: **Scatterplot**
➢ Dependent Variable: **82) POOR LAZY**
➢ Independent Variable: **83) INJUSTICE**
➢   View: **Reg. Line**

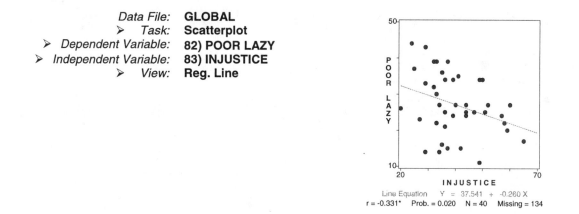

This is a weak but statistically significant correlation ($r = -.331$, $p < .05$) among the countries for which we have data. This shows that in countries where people believe that people are poor because they are lazy, these people do not believe that people are poor because there are injustices in society. Of course, this is a weak correlation with a small subset of nations. Out of 174 nations, we have data for both variables from only 40 countries. There are another 134 nations for which we have no data to analyze. As discussed in Chapter 6, when you are missing data on 70% of your sample, it is unwise to draw conclusions and generalize from this small subgroup to the entire sample of 174 nations. When reporting this type of finding, we generally say something like, "*Among the countries for which we have data, there is a weak but significant relationship.*" This alerts the reader that there is a substantial amount of missing data that probably affected the analysis and the findings. This gives the reader the option to accept the findings or reject them. Typically, if there is a good bit of missing data, such as in this case, I view the findings as suggestive. If I had data on all the countries, it *might* show that this is a true relationship, but without more data I will never know.

As we have seen before, however, there can be a big difference between First, Second, and Third World countries. In the above analysis we used all the countries that we had data for, and it included only 40 countries. Even so, let's see what people in Second and Third World countries think about poor people. On the one hand, I would think that if they buy into the idea that poor people are lazy, they have bought into the *Horatio Alger* myth. Horatio Alger (1832–1899) was an American writer in the second half of the 19th century. The theme that ran through his books and stories was about poor boys who grew up following high moral standards, working hard, and in the end attained wealth and respect. If people buy into the *Horatio Alger* myth, I would expect them to view the poor as lazy. On the other hand, people, such as those living in South Africa who have been deprived the opportunity to participate in the economy of their country, will believe that people are poor because of social and economic injustice.

Although we have data for only 40 countries, let's see if the *Horatio Alger* hypothesis is observable in the data that we do have. I wish we had data on all the countries, but this is the real world and things are not always the way I want them to be.

To begin, we will do the same analysis but this time we will do the analysis with several subsets of countries. I will break them into Second and Third, and First World countries.

Research Hypothesis/Question   9.4:
People in First World countries who think that the poor are lazy do not think that the people are poor because there are injustices in society.

Data File:	**GLOBAL**
Task:	**Scatterplot**
Dependent Variable:	**82) POOR LAZY**
Independent Variable:	**83) INJUSTICE**
➤ *Subset Variable:*	**25) THREEWORLD**
➤ *Subset Category:*	**Include1) 1ST WORLD**
➤ *View:*	**Reg. Line**

[Subset]

DENMARK

X = 29
Y = 14
New r Value
if Removed = -0.532*
Prob. = 0.017

Line Equation   Y = 40.377 + -0.472 X
r = -0.434*   Prob. = 0.041   N = 18   Missing = 8

What happens if we drop a couple of these First World countries to make the relationship more linear? This will make the scatter much tighter around the regression line. To find out what will happen when you have a tighter scatterplot, drop Demark and the United States from the scatterplot. I have marked Demark for you. The United States is represented by the point located at the top of the scatterplot. This identifies the country (the United States) with the highest number of people who believe that the poor are poor because they are lazy. To remove these two countries from the analysis, while viewing the scatterplot in MicroCase, highlight Denmark and then click on the [Remove] button. Then do the same with the point that represents the United States. You will notice that the correlation goes from -.43 to -.57. This indicates that people in First World countries, the ones for which we have data, who believe that poor people are poor because they are lazy discount social and economic injustice as a cause for poverty.

9.4   The Highest Disparity Rate in the World

Latin America has the highest disparity rate in the world between the rich and the poor. The foreign policy of the United States in Central and South America has often been criticized for failing to help improve the conditions of the poor in that region. Critics, both in the United States and abroad, suggest that the only reason the United States is involved in South America is to enhance United States national interests. This includes interference that affects the course and direction of the nations in the region through overt and covert destabilization (often in the cry against communism, but in reality to prevent substantial development so that the United States may continue its influence and control, and ensure cheap resources) (Youngers, 1999).

Before we leave First World countries, I am going to do the same analysis and remove the country that is the first outlier. The United States and Demark were not outliers. I removed them because I wanted to show you what would happen if we tightened the scatterplot around the regression line. As you saw, it increased the correlation coefficient from -.43 to -.57. What would happen, however, if I dropped the country with the highest score on the question about people being poor because of social injustice? In this case that country is Norway.

Research Hypothesis/Question   9.5:
Removing a single outlier country will reduce the correlation between people in First World countries who think that the poor are lazy and people who think that injustices in society cause poverty.

Data File:	**GLOBAL**
Task:	**Scatterplot**
Dependent Variable:	**82) POOR LAZY**
Independent Variable:	**83) INJUSTICE**
Subset Variable:	**25) THREEWORLD**
Subset Category	**Include1) 1ST WORLD**
➢ *View:*	**Reg. Line**
➢ *Find:*	**Outlier/Remove**

To replicate these results, first click on the select variables button [🔙] and then click [OK] to restore the previously deleted cases to the scatterplot. Select Reg. Line and then continue with the instructions below to identify and remove the outlier.

For this analysis, I used MicroCase to identify the outlier country. I did this by clicking on the [Outlier] button in the Find box. MicroCase then selected Norway as the outlier. When Norway was removed from the analysis, there was no statistically significant relationship, neither *positive* nor *inverse*, between the variables: *the poor are lazy* and *injustice causes poverty* ($r = -.294$, $p < $ NS). Of all First World countries, Norway's people strongly believe in the *social injustice* explanation for poverty. This finding suggests that people in most First World countries do not accept that people are poor because they are *lazy* nor do they believe people are poor because of an *unjust society*. People in First World countries may think there are other explanations for people being poor, but we can rule out *laziness* and *injustice* as explanations. Now let's look at Second and Third World countries and see how they view people living in poverty. It will surely be different.

Research Hypothesis/Question   9.6:
People in Second and Third World countries who think that the poor are lazy do not think that the people are poor because there are injustices in society.

Data File:	**GLOBAL**
Task:	**Scatterplot**
Dependent Variable:	**82) POOR LAZY**
Independent Variable:	**83) INJUSTICE**
➢ *Subset Variable:*	**25) THREEWORLD**
➢ *Subset Categories:*	**Include 2) 2nd WORLD,**
	3) 3rd WORLD
➢ *View:*	**Reg. Line**
➢ *Find:*	**Outlier/Remove**

To see the previous graph you will need to remove the outlier nation China from the scatterplot. While viewing the scatterplot, click on the [Outlier] option. China will be circled in red. Then click the [Remove] button. After you remove China from the analysis, you will almost have a perfect inverse correlation ($r = -.849$, $p < .000$). You will note that the diagonal is running almost perfectly from the top left corner to the lower right corner. This correlation shows that among the 21 Second and Third World countries for which we have data, the people in these countries view the two conditions that are used to explain poverty (*laziness* and *social injustice*) in a very diametric way. You can also try removing a few other outliers to see what happens to the correlation. If you do remove outliers identified by the scatterplot procedure, you will notice that the correlation decreases but it continues to remain quite strong even after removing five outlier countries.

Residuals and Their Role in Understanding the Results

Read this section, please! It will be easy to understand; I use pictures. Before moving on in our analysis of world poverty, I want to show you how the correlational and regression analysis is figured. It's not difficult to understand if we use two visuals. Use the following to do this in MicroCase.

If you add up the distances between the scores below the diagonal line (this line is the combined mean of the two variables—it is also called the *regression line*) and subtract that total from the sum of distances of scores above the diagonal line, the answer will be *zero*. The correlation and regression procedures split the scores so that the plot of the regression line is down the middle of the plotted scores.

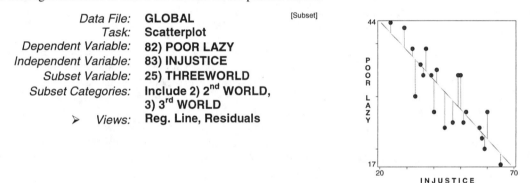

		[Subset]
Data File:	**GLOBAL**	
Task:	**Scatterplot**	
Dependent Variable:	**82) POOR LAZY**	
Independent Variable:	**83) INJUSTICE**	
Subset Variable:	**25) THREEWORLD**	
Subset Categories:	**Include 2) 2nd WORLD, 3) 3rd WORLD**	
➢ *Views:*	**Reg. Line, Residuals**	

Line Equation   Y = 55.484 + -0.560 X
r = -0.849**   Prob. = 0.000   N = 21   Missing = 127

For contrast, use MicroCase to create the following graph:

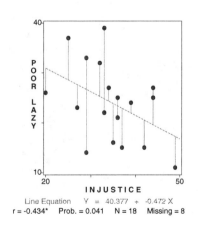

		[Subset]
Data File:	**GLOBAL**	
Task:	**Scatterplot**	
Dependent Variable:	**82) POOR LAZY**	
Independent Variable:	**83) INJUSTICE**	
➢ *Subset Variable:*	**25) THREEWORLD**	
➢ *Subset Category:*	**Include 1) 1ST WORLD**	
➢ *Views:*	**Reg. Line, Residuals**	

Line Equation   Y = 40.377 + -0.472 X
r = -0.434*   Prob. = 0.041   N = 18   Missing = 8

As you can see, the distances between the scores and the regression line are much greater than the distances in the scatterplot among Second and Third World countries. This is why the correlation among First World countries ($r = -.434$, $p < .05$) is so much lower than the correlation between Second and Third World countries ($r = -.849$, $p < .000$). As well, you will notice that the diagonal line or regression line in the scatterplot does not run from corner to corner. It is more from side to side. See! I told you it is not that hard to understand. Now doing the math, called linear math, is a bit more complicated. For that reason, however, we let computers do the math. Computers do not do a lot, but they sure do these kinds of math problems easily.

Injustice and Reform

There is a problem with believing that people are poor because of social injustice. One has a clear ethical and moral obligation to help correct an injustice. On a global scale this may seem impossible, but we need to continue to point out the injustices, and we need to continue to ask that conditions be made equitable for all.

Karl Marx (1818–1883) predicted in 1847 that the workers of the would one day rise up in revolt against the wealthy owners of industrial production and take it for themselves. Then the workers would organize themselves under a socialist government he called *communism*. This was his vision of how the injustices of the Industrial Revolution would be corrected. Today, for the most part, when people call for a revolution, they mean a political revolution, not a violent revolution. Using nonviolent political protest was perfected by Mohandas K. Gandhi of India (1869–1948) in the early 1900s and Martin Luther King, Jr., of the United States (1929–1968) in the 1960s.

9.5	We Have the Resources to Eradicate Poverty
•	Providing universal access to basic social services and transfers to alleviate income poverty would cost about $80 billion U.S. dollars. This is less than the net worth of the seven richest men in the world.
•	Debt relief for 20 of the poorest countries would cost $5.5 billion–the cost of building Euro Disney.
•	The cost of eradicating poverty is 1% of global income (UNDP, 2001).

We can use a few variables to test our statement that *people who think poverty is the result of an unjust society are people who are more willing to participate in activities to correct social injustice.*

Research Hypothesis/Question   9.7:
People in countries who think that people are poor because of social injustice also think that "the entire way our society is organized must be radically changed by revolutionary action."

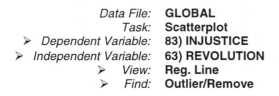

Data File:	**GLOBAL**
Task:	**Scatterplot**
➤ Dependent Variable:	**83) INJUSTICE**
➤ Independent Variable:	**63) REVOLUTION**
➤ View:	**Reg. Line**
➤ Find:	**Outlier/Remove**

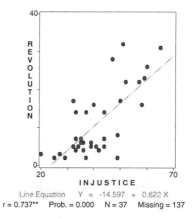

Line Equation   Y = -14.597 + 0.622 X
r = 0.737**   Prob. = 0.000   N = 37   Missing = 137

To see the preceding graph you will have to remove two countries that are outliers. While viewing the scatterplot, click on the [Outlier] option. The Czech Republic will be circled in red. Then click the [Remove] button. While still viewing the scatterplot, click on the [Outlier] option a second time. The Slovak Republic will be circled in red. Then click the [Remove] button. These two countries were very different from all of the others, as people in both countries believe that "the entire way our society is organized must be radically changed by revolutionary action" and they also do not believe people are poor because of social injustice.

Once the two outliers are removed, the correlation between countries where people believe that people are poor because of social injustice and countries where people believe that "the entire way our society is organized must be radically changed by revolutionary action" is very high ($r = .737$, $p < .000$). **Remember, however, we found this relationship exists with only 37 countries. We cannot generalize this finding to the 135 countries that we have no data for and thus are not in the analysis.**

Poverty and the Distribution of Wealth in the United States

There are only three times in the history of the United States when the people of the United States felt and acted as one: when a German submarine sunk the Lusitanian resulting in the United States' entering World War I; when the Japanese bombed Pearl Harbor, resulting in the United States' entering World War II; and when the World Trade Center was destroyed and the Pentagon attacked with our own domestic passenger planes. During these periods, petty differences were put aside to accomplish the goal of regaining our security. It would be great if we could come together as a country to put a stop to social and economic injustice in the United States.

Poverty in the United States is unnecessary and it is as destructive to the people who are deprived as it is to those of us who probably have too much. When large subgroups of people in the United States struggle for the means needed for a fair chance for a decent life: a stable income, a stable social environment, equitable ownership of housing and land, and basic rights and freedom, it denigrates us all. In our hearts, we know there is enough to go around, but we feel helpless to do anything about it. What each of us can do is to learn the facts about poverty in the United States and around the world. Then, when political leaders suggest that there is nothing that can be done to stop the deprivation of people in the United States and the world of the means to pursue a decent life, you and I can speak out with the knowledge that people do not have to live in poverty to maintain our high standard of living.

9.6	The Global Distribution of Wealth
•	In 1960, 20% of the people in the world's richest countries had 30 times the income of the poorest 20% in those countries. In 1997, the same 20% had 74 times as much income as the poorest 20% did in these rich countries.
•	It is estimated that 7 million children die each year as a result of the world debt crisis. Between January 2000 and April 2001, over 8.55 million children are believed to have died because of the debt crisis (UNDP, 2001).

Poverty in Your County

To begin our study of poverty in the United States, let's look at where impoverished families live in the United States. In our **COUNTIES** data file, there are several variables that can help us increase our knowledge about those who are poor and living in the United States.

Research Hypothesis/Question   9.8:
There is a great deal of variation from county to county in the United States in terms of the percentage of people living below the poverty level.

> ➤ *Data File:* **COUNTIES**
> ➤ *Task:* **Mapping**
> ➤ *Variable 1:* **7) %POOR 89**
> ➤ *View:* **Map**

%POOR 89 -- 1989: PERCENT BELOW POVERTY LEVEL

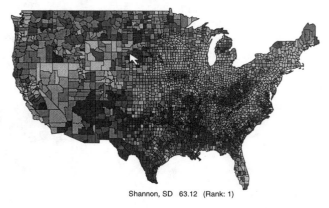

Shannon, SD 63.12 (Rank: 1)

As you will notice, the data for the 3,141 counties are based on 1989 census data. It may be several years before 2000 census data by county are completed. Even so, using the data available, let's see where the poor lived.

Shannon, South Dakota, was the poorest county in the United States in 1989. In the late 1970s, Green County, Alabama, was the poorest country in the United States. Then they were allowed to open a Greyhound Race track. This simulated the economy and Green County moved from being the poorest county in the country to being the 22nd poorest county in 1989. Even then, Green County remained the poorest county in Alabama. By 2001, the race track was doing poorly and I expect Green County is still one of the poorest counties in the United States.

Using this map, find out where your county ranks in terms of the percentage of people living below the poverty level. How do you explain the number of people living below the poverty level in your county?

The Effects of Poverty and Discrimination Against American Indians

Among the neglected poor in the United States, and the Americas as a whole, are the American Indians. They have been discriminated against by Europeans since the time of Columbus. Native Americans are indigenous to the Americas. Anthropologists believe that American Indians are descendents of Asian people who migrated across the Bering land bridge some 30,000 years ago. When Columbus planted the Spanish flag in the sand of a beach on a tiny Caribbean island, there were 90 million Indians living in North, Central, and South America. This means that 90 million people discovered the Americas before Columbus stumbled on it.

Which comes first, discrimination and then poverty, or poverty and then discrimination? Of course, both are devastating to the individual, families, and the group being discriminated against at the time. Over the centuries, discrimination has been used to deprive segregated groups of needed resources; this results in a drift into poverty. In an economy organized on the principles of Adam Smith (1723–1790), (a capitalist) *poverty* breeds contempt from those who are better off and results in discrimination (Smith, 1965). I suggest both are a serious threat to children and adults. Given the perverse nature of poverty and discrimination, how do you think it will affect the high school graduation rates among adolescents from poor American Indian families? Shall we see if there is a correlation between counties with people living below the poverty level and the percentage of Native Americans living in each county?

Research Hypothesis/Question   9.9:
A statistically significant correlation will exist between counties with a high percentage of people living below the poverty level and a high percentage of people who are American Indian.

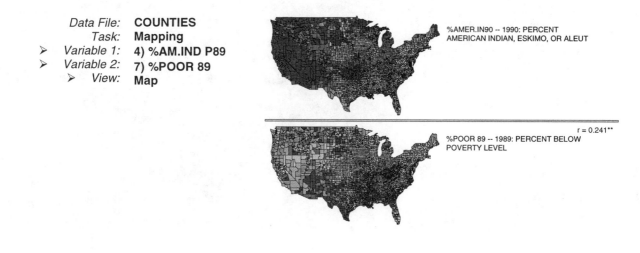

Data File: **COUNTIES**
Task: **Mapping**
➤ Variable 1: **4) %AM.IND P89**
➤ Variable 2: **7) %POOR 89**
➤ View: **Map**

%AMER.IN90 -- 1990: PERCENT AMERICAN INDIAN, ESKIMO, OR ALEUT

%POOR 89 -- 1989: PERCENT BELOW POVERTY LEVEL

r = 0.241**

The findings show that there is a small correlation between the percentage of American Indians in a county and counties with higher rates of people living below the poverty level, but the relationship is still statistically significant ($r = .241$, $p < .01$). When we find high percentages of people living below the poverty level, and there are American Indians living in the county, you will find substantial numbers of American Indians living below the poverty level. The exceptions are counties such as Broward, Miami-Dade, and Palm Beach located in southeastern Florida. The American Indians in this area are the Miccosukee and the Seminoles. These tribes are a vital part of the tourism industry and have income from legalized gambling on their reservations, which are covered under a federal law that allows gambling, even though state laws forbid legal gambling. The numbers are small, which means that there is more income for each family from tribal businesses and investments. Because of the oil wells on the northern shores of Alaska, the Eskimo and Aleut also have an income that puts them at an income level far above the poverty level. Nevertheless, for the majority of American Indians, poverty and discrimination are as serious a threat to them today as William Tecumseh Sherman's campaign to starve the Plains Indians into submission by destroying their major food source, the American Buffalo (Athearn, 1956). If you have not read about what happened to the American Indians in the late 1800s, you can still imagine what happened when starvation was used as a weapon against not just the Plains Indians but against all Indians in the United States. There were many Indians, both adults and children, who starved to death. Sherman is the general who marched through the South during the Civil War, burning a broad path through Georgia that included the burning of Atlanta. After the American Civil War, President Grant assigned him the job of moving the remaining American Indians from their traditional homelands onto reservations. This gave white settlers the chance to take what had been Indian land in the west. This was the same process that was used to take Indian lands in the northeast from the Iroquois, Lenape (known as the Delaware), Shawnee, and other tribes. In the south the Creek, the Cherokee, and other tribes lost their land, and in the west land was taken from the Sioux, the Cheyenne, and others. Sherman's strategy of starving the Indians into submission worked.

9.7	**The Number of People Living Below the Poverty Level Has Changed Little Since 1981**
•	In 1981, in the United States, there were approximately 36 million people living below the poverty level, or about 14.2% of all people, including children.
•	In 1997, in the United States, there were approximately 37 million people living below the poverty level. This is approximately 13.3% of the population (U.S. Bureau of the Census, 2000).

What kind of effect have the years of discrimination and poverty had on the American Indian? What has been the effect of both overt and covert federal programs designed to destroy Indian heritage and their culture? How is it affecting American Indian children today?

Research Hypothesis/Question   9.10:
More adolescents between 16 and 19 years old will be out of school in areas where there are high percentages of American Indian families living below the national poverty level.

Data File: **COUNTIES**
Task: **Mapping**
➢ Variable 1:   **10) %AM.IND P89**
➢ Variable 2:   **19) NOT N HS90**
➢   View: **Map**

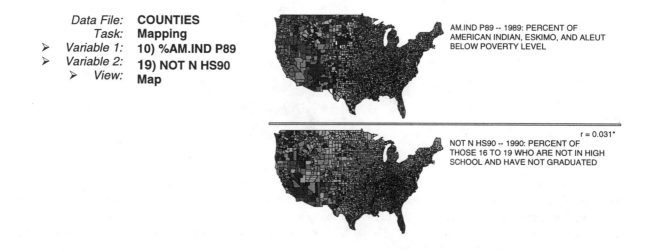

AM.IND P89 -- 1989: PERCENT OF AMERICAN INDIAN, ESKIMO, AND ALEUT BELOW POVERTY LEVEL

r = 0.031*

NOT N HS90 -- 1990: PERCENT OF THOSE 16 TO 19 WHO ARE NOT IN HIGH SCHOOL AND HAVE NOT GRADUATED

Although the correlation is very small, it is statistically significant because, even though it only happens occasionally, both tend to consistently occur together ($r = .031$, $p < .05$). My hypothesis was based on the knowledge that discrimination is harmful to children and adults, and that American Indians have a history of being discriminated against. The findings are interesting and support the hypothesis that discrimination is harmful to children when they experience it. One could speculate that the findings suggest that American Indian children from poor families, in areas where poverty among American Indians is common, do not experience as much discrimination as American Indian children living in regions where there are few poor American Indian families. In cases where there are few poor American Indian families, the discrimination makes it more difficult for children and their families in these communities to take advantage of resources, such as education, health services, and social services.

If this is a true phenomenon associated with poverty and discrimination, we should be able to find it operating among other groups of people that are discriminated against, such as African Americans. If it does exist, we would expect to find counties with a high percentage of people living below the poverty level and a high percentage of those people will be African Americans. Let's test to see if the phenomenon is operating among African American adolescents.

9.8   Everyone Has the Right to Work

Although many may blame the poor for their poverty, the poor are often victims of unemployment and under-employment. However, "Everyone has the right to work, to just and favorable conditions of work and to protection for himself and his family [and] an existence worthy of human dignity. Everyone has the right to a standard of living adequate for the health and well being of himself and his family, including food, clothing, housing and medical care."—*Universal Declaration of Human Rights*

Research Hypothesis/Question   9.11:
A statistically significant correlation will exist between counties with a high percentage of people living below the poverty level and a high percentage of people who are African Americans living below the national poverty level.

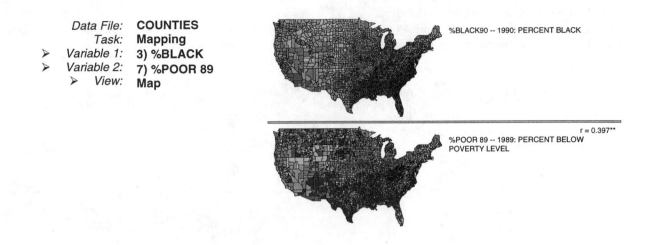

Data File: **COUNTIES**
Task: **Mapping**
➤   Variable 1:   **3) %BLACK**
➤   Variable 2:   **7) %POOR 89**
➤   View: **Map**

%BLACK90 -- 1990: PERCENT BLACK

r = 0.397**

%POOR 89 -- 1989: PERCENT BELOW
POVERTY LEVEL

This correlation between counties with high percentages of African Americans and high percentages of people living below the poverty level leaves little doubt that many African Americans are living in poverty ($r = .397$, $p < .01$). As we saw in the chapter on families (Chapter 2), African Americans still tend to live in the region of their forebearers in the southeastern United States.

Research Hypothesis/Question   9.12:
More adolescents between 16 and 19 years of age will be out of school in areas where there are high percentages of African Americans.

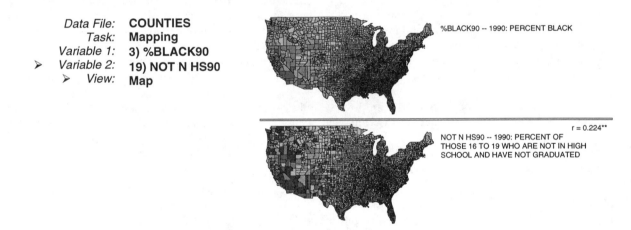

Data File: **COUNTIES**
Task: **Mapping**
Variable 1:   **3) %BLACK90**
➤   Variable 2:   **19) NOT N HS90**
➤   View: **Map**

%BLACK90 -- 1990: PERCENT BLACK

r = 0.224**

NOT N HS90 -- 1990: PERCENT OF
THOSE 16 TO 19 WHO ARE NOT IN HIGH
SCHOOL AND HAVE NOT GRADUATED

This is not the kind of hypothesis we want to find supported by the data. It shows us that in counties where there are high numbers of African Americans, there are also high numbers of adolescents between 16 and 19 years old who are *not* in school and who did not graduate from high school. It is a weak correlation, meaning that the two conditions do not occur in every case, but it is very statistically significant ($r = .224$, $p < .01$), which means that in many cases when they do occur, they occur together.

The Urban Poor

One of the largest groups of poor in the United States is the urban poor. They are not the only group of poor in this country. There are a large number of rural poor, but these impoverished rural people are for many of our political leaders *out of sight, out of mind.* This is much harder when politicians try to ignore the urban poor. The urban poor are a more *in your face* kind of group (to use a phrase from the urban poor). They are more mobile and have more access to social, legal, and political resources than the rural poor. Moreover, to the chagrin of many local politicians, the urban poor take advantage of these resources to shape public policy. It is slow, but there is no doubt in any politician's mind that the urban poor are a powerful force in shaping public policy.

9.9   Facts About the Urban Poor

- The urban poor are concentrated in the central cities in the United States. The areas defined as poverty areas in our metropolitan community are actually designated census tracts. A census tract where the poverty rate is 20% or more is considered a poverty area. Census tracts have between 2,500 to 8,000 people in small areas referred to as neighborhoods. In rural areas the whole county is designated a poverty area if the county has a poverty rate of 20% or more and the rural area does not have a census tract (O'Hare, 1996).

- Approximately 45% of poor people live in pockets in the central cities. Another 33% live in the suburbs, and 20% live in rural areas (O'Hare).

Given the available facts, I would hypothesize that although there are large numbers of urban poor, the poor in the United States are not concentrated just in the inner cities.

Research Hypothesis/Question   9.13:
There will *not* be a statistically significant correlation between counties with a high percentage of people living below the poverty level and counties with a high percentage of urbanization.

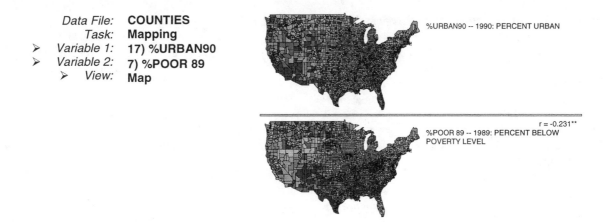

Data File:	**COUNTIES**
Task:	**Mapping**
➤ Variable 1:	**17) %URBAN90**
➤ Variable 2:	**7) %POOR 89**
➤ View:	**Map**

The reason I hypothesized that there would be *no* correlation between the high percentage of people living below the poverty level and counties with a high percentage of urbanization is because a lot of poor people live in the suburbs and in rural areas. My hypothesis was based on the observation that the poor are not particularly concentrated only in the inner cities. Although it is a small correlation, there is support for this observation that the poor are not all concentrated in the inner city ($r = -.231, p < .01$).

Poverty and Its Effect on Children

Given the relationships between poverty and education among American Indian and Africa American adolescents (poverty puts these children at risk of not finishing high school), does poverty affect all children despite race or ethnic group from finishing high school? We can find out the answer to the question using this data file.

Research Hypothesis/Question   9.14:
A statistically significant correlation will exist between counties with a high percentage of families living below the poverty level and a high percentage of adolescents between 16 and 19 years of age who are not in school and have not graduated from high school.

Data File: **COUNTIES**
Task: **Mapping**
➢ Variable 1:   **13) POOR FAM89**
➢ Variable 2:   **19) NOT N HS90**
➢ View: **Map**

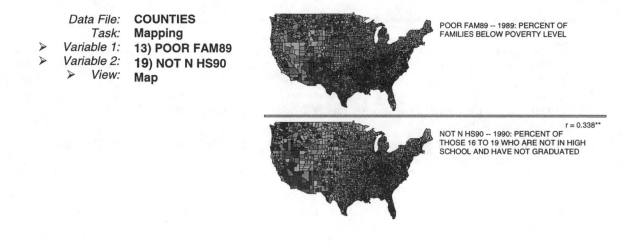

POOR FAM89 -- 1989: PERCENT OF FAMILIES BELOW POVERTY LEVEL

r = 0.338**

NOT N HS90 -- 1990: PERCENT OF THOSE 16 TO 19 WHO ARE NOT IN HIGH SCHOOL AND HAVE NOT GRADUATED

This correlation supports the literature that says poverty is harmful in more ways than simply depriving people of the means to pursue a decent life ($r = .338$, $p < .01$). This set of analyses suggests that poverty may also steal the future of a child living in a poor family.

Opinion About the Poor and Poverty in the United States

The book *The Reluctant Welfare State* (Jansson, 2001) says it all in the title. The federal government (with the exception of the Depression legislation and the "War on Poverty") has been opposed to policy that would move the United States closer to being a *welfare state.* Jansson's point is that the United States is a welfare state whether it wants to be or not. A major change in welfare in the United States took place when *The Personal Responsibility and Work Opportunity Reconciliation Act* was signed into law on August 22, 1996. This law ended entitlement of impoverished people to government assistance, a right guaranteed by the government since the 1930s. At the time the law took effect, few of us really thought it was an opportunity for the poor, but few protested this change in welfare.

While the traditional advocates for the poor in the United States protested TANF (Temporary Assistance for Needy Families), they warned of dire consequences, and most advocates vowed to monitor the progress or plight of TANF recipients. This legislative package was passed by both houses of Congress and signed by the president because the truth is, a *plurality* of the people in the United States do not believe that the poor do enough to help themselves. If people believe this, they would not be supportive of welfare assistance to the poor. We have all heard this a number of times before; it is akin to telling a poor person that other people have "pulled themselves up by their boot straps and you can also." Do many people think this way?

9.10   Plurality
A *plurality,* in political terms, means that although a group may not be a majority, it is larger than all opposing groups. For example, George W. Bush in the 2000 election did not win a majority of the votes. The votes were basically split three ways. Neither Bush nor Al Gore had a majority of the votes. George W. Bush, through hook and crook, had a slight *plurality.* Although there is a big difference between winning an election with a majority of voters supporting a president and winning with a plurality, George W. Bush is still the president.

Research Hypothesis/Question   9.15:
A plurality of people interviewed for the GSS will think the poor do not do enough to help themselves.

> *Data File:*   **GSS**
> *Task:*   **Univariate**
> *Primary Variable*   **78) WHY POOR 2**
> *View:*   **Pie**

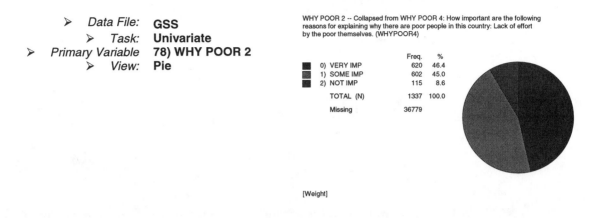

WHY POOR 2 -- Collapsed from WHY POOR 4: How important are the following reasons for explaining why there are poor people in this country: Lack of effort by the poor themselves. (WHYPOOR4)

		Freq.	%
■	0) VERY IMP	620	46.4
▨	1) SOME IMP	602	45.0
■	2) NOT IMP	115	8.6
	TOTAL (N)	1337	100.0
	Missing	36779	

[Weight]

A plurality of 46.4% of the 1,337 people who were asked the question thought that a very important reason for people being poor is that they do not do enough to help themselves. In fact, the vast majority of people surveyed (91.4%) thought that a lack of effort was a very important or a somewhat important explanation for some people being poor in the United States.

Few of us have any idea how much money the federal government is spending on welfare. This is especially true if we add in the welfare payments made to corporate America (i.e., Bowing, Exxon, McDonalds, Microsoft, etc.). Nevertheless, almost all people in the United States have an opinion about welfare and aid to the poor in the United States, and for that matter, the poor around the world. Some of these opinions are informed, others are less informed.

Do Education and Income Modify People's Opinion About the Poor?

Many people believe that the more education a person has, the more liberal he or she will be in his or her thinking. If this is true, it suggests that people with higher levels of education tend to think that poor people are trying very hard to help themselves. We have all heard this before, but does this education-based hypothesis really hold up under examination? We can use the GSS date file to test this phenomenon. We will use the multivariate analysis of variance (MANOVA) procedure to see if there is a significant difference in education by attitude toward the poor while controlling for other influences. The MANOVA works much like the ANOVA procedure. With MANOVA, we are able to test for significant differences in means on a ratio-level dependent variable across the levels of two or more categorical independent variables. If you have only one independent variable, the ANOVA task is the best procedure to use.

In the following analysis, we will use the MANOVA to build a model to explain conditions that modify or intensify the attitude of the people surveyed toward the poor. Education, as we have seen before, has a major effect on behavior. People are more willing to listen and are not as swayed by emotional arguments. Using the MANOVA we can test for the effect of education, and control for the influence of another important variable that influences attitudes, *income*. While we are at it, we can examine the relationship in subgroups, such as by race.

First, let us see if education does affect a person's attitude toward the poor.

Research Hypothesis/Question   9.16:
The higher a person's education, the *less* she or he will think that the poor do not do enough to help themselves.

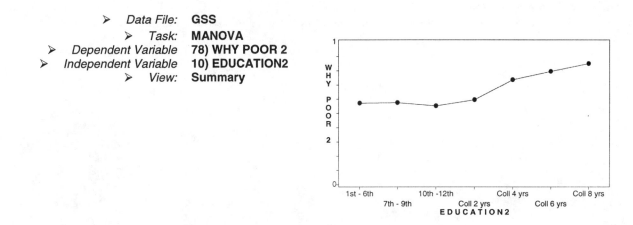

> Data File: **GSS**
> Task: **MANOVA**
> Dependent Variable **78) WHY POOR 2**
> Independent Variable **10) EDUCATION2**
> View: **Summary**

The MANOVA task is found on the Advanced Statistics Screen. Enter your dependent variable 78) WHY POOR 2 and your independent variable 10) EDUCATION2 and then click OK to generate the results.

This MANOVA summary shows that the more education a person has, the *less* they tend to think that the poor do not do enough to help themselves [select the ANOVA view ($F = 4.554$, df $= 6$, $p < .000$)]. In this case, education does have a positive effect. The more education, the less they see the poor as not helping themselves. Is income, however, influencing the relationship between education and attitude toward the poor? It could be that income is affected by education, and income rather than education is causing the changes in attitude toward the poor. To test for this possibility and to continue to build the best model for explaining people's attitudes toward the poor, we will next examine the two variables and control for *income*. In other words, if everyone has the same income, will people with more education still be more positive toward the poor?

9.11   TANF Outcome Studies

- In a 1997 study of families no longer receiving TANF (Temporary Assistance for Needy Families), which replaced Aid for Dependent Children, conducted in 10 large states (California, Florida, Illinois, Massachusetts, Michigan, New Jersey, New York, Ohio, Pennsylvania, and Texas), 36% of the families surveyed reported that their children were eating less or skipping meals due to the cost of food (Network, 1998).

- Some 78% of cities surveyed by the United States Conference of Mayors' Status Report on Hunger and Homelessness in American Cities reported increases in requests for emergency food in 1998. On average, request for emergency food increased by 14%. At least 84% of these cities surveyed reported increased need for emergency food among families with children. Moreover, 37% of persons requesting emergency food assistance were employed (FRAC, 1998).

- Second Harvest National Food Bank's study of emergency food clients, in 1997, found that more than one in eight (1:8) persons requesting emergency food had been cut from cash assistance in the prior two years as a result of TANF. Of the people requesting the food, 40% of their households had one or more adults working (SHFB, 1998).

Research Hypothesis/Question   9.17:
The higher a person's education, even when income is controlled, the less she or he will think that the poor do not do enough to help themselves.

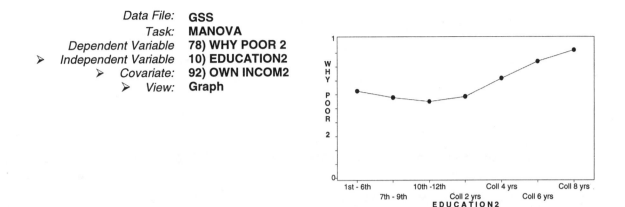

Data File:	GSS
Task:	MANOVA
Dependent Variable	78) WHY POOR 2
➢ Independent Variable	10) EDUCATION2
➢ Covariate:	92) OWN INCOM2
➢ View:	Graph

As we suggested, income is an influence on people's attitude toward the poor, but not like we hypothesized. When everyone in the analysis is made to statistically have the same income so as to control for differences in the level of income, there is an even greater difference for the effect of *education*. In this case, income has a negative effect on people's attitudes toward the poor, not a positive effect like I hypothesized. When income is controlled, people with more education are even more positive to people who are poor. When income is not controlled, the *F* value is 4.554; when the influence of income is removed, the *F* value increases to 5.061.

Research Hypothesis/Question   9.18:
People who self-identify as white and have higher levels of education will think that the poor do all they can to help themselves.

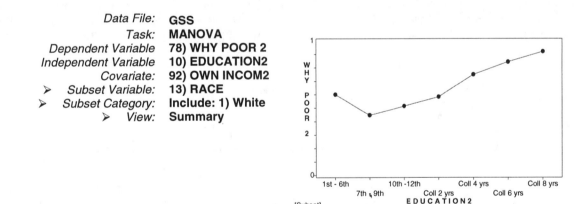

Data File:	GSS
Task:	MANOVA
Dependent Variable	78) WHY POOR 2
Independent Variable	10) EDUCATION2
Covariate:	92) OWN INCOM2
➢ Subset Variable:	13) RACE
➢ Subset Category:	Include: 1) White
➢ View:	Summary

There are two ways to change the subset category from the variable selection screen: 1) select the subset variable, press <Delete>, and the reselect the subset variable 13) RACE and select the new category Include: 2) Black. Or 2) Left-click once on the subset variable to select it, then right-click once and select the option Modify from the menu that appears. You can then unselect the category 1) White and select the category 2) Black. Click [OK] to continue.

This summary of the MANOVA shows that as education increases for self-identified whites, their attitude is significantly more positive toward the poor ($F = 6.411$, df = 6, $p < .000$) than those with less education. See the ANOVA statistics for the *F* value.

Now let's control for education among white respondents to see if their opinions about the poor change or remain the same as when we controlled for income.

Research Hypothesis/Question   9.19:
People who self-identify as white, who have high levels of income, and who have the same level of education will think that the poor do not do enough to help themselves.

Data File:	**GSS**
Task:	**MANOVA**
Dependent Variable	**78) WHY POOR 2**
Independent Variable	**92) OWN INCOM2**
Covariate:	**10) EDUCATION2**
➢ *Subset Variable:*	**13) RACE**
➢ *Subset Category:*	**Include: 1) White**
➢ *View:*	**Summary**

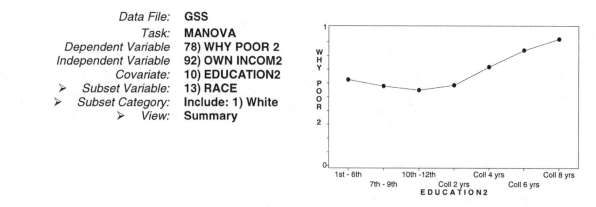

If you want to learn additional information about the MANOVA task in MicroCase, use the online help (F1).

This is quite different from the analysis when we controlled for income and let education vary. When looking at the effect of income on people's opinion, those that make between $15,000 and $19,000 are the least likely to blame the poor for the situation. And, although people who identified themselves as white who earn $20,000 or more are more inclined to think that the poor are not doing enough to help themselves, they are not as harsh in their opinion as people who earn under $14,999. The next question we would want to answer is related to the effects of race and ethnicity. Do African Americans and those identified as white have similar attitudes toward people who are poor? We can do the same analysis for both groups to find out if the effects of education are the same. First, we will do a set of analyses to determine the view of people who self-identify as white. Then we will do a set of the same analyses with people who self-identified as African American.

9.12   TANF State Studies

- *South Carolina*: A South Carolina Department of Social Services survey found 17% of former welfare recipients had no way to buy food some of the time since leaving TANF. This is twice as many families as reported such difficulties while receiving cash assistance (South Carolina DSS, 1998).

- *Massachusetts:* A 1998 statewide study by Project Bread and the Center on Hunger and Poverty at Tufts University found that 35% of those receiving emergency food were children. Almost 50% of providers that distribute emergency food reported an increase in need among families with children over the previous year. Almost 30% of the adults requesting emergency food assistance were employed full- or part-time (Project Bread, 1998).

- *New Jersey:* A survey by the New Jersey Statewide Emergency Food Assistance Network found a substantial increase in demand for emergency food between 1996 and 1997, despite a booming economy and an unprecedented low unemployment rate (FRAC, 1998).

- *Virginia:* A survey of emergency food providers in Virginia found that half the people relying on food pantries and soup kitchens had held a job in the past six months (FRAC, 1998).

- *Wisconsin:* Among people who left TANF under Wisconsin's W-2 program, over one-third of former welfare recipients had trouble paying for food, despite a high level of employment (Wisconsin, 1999).

Research Hypothesis/Question   9.20:
People who self-identify as black and have higher levels of education will think that the poor do all they can to help themselves.

Data File:	**GSS**
Task:	**MANOVA**
Dependent Variable	**78) WHY POOR 2**
Independent Variable	**10) EDUCATION2**
Covariate:	**92) OWN INCOM2**
➤ *Subset Variable:*	**13) RACE**
➤ *Subset Category:*	**Include: 2) Black**
➤ *View:*	**Summary**

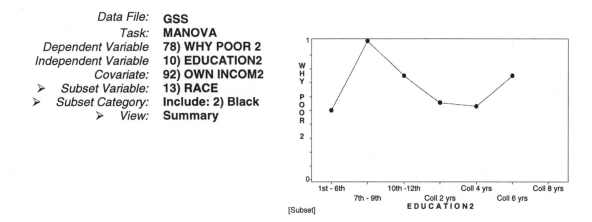

These analyses tell us an interesting story. The attitudes of people who self-identify as *white* change and become more positive toward the poor as their level of education increases ($F = 6.411$, df = 6, $p < .000$). Education, however, does not change the minds of African Americans ($F = .667$, df = 6, $p = $ NS). This may mean that African Americans, particularly those with less than a high school education, know that they and their neighbors are trying as hard as they can to help themselves; yet, they continue to struggle to make ends meet.

Of course, you could argue that it is not education among African Americans that shapes their attitudes toward the poor; this may vary by their income level. In other words, the more income an African American has, the less sympathetic he or she is to the poor. We can test this by using the same set of variables. The independent variable in this case will be OWN INCOM2. We will control for education.

Research Hypothesis/Question   9.21:
People who self-identify as African American, who have high levels of income, and who have the same level of education will think that the poor do not do enough to help themselves.

Data File:	**GSS**
Task:	**MANOVA**
Dependent Variable	**78) WHY POOR 2**
➤ *Independent Variable*	**92) OWN INCOM2**
➤ *Covariate:*	**10) EDUCATION2**
➤ *Subset Variable:*	**13) RACE**
➤ *Subset Category:*	**Include: 2) Black**
➤ *View:*	**Summary**

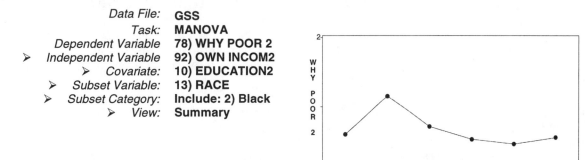

As you can see, attitudes toward the poor, when the person responding is earning between $5,000 and $9,999, are very positive. Then the line drops as income increases until reaching those earning $25,000 and above. Then attitudes toward the poor improve. Even so, this could be a spurious finding, a fluke. There are no statistically significant differences by income group. African Americans do not believe that people are poor because they don't try hard enough to help themselves ($F = 2.233$, df = 5, p = NS).

What we have found out from the people who answered these GSS questions about the cause for people being poor in the United States was that as a group, they feel that the poor in the United States are not trying hard enough to help themselves. This attitude, however, can be modified for whites by increasing their level of education. Apparently, however, African Americans, for the most part, who experience poverty on more of a first-hand basis than whites, do not change their attitudes about poverty with or without the benefit of additional education.

9.13   African American Poverty

Among African Americans in the United States, the number of poor dropped from 9.1 million in 1998 to 8.4 million in 1999. The poverty rate fell from 26.1% in 1998 to 23.6% in 1999. The 1999 poverty rate for African Americans was the lowest ever measured by the Census Bureau. Despite this decrease, the poverty rate among Africans Americans is still three times that of white non-Hispanics (U.S. Bureau of the Census, 2000).

End Note: As we have seen in this chapter, poverty in developed countries such as the United States is alive and well. Furthermore, few federal or state policies are currently in place that will provide a means for the poor to improve their situation. We also found that poverty in the developed countries is far different than in developing countries. It was also instructive to look at how poverty is viewed in the First World countries in comparison to Third World countries. It was even more instructive, once we removed the outlier nation, Denmark, from the group of First World countries. Once the outlier nation was removed, the correlation between people in the remaining countries was very small ($r = .43$ to $r = 29$). This indicates that people in these First World countries were not convinced that either being lazy or social injustice explained poverty. The look at residuals in this comparison was also important. As you noticed, some countries in the Third World are persuaded that the poor are lazy while others are convinced that poverty is caused by injustice ($r = .85$). As you can see, the residuals are smaller among Third World nations than for First World countries. Next, do the exercises and then we will take a look at criminal justice.

Other Issues Related to Poverty and the Distribution of Wealth

There are a number of issues related to poverty and the distribution of wealth that I could not examine in this chapter. However, with the data files provided with this book, you can analyze many of these issues on your own. To learn more about other issues related to poverty, enter the following search terms in the InfoTrac College Edition.

Poverty	**Malnutrition**
Unemployment	**Working poor**
Homeless	**World Bank**
International economic relations	**Immunization**
Legal assistance to the poor	**Rural poverty**

NAME:

COURSE:

DATE:

Workbook exercises and software are copyrighted. Copying is prohibited by law.

Review Questions

Based on the work you've done so far on the issue of poverty, see how well you do on this short True or False quiz.

If people in countries, for which we have data, tended to believe that poor people were lazy, they did not believe poor people were poor because of social injustice.　　T　F

After removing Norway from the analysis, people in countries identified as First World countries did not tend to believe that poor people were lazy, nor did they believe poor people were poor because of social injustice.　　T　　F

There was a strong correlation between countries where people believed that poverty was caused by an unjust society and countries where the people believed that a revolution was needed to change society.　　T　　F

The correlation between countries where people believe that poverty is caused by social injustice and countries where people believe that a revolution is needed to change society is correlated at $r = .737$.　　T　　F

In the United States, there is a significant correlation between counties with large populations of American Indians and counties with large populations of adolescents who are not attending school but never graduated high school.　　T　F

In the United States, *no* similar significant correlation (as seen among American Indians) was found between counties with large populations of African Americans and counties with large populations of adolescents who are not attending school but never graduated.　T　F

The majority of people in the United States believe the poor are doing all they can do to help themselves.　　T　F

Although African Americans and white non-Hispanics are two separate and distinct groups, they both have a very negative attitude toward the poor. However, this attitude changes as individuals obtain more education.　　T　F

MicroCase QUESTIONS

Use the following data files, variables, and analytical approaches to answer the MicroCase questions.

1.　　Using the STATES data file, map out a correlation between states with high numbers of children living with both parents and states with high percentages of households receiving food stamps.

> ➢ *Data File:* **STATES**
> ➢ *Task:* **Mapping**
> ➢ *Variable 1:* **79) %FS 95**
> ➢ *Variable 2:* **87) BOTH PAR92**
> ➢ *View:* **Map**

a.   The correlation between states with large percentages of households receiving food stamps and states where high percentages of children report living with both parents is $r =$ _____. The correlation is _____ (positive or inverse).

b.   The correlation between these two variables was significant, with $p <$ _____.

2.   Now, turn your attention to the impact of work on poverty. How does the type of work that is available affect the percentage of households receiving food stamps? Use the following two analyses to answer the questions.

> *Data File:* **STATES**
> *Task:* **Mapping**
> *Variable:1:* **79) % FS 95**
> ➢ *Variable 2:* **85) % AGRI.EM90**
> ➢ *View:* **Map**

a.   What are the $r =$ _____ and the $p <$ _____ from this analysis?

> *Data File:* **STATES**
> *Task:* **Mapping**
> *Variable:1:* **79) % FS 95**
> ➢ *Variable 2:* **84) %MANUF.E94**
> ➢ *View:* **Map**

b.   What are the $r =$ _____ and the $p <$ _____ from this analysis?

c.   The type of work people have available to them in a state (agricultural or industrial) makes a lot of difference in terms of the percentage of households that receive food stamps. Use the findings from the statistical analyses to explain why the findings support this statement.

_____

_____

I would leave you with an observation by *Dom Helda Camara,* a South American apostle of Liberation Theology who died in 1998:

"When I give food to the poor, they call me a saint.
When I ask why the poor have no food, they call me a communist."
As found on: www.globalissues.org/

Variable Lists Related to Poverty and the Distribution of Wealth

The following is a partial list of the variables in your data files. You can examine them as individual variables or several variables at a time using the approaches you learned in this chapter. To see a list of all of the variables, the question the variable asks, and the range of values, press [F3] to open the variable list window from anywhere in the software. Try using some of the variables below with the variables you have already tested.

GLOBAL

37) INFLATRT
    ANNUAL INFLATION RATE (TWF, 1997)
41) LITERACY
    LITERACY RATE. NUMBER OF PEOPLE OVER 15 YEARS OF AGE PER 1,000 POPULATION
64) LEFT/RIGHT
    NUMBER OF LEFTISTS PER RIGHTIST (CALCULATED)

STATES

50) %MENT.HS90
    PERCENT LIVING IN MENTAL HOSPITALS
51) %JUV.INS90
    PERCENT LIVING IN JUVENILE INSTITUTIONS
52) %COL.DRM90
    PERCENT LIVING IN COLLEGE DORMITORIES

GSS

27) EQUALIZ $2
    Some people think that the income differences between the rich and the poor ought to be reduced.
76) HELP POOR?
    Place self on scale: (1) I strongly agree, government should improve living standards; to (5) I strongly agree that people should take care of themselves.
80) SOC.DIF.1
    Only if differences in income are large enough is there an incentive for individual effort.
81) RACE QUOTA
    Do you favor or oppose forbidding the use of racial quotas in hiring and employment?

Web Pages Related to Poverty and the Distribution of Wealth

If you wish to find a world of resources that are available over the Internet, the following list of Web sites will get you started. Once you visit these Web sites, you will find many interesting links to other useful Web sites.

Infoplease.com
ln.infoplease.com/index.html

The Urban Institute
www.urban.org

Center for Public Policy Priories
www.cppp.org/policy/welfare-reform/

American Bar Association
www.abanet.org/homeless/home.html

U.S. Dept. of Labor
www.doleta.gov/

The Kansas City Star: Welfare Reform & Reality
www.kcstar.com/projects/welfare/links.htm

American Public Human Services Association
www.usaid.gov/

Habitat for Humanity International
www.habitat.org/

References

Athearn, R. G. (1956). *William Tecumseh Sherman and the Settlement of the West.* Norman, OK: University of Oklahoma Press.

Cherry, A. L. (1994). *The Socialization Instinct: Individual, Family, and Social Bonds.* Westport, CT: Praeger Press.

Cherry, A. L., Dillon, M. E., and Rugh, D. (eds.). (2001). *Teenage Pregnancy: A Global View.* Westport, CT: Greenwood Pub.

FRAC. (1998). *The hunger of poor people in the United States: 1998.* World Hunger Education Service Associates. Retrieved September 18, 2001, from www.worldhunger.org/articles/us/frac.htm.

Global Issues. (2001). *Causes of poverty: Poverty around the world.* Retrieved September 18, 2001, from www.globalissues.com.

Jansson, B. S. (2001). *The Reluctant Welfare State* (4th ed.). Belmont, CA: Wadsworth Publishing Company.

Network. (1998). *Welfare reform: How do we define success?* Washington DC: A Catholic Social Justice Lobby. Retrieved September 19, 2001, from www.networklobby.org/wrwp.htm.

O'Hare, W. P. (1996). A new look at poverty in America. *Population Bulletin, 51*(2), 2–46.

Paxman, J. (2001). *Jeremy Paxman of the BBC—Interview of Tony Blair.* London: The British Broadcasting Company, June 7.

Project Bread (1998). *Hidden Hunger, Fragile Futures.* Boston, MA: Tufts University, Center on Hunger, Poverty and Nutrition Policy.

SHFB. (1998). *Hunger 1997: The Facts and Faces.* Santa Clara, CA: Second Harvest National Food Bank Network.

Smith, A. (1965). *The Wealth of Nations.* New York: Random House.

Smith, J. W. (1994). *The World's Wasted Wealth 2.* Santa Maria, CA: Institute for Economic Development.

South Carolina DSS. (1998). *Survey of Former Family Independence Program Clients Whose Cases Were Closed Between January and March, 1997.* South Carolina, Department of Social Services.

UNDP (2001). *Facts and figures on poverty.* United Nations Development Programme. Retrieved September 18, 2001, from www.undo.org/tems/english/facts.htm.

The United States Conference of Majors. (1999). *A status report on hunger and homelessness in American cities 1999.* Retrieved September 19, 2001, from www.usmayors.org/uscm/homeless/hunger99.pdf.

U.S. Bureau of the Census. (2000). Poverty statistics on population growth. *Current Population Survey.* Washington, DC: Population Division, U.S. Census Bureau.

WDW. (1999). *Survey of Those Leaving AFDC or W-2 January to March, 1998: Preliminary Report.* Madison, WI: Wisconsin, State of, Department of Workforce Development.

Youngers, C. (1999). U.S. policy in Latin America and Caribbean. *The Progressive Response, 3*(7), 2. Retrieved September 18, 2001, from www.foreignpolicy-infocus.org/.

Additional Material That May Be of Interest

Dyke, N. B. (ed.) (2001). *Alleviating Global Poverty: Technology for Economic and Social Uplift.* Washington, DC: Aspen Institute (distributed by the Brookings Institution Press).

Hartman, C. (ed.) (2001). *Challenges to Equality: Poverty and Race in America.* Armonk, NY: M. E. Sharpe.

Rwomire, A. (ed.) (2001). *African Women and Children: Crisis and Response.* Westport, CT: Praeger Press.

Chapter 10

Crime and Justice

Tasks: Mapping, Scatterplot, Correlation, Times Series, Curve Fitting

Data Files: STATES, GLOBAL, US TRENDS

Overview of Chapter 10

This last chapter deals with one of human's most enduring problems: crime and justice. In part, it is because of the unpredictable and volatile nature of human relationships. Justice, however, is a concept that is intended to control acts of vengeance by one person on another or by one group on others. Justice is needed because too often crime is defined by the powerful to control the less fortunate. While we are looking at the role that social and political variables play in crime, justice, and punishment, we will spend a bit more time working with time-series data doing something called *curve fitting*. This will help us identify if changes in the crime rate are influenced and fluctuate with the divorce rate, unemployment, and the percentage of people who feel that their politicians are crooked. In this final chapter, you will use many of the basic procedures you used in the preceding chapters. You will also visit with residuals again to see what they tell us about statistical relationships. Of course, the *curve-fitting* approach is new, but it gives you yet another view of reality. It gives you another question to ask when engaging in critical thinking: what has been the relationship between two or more conditions over time?

P risons are places that house people defined as criminals. People are defined as criminals because they participated in an act or they exhibited a behavior that the larger social group prohibits. Prisons have been used throughout human history as a survival strategy, much like the leper colony mentioned in Chapter 9. Prisoners in antiquity, once incarcerated or thrown into a dungeon, were not expected to ever leave (Cherry, 1994).

The definition of crime is typically based on strongly held beliefs by the larger society. Based on norms and values of the dominant society, laws are enforced by agents of the courts who are the enforcement arm of the political organization in power. Because of the changing beliefs and norms, laws change and this changes the definition of who is a criminal. Some crimes, however, have been defined in a similar way down through the ages. Long before recorded history, homicide, for instance, was considered a serious crime in all families, tribes, and social organizations. Yet even homicide is based on a definition. While it is a crime to murder one of your own kind, it may be perfectly okay with the controlling political or social group to take the life of someone from a different troop, religion, or political persuasion. Even then, the right to take another's life is usually situational. In most modern societies, if you are in a war and fighting for your country, killing the *enemy* is an accepted behavior. It may even be laudable and result in one winning metals and honor. If, however, after the battle, you kill a captured enemy who *spits* on you, you will be prosecuted for murder. You would probably be given a long prison term and you may even be executed for the murder of such an enemy. Killing during battle is okay; killing after it is over is murder.

Among the early theories to explain crime, demonology was probably the first. It is akin to the statement that *the devil made me do it*. The classical theory suggests that the decision to commit a crime is based on the pleasure and pain of the act for the person committing the crime. Karl Marx viewed crime as a behavior that resulted from an intense competition for resources, and this competition was based on class differences. Later, criminals were considered to be mentally deficient. Even Freud's psychoanalytic approach was used to explain criminal behavior. Social control theory, another *devil theory,* assumes that everyone would be a criminal if they were not stopped by the threat of harsh punishment. Anomie, of course, has been a popular theory used to explain many human deviate behaviors. Labeling has been a popular explanation for people committing a criminal act, especially in the case of children (Zastrow, 2000).

Even though homicide is defined and sanctions against murder are enforced by the politically powerful, aggression is a human condition often associated with homicide. It is a biological condition found to some degree in all individuals. Some social scientists believe that the control of individual aggression was the basis for the development of human society and laws. Evolutionary law and its derivative *social bond theory*, however, would suggest another explanation. The variations of aggressiveness found among individuals have an evolutionary advantage. During periods of threat to the larger group of individuals, those who are more aggressive are useful in defending the group. Their aggression gives the larger group a better chance of survival. It may be, however, the end of a large number of aggressive people such as those killed in war. High levels of aggression among the individuals, even though useful when facing an attacker, can be harmful to the survival of the group when no threat is present. For this reason, there are jails and prisons with which to both threaten and confine aggressive people. What I am proposing is that aggression results from competition for scarcest resources, competition for sexual partners, because of crowding, anomie (social upheaval), and a weakening of bonds to the social group. This construct also suggests that to modulate aggression in an individual or group toward another, strengthen the bonds between those who are the aggressor and those who are the target of the aggressor. In kidnapping and hostage situations, it is called the *Stockholm syndrome* (with the exception of the movie "Die Hard," where a movie character mistakenly refers to it as the Helsinki syndrome). The *Stockholm syndrome* is a situation that develops after a period of time where the hostages begin to sympathize with the captors and the captors begin to see the hostages as supporters of their cause. In a hostage situation, as time passes, an odd type of bond forms between hostages and their captors. The *Stockholm syndrome* develops when a captive cannot escape; he or she is isolated with the captive, and the captors threatens to kill the hostage. It takes small tokens of kindness by the captor and two to four days for the syndrome to develop. In many ways, in these situations, the captors and hostages have more in common with each other than with the rest of us.

In the early days of the year 2000, for the first time in human history one nation, the United States, was holding in its jails and prisons 2 million people defined as criminal. What is crime? Does it vary with changes in social conditions? These are questions that will be addressed in this last chapter.

Examining Crime and Justice Using Social Bond Theory

The overarching hypothesis for this examination is that criminal activity varies with specific social conditions that reduce the social bond of the individual to his or her community and social group. This concept is based on evolutionary law that supports the notion that when a person's bonds to their community and social group are weakened, the person's obligation to the community is lessened, which allows the person to perpetrate acts against the community and individuals in that community (Cherry, 1994). Social bond theory explains crime in a similar way to Durkheim's theory of anomie. The difference with social bond theory is that it helps us understand the operations involved in a person's reaction to anomie. It is not enough that the social order is in disarray; it is that the attachment of the individual to the society is damaged by the society that is in disarray. This allows the alienated person to act in his or her own best interest even when it is a crime in the larger society to do so. In such cases, the person is free of the psychological restraints that prevent criminal acts. What I am proposing is that crime is a social condition and as such, laws, concepts of justice, and punishment must be guided by ethical standards to exact justice.

10.1   The Stockholm Syndrome

In the summer of 1973, four hostages were taken in a botched bank robbery in Stockholm, Sweden. At the end of their captivity, six days later, the hostages resisted rescue. The hostages refused to testify against their captors, and they raised money for their captors' legal defense. Some accounts even report that one of the hostages eventually became *engaged* to one of her jailed captors (Cockburn, 1985). An example of the depth of this bizarre bond that develops is reflected in the statement of a hostage from Flight 847, "They weren't bad people. They let me eat, they let me sleep, they gave me my life." The flight crew and passengers were held hostage for 17 days in 1986 by terrorists (Strasser, 1987).

Ethical Foundation for Crime and Justice

Some take the position that those who commit a criminal act or who live a life of crime have given up any rights they have to be treated ethically and justly. Often, this conceptualization is based on the primitive view of justice, *an eye for an eye*. Yet, there have always been others who have studied law and have tried to determine a just penalty when those laws are broken. A few of these groups that are active in the United States are the Victim-Offender Reconciliation Program, the Families to Amend California's Three-Strikes Law, and The Sentencing Project, to mention a few (the Web sites for these and others organizations can be found at the end of this chapter).

10.2   Ethical Ground Zero: Crime and Justice

Many of us feel fairly secure in our community. We are not involved in any criminal activities, and we have never broken the law, with the exception of driving over the speed limit whenever we think we can get away with it. Suppose this was you. You have never been involved in a crime nor have you ever been a victim. Yet, one day your neighbor was murdered; the police found the weapon in your car; a neighbor said you and the victim were sexually involved, and he had heard you yelling at her the night she was murdered. Worst of all, you had no one that could put you somewhere else when the murder occurred. You were found guilty and sentenced to death. Through the years your legal appeals were unsuccessful. You were on death row. You were let out for one hour a week. You were allowed a bath twice a week. The only thing that broke the boredom was a prison guard who harassed and tormented you unmercifully. Year after year the guard made your life a living hell. The more you complained, the worse the guards treated you. Finally, when your last appeal failed, another date was set for your execution. Several days before you were to die, you had the chance, and you killed your tormentor. The other guards came to his rescue, but not in time. Because of the murder, your execution was postponed so that you could be charged and stand trial for the guard's murder. During the second trial, a newspaper investigator found out that the neighbor who testified against you in the first murder trial had been in prison in the past for killing a girlfriend. In that case, he had accused his brother of the crime. Under pressure from the police, your one-time neighbor confessed. You found out about his confession the day the jury sentenced you to death for killing the prison guard. If you knew something like this could happen to an innocent person, what kind of justice system would you devise? In light of the fact that you were innocent of the crime that sent you to prison where you killed a guard, how would you want to be judged?

A Global View of Crime and Justice

If crime were a part of the human character, crime would have similar features to that of gender. In the case of gender, for instance, social circumstances and culture define *female behavior* in different ways. Even so, women act and are treated in recognizable ways around the world. People defined as criminal, however, have no physical traits and often the same behavior is criminal one day and patriotic the next.

Through the ages people have also recognized this phenomenon (a crime to one group may be an act of heroism to another group). The literature is replete with criminal Robin Hoods and Jessie James-type characters. Books and movies romanticize the life of the outlaws. The truth is, of course, there are people who commit serious crimes and need to be incarcerated to protect society from future harm. Even so, most of us realize that prisons are often inhumane places, are unsafe, and in many ways represent the failure of the political system to provide access to resources and sustenance to all of its citizens.

Testing the Observation That Crime Is Socially Defined

Given the data files we have available to us, how could we test the statements made above? We have variables on crime, but the question is, how can we use variables on crime in different countries to support the hypothesis that crime is the function of a social definition? One approach that works fairly well in science is to identify what conditions would look like if there were no outside influences. This can be called the *null hypothesis*. Again take sex. As a child develops, his or her sexual organs develop. We expect them to develop. That is the normal process. If they do not develop normally, we suspect that their development has been interfered with by outside forces not a part of the normal process of child development. Using this approach, describing the null hypothesis, what would we expect if homicide were like the development of the sexual organ, a part of our biology? If this were a theoretical proposition, it would suggest that all human groups would have about the same number of criminals in each crime group. This would mean that each country would have approximately the same percentage of murders and thefts per year. If an outside influence were at work, we would expect to see big differences between countries. Let's see if this null hypothesis is supported by the data.

Research Hypothesis/Question   10.1:
All countries will have approximately the same percentage of murders and thefts each year.

> ➢ *Data File:* **GLOBAL**
> ➢ *Task:* **Mapping**
> ➢ *Variable 1:* **69) MURDER 90**
> ➢ *Variable 2:* **72) THEFT 90**
> ➢ *View:* **Map**

MURDER 90 -- 1990: NUMBER OF HOMICIDES PER 100,000 POPULATION (UNCRIME)

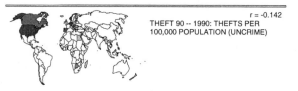

r = -0.142
THEFT 90 -- 1990: THEFTS PER 100,000 POPULATION (UNCRIME)

There are a large number of countries that we do not have data for, but it is still evident that neither the number of murders nor thefts is equally distributed across the countries for which we have data. Thus, it disproves the null hypothesis. Data from more countries would not reduce the variation found among this handful of countries. More than likely the variation from country to country would be even greater.

You will also notice that murder rates and the number of thefts are not correlated. Any correlation, however, that is calculated with this much missing data should not be reported. The likelihood that it is incorrect is very high. At times when I see these analyses, I ask myself what the correlation would be if I had more complete data, but until I have more complete data, I view the correlation as an unsupported observation.

This analysis not only disproves the hypothesis, but incomplete data and all, it presents a challenge to many of the past and recent theories of criminology. The social control-type theories, for example, easily explain why there are few murders in China, but it does not work as well in explaining the low number of murders in Australia. China is a totalitarian government, while Australia is a democracy. Could there be another variable at work here? Could it be that both countries have homogenous populations?

10.3   Germany's Law Against Homosexual Behavior

At the end of WWII, and after the liberation of the Nazi concentration camps, there were countless numbers of homosexuals who were not liberated or released but sent to German prisons because of a law on the books, Paragraph 175, which remained law in West Germany even after the war. Paragraph 175 was a clause in German law prohibiting homosexual relationships. It was revised by Hitler in 1935 to include (in addition to prohibiting a homosexual act) sanctions against men kissing and embracing other men, and even having gay fantasies. There were an estimated 25,000 people convicted for breaking one of the provisions of this law between 1937 and 1939. People convicted of gay behavior were first sent to prison, but later they were sent to Hitler's concentration camps. The sentence for being convicted of a gay act was sterilization. The procedure most often used to sterilize the convicted person was castration. In 1942, Hitler increased the punishment for homosexual behavior to include a death sentence. This Nazi era law, Paragraph 175, was not repealed until 1969 (Plant, 1986).

Another relationship that we would expect to find in the data is that the number of police per country will be related to the number of people in prison. Logically, one would reason that the more people that are held in prison, the more police that would be needed to make sure that the prisoners stayed in jail. All things being equal, then we would expect to see a similar number of police in countries with similar numbers of people in prison. We do not really think that this is the situation, but if it were, it would indicate that no political, cultural, or social influences were at work.

Research Hypothesis/Question   10.2:
The greater the number of people in prison, the greater the number of police that will be employed in countries around the world.

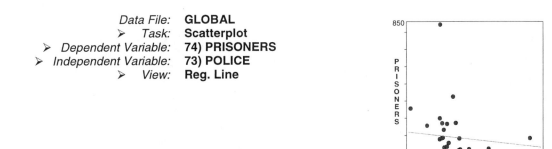

Data File:	**GLOBAL**
➤ *Task:*	**Scatterplot**
➤ *Dependent Variable:*	**74) PRISONERS**
➤ *Independent Variable:*	**73) POLICE**
➤ *View:*	**Reg. Line**

Line Equation   Y = 219.570 + -0.879 X
r = -0.103   Prob. = 0.301   N = 29   Missing = 145

This correlation is not significant, which indicates that as a group, the numbers of prisoners have nothing whatsoever to do with the number of police ($r = -.103$, $p = $ NS). This is probably because of the different standards for prisons from one country to another. Nevertheless, if we thought that there would be a significant correlation between the number of people in prison and the number of police needed to put criminals in jail and to keep them there, it is not supported by the data that we have in our data files. Again, I would point out that we have data on only 29 of the 174 countries that are available to us. This means that we have to be careful how we view this finding. If we had more data, we might have found something different. So this outcome is considered a single observation, not a finding.

Even so, let's move away from the proposition that the number of police in a given country can predict the prison population of that country and test the possibility that even the number of murders that occur in a given country will not predict the number of police in that country. This hypothesis is based on the findings to this point in the analysis, but it is also based on a strong belief that I developed after years of study. Crime, for me, is a set of behaviors that, while typically are harmful to others, are still socially defined behaviors.

10.4   Theory Development

Robert K. Merton, an American sociologist, borrowed Durkheim's concept of anomie to form his own theory, called Strain theory. It differs somewhat from Durkheim's in that Merton argued that the real problem is not created by a sudden social change, as Durkheim proposed, but rather by a social structure that holds out the same goals to all its members without giving them equal means to achieve them. This lack of integration between what the culture calls for and what the structure permits causes deviant behavior. Deviance then is a symptom of the social structure. Merton borrowed Durkheim's notion of anomie to describe the breakdown of the normative system (Merton, 1957).

Research Hypothesis/Question   10.3:
The number of murders reported by a given country per year will not predict the number of police in that country.

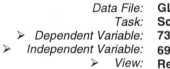

Data File: **GLOBAL**
Task: **Scatterplot**
➢ Dependent Variable: **73) POLICE**
➢ Independent Variable: **69) MURDER90**
➢ View: **Reg. Line**

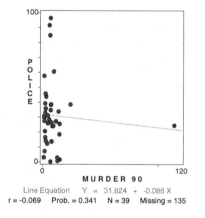

The story is in the numbers. There is no correlation, using global data, between the number of murders that occur in a country during a year and the number of police in that country supposedly needed to control crime ($r = -.069$, p = NS). This supports the hypothesis that crimes of all kinds tend to be socially defined, thus having no relationship to the number of crimes committed.

10.5   Causation Versus Association?

Too often news reporters commit the statistical sin of confusing correlation with causation. In an editorial in the *Boston Herald*, 9-4-2001, the editor, while commenting on a Justice Department report that a record 6.47 million Americans, one out of every 32 adults, are under correctional supervision (serving time behind bars or on probation or parole), proposed that the recent decline in crime was a result of locking up more criminals under the "three-strikes" law. The reality is, however, as pointed out in a letter to the editor, that most of the

1990s crime drop, in Boston and elsewhere, was *not* solely the result of putting more people in prison. Investment in prevention programs, the decrease in crack use, a booming economy, the shift to community-oriented policing, and an aging criminal population also contributed to the decrease in crime. Prison populations had been increasing long before the crime rate started its nose-dive in the 1990s. From 1985 to 1991, the count of U.S. prisoners increased 63% while the crime rate rose 13%. This increase in prison population had some effect on crime; about 25% of the drop in crime in the 1990s can be linked to locking up more criminals in prison and giving criminals longer sentences. Even so, there was a lot more involved in the drop in crime in the 1990s than simply putting more people in prison. The Sentencing Project organization reported that California's three-strikes law, one of the toughest in the United States, had no impact on the state's crime rate (Fox, 2001). While it may seem logical to think that incarcerating criminals for long periods of time will reduce their criminal activity, like the California study shows, it does not necessarily mean that there is a causal relationship between more prisoners and less crime.

Now, to finish up this *quick and dirty* analysis of global crime, we will look at the correlation of two environmental variables that numerous social scientists have identified as instrumental in causing variations and cycles of crime: unemployment and government corruption.

Research Hypothesis/Question   10.4:
Social conditions are associated with criminal behavior.

> Data File: **GLOBAL**
> Task: **Correlation**
> Variables: **38) UNEMPLYRT**
> **60) NO CORRUPT**
> **68) ASSAULT 90**
> **69) MURDER 90**
> **71) BURGLARY90**
> **72) THEFT 90**
> **73) POLICE**
> **74) PRISONERS**
> Deletion: **Pairwise**
> Test: **2-tailed**

Correlation Coefficients Table

	UNEMPLYRT	NO CORRUPT	ASSAULT 90	MURDER 90	BURG-LARY90	THEFT 90	POLICE	PRISON ERS
UNEMPL-YRT	1.000 (124)	-0.268 * (80)	0.469 ** (45)	0.224 (46)	0.073 (39)	-0.172 (24)	-0.153 (38)	0.189 (32)
NO CORRUPT	-0.268 * (80)	1.000 (88)	0.437 ** (36)	-0.329 (53)	0.713 ** (31)	0.492 * (19)	-0.151 (30)	0.486 * (27)
ASSAULT 90	0.469 ** (45)	0.437 ** (36)	1.000 (51)	0.486 ** (47)	0.335 * (39)	0.122 (26)	0.022 (39)	0.680 ** (31)
MURDER 90	0.224 (46)	-0.329 (35)	0.486** (47)	1.000 (53)	0.110 (42)	-0.142 (25)	-0.069 (39)	0.797 ** (31)
BURGLARY 90	0.073 (39)	0.713 ** (31)	0.335 * (39)	0.110 (42)	1.000 (44)	0.393 (23)	-0.076 (32)	0.109 (27)
THEFT 90	-0.172 (24)	0.492 * (19)	0.122 (26)	-0.142 (25)	0.393 (23)	1.000 (27)	-0.156 (25)	0.582 * (18)
POLICE	-0.153 (38)	-0.151 (30)	0.022 (39)	-0.069 (39)	-0.076 (32)	-0.156 (25)	1.000 (44)	-0.103 (29)
PRISONERS	0.189 (32)	0.486 * (27)	0.680 ** (31)	.797 ** (39)	0.109 (27)	0.582 * (18)	-0.103 (29)	1.000 (34)

Pairwise deletion (2-tailed test)   Significance Levels: ** =.01, * =.05

To quickly identify the important correlations from our hypothesis, look down the two columns for *unemployment* and *no corruption*. Are there any asterisks by the coefficients? If there are, these are the first correlations to examine. In this case, we will start with *unemployment*. The first correlation is an inverse relationship between *unemployment* and *no corruption* ($r = -.268$, $p < .05$). The variable *no corruption* has values that run from 0 to 10. The value 10 indicates *highly clean* while 0 indicates *highly corrupt*. This is a weak correlation, but this relationship suggests that as corruption increases the unemployment level rises.

This is not a test of our hypothesis, but it is an interesting relationship. Could it be that a corrupt government is more willing to support employment programs to pacify their people? The next significant correlation, which is a bivariate test of the hypothesis, is between the variables *unemployment* and *assaults* ($r = .469$, $p < .01$). This is a moderately strong positive correlation indicating that as *unemployment* increases, the number of *assaults* increases. This tends to support the hypothesis that social conditions are related to crime.

Next, we will look at the column of the variable *no corruption*. In this second column, the correlation between *unemployment* and *no corruption* ($r = -.268$, $p < .05$) was reported above. There are four significant correlations that may help test the hypothesis between the level of *corruption* in a country and crime. The first significant relationship is between the variables *corruption* and *assaults* ($r = .437$, $p < .01$). This indicates that as *corruption* decreases in a country, the number of assaults in that country increase. This does *not* seem to support a theoretical link between the weakening of social bonds between the country and individuals, which allows for behavior that is more antisocial. The next significant correlation is between *burglary* and *no corruption* ($r = .713$, $p < .01$). This strong correlation clearly does *not* support the *social bond hypothesis*. There is also a moderately strong significant correlation between *no corruption* and *theft* ($r = .492$, $p < .05$). This suggests the greater the level of *no corruption* the greater the number of *thefts*. The final significant correlation is between the number of *prisoners* and the level of *no corruption* in a country ($r = .486$, $p < .05$). This moderately strong correlation indicates that as a country becomes less corrupt, the number of people in prison increases.

In this case, the relationship between corruption and crime does not seem to support our *social bond* hypothesis; however, if corruption is just another form of crime, it may not be the best variable to use to test the hypothesis. Moreover, the *no corruption* variable may be a condition that restrains certain other crimes like *assaults* and *thefts*. Interestingly, however, the *no corruption* variable had no relationship to the number of police per country, which I would assume is needed to control the population in a corrupt government. This *none significant* correlation suggests that the number of police has little or nothing to do with the level of *corruption*.

We could speculate as to why these conditions are different than hypothesized, but we do know for sure that the level of corruption in the countries for which we have data is not associated with an increase in the number of *reported* crimes. We do have a glimmer of support for the hypothesis in the relationship between *unemployment* and *assaults*. I would rather have had a strong correlation between *unemployment* and *burglary* or *thefts*, but that did not happen. Of course, the data file—an inanimate object—is not interested in my hypotheses or my ideas; it only provides the numbers available for analysis. Next, we will continue to test the social bond hypothesis, but with a more homogeneous group of people, people in the United States.

Crime and Justice in the United States

At the beginning of the 21st century, 49% of the prisoners in the United States were locked up for nonviolent crimes: drug offenses, property crimes, and offenses against public order (for instance, drunken driving, and weapons violations). A more selective sentencing program would save these expensive prison cells for dangerous felons and use devices such as electronic monitoring and probation for those law breakers who are not dangerous. Giving a judge discretion is more rational and effective than using a number like *three* to dictate a prison term. The type of offense should guide sentencing decisions, not the number of the offenses committed by an individual.

There are many people in prison who are first- and second-time offenders who are far more dangerous than many of the three-time losers. Another point is that keeping felons incarcerated after their prime years for criminal behavior is not the best use of correctional resources. Three-strikes laws have resulted in a growing number of aging prisoners and longer sentences for nonviolent offenders (Fox, 2001).

NOTE ON VARIABLES: In the following analyses you will note that the same variables may have different dates. This is because data on the variables are collected in different years. This also happened when data on the variables come from different sources. For instance, in the analysis 10.9 the variable %BLACK92 is compared to #POLICE96. This is as close in time as there is data. In the next analysis (10.10), I use a different variable to measure the percentage of African Americans, %BLACK90. I use this 1990 variable because it is from the same year as the variable that gives us a count of people in prison. I am trying to compare conditions with some logical time order in mind. It is my preference that data for all the variables come from the same year. With *real data*, however, this is not always possible. In these cases, we want to use the best data available. In spite of these problems, there is still much we can learn about crime and justice.

As we did in the section on global crime, let us start with the same *null hypothesis*. If crime were not a function of social conditions, we would expect to see approximately the same number of people in prison, and each state would need approximately the same number of police to arrest a similar number of criminals.

Research Hypothesis/Question   10.5:
A statistically significant correlation will exist between states with a high percentage of murders and the number of police employed by state and local governments.

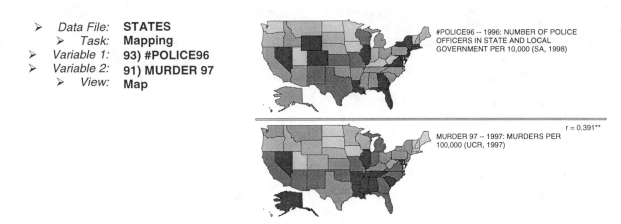

> *Data File:* **STATES**
> *Task:* **Mapping**
> *Variable 1:* **93) #POLICE96**
> *Variable 2:* **91) MURDER 97**
> *View:* **Map**

#POLICE96 -- 1996: NUMBER OF POLICE OFFICERS IN STATE AND LOCAL GOVERNMENT PER 10,000 (SA, 1998)

r = 0.391**

MURDER 97 -- 1997: MURDERS PER 100,000 (UCR, 1997)

This is a weak correlation, but it is significant ($r = .391$, $p < .01$). This indicates that there is some logic in the number of police hired by a community in the United States. Using regression I found that the number of murders in a state explains slightly over 15% ($r^2 = .153$) of the reason a state hires more police.

What other reasons could explain the remaining 85% of the decision to hire more police? Perhaps it is the number of rapes in a given state. Surely, if a state has a high number of rapes per person, it will mean that the state and local authorities will hire more police.

Research Hypothesis/Question   10.6:
A statistically significant correlation will exist between states with a high percentage of rapes and the number of police employed by state and local governments.

Data File:	STATES
Task:	Mapping
Variable 1:	93) #POLICE96
➢ Variable 2:	92) RAPE 97
➢ View:	Map

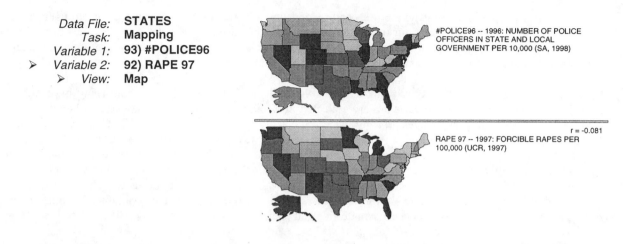

#POLICE96 -- 1996: NUMBER OF POLICE OFFICERS IN STATE AND LOCAL GOVERNMENT PER 10,000 (SA, 1998)

r = -0.081

RAPE 97 -- 1997: FORCIBLE RAPES PER 100,000 (UCR, 1997)

This should embarrass us all. The number of rapes in a state has absolutely no influence on the number of police hired by state and local authorities ($r = -.181$, $p = NS$). A cynic could use this finding to support the observation that rape has been and is often used as a political weapon to exert control over women and as a way of reducing their participation in society and the political activities of their community.

If it is not rape, what else could explain the difference in the number of police per state? One phenomenon that continues to rear its ugly head is called *profiling*. It is the practice of using a person's race or ethnic group to determine if he or she should be stopped and searched by the police. It is one thing for an individual police officer to be suspicious of blacks, foreigners, and immigrants. It is another thing, altogether, for a police department to support or promote racial profiling. If this is a part of the explanation of why one state hires more police than another state, then we would expect to see a significant correlation between states with higher percentages of immigrants and states with higher percentages of police.

Research Hypothesis/Question   10.7:
A statistically significant correlation will exist between states with a high percentage of immigration and the number of police employed by state and local governments.

Data File:	STATES
Task:	Mapping
➢ Variable 1:	15) IMMIGRAN94
➢ Variable 2:	93) #POLICE96
➢ View:	Map

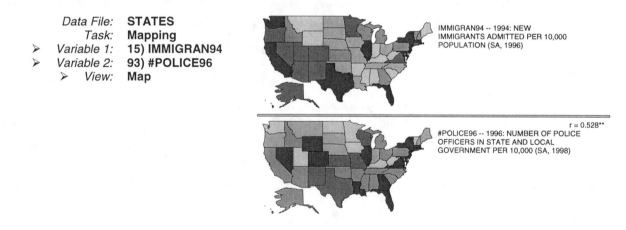

IMMIGRAN94 -- 1994: NEW IMMIGRANTS ADMITTED PER 10,000 POPULATION (SA, 1996)

r = 0.528**

#POLICE96 -- 1996: NUMBER OF POLICE OFFICERS IN STATE AND LOCAL GOVERNMENT PER 10,000 (SA, 1998)

Well, there is little doubt that in states with large immigrant populations, the authorities hire a greater percentage of people as police ($r = .528$, $p < .01$). This is a moderately strong correlation that suggests some force or forces, like racial and ethnic profiling, discrimination, or a lack of access to resources (financial or legal, or both), is resulting in immigrants being targeted by the authorities. But are they really arresting more immigrants? Are there a disproportionate number of immigrants in prison in the United States?

Research Hypothesis/Question   10.8:
A statistically significant correlation will exist between states with a high percentage of immigrants and states with large percentages of people in prison.

Data File:	**STATES**
Task:	**Mapping**
➤ *Variable 1:*	**33) IMMIGRAN89**
➤ *Variable 2:*	**48) %PRISON90**
➤ *View:*	**Map**

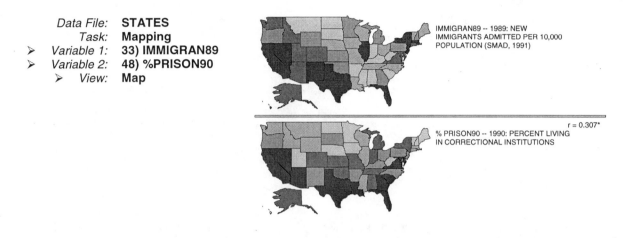

IMMIGRAN89 -- 1989: NEW IMMIGRANTS ADMITTED PER 10,000 POPULATION (SMAD, 1991)

r = 0.307*

% PRISON90 -- 1990: PERCENT LIVING IN CORRECTIONAL INSTITUTIONS

As you can see, there is a significant correlation, albeit small, between states with large immigrant populations and states with high percentages of people in prison (*r* = .307, *p* < .05). This small correlation means only that states with high immigrant populations have more people in prison than states with fewer immigrants. The truth is, we do not know if the people in prison are immigrants are not.

Let's see if this hypothesis holds up when the population is African American. Traditionally, African Americans have been one of the main groups enduring open discrimination in the United States. Did this change in the 1990s? Reason and general observation would suggest that African Americans are still discriminated against in many ways. We will do two analyses before drawing any conclusions.

Research Hypothesis/Question   10.9:
A statistically significant correlation will exist between states with a high percentage of people who are African Americans and the number of police employed by state and local governments.

Data File:	**STATES**
Task:	**Mapping**
➤ *Variable 1:*	**13) %BLACK92**
➤ *Variable 2:*	**93) #POLICE96**
➤ *View:*	**Map**

%BLACK92 -- 1992: PERCENT BLACK (SA,1996)

r = 0.454**

#POLICE96 -- 1996: NUMBER OF POLICE OFFICERS IN STATE AND LOCAL GOVERNMENT PER 10,000 (SA, 1998)

Now we will examine the number of people in prison in states with high percentages of African Americans.

Research Hypothesis/Question   10.10:
A statistically significant correlation will exist between states with a high percentage of African Americans and states with a high percentage of people in prison.

Data File:	**STATES**
Task:	**Mapping**
➢ *Variable 1:*	**29) %BLACK90**
➢ *Variable 2:*	**48) % PRISON90**
➢ *View:*	**Map**

%BLACK90 -- 1990: PERCENT BLACK

r = 0.557**

% PRISON90 -- 1990: PERCENT LIVING IN CORRECTIONAL INSTITUTIONS

These two analyses show that the same patterns are found in all four analyses. Again, a cynic or a realist might use these analyses to point out that in the United States, if you are different from the dominant group you will be watched by more police and you will live in a state with larger prison populations.

The Number of Minorities Being Arrested

To see if the number of people arrested are still disproportionately immigrants and African American, go to the Federal Bureau of Investigation *Uniform Crime Reports* (www.fbi.gov/ucr/ucr.htm) for the latest statistics on crime in the United States. When I looked at the latest statistics on race distribution for the total number of arrests in the United States during the year 2000, I found that that "69.7% of the arrestees were white, 27.9% were black, and the remainder were of other races. Whites made up 64.5% of the *Index* crime arrests, 66.2% of the property crime arrests, and 59.9% of the violent crime arrests." African Americans make up slightly under 13% of the population of the United States. All things being equal, one would expect that the arrests of African Americans would be about 13%. In fact, it is 27.9%, or double the percentage of African Americans in the general population.

Minorities in Prison

To see if there is a disproportionate number of minorities in prison, go to the report on *Prison Statistics* (www.ojp.usdoj.gov/bjs/prisons.htm). There you will find the latest statistics on people in prison in the United States. For instance, when I looked up the numbers, I found that on December 31, 2000, there were 478 people per 100,000 U.S. residents in federal and state prisons. This was an increase from 292 people per 100,000 in 1990. This is almost a 40% increase over a 10-year period. The racial and ethnic breakdown is even more informative. At year's end, there were 3,457 African American male inmates per 100,000 African American males. There were 1,220 Hispanic males inmates per 100,000 Hispanic males, and there were 449 white male inmates per 100,000 while males. A reasonably intelligent person would ask, "Why are there 8 times the number of African American males in prison per 100,000 African American men than white male inmates?" These differences are no statistical fluke. It is the reason almost all African Americans know of someone who has been sent to prison. The chances of an African American male being incarcerated in prison at any given time in the United States is 3.5 out of 100. For white males, it is 1 out of 200.

Exploring Global Social Welfare

To continue the examination, let's see what other social conditions might be involved in increasing the crime rate.

Research Hypothesis/Question   10.11:
A statistically significant correlation will exist between states with a high rate of unemployment and property crimes.

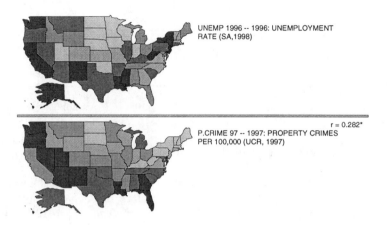

Data File:	**STATES**
Task:	**Mapping**
➢ Variable 1:	**81) UNEMP 1996**
➢ Variable 2:	**90) P.CRIME 97**
➢ View:	**Map**

It is a weak correlation, but it does suggest that unemployment is a factor that explains part of the variation that occurs in crime from year to year. If this is a real relationship today, it has probably been related to crime in the past to keep the relationship between crime and unemployment in mind. When we turn to our US TRENDS data file, we will use a measure of unemployment to see if it has truly been associated with crime in the past.

Juvenile Incarceration

The number of juveniles in jail or detention is more of a measure of the social condition under which they live than it is a behavioral problem. So let's look at a correlation matrix with several variables related to juveniles in institutions and see what other social conditions are correlated with juvenile crime.

Research Hypothesis/Question   10.12:
There will be a statistically significant correlation between the number of young people in juvenile detention centers and states with higher immigration, a greater percentage of African American, a greater percentage of the population under 18 years of age, a greater percentage of males, and a greater percentage of female-headed households.

Data File:	**STATES**
➢ Task:	**CORRELATION**
➢ Variables:	**51) %JUV.INS90**
	15) IMMIGRAN94
	29) %BLACK90
	22) %<18 90
	25) %MALE90
	42) FEM.HEAD90
➢ Deletion:	**Pairwise**
➢ Test:	**2-tailed**

Correlation Coefficients Table

	%JUV. INS90	IMMI-GRAN94	%BLACK 90	%<18 90	%MALE 90	FEM. HEAD90
%JUV. INS90	1.000 (50)	-2.222 (50)	-0.129 (50)	0.371 (50)	0.268 (50)	-0.221 (50)
IMMIGRAN 94	-0.222 (50)	1.000 (50)	-0.024 (50)	-0.339 * (50)	0.177 (50)	0.172 (50)
%BLACK 90	-0.129 (50)	-0.024 (50)	1.000 (50)	-0.143 (50)	-0.465 ** (50)	0.880 ** (50)
%<18 90	0.371 ** (50)	-0.339 * (50)	-0.143 (50)	1.000 (50)	0.453 ** (50)	-0.218 (50)
%MALE90	0.268 (50)	0.177 (50)	-0.465 ** (50)	0.453 ** (50)	1.000 (50)	-0.495 ** (50)
FEM. HEAD90	-0.221 (50)	0.172 (50)	0.880 ** (50)	-0.218 (50)	-0.495 ** (50)	1.000 (50)

PAIRWISE deletion (2-tailed test)   Significance Levels: ** =.01, * =.05

Again, the best way to deal with these correlation matrixes is to look down the column for juveniles in institutions, the variable %JUVINS90. When you do, you will see that the only correlation is with the age group that is under 18 years of age. This correlation implies that the number of juveniles in institutions is more a function of a state having a large percentage of people younger than 18, than having a higher percentage of *immigrants* (*r* = -.222, *p* = NS), *African Americans* (*r* = -.129, *p* = NS), *males* (*r* = .268, *p* = NS), or *children living in female headed households* (*r* = -.221, *p* = NS).

This should give us pause. If the only correlation among these variables (that are thought to be involved in causing higher rates of juvenile incarceration) is age, it suggests that the dominant group views juveniles much like they view African Americans and immigrants; juveniles are viewed as one of the *outgroups* that are a potential threat to the dominant group. You will *not* find a similar correlation between the percentage in prison and people 65 and older. To test this statement, do a correlation with 48) %PRISON90 and 7) %>64 96. If you do the analysis, you will find that unlike states with a high percentage of people under 18 years of age, in states with high percentages of people 65 and older there is a slight inverse relationship between people in prison and age (*r* = -.291, *p* < .05).

Before quitting this line of inquiry, let us look at a map comparison of states that have high numbers of children under 18 years of age and states with large numbers of juveniles in detention.

Research Hypothesis/Question   10.13:
There will be a statistically significant correlation between the number of young people in juvenile detention centers and the number of police employed by state and local governments.

Data File:	**STATES**
➤ *Task:*	**Mapping**
➤ *Variable 1:*	**51) %JUV.INS90**
➤ *Variable 2:*	**22) %<18 90**
➤ *View:*	**Map**

%JUV.INS90 -- 1990: PERCENT LIVING IN JUVENILE INSTITUTIONS

r = 0.371**

%<18 90 -- 1990: PERCENT OF POPULATION 17 YEARS OR YOUNGER

If you look at the rank-order list you will see that the northwestern states of South Dakota, Wyoming, Alaska, and Montana are in the top 10 on both lists. These states tend to have large populations of children under 18 years of age, and they are the states that lock up the most juveniles. Are juveniles locked up for committing crimes, or are there more juveniles in detention simply because there are more juveniles in a state? It is some of each according to this analysis.

Females in Prison

Although some would argue that women are becoming more violent and criminal, there is little aggregate data to suggest this is a trend. Evolutionary law would suggest otherwise. Based on evolutionary law, I would theorize that females will continue to be less violent and more nurturing than men. In most First World countries, women are often put in prison for the same crimes for which men are given probation. Passing *bad paper* (bad checks) has meant prison time for many women in the United States. On December 31, 2000, there were 91,612 women in federal and state prisons out of a total population of 143,243,750 females in the United States (Bureau of the Census, 2001; Bureau of Justice Statistics), or 6.4 females per 100,000 females of all races and ethnic groups in the United States. This is quite a contrast to the number of men in prisons, which approaches 450 men per 100,000.

10. 6	Stanford Prison Experiment

The Stanford Prison Experiment of August 1971 is a classic. It showed how easy it was to create a prison atmosphere that transformed the voluntary participants, young men who played prisoners and guards, into guards and prisoners. It showed how circumstances can distort individual personalities and suggested that almost anyone, when given complete control over others, can become a monster (Haney and Zimbardo, 1998).

Crime Over the Years

When people talk about the "good old days," they often lament that crime was not as bad in the past as it is today. This may be true or it may be that our memory fades over time and yesteryear looks much better in retrospect than it did when we were living through it. Another factor that may have contributed to increased crime is the increase in population. As the population increases, so does the number of those who commit a crime and thus so too does the prison population. One of the ways to test this type of speculation is to use data collected over the years and organize it by year. Our US TRENDS data file is organized to reflect changes or the lack of change over the years.

10.7	There Are 3,500 People on Death Row in the United States

The focus of human rights groups around the world is centered more and more upon the United States. Our continued use of the death penalty is a major human rights issue in many countries and the European Union. In 2000, Governor Ryan of Illinois declared a moratorium on executions while the fairness, the racial inequities, and the possibility of executing innocent people were evaluated. Debates over the death penalty being cruel and unusual punishment, not to mention the questionable deterrent value of capital punishment, rage across the nation. There were 3,500 people on death row in the United States on December 31, 2000. Please take a little time to think about what state murder of these prisoners does to us all (Pierce, 2001).

Again, murder is a behavior that should have little association with social or political conditions. Nevertheless, most of us realize that the number of homicides has varied over the years. The question that is in need of an answer is whether or not homicide changes as the population increases or whether the number of homicides is about the same from year to year. Cyclical changes in the number of murders per year would indicate that there are environmental forces at work that promote homicide in the United States. That would be a terrible situation if it were true. To murder another person seems like such a personal decision that outside influences would be irrelevant. We can hope.

Research Hypothesis/Question   10.14:
The number of murders over the years will occur in cycles.

> *Data File:* **US TRENDS**
> > *Task:* **Historical Trends**
> *Variable:* **16) HOMICIDE**

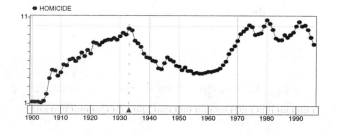

Not only is the number of homicides cyclical, the period starting with the Harrison Narcotic Act (1914) which made many drugs illegal in the United States, and the 18th Amendment (Prohibition) making the sale of alcoholic beverages illegal (1920–1933) saw a sharp increase in homicides. The increase continued until the 21st Amendment repealing prohibition became law (Brecher, 1972). Homicides again increased when illegal drugs gained popularity in the late 1960s and during the Vietnam War. This analysis over time leaves little doubt that homicide is cyclic. Will we find the same type of phenomena at work with other crimes, say like property crime?

Research Hypothesis/Question   10.15:
The number of property crimes over the years will occur in cycles.

> *Data File:* **US TRENDS**
> *Task:* **Historical Trends**
> *Variable:* **19) PROP.CRIME**

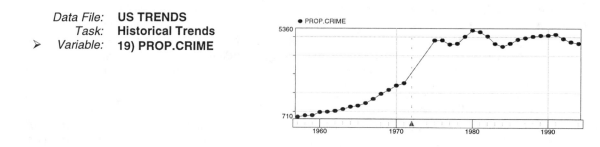

Although there was a major increase in property crime between 1960 and 1970, after the Watergate break in and the subsequent impeachment trial of then-President Richard Nixon, property crime took a major leap. This would support our hypothesis that when people believe their government officials are *crooks*, their bonds to the social group and by extension their bond to the social order are weakened and thus property crime increases. Crime appears to have leveled off after 1980, and today property crime is lower than it was in 1975. There is an important difference between the two phenomena; the graph reflecting homicide rates per 1,000 people runs from 1900 to approximately the year 2000. The graph reflecting property crime runs from 1955 to approximately 2000. The additional 55 years of homicide data allow more time for long cycles to appear, as it does in the graph of the number of homicides per thousand in the United States.

So, just what is causing the cyclical changes in homicide? Social bond theory would suggest that homicide in a population is caused by social and political conditions. Let's select a few of the social conditions that seem to impact human behavior. Divorce rate and unemployment are good candidates of inclusion. Divorce rate and unemployment will result in a weakening of individual and social bonds. Politically, the percentage who thinks the government is crooked would be a condition that would help a person rationalize criminal behavior. We also need to include population growth to see if the murder rate increases because of an increase in population.

We can look at these conditions over time as we have done in the past chapter. We can also look at the changes in these variables over time using the time-series analytical procedure. We will select variables that measure crime and social conditions that may increase or decrease crime such as social conditions that affect the individual.

Research Hypothesis/Question   10.16:
Do the number of homicides per capita vary over time with changes in population, changes in the divorce rate, changes in unemployment, and changes in the perception of people in the United States that government officials are dishonest?

Data File:	**US TRENDS**
➢ *Task:*	**Time Series**
➢ *Dependent Variable:*	**16) HOMICIDE**
➢ *Independent Variables:*	**2) POPULATION**
	4) DIV RATE
	22) UNEMP MALE
	29) GOV.CROOK?
➢ *Graph:*	**Data (z)**
➢ *View*	**Graph**

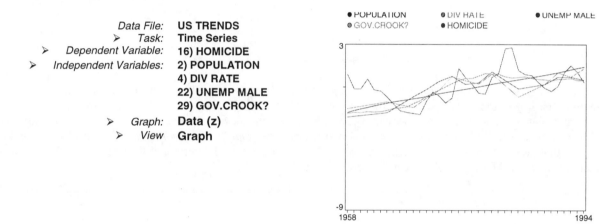

Time series is found on the ADVANCED STATISTICS menu. To create this graph, select the dependent variable and independent variables and click [OK]. Click [OK] for the next two screens that appear to view the graph. Once the graph appears, select Data (z) from the Graph options on the left side of your screen to view the results shown above.

This graph view has converted all raw scores on the five variables to *z-scores*. Using *z-scores* (also called *standard scores*), we can better compare the values of each variable over time. If you wish to see the graph using raw scores, point and click on the button *Data (raw)* in the graph box. It is the button above the button *Data(z)*.

z-Score or Standard Score

We use *z-scores* when the raw data scores or the original score of the variables in the analysis are so different that they cannot be easily compared. We convert a raw score of a variable into a *z-score* by determining the score's position around the mean. For instance, Nevada has a *z-score* on the *murder* variable of 1.5. Nevada has a raw score on *murder* that is one-and-a-half standard deviations above the mean. Utah has a *z-score* on the *murder* variable of –1. Utah has a raw score that is one (1) standard deviation below the mean. By expressing raw scores as *z-scores*, like we did in the graph above, we can see if there are cycles among the variables and we can see if the variables vary at about the same time. As you can see in the *Data (raw)* view, the only line you can see represents the *population* variable. The remaining variables run along the bottom. This occurs because the population increases yearly by the millions while there are only a few thousand murders in the United States per year. Laying out both variables on a graph offers little visual assistance in understanding any relationship between the variables. The graph is much clearer when the scores are expressed in *z*-scores. They allow us to inspect the relationships both visually and statistically.

Using *z*-scores, we can also calculate a grand mean for all the variables and a predicted mean. You can see the graph below in the *summary view.*

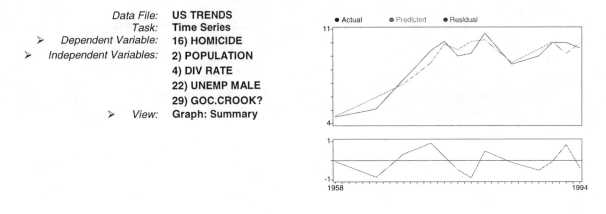

Data File:	**US TRENDS**
Task:	**Time Series**
➢ *Dependent Variable:*	**16) HOMICIDE**
➢ *Independent Variables:*	**2) POPULATION**
	4) DIV RATE
	22) UNEMP MALE
	29) GOC.CROOK?
➢ *View:*	**Graph: Summary**

In the time-series analysis of these five variables, both the *Summary* graph and the *Data (z)* graph support our hypothesis. If you look at the statistics by clicking on the *ANOVA* button, you will see that the R^2 is .898. This indicates that the four independent variables can predict the tendency in the dependent variable (homicide) with almost 90% accuracy. This means that if I know the scores on *population, divorce rate, unemployment,* and the degree that people think that politicians are *crooked,* for a given year, I can predict how many murders occurred that year and I will be within about 10% of being correct.

10.8   Study on the "Three-Strikes" Law

- A study conducted by the Presley Center for Crime and Justice Studies at the University of California, Riverside, shows that Californians are less likely to support the imposition of the "three-strikes" law if the three felony convictions are not violent, but relate to drug or property offenses. As it stands, the "three-strikes" law of 1994 applies to all felonies regardless of the type of crime committed. This survey found that Californians are more logical than their political leaders. Despite racial or ethnic background, 93% of those surveyed agree that people convicted of three violent, serious felonies deserve sentences of 25 years to life. Support for the law diminishes, however, as the survey probes opinions about crimes against property or drug-related crimes.

- When asked about a conviction of three serious drug-related crimes, support for a 25-year to life sentence drops to 65%, and when asked about a conviction for three serious property crimes, just 47% of Californians agreed that a sentence of 25 years to life is appropriate. Support for "three-strikes" erodes further as the crimes are described as "less serious." For instance, just 13% of those surveyed supported a 25-year to life sentence for three "less serious" property crimes.

- The survey also asked questions about state spending priorities. Participants were asked how they would allocate $100 among colleges and universities, prisons, probation departments, health care, and highways. Californians surveyed were significantly more likely to favor spending money on health care and colleges as opposed to prisons, highways, and probation departments. Respondents decided to allocate $56 on the former, splitting the remaining money equally among the latter (Parker, 2001).

Curve Fitting

As we see in the time-series analysis, many variables run in cycles. Many conditions such as the number of murders per year in the United States will ebb and flow from low numbers to high numbers of murders from year to year. The same goes for people's opinion of their politicians. This means that we might be able to better predict the relationship between these two conditions if we analyzed them using a curve-fitting approach. Most statistical procedures are based on the concept of a straight-line linear correlation. Procedures such as regression assume that the relationship between the independent and dependent variables in question is linear. Often, however, these relationships are *not* linear. If you see a nonlinear relationship in a scatterplot of two variables, you would want to see if the association fits a predicted nonlinear form. Frequently, the shape of the relationship is not anticipated in advance and the analyst faces the challenge of determining not only the extent to which the association deviates from simple linearity, but whether there is a better form with which to approximate the association. Let's see what this looks like using real data.

Research Hypothesis/Question   10.17:
There will be a statistically significant linear relationship between people's perception that politicians are crooked and the number of murders committed per year.

Data File:	**US TRENDS**
➤ *Task:*	**Curve Fitting**
➤ *Dependent Variable:*	**16) HOMICIDE**
➤ *Independent Variable :*	**29) GOV.CROOK?**
➤ *View:*	**Function: Linear**

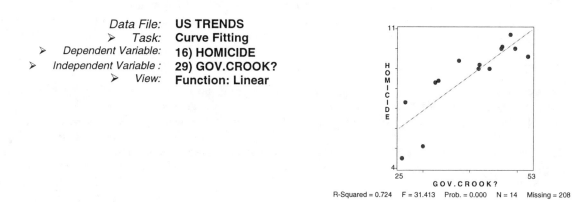

R-Squared = 0.724   F = 31.413   Prob. = 0.000   N = 14   Missing = 208

You can find Curve Fitting by returning to the ADVANCED STATISTICS menu. To create this graph, select the dependent variable 16) HOMICIDE and independent variable 29) GOV.CROOK? and click [OK]. Once the graph appears, select Linear from the Functions options on the left side of your screen to view the results shown above. Be sure to note that selecting a new function does not unselect a previously selection function. You must unselect the functions manually when you no longer wish to use them.

In this analysis, you will notice that the R-square coefficient is .724. This is a great deal of variance to account for in a dependent variable. Even so, the linear line does not look like a very *good fit*. In this case, we might want to use a different analysis. While viewing in the scatterplot created by the *Curve Fitting* procedure, in the Functions box unselect **[Linear]** and select **[Recipro]**. There are six different functions that you can apply to your data in the analysis: linear, square, cube, log, square root, and reciprocal. To apply a function, click on it to to see the change in the statistics and the R-square value. Click on a function again to uncheck it and remove its effects. You may apply as many different functions as you like. In this case, to see the graph presented ahead, select the function **[Recipro]**.

Research Hypothesis/Question   10.18:
There will be a statistically significant curvilinear relationship between people's perception that politicians are crooked and the number of murders committed per year.

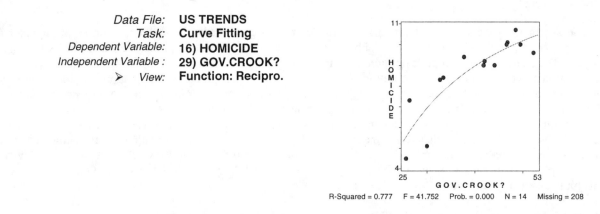

Data File:	US TRENDS
Task:	Curve Fitting
Dependent Variable:	16) HOMICIDE
Independent Variable :	29) GOV.CROOK?
➢ View:	Function: Recipro.

R-Squared = 0.777   F = 41.752   Prob. = 0.000   N = 14   Missing = 208

Be sure you have unselected the [Linear] function before continuing.

In this case, the curve-fitting analysis improved our R^2 from a .724 to a .777. This is not a great improvement, but it helps to illustrate the concept of curve fitting. Remember, not everything we study is going to be linear. There is a lot of missing data in this analysis, so we must consider this relationship as an observation, not a true finding.

What Residuals Can Tell Us

There is another issue that needs to be touched on before wrapping up this section using advanced research statistical procedures—and that is the role of *residuals*. In the time-series analysis used to test Hypothesis 10.16 above, the *Summary* view has two graph layouts. The bottom graph is a plot of the residuals. A residual is the difference between the observed value of a variable score and the value predicted using least-squares regression with one or more independent variables. There are several assumptions about the distribution of the residuals, or errors, in regression analysis. When these assumptions are violated, the results of the analysis may be inaccurate. One of these assumptions is that the residuals are statistically independent of one another. This means that the *residuals* (Rs1:V73) of the combined variables HOMICIDE and GOV.CROOK should not correlate with either variable, HOMICIDE or GOV.CROOK. I saved the residuals as a variable (Rs1:V73). If the residuals are not correlated, the assumption that the data are not autocorrelated is met. This finding supports the claim that the independent variable GOV.CROOK is causing the change in the dependent variable HOMICIDE.

Research Hypothesis/Question   10.19:
The residuals (Rs1:V73) of the combined variables HOMICIDE and GOV.CROOK will not correlate with the variables HOMICIDE and GOV.CROOK.

Data File:	US TRENDS
➢ Task:	Correlation
➢ Variables:	16) HOMICIDE
	29) GOV.CROOK?
	30) *Rs1:V73*
➢ Deletion:	Pairwise
➢ Test:	2-tailed

Correlation Coefficients Table

	HOMICIDE	GOV. CROOK?	Rs1:V73
HOMICIDE	1.000 (97)	0.851 ** (14)	0.473 (14)
GOV.CROOK?	0.851 ** (14)	1.000 (14)	-0.033 (14)
RS1:V73	0.473 (14)	-0.033 (14)	1.000 (14)

PAIRWISE deletion (2-tailed test)   Significance Levels: ** =.01, * =.05

This lack of any significant correlations between the residuals (variable Rs1:V73) and the two variables of interest supports our hypothesis. The analysis suggests that the independent variable GOV.CROOK is causing the change in the dependent variable HOMICIDE. Overall, these analyses taken together support the predictions of social bond theory.

To make the point visually, let's use each of the variables as a dependent variable and use the residual variable as the dependent variable in a scattergram to see if the residual variable *residuals* (Rs1:V73) can predict variation of the two variables of interest. First we will use HOMICIDE as the dependent variable.

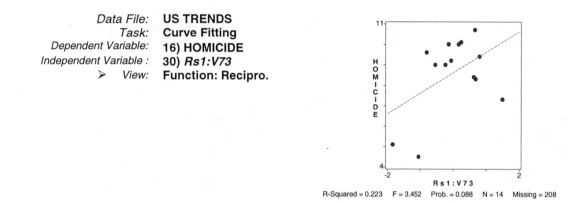

Data File:	**US TRENDS**
Task:	**Curve Fitting**
Dependent Variable:	**16) HOMICIDE**
Independent Variable :	**30) *Rs1:V73***
➤ *View:*	**Function: Recipro.**

R-Squared = 0.223   F = 3.452   Prob. = 0.088   N = 14   Missing = 208

Now we will use GOV.CROOK? for the dependent variable.

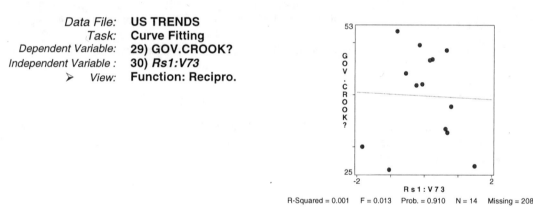

Data File:	**US TRENDS**
Task:	**Curve Fitting**
Dependent Variable:	**29) GOV.CROOK?**
Independent Variable :	**30) *Rs1:V73***
➤ *View:*	**Function: Recipro.**

R-Squared = 0.001   F = 0.013   Prob. = 0.910   N = 14   Missing = 208

These scattergrams clearly show that there is no significant correlations between the residuals (variable Rs1:V73) and the two variables of interest. Again, this supports our hypothesis, and taken together they support the predictions of social bond theory.

As these analyses show, crime varies with changes that weaken a person's bonds to his or her social group and society. This effect can be seen when the public loses confidence in its political leaders, crime—even murder—increases. Social bonds also help us understand why outgroups are segregated and discriminated against in a society. The dynamics of social bonds are often visible when the number of people in an outgroup increases. This creates pressure on the dominant group to control outgroup members, to apply sanctions, or to imprison members of the outgroup in an effort to maintain the dominant group bonds.

Moving Beyond Learning to Discovering Knowledge

In the first chapter, I made the point that we begin our study or research with a question. I recommended this activity and discipline as a way to help you develop your critical thinking skills. When we ask a question or state a hypothesis about a relationship that we can test with honest and real data, we are also testing our analytical thinking skills. When you call on your knowledge of a theory to explain a phenomenon by hypothesizing a relationship, you are testing more than your hypothesis. You are testing your critical thinking skills and the theory you used to explain the relationship. As you continue the process of asking questions and hypothesizing about the relationship between conditions such as crime and justice, you can expect your critical thinking skills to continue to improve. Practitioners in the helping professions who develop their knowledge of applicable theory and who are disciplined in their inquiry can expect to move from simply learning new facts from teachers, supervisors, and workshop/conference presenters, to discovering new knowledge on their own.

End Note: This brings to an end the chapters of this workbook. Of course, you still have a few exercises to do and I hope you will continue to practice using these statistical procedures with the data file to improve your research and analytical and critical thinking skills. There are still a great deal of analyses you can do with the data files on the CD that came with this workbook. I hope you will continue playing around with it. You will more than likely learn something new each time you test a new hypothesis. As I hope you see, research and statistical analysis can be extremely helpful for validating or eliminating the hypotheses that we construct from the literature and our own observations. What I also hope it taught you was that simply because we have an idea that seems compelling, it still needs to be tested in some way. Although it is not always possible to test a supposition using statistical approaches, nevertheless, we need to put it to the test and it needs to withstand testing.

I hope you also learned that asking well-thought-out questions is as important as knowing how to use statistical methods. It is a waste of time as you observed in the first chapter to ask a poorly thought-out question. The most sophisticated research procedures and statistical analysis cannot make up for a poorly thought-out question.

I also hope that the work you did in these chapters has alerted you to the existence of another way to view reality, and made you a bit more cynical and able to recognize politically motivated policies and procedures. There is nothing inherently wrong with pushing an agenda, but we need to know when policy and procedures are based on ideology and not on information that matches environmental and psychological circumstances.

Finally, I would remind you that insight only occurs to those who keep an open mind. It can only occur where one assesses a situation and willingly reassesses the situation as new information becomes available. Moreover, it comes readily to those who keep an open mind, reassess, and seek new knowledge and information.

Other Issues Related to Crime and Justice

There are a number of issues related to crime and justice that I could not examine in this chapter. However, with the data files provided with this book, you can analyze many of these issues on your own. To learn more about other issues related to crime and justice, you can enter the following search terms in the InfoTrac College Edition.

Crime	**Prisoners**
Sex offenders	**Prison violence**
White-collar crime	**United States Bureau of Prisons**
Female delinquents	**Adolescent crime prevention programs**
Justice	**Prisons for women**
Criminal courts	**Prison race relations**
Death penalty	**HIV/AIDS prisoners**

NAME: _____

COURSE: _____

DATE: _____

Workbook exercises and software are copyrighted. Copying is prohibited by law.

Review Questions

Based on the work you've done so far on the issue of crime and justice, see how well you do on this short True or False quiz.

The global analysis that examined social and crime variables in a correlational analysis was trying to find support for the hypothesis that crime is affected by social events and conditions.　　　　　　　　　　　　　　　　　　　T　F

Unlike the global analysis, the analysis of data on the number of police and the numbers of murders per state in the United States was weakly correlated.　　　T　F

The correlation between states with a high percentage of immigrants and states with higher numbers of police was moderately correlated ($r = .528$, $p < .001$).　　T　F

When using data collected over time in an analysis, it is likely that the changes in the values of a variable will be cyclical. Even so, a linear analysis is still the best analytical approach to use with this data.　　　　　　　　　　　　　　　　T　F

In the United States, crime is not affected by social conditions. This was evident in the set of analyses at the end of this chapter. Instead, crime in the United States is solely an individual decision. Thus, there were no correlations between the crime variables used in the analysis and the variables used that measured social conditions.　　T　F

MicroCase QUESTIONS

If you want to learn additional information about the Time Series or Curve Fitting tasks in MicroCase, use the online help (F1).

Use the following data files, variables, and analytical approaches to answer the MicroCase questions.

1.　　Using the STATES data file, map out a correlation between states with a high percentage of adolescents in juvenile institutions and states with a high percentage of people in prison.

> ➤　*Data File:*　**STATES**
> ➤　*Task:*　**Mapping**
> ➤　*Variable 1:*　**51) %JUV.INS90**
> ➤　*Variable 2:*　**48) %PRISON90**
> ➤　*View:*　**Map**

    a.   The correlation between states with large percentages of juveniles in institutions and states with high percentages of people in prison is $r =$ _____. The correlation is _____ (positive or inverse).

    b.   The correlation between these two variables was significant at $p <$ _____.

2.   Race often plays an important role in the number and type of people who go to prison. Using the STATES data file, map out a correlation between states with a high percentage of adolescents in juvenile institutions and states with a high percentage of African Americans.

>   Data File: **STATES**
>   Task: **Mapping**
>   Variable:1: **51) %JUV.INS90**
> ➢ Variable 2: **29) %BLACK90**
> ➢   View: **Map**

    a.   The correlation between states with large percentages of juveniles in institutions and states with high percentages of African Americans is $r =$ _____. The correlation is _____ (positive or inverse).

    b.   The correlation between these two variables was significant at $p <$ _____.

3.   For the next set of questions, use the Time Series procedure to find out if the *divorce rate* increases the rate of *violent crime*.

> ➢   Data File: **US TRENDS**
> ➢   Task: **Time Series**
> ➢ Dependent Variable: **18) VIOL.CRIME**
> ➢ Independent Variable: **4) DIV RATE**
> ➢   View: **Data (z)**

Hint: You will need to use the ANOVA view to respond to some questions.

    a.   The time-series analysis between violent crime and divorce rate has an $R^2 =$ _____, and it is significant at $p <$ _____.

    b.   The trend relationship found between violent crime and divorce rate suggests that...

    _____

I will leave you with this thought: No one can take from us what we have learned. It is also true that no one can give to us what we have missed or chose to ignore.

Variable Lists Related to Crime and Justice

The following is a partial list of the variables in your data files. You can examine them as individual variables or several variables at a time using the approaches you learned in this chapter. To see a list of all of the variables, the question the variable asks, and the range of values, press [F3] to open the variable list window from anywhere in the software. Try using some of the variables below with the variables you have already tested.

US TRENDS

7) #MALES
    MALE RESIDENT POPULATION IN THOUSANDS FROM TABLE 12, SA96
8) #FEMALES
    FEMALE RESIDENT POPULATION IN THOUSANDS FROM TABLE 12, SA96
9) #WHITE
    WHITE RESIDENT POPULATION IN THOUSANDS FROM TABLE 12, SA96
10) #BLACK
    BLACK RESIDENT POPULATION IN THOUSANDS FROM TABLE 12, SA96
13) #HISPANIC
    HISPANIC ORIGIN RESIDENT POPULATION IN THOUSANDS FROM TABLE 12, SA96
15) SUICIDE RT
    SUICIDES PER 100,000 (1970 AND BEFORE, HSUS, SERIES H 971-986; AFTER 1970, SA)
17) CIRRHOSIS
    DEATHS PER 100,000 FROM CIRRHOSIS OF THE LIVER (DISEASE ASSOCIATED WITH ALCOHOLISM) (BEFORE 1970, HSUS, TABLE B149-166; AFTER 1970, SA)
20) AUTO THEFT
    Auto Thefts per 100,000 population (1970 and before, Series H952-961, HSUS; after 1970, SA)
21) LAB FRC M
    Labor Force Participation Rate—Civilian Population Male 20 Years and Older Series ID: LFU601701, Bureau of Labor Statistics, 1999
26) LAWYER/CAP
    Number of lawyers per 10,000 population

Web Pages Related to Crime and Justice

If you wish to find a world of resources that are available to you over the Internet, the following list of Web sites will get you started. Once you visit these Web sites, you will find many interesting links to other useful Web sites.

Victim-Offender Reconciliation Program (VOCP)
www.vorp.com

The Sentencing Project
www.sentencingproject.org

Families to Amend California's Three-Strikes Law
www.facts1.com

Bureau of Justice Statistics
www.ojp.usdoj.gov

Death Penalty Information Centers
www.deathpenaltyinfo.org

HIV/AIDS in Prison
users.javant.com

Crime and Justice International
www.oicj.org/public/toc.cfm?series=CJI

American Civil Liberties Union
www.aclu.org/

References

Brecher, E. M. (1972). *Licit & Illicit Drugs*. Boston: Little, Brown and Company.

Bureau of Justice Statistics. (2001). *Prison statistics: Summary findings*. Retrieved September 30, 2001, from www.ojp.usdoj.gov/bjs/prisons.htm.

Cherry, A. L. (1994). *The Socialization Instinct: Individual, Family, and Social Bonds*. Westport, CT: Praeger Press.

Cherry, A. L., Dillon, M. E., and Rugh, D. (eds.). (2001). *Teenage Pregnancy: A Global View*. Westport, CT: Greenwood Pub.

Cockburn, A. (1985). Beyond Stockholm syndrome. *The Nation, 241* (July 20–27), 38.

Federal Bureau of Investigation. (2001). *Uniform Crime Reports*. Washington, DC: Government Printing Office. Retrieved September 28, 2001, from www.fbi.goc/ucr/ucr.htm.

Fox, J. A. (2001). Prisons alone are no lockbox for crime. *The Boston Herald*. Letter to the Editor, September 4. James Alan Fox is the Lipman Family Professor of Criminal Justice at Northeastern University.

Haney, C. and Zimbardo, P. G. (1998). The past and future of U.S. prison policy: twenty-five years after the Stanford Prison Experiment. *American Psychologist, 53*(7), 709-727.

Merton, R. K. (1957). *Social Theories and Social Structure*. New York: Free Press.

Parker, R. N. (2001). *UCR study sheds light on "Three Strikes" law*. Riverside, CA: Presley Center for Crime and Justice Studies at the University of California, Riverside. Retrieved September 30, 2001, from www.ucr.edu/SubPages/2CurNewsFold/UnivRelat/strikes.html.

Pierce, A. R. (2001). *Abolish the death penalty*. Prison Reform Unity Project. Retrieved September 28, 2001, from arpofasy.freeyellow.com/.

Plant. R. (1986). *The Pink Triangle: The Nazi War Against Homosexuals*. New York: Henry Holt and Company.

Strasser, S. (1987). The kidnappers strike again. *Newsweek, 109* (February 2), 20–22.

Zastrow, C. (2000). *Introduction to Social Work and Social Welfare*. (7th ed.). Belmont, CA: Wadsworth Publishing Company.

Additional Material That May Be of Interest

Austin, J. and Coventry, G. (2001). *Emerging Issues on Privatized Prisons*. Washington, DC: U.S. Dept. of Justice, Office of Justice Programs, Government Printing Office.

Barak, G., Flavin, J., and Leighton, P. (2001). *Class, Race, Gender and Crime: Social Realities of Justice in America*. Los Angeles: Roxbury.

Cook. J. R. (2001). *Asphalt Justice: A Critique of the Criminal Justice System in America*. Westport, CT: Praeger Press.

Dickey. W. J. (2001). *Community Justice in Rural America: Four Examples and Four Futures*. Washington, DC: U.S. Dept. of Justice, Office of Justice Programs, Bureau of Justice Assistance, Government Printing Office.

Karmen, A. *Crime Victims: An Introduction to Victimology* (4th ed.). Belmont, CA : Wadsworth/Thomson Learning.

Salvatore, R. D., Aguirre, C., and Joseph, G. M. (eds). (2001). *Crime and Punishment in Latin America: Law and Society Since Late Colonial Times*. Durham, NC: Duke University Press.

Vellani, K. H. and Nahoun, J. D. (2001). *Applied Crime Analysis*. Boston: Butterworth-Heinemann.

INDEX

APPENDIX A:
VARIABLE NAMES AND SOURCES

Data File: COUNTIES

1) NAME
2) %WHITE90
3) %BLACK90
4) %AMER.IN90
5) %ASIAN/P90
6) %HISPANC90
7) %POOR 89
8) WHT POOR89
9) BLK POOR89
10) AM.IND P89
11) ASIA POR89
12) HISP.POR89
13) POOR FAM89
14) F.HEAD P89
15) CHLD POR89
16) FEM.HD.F89
17) %URBAN90
18) %RURAL90
19) NOT N HS90
20) SCH0-8YR90
21) SOME H.S90
22) HIGHSCH 90
23) H.S.GRAD90
24) COLLEGE 90
25) COL.DEGR90
26) %IN COLL90

Data File: GLOBAL

1) COUNTRY
2) POPULATION
3) DENSITY
4) URBAN %
5) URBAN GRWT
6) CITY POP
7) POP GROWTH
8) NETMIGRT
9) BIRTH RATE
10) FERTILITY
11) LARGE FAML
12) INF. MORTL
13) CONTRACEPT
14) ABORTION
15) MOM HEALTH
16) DEATH RATE
17) LIFE EXPCT
18) LIFEX MALE
19) LIFEX FEM
20) SEX RATIO
21) % UNDER 15
22) % OVER 64
23) HUMAN DEV.
24) ECON DEVEL
25) THREEWORLD
26) QUAL. LIFE
27) CALORIES
28) MEAT CONS.
29) %UNDRWGHT
30) DOCTORS
31) PUB EDUCAT
32) PUB HEALTH
33) $ RICH 10%
34) GDP GROWTH
35) GDP/CAP
36) EXPND/CP
37) INFLATRT
38) UNEMPLYRT
39) %WORK AG
40) %WORK IN
41) LITERACY
42) TLVSN/CP
43) PRIM.SCH
44) SEC.SCH
45) SEC/CP
46) % GO 5TH
47) FEM.PROF.
48) %FEM.LEGIS
49) %FEM.HEADS
50) %WKR WOMEN
51) M/F EDUC.
52) GENDER EQ
53) FEM POWER
54) SEX MUTIL
55) SINGLE MOM
56) HOME&KIDS
57) WED PASSE'
58) CIVIL LIBL
59) FREEDOM
60) NO CORRUPT
61) MULTI-CULT
62) C.CONFLICT
63) REVOLUTION
64) LEFT/RIGHT
65) DEFNS/CP
66) ARMY/DOCTR
67) CH.ATTEND
68) ASSAULT 90
69) MURDER 90
70) RAPE 90
71) BURGLARY90
72) THEFT 90
73) POLICE
74) PRISONERS
75) CAP PUNISH
76) ANTI-SEM.
77) ANTI-FORGN
78) ANTI-MUSLM
79) RACISM
80) ANTI-GAY
81) HOME LIFE?
82) POOR LAZY
83) INJUSTICE
84) TRUST KIN?
85) CIRRHOSIS
86) SUICIDE NO
87) EUTHANASIA

Data File: GLOBAL (cont.)

88) AIDS
89) ALCOHOL
90) BEER DRINK
91) WINE DRINK
92) CIGARETTES
93) VERY HAPPY

94) FAMILY IMP
95) KID INDEPN
96) KID OBEY
97) AS/AFR/LAT
98) EUROPE
99) C.CONFLIC2

100) C.CONFLIC3
101) THIRDWORLD
102) FIRSTWORLD
103) SECONDWORL

Data File: GSS

1) ID
2) WORKING?
3) WORKING?2
4) PRESTIGE
5) MARITAL
6) #CHILDREN
7) AGE
8) AGE2
9) EDUCATION
10) EDUCATION2
11) DEGREE
12) SEX
13) RACE
14) PAR. BORN
15) HH SIZE
16) FAM.INCOME
17) FAM.INCOM2
18) INCOME98
19) PART/FULL
20) IF:WHO 92?
21) EDUCATE $
22) SOC.SEC.$
23) DRUGS $ 2
24) WELFARE $2
25) WELFARE $3
26) LIVE WELL
27) EQUALIZ $2
28) CRIME IMP?
29) GRASS? 2
30) HOW RELIG?
31) AFTERLIFE?

32) INTERMAR72
33) INTERMAR98
34) RACE NAME
35) RACE NAME2
36) HEALTH
37) LIFE
38) HELP OTH
39) DRINK?
40) OVERDRINK
41) OVERDRINK2
42) SMOKE?
43) TRY QUIT?
44) CIGGIES?
45) CIG.WEEK?
46) EVER SMOKE
47) ANOMIA 6
48) FIND JOB?
49) LIKE JOB?
50) SEC.IMP2
51) TIME IMP?
52) $ RANK
53) $NEEDED?
54) EVER UNEMP
55) EVER WELF?
56) AFDC?
57) UNIONIZED?
58) GET AHEAD?
59) ABORT.WANT
60) IDEAL#KIDS
61) TEEN BC 86
62) TEEN BC 98

63) SUP.PAID?
64) TEEN SEX86
65) TEEN SEX98
66) EUTHANASIA
67) EUTHANAS 2
68) SPANKING
69) SUIC.ILL
70) EVER HIT?
71) WHEN HIT?
72) # HITS
73) THREAT GUN
74) ERA?
75) RUSHED
76) HELP POOR?
77) MEM.UNION
78) WHY POOR 2
79) WHY POOR 4
80) SOC.DIF.1
81) RACE QUOTA
82) DRUG TEST
83) SELL SEX
84) HMO1
85) HMO3
86) HMO4
87) KID DRUGS
88) KID TRUANT
89) FEM.WK.SUP
90) SINGL.PRNT
91) Pi1:V59
92) OVERSAMP
93) YEAR

Data File: STATES

1) STATE NAME
2) POP 96
3) POP GO 96

4) NIM 90-99
5) %<5 96
6) %<20 96

7) %>64 96
8) %65-69 96
9) %65-84 96

10) %>85 96
11) DENSITY 95
12) %WHITE92
13) %BLACK92
14) %ASIAN/P92
15) IMMIGRAN94
16) %NON-ENG90
17) %NO MOVE90
18) %FOREIGN90
19) SAME HSE90
20) %URBAN90
21) %RURAL90
22) %<18 90
23) %>17 90
24) POP<18 98
25) %MALE90
26) %FEMALE90
27) %FEMALE96
28) %WHITE90
29) %BLACK90
30) %AMER.IN90
31) %ASIAN/P90
32) %HISPANC90
33) IMMIGRAN89
34) MARRIAG 94
35) MARRIAG94B
36) DIVORCE 94
37) %SNG.MEN90
38) %WIDOWR90
39) %SNG.FEM90

40) %WIDOWS90
41) MLE HEAD90
42) FEM.HEAD90
43) F HEAD/C90
44) ONE P.HH90
45) MARRIAGE80
46) %BIG UNT90
47) HOUSE $90
48) % PRISON90
49) %NURS.HM90
50) %MENT.HS90
51) %JUV.INS90
52) %COL.DRM90
53) %MIL.QRT90
54) %EMERG.90
55) CH.MEMB 90
56) SUICIDE 96
57) MA <20 93
58) CHLD MRT96
59) RITALIN
60) COKEUSER90
61) BEER 95
62) WINE 95
63) ALCOHOL 89
64) AIDS 95
65) HEART DD95
66) % FAT 95
67) SYPHILIS91
68) DR.RATE96
69) HLTH INS96

70) HSP.B RT94
71) SHRINKS 90
72) PUB.TRNS90
73) BUS90
74) %POOR 96
75) MED.FAM$96
76) MED.FAM$94
77) WELFARE
78) POV. LINE
79) % FS 95
80) CHLD POR89
81) UNEMP 1996
82) FEM UNE 96
83) MAL UNE 96
84) %MANUF.E94
85) %AGRI.EM90
86) %HLTH EM90
87) BOTH PAR92
88) DRUG ED 90
89) HLTH.SV$87
90) P.CRIME 97
91) MURDER 97
92) RAPE 97
93) #POLICE96
94) HEALTH $87
95) SS DSAB$94
96) SEX RAT.96
97) HLTH$/CP94

Data File: US TRENDS

1) Date
2) POPULATION
3) MAR. RATE
4) DIV RATE
5) BIRTH RATE
6) LIFE EXP
7) #MALES
8) #FEMALES
9) #WHITE
10) #BLACK

11) #AMERIND
12) #ASIAN
13) #HISPANIC
14) %HS
15) SUICIDE RT
16) HOMICIDE
17) CIRRHOSIS
18) VIOL.CRIME
19) PROP.CRIME
20) AUTO THEFT

21) LAB FRC M
22) UNEMP MALE
23) LAB FRC F
24) UNEMP FEM
25) MOM LAB
26) LAWYER/CAP
27) % BLK PRES
28) %F F.PRES
29) GOV.CROOK?
30) Rs1:V73

SOURCES

COUNTIES – The Counties of the United States

The data in the Counties file are from a variety of sources. The variable description for each variable uses the following abbreviations to indicate the source. If no abbreviation or source is shown in the variable description, the source is Census publications.

AHA: American Hospital Association
AMA: American Medical Association
BEA: Bureau of Economic Analysis
BLS: Bureau of Labor Statistics
CENSUS: The summary volumes of the U.S. Census
ERC: Elections Research Center
FBI: Federal Bureau of Investigation
NCHS: National Center for Health Statistics
SSA: Social Security Administration

GLOBAL – The 174 Largest Nations of the Globe

The data in the GLOBAL file are from a variety of sources. The variable descriptions for each variable use the following abbreviations to indicate the source.

SOURCES:

CA: *Church Almanac*, published biannually by the *Salt Lake City Desert News*.
FITW: *Freedom in the World*, published annually by Freedom House.
HDR: *Human Development Report*, published annually by the United Nations Development Program.
IDB: International Data Base, 1998, U.S. Bureau of the Census.
IDEA: Institute for Democracy and Electoral Assistance. Turnout data are from the institute's "Global Report on Political Participation (Stockholm, 1997). Electoral system data and coding from *The International Handbook of Electoral System Design.*
IP: *International Profile: Alcohol and Other Drugs*, published by the Alcoholism and Drug Addiction Research Foundation (Toronto), 1994.
JWY: *The Yearbook of Jehovah's Witnesses*, published annually.
KIDRON & SEGAL: *State of the World Atlas*, 5th ed., London: Penguin, 1995.
LE ROY: Coded and calculated by Michael K. Le Roy.
McCORMICK: Coded by John McCormick, *Comparative Politics in Transition*, New York: Wadsworth, 1995, p. 9.
NBWR: *The New Book of World Rankings*, 3rd ed., Facts on File, 1991.
PON: The Progress of Nations, UNICEF, 1996.
SAUS: *Statistical Abstract of the United States*, published annually by the U.S. Department of Commerce.
STARK: Coded and calculated by Rodney Stark.
SWPA: Dan Smith, *The State of War and Peace Atlas*, 1st ed., London: Penguin, 1997.
TI: *Corruption Perceptions Index*, Transparency International, 1998.
TWF: *The World Factbook*, published annually by the Central Intelligence Agency.
TWW: The World's Women, published by the United Nations, 1995.
UNCRIME: United Nations. THE FOURTH UNITED NATIONS SURVEY OF CRIME TRENDS AND OPERATIONS OF CRIMINAL JUSTICE SYSTEMS, 1986–1990 (Computer files). Vienna, Austria: Crime Prevention and Criminal Justice Branch, United Nations Office at Vienna, 1994. The United States did not

provide data for the Fourth Survey. Therefore, the crime rates for the United States were taken from the *Statistical Abstract of the United States*, 1996.

UNSY: *United Nations Statistical Yearbook*, 1997, United Nations.

WCE: *World Christian Encyclopedia*, David B. Barrett, editor, Oxford University Press, 1982.

WDI: *World Development Indicators*, published annually by the World Bank.

WDR: *World Development Report*, published annually by the World Bank.

WR: *World Resources, 1994—1995*, World Resources Institute

WVS: World Values Study Group. WORLD VALUES SURVEY, 1981–1984 AND 1990–1993 (Computer files). ICPSR version. Ann Arbor, MI: Institute for Social Research (producer), 1994. Ann Arbor, MI: Inter-university Consortium for Political and Social Research (distributor), 1994.

GSS – The General Social Survey

The GSS data file is based on selected variables from the National Opinion Research Center (University of Chicago) General Social Surveys for the years 1972–1998, distributed by the Roper Center and the Inter-university Consortium for Political and Social Research. The principal investigators are James A. Davis and Tom W. Smith.

STATES – The Fifty States of the United States

The data in the STATES file are from a variety of sources. The variable description for each variable uses the following abbreviations to indicate the source.

AMERICAN LEGION: Data published by the American Legion.

ABC: Audit Bureau of Circulation Blue Book for the indicated year.

BADER: Coded and calculated by Chris Bader, MicroCase.

BEA: Bureau of Economic Analysis.

CENSUS: The summary volumes of the U.S. Census for the indicated year.

CHRON.: *The Chronicle of Higher Education Almanac* for the indicated year.

CHURCH: *Churches and Church Membership in the United States*, published every 10 years by the Glenmary Research Center, Atlanta, for the year indicated.

DEA: Drug Enforcement Administration.

DES: U.S. Dept. of Education, Digest of Education Statistics for the indicated year.

E & E: Bureau of Labor Statistics, Employment and Earnings for the date indicated.

FEC: Federal Election Commission for the indicated year.

HCSR: Health Care State Rankings (Morgan Quitno, Lawrence, KS) for the indicated year.

HEAVEN'S GATE: Data taken from a publication, "How and When Heaven's Gate May Be Entered," posted by Heaven's Gate on the Internet.

HIGHWAY: Federal Highway Administration, Highway Statistics for the indicated year.

KINKO'S: Data published by Kinko's, Incorporated.

KOSMIN: Kosmin, Barry A. 1991. *Research Report: The National Survey of Religious Identification*, New York: CUNY Graduate Center.

MELTON: Melton, Gordon. 1993. *Encyclopedia of American Religion*.

MMWR: Morbidity and Mortality Weekly Report for the date indicated.

NCHS: National Center for Health Statistics.

NEA: National Endowment for the Arts.

RETAIL: *Census of Retail Trade*, published every five years by the Bureau of the Census, for the indicated year.

SA: *Statistical Abstract of the United States* for the indicated year.

SMAD: *State and Metropolitan Area Data Book* for the indicated year.

S.P.R.: *State Policy Reference* for the indicated year.

S.R.: *State Rankings* (Morgan Quitno Corp., Lawrence, KS) for the indicated year.
SSA: Data published by the Social Security Administration.
UCR: Uniform Crime Reports for the indicated year.
UFO NEWSCLIPPING SERVICE: (The UFO Newsclipping Service, AR) 1994–1996.
U.S. FISH & WILDLIFE: Data provided by U.S. Fish and Wildlife Service.
WA: The *World Almanac* for the indicated year.

US TRENDS – TRENDS IN THE UNITED STATES, 1789-2001

The data in the US TRENDS file are from a variety of sources. The variable description for each variable uses the following abbreviations to indicate the source.

SA: *Statistical Abstract of the United States*, published yearly by the Department of Commerce.

HSUS: *Historical Abstracts of the United States, Colonial Times to 1970*, published by the Department of Commerce.

DES: *Digest of Education Statistics*, published yearly by the U.S. Department of Education.

GSS: General Social Survey, National Opinion Research Council, Chicago, IL Results are aggregated by year to generate percentages.

NES: National Election Studies, Institute of Social Research, University of Michigan. Results are aggregated by year to generate percentages.

APPENDIX B:

Matrix: Workbook chapters that supplement chapters in selected Brooks/Cole social work texts

Text by Author(s) & Title*	Chp1) Pop Explosion	2) The Family	3) The Children	4) Aging	5) Health Care	6) Substan Abuse	7) Gender Equality	8) Race/ Ethnic Diversity	9) Poverty	10) Crime &Jus Tice
A) Ambr& Heffer: S. W. & S. Welfare	17	5, 12	11, 12	13	10	9	4	4	8	14
B) Zastrow: Intro. S. W. & Social Welfare	17	6	6	14	15, 16	8	7, 13	12	4	
C) Jansson: Reluctant Welfare State	5	8, 14	8, 14	10	6	14	10, 14	9, 14	7, 8	12
D) KrstAsh & Hull-2: Gen. Prac. Org & Comm.			15			9. 18		12	11	13
E) Hepwoth et al.: Direct S. W. Pract.		10, 16	15		9	9	15	9, 15		
F) Jasson: Policy	3	5	7	6	13		7		5	
G) Ashford Et al.: HBSE	5	4	3, 5, 8	12	11, 12	9	4, 8, 11	4, 12	11	9
H) Zastrow &Kirst: HBSE		4	2, 3	15, 16	10	8, 11	9	5	12	8
I) Cherry: Research	1, 3, 12	13, 4, 15	19	21	14	17,18, 20	26	22	20	26
J) Marlow: Research	3, 4, 12	8, 9	12	15	12, 13	15				
K) Rubin & Babbie: Research	1, 14	15	16	17	18	16				

MATRIX of CHAPTERS (Cond.)

-A- Ambrosino, R., Heffernan, J., Shuttlesworth, G. and Ambrosino, R. (2001). *Social Work and Social Welfare: An Introduction* (4th ed.). Belmont, CA: Wadsworth Publishing.

-B- Zastrow, C. (2000). *Introduction to Social Work and Social Welfare.* (7th ed.). Belmont, CA: Wadsworth Publishing.

-C- Jansson, B. S. (2001). *The Reluctant Welfare State* (4th ed.). Belmont, CA: Wadsworth Publishing.

-D- Kirst-Ashman, K. K. and Hull, G. H. (2001). *Generalist Practice with Organizations & Communities* (2nd ed.). Belmont, CA: Wadsworth Publishing.

-E- Hepworth, D. H., Rooney, R. H. and Larsen, J. A. (1997). *Direct Social Work Practice: Theory and Skills* (4th ed.). Pacific Grove, CA: Brooks/Cole Publishing Company.

-F- Jansson, B. S. (1999). *Becoming an Effective Policy Advocate: From Policy Practice to Social Justice.* Pacific Grove, CA: Brooks/Cole Publishing Company.

-G- Ashford, J. B., Lecory, C. W. and Lortie, K. L. (2001). *Human Behavior in the Social Environment* (2nd ed.). Belmont, CA: Wadsworth Publishing.

-H- Zastrow, C., Kirst-Ashman, K. K. (2001). *Understanding Human Behavior in the Social Environment* (5th ed.). Belmont, CA: Wadsworth Publishing.

-I - Cherry, A. L. (2000). *A Research Primer for the Helping Professions: Methods Statistics and Writing.* Pacific Grove, CA: Brooks/Cole Publishing Company.

-J- Marlow, C. (2001). *Research Methods for Generalist Social Work* (3rd ed.). Pacific Grove, CA: Wadsworth Publishing.

-K- Rubin, A. and Babbie, E. (2001). *Research Methods for Social Work.* Belmont, CA: Wadsworth Publishing.

License Agreement for Wadsworth Group, a Division of Thomson Learning, Inc.

You the customer, and Wadsworth Group incur certain benefits, rights, and obligations to each other when you open this package and use the materials it contains. BE SURE TO READ THE LICENSE AGREEMENT CAREFULLY, SINCE BY USING THE SOFTWARE YOU INDICATE YOU HAVE READ, UNDERSTOOD, AND ACCEPTED THE TERMS OF THIS AGREEMENT.

Your rights:

1. You enjoy a non-exclusive license to use the enclosed materials on a single computer that is not part of a network or multi-machine system in consideration of the payment of the required license fee (which may be included in the purchase price of an accompanying print component) and your acceptance of the terms and conditions of this agreement.

2. You own the CD-ROM on which the program/data is recorded, but you acknowledge that you do not own the program/data recorded on the CD-ROM. You also acknowledge that the program/data is furnished "AS IS," and contains copyrighted and/or proprietary and confidential information of Wadsworth Group, a division of Thomson Learning, Inc.

3. If you do not accept the terms of this license agreement you must not install the CD-ROM and you must return the CD-ROM within 30 days of receipt with proof of payment to Wadsworth Group for full credit or refund.

There are limitations on your rights:

1. You may not copy or print the program/data for any reason whatsoever, except to install it on a hard drive on a single computer, unless copying or printing is expressly permitted in writing or statements recorded on the disk.

2. You may not revise, translate, convert, disassemble, or otherwise reverse engineer the program/data.

3. You may not sell, license, rent, loan, or otherwise distribute or network the program/data.

4. You may not export or re-export the CD-ROM, or any component thereof, without the appropriate U.S. or foreign government licenses. Should you fail to abide by the terms of this license or otherwise violate Wadsworth Group's rights, your license to use it will become invalid. You agree to destroy the CD-ROM immediately after receiving notice of Wadsworth Group's termination of this agreement for violation of its provisions.

U.S. Government Restricted Rights:

The enclosed multimedia, software, and associated documentation are provided with RESTRICTED RIGHTS. Use, duplication, or disclosure by the Government is subject to restrictions as set forth in subdivision (c)(1)(ii) of the Rights in Technical Data and Computer Software clause at DFARS 252.277.7013 for DoD contracts, paragraphs (c) (1) and (2) of the Commercial Computer Software-Restricted Rights clause in the FAR (48 CFR 52.227-19) for civilian agencies, or in other comparable agency clauses. The proprietor of the enclosed multimedia, software, and associated documentation is Wadsworth Group, 10 Davis Drive, Belmont, California 94002.

Limited Warranty

Wadsworth Group also warrants that the optical media on which the Product is distributed is free from defects in materials and workmanship under normal use. Wadsworth Group will replace defective media at no charge, provided you return the Product to Wadsworth Group within 90 days of delivery to you as evidenced by a copy of your invoice. If failure of disc(s) has resulted from accident, abuse, or misapplication, Wadsworth Group shall have no responsibility to replace the disc(s). THESE ARE YOUR SOLE REMEDIES FOR ANY BREACH OF WARRANTY.

EXCEPT AS SPECIFICALLY PROVIDED ABOVE, WADSWORTH GROUP, A DIVISION OF THOMSON LEARNING, INC. AND THE THIRD PARTY SUPPLIERS MAKE NO WARRANTY OR REPRESENTATION, EITHER EXPRESSED OR IMPLIED, WITH RESPECT TO THE PRODUCT, INCLUDING ITS QUALITY, PERFORMANCE, MERCHANTABILITY, OR FITNESS FOR A PARTICULAR PURPOSE. The product is not a substitute for human judgment. Because the software is inherently complex and may not be completely free of errors, you are advised to validate your work. IN NO EVENT WILL WADSWORTH GROUP OR ANY THIRD PARTY SUPPLIERS BE LIABLE FOR DIRECT, INDIRECT, SPECIAL, INCIDENTAL, OR CONSEQUENTIAL DAMAGES ARISING OUT OF THE USE OR INABILITY TO USE THE PRODUCT OR DOCUMENTATION, even if advised of the possibility of such damages. Specifically, Wadsworth Group is not responsible for any costs including, but not limited to, those incurred as a result of lost profits or revenue, loss of use of the computer program, loss of data, the costs of recovering such programs or data, the cost of any substitute program, claims by third parties, or for other similar costs. In no case shall Wadsworth Group's liability exceed the amount of the license fee paid. THE WARRANTY AND REMEDIES SET FORTH ABOVE ARE EXCLUSIVE AND IN LIEU OF ALL OTHERS, ORAL OR WRITTEN, EXPRESS OR IMPLIED. Some states do not allow the exclusion or limitation of implied warranties or limitation of liability for incidental or consequential damage, so that the above limitations or exclusion may not apply to you.

This license is the entire agreement between you and Wadsworth Group and it shall be interpreted and enforced under California law. Should you have any questions concerning this License Agreement, write to Technology Department, Wadsworth Group, 10 Davis Drive, Belmont, California 94002.